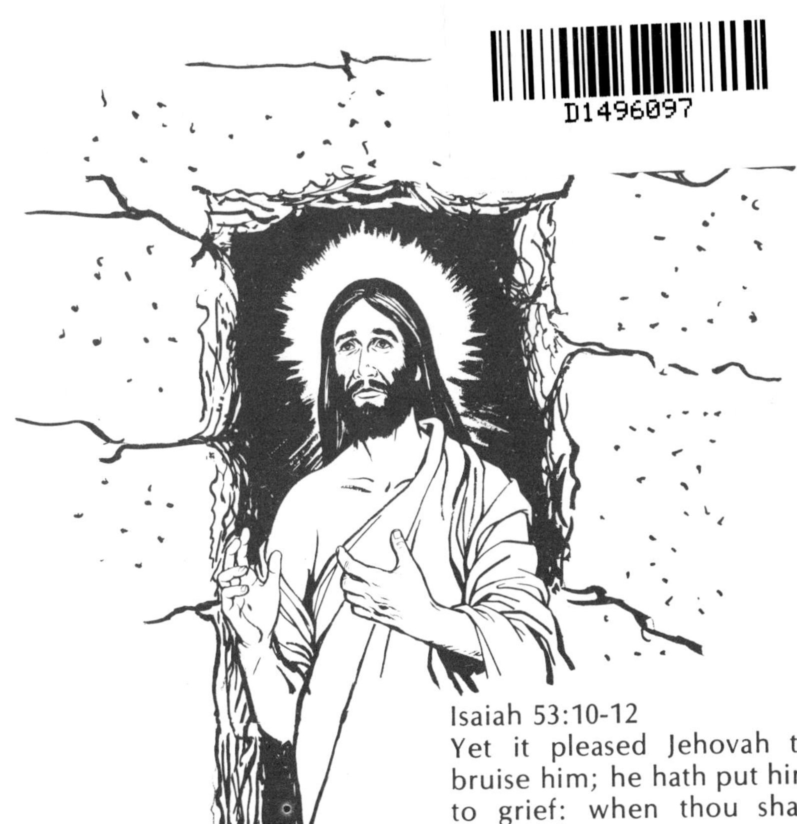

Isaiah 52:13-15
Behold, My servant shall deal
wisely, he shall be exalted
and lifted up, and shall be
very high. 14 Like as many
were astonished at thee (his
visage was so marred more
than any man, and his form
more than the sons of men),
15 so shall he startle many
nations; kings shall shut their
mouths at him: for that
which had not been told
them shall they see; and that
which they had not heard
shall they understand.

Isaiah 53:10-12
Yet it pleased Jehovah to
bruise him; he hath put him
to grief: when thou shalt
make his soul an offering for
sin, he shall see his seed, he
shall prolong his days, and
the pleasure of Jehovah shall
prosper in his hand. 11 He
shall see of the travail of his
soul, and shall be satisfied: by
the knowledge of himself
shall my righteous servant
justify many; and he shall
bear their iniquities. 12
Therefore will I divide him a
portion with the great, and
he shall divide the spoil with
the strong; because he
poured out his soul unto
death, and was numbered
with the transgressors: yet he
bare the sin of many, and
made intercession for the
transgressors.

ISAIAH

Volume III

The Bible Study Textbook Series

NEW TESTAMENT

The Bible Study New Testament Ed. By Rhoderick Ice	**The Gospel of Matthew** In Four Volumes By Harold Fowler (Vol. IV not yet available)	**The Gospel of Mark** By B. W. Johnson and Don DeWelt
The Gospel of Luke By T. R. Applebury	**The Gospel of John** By Paul T. Butler	**Acts Made Actual** By Don DeWelt
Romans Realized By Don DeWelt	**Studies in Corinthians** By T. R. Applebury	**Guidance From Galatians** By Don Earl Boatman
The Glorious Church (Ephesians) By Wilbur Fields	**Philippians · Colossians Philemon** By Wilbur Fields	**Thinking Through Thessalonians** By Wilbur Fields
Paul's Letters To Timothy & Titus By Don DeWelt	**Helps From Hebrews** By Don Earl Boatman	**James & Jude** By Don Fream
Letters From Peter By Bruce Oberst	**Hereby We Know (I-II-III John)** By Clinton Gill	**The Seer, The Saviour, and The Saved (Revelation)** By James Strauss

OLD TESTAMENT

O.T. History By William Smith and Wilbur Fields	**Genesis** In Four Volumes By C. C. Crawford	**Exploring Exodus** By Wilbur Fields	**Leviticus** By Don DeWelt
Numbers By Brant Lee Doty	**Deuteronomy** By Bruce Oberst	**Joshua · Judges Ruth** By W. W. Winter	**I & II Samuel** By W. W. Winter
I & II Kings By James E. Smith	**I & II Chronicles** By Robert E. Black	**Ezra, Nehemiah & Esther** By Ruben Ratzlaff & Paul T. Butler	**The Shattering of Silence (Job)** By James Strauss

Psalms In Two Volumes By J. B. Rotherham	**Proverbs** By Donald Hunt	**Ecclesiastes and Song of Solomon** – By R. J. Kidwell and Don DeWelt
Isaiah In Three Volumes By Paul T. Butler	**Jeremiah and Lamentations** By James E. Smith	**Ezekiel** By James E. Smith
Daniel By Paul T. Butler	**Hosea · Joel · Amos Obadiah · Jonah** By Paul T. Butler	**Micah · Nahum · Habakkuk Zephaniah · Haggai · Zechariah Malachi** – By Clinton Gill

SPECIAL STUDIES

The Church In The Bible By Don DeWelt	**The Eternal Spirit** By C. C. Crawford	**World & Literature of the Old Testament** Ed. By John Willis	**Survey Course In Christian Doctrine** Two Bks. of Four Vols. By C. C. Crawford

New Testament History – Acts By Gareth Reese	**Learning From Jesus** By Seth Wilson	**You Can Understand The Bible** By Grayson H. Ensign

BIBLE STUDY TEXTBOOK SERIES

ISAIAH

Volume III

by

Paul T. Butler

College Press, Joplin, Missouri

Second Printing - 1983

Printed and Bound in the
United States of America

International Standard Book Number: 0-89900-022-3

THIS VOLUME

IS

DEDICATED

TO

Sandra VanNortwick
Charlene Martin Schell
Becky Blodgett Holt
Linda Thurman Rush
Darlene Ashcraft
Sherry Butler Lankford
Elizabeth Weeks

my lovely secretaries

through whose outstanding efficiency and cooperation
my writing ministry has been made possible

and

James R. Marcum

teaching assistant

whose aid has been
a great encouragement and contribution.

TABLE OF CONTENTS

SEVENTEEN ARGUMENTS THAT THE BOOK OF ISAIAH WAS WRITTEN BY ONE AUTHOR

Isaiah, the son of Amoz, is the author of the entire prophecy, because:

1. N.T. quotations leave no room for doubt that in the eyes of the N.T. writers Isaiah was the author of the entire prophecy.
2. Traditions, as early as Ecclesiasticus, attribute one authorship for Isaiah.
3. The heading of the prophecy (1:1) is intended to stand for the entire book.
4. The author of Isaiah 40-66 was a Palestinian—not showing familiarity with the land or the religion of Babylon such as we might expect from one of the exiles.
5. There are historical passages in chapters 40-66 which do not fit the time of the exile.
6. Once "higher critics" begin separating or dividing Isaiah, it is impossible to rest with two or even three large divisions, which ends in absurdity.
7. Passages in Zephaniah, Nahum, Jeremiah and Zechariah seem to indicate that the latter portion of Isaiah (40-66) was in existence when these prophets wrote.

Isaiah	Jeremiah
44:12-15	10:1-16
46:7	10:1-16
48:6	33:3
53	11:19
56:11	6:15
56:9—57:11a	6:15
65:17	3:16
66:15	4:13

Cf. also Isa. 47:8-10 with Zeph. 2:15; and Isa. 17:1, 7; 66:20 with Zeph. 3:10.

8. After nearly 200 years of intense research by negative critics, scholarship has not been able to present a satisfactory account of the authorship of Second Isaiah (40-66).

9. No two critics agree on the identity of the author of Deutro-Isaiah (even assuming that there is such an author).
10. Even critics make many admissions to valuelessness of style as a vehicle of evidence for two Isaiahs.
11. Critics cannot account adequately for ancient tradition which says Isaiah is the author.
12. The Isaiah Scroll of the Dead Sea Scrolls gives only positive evidence for one authorship of Isaiah (these scrolls date somewhere between 100-200 B.C.).
13. Claims for Isaiah's authorship of the entire book from N.T. quotations

Isaiah	Quoted	Attributed by critics to:
40:3	Mt. 3:3	II
53:4	Mt. 8:17	II, III
42:1	Mt. 12:17	II
6:9-10	Mt. 13:14	I
29:13	Mt. 15:7	I
40:13	Mk. 1:2	II
29:13	Mk. 7:6	I
40:3-5	Lk. 3:4	II
61:1-2	Lk. 4:17	III
40:3	Jn. 1:23	II
53:1	Jn. 12:38	II, III
6:9-10	Jn. 12:39	I
53:1; 6:9-10	Jn. 12:41	I, II
53:7-8	Acts 8:28	II, III
53:7-8	Acts 8:32	II, III
53:7-8	Acts 8:30	II, III
6:9-10	Acts 28:25	I
10:22, 23; 11:5	Rom. 9:27	I
1:9	Rom. 9:29	I
53:1	Rom. 10:16	II, III
65:1	Rom. 10:20	III

That the writers of the New Testament claimed Isaiah to

be the author of the entire book is the strongest of all arguments that Isaiah was indeed the only author of the book.

14. *Circle of ideas*—strikingly the same throughout the entire book; e.g., the characteristic name for God, "the Holy One of Israel," (25 times in Isaiah and only six in rest of O.T.).

    Another idea unique with the whole book is "a highway." (cf. Isa. 11:16; 35:8; 40:3; 43:19; 49:11; 57:14; 62:10).

    Another characteristic is the idea of "a remnant." (cf. Isa. 1:9; 10:20-22; 11:11-16; 14:22-30; 15:9; 16:14; 17:3; 21:17; 28:5; 37:31; 46:3; 65:8-9).

    Another characteristic idea is that of "Zion." (cf. Isa. 2:3; 4:5; 18:7; 24:23; 28:16; 29:8; 30:19; 31:9; 33:5-20; 34:8; 46:13; 49:14; 51:3-16; 52:1; 59:20; 60:14; 62:1-11; 66:8).

    Another oft-repeated expression is, "pangs of a woman in travail." (cf. Isa. 13:8; 21:3; 26:17-18; 42:14; 54:1; 66:7).

    These, and many other characteristics . . . stamp the book with an individuality which it is difficult to account for, if it be broken up into countless fragments and distributed, as some do, over the centuries.

15. *The literary style:* Although literary style is not a sure criterion of authorship, yet it is certainly remarkable that the clause "for the mouth of Jehovah hath spoken it" should be found three times in the Book of Isaiah, and nowhere else in the entire O.T. (cf. 1:20; 40:5; 58:14).

    The phrase, "streams of water," occurs twice in Isa. and nowhere else (cf. 30:25; 44:4 in the Hebrew).

    Another literary peculiarity is the prophet's tendency to reduplication (cf. 2:7-8; 6:3; 8:9; 24:16-23; 40:1; 43:11-25; 48:15; 51:12; 57:19; 62:10).

    Isaiah's style differs widely from that of every other O.T. prophet, and is as far removed as possible from that of Ezekiel and the post-exilic prophets.

16. *Historical references:* The prophet's constant reference to

Judah and Jerusalem, his country and its capital (1:7-9; 3:8; 24:19; 25:2; 40:2-9; 62:4). His reference to the temple and its ritual of worship and sacrifice. When there was prosperity and the people were profuse and formal in their ceremonies, the prophet brings God's complaint, 1:11-15; when the country had been devastated by Sennacherib and the Assyrian hosts, the prophet reminds them that they had not brought to Jehovah the sheep of their burnt offerings, 43:23-24, nor honored Him with their sacrifices; while in 66:1-3, 6:20, the temple and its services are certainly presupposed to be in existence (which was not the case in post-exilic times until rebuilt).

Isaiah's attitude throughout the book toward the captivities is that of both anticipation and realization (in 57:1 judgment is only threatened, not yet inflicted). While in the first part of the book (3:8) the destruction of Judah and Jerusalem is described as in the past.

17. *Predictive Element:* This is the strongest proof of the unity of the book.
    a. Predicted the breaking to pieces of Ephraim (7:8)
    b. Carrying away of spoils of Damascus and Samaria (8:4; 7:16)
    c. That Tyre would be forgotten 70 years (23:15-18)
    d. That suddenly Jerusalem's foes should be as dust (29:5)
    e. That Assyria should be dismayed and fall by the sword (30:17-31; 31:8).
    f. Reminded the people after the siege by Sennacherib that he had predicted it (41:21-23, 26).
    g. Cf. also, 42:9-23; 43:9-12; 44:7-28; 45:3-13; 46:10-11; 48:3-5; 48:6-16.

VII. SALVATION THROUGH GOD'S SERVANT
CHAPTERS 40 - 53

A. PURPOSE OF THE LORD'S SERVANT
CHAPTERS 40 - 43

1. COMFORT, CHAPTER 40

a. PREPARE FOR THE COMING OF THE LORD

TEXT: 40:1-11

1 Comfort ye, comfort ye my people, saith your God.
2 Speak ye comfortably to Jerusalem; and cry unto her, that her warfare is accomplished, that her iniquity is pardoned, that she hath received of Jehovah's hand double for all her sins.
3 The voice of one that crieth, Prepare ye in the wilderness the way of Jehovah; make level in the desert a highway for our God.
4 Every valley shall be exalted, and every mountain and hill shall be made low; and the uneven shall be made level, and the rough places a plain:
5 and the glory of Jehovah shall be revealed, and all flesh shall see it together; for the mouth of Jehovah hath spoken it.
6 The voice of one saying, Cry. And one said, What shall I cry? All flesh is grass, and all the goodliness thereof is as the flower of the field:
7 the grass withereth, the flower fadeth, because the breath of Jehovah bloweth upon it; surely the people is grass.
8 The grass withereth, the flower fadeth; but the word of our God shall stand forever.
9 O thou that tellest good tidings to Zion, get thee up on a high mountain; O thou that tellest good tidings to Jerusalem, lift up thy voice with strength; lift it up, be not afraid; say unto the cities of Judah, Behold, your God!
10 Behold, the Lord Jehovah will come as a mighty one, and his arm will rule for him: behold, his reward is with him, and his recompense before him.
11 He will feed his flock like a shepherd, he will gather the

lambs in his arm, and carry them in his bosom, and will gently lead those that have their young.

QUERIES

a. Who is to do the comforting in verses 1 - 27?
b. Why cry, "All flesh is grass"?
c. When is God going to feed his flock like a shepherd?

PARAPHRASE

Encourage and strengthen my people says your God. Speak to the heart of Jerusalem and call out to her that her warfare and her struggle is fulfilled—it is over; her iniquity is paid for; God's wrath is abundantly satisfied. Hark, a voice crying! In the wilderness prepare a way for Jehovah; make smooth and level in the desert a highway for our God. Every dark valley will have to be filled in and raised up and every mountain and hill scraped off and lowered. Everything that is uneven must be made level, and the rough places must be smoothed out like a plain. When the way is prepared then the glory of the Lord will be made manifest and all the human race will have His glory shown to them together. The Lord has promised this and it shall certainly come to pass. Hark, a second voice saying, Cry! And I said, What shall I cry? Cry out that all the human race is frail like grass and the flowers of the field. When the breath of God blows upon the grass in the hot, dry winds of summer, the grass withers and the flowers fade. That is just how fragile man is. He and grass and flowers wither and fade, but the word of our God stands forever.

O Zion, bringer of good news, get yourself up on a high mountain where you can really cry the good news to Jerusalem, as a bringer of good news and shout with a strong voice. Do not be afraid to cry loudly to all the cities of Judah, Behold, your God! Behold indeed! For the Lord Jehovah is coming like a strong and powerful ruler and His arm will rule for Him. He is bringing His rewards and compensations with Him for His people. He is going to provide food for His people like a shepherd; He is going to provide safety and protection for His people like a shepherd; He is going to show compassion and gentleness to all those who need help.

COMMENTS

v. 1-2 STRENGTHEN: There is definitely a division of Isaiah's book at chapter 40. This, however, does not mean the book has two different authors any more than there were two different authors for the Pentateuch (first five books of the O.T.). Moses, author of the Pentateuch, had different purposes in mind for his books and so used a different style. Isaiah has a different purpose in mind for the last half of his book and so uses a different style. For evidence of one authorship of Isaiah see Special Study, "Seventeen Arguments That The Book of Isaiah Was Written By One Author," pages 1-4. Isaiah's main purpose in chapters 1-39 was to preach against the sin of Israel and predict judgment. His main purpose in chapters 40-66 is to preach of peace and predict the nature of the future Israel of God, the Church. Edward J. Young calls chapters 40-66, "The Salvation and Future Blessing of The True Israel of God." These latter chapters are intensely Messianic! Isaiah 40:3-4; 40:6-8; 53:1-12; 55:1-3; 61:1-2 are specifically fulfilled in the New Testament. We have emphasized the Messianic nature of chapters 40-66 in our outline (see also the chart, Vol. I, pgs. 64-65).

These first two verses of chapter 40 form a prologue for the rest of the entire book. Some have outlined chapters 40-66 in a threefold division to correspond to the prologue thusly:

1. 40:1—48:22 — "her warfare is ended."
2. 49:1—57:21 — "her iniquity is pardoned."
3. 58:1—66:24 — "she hath received . . . double for all her sins."

Nakhamu is the Hebrew word translated *comfort.* It is also translated *repent* in many places in the O.T. The authors of the Septuagint (Greek version of the Hebrew Old Testament) used the Greek word *parakaleo* which is the word Paraclete or Comforter in John's Gospel. In Greek it means "one called alongside to help, aid or strengthen." The command in verse one is for someone to "strengthen, help or aid" God's people.

Who is to do this "strengthening"? It is all the prophets from Isaiah to the Messiah. It is probably correct to say that the initial comforting was for the Israel of Isaiah's day or the Israel of the captivities (although the captivity in Babylon has not yet occurred). However, the ultimate target is the Messianic Israel. The fulfillment is for the days of John the Baptist and the Messiah. The true Israel's warfare was not ended and her iniquity pardoned until accomplished in Christ (cf. Lk. 1:67-79) and John the Baptist was born especially to announce this. In 40:1-11 there are two texts specifically quoted in the New Testament as finding their fulfillment there (40:3-4 and 40:6-8). The prophets from Isaiah to Malachi must strengthen Israel that those who believe may prepare a remnant through which the Incarnate Son may come and establish His kingdom. John the Baptist was the one who was "more than a prophet" (Mt. 11:9), the one whose crying in the wilderness signaled the fulfillment of "the law and the prophets" (Mt. 11:13). The Messiah-Servant was the one to whom this prophecy pointed. (See Isa. 49:13.)

The Hebrew phrase *dabberu 'al—lev* translated "speak ye comfortably" or "speak tenderly" means literally, "speak upon the heart." It is a phrase meaning to "win someone over" in Gen. 34:3 and Judges 19:3. In Gen. 50:21 Joseph "spoke upon the heart" of his brothers to build their confidence in his kind intentions toward them. This is the manner in which the strengthening is to be done. The comforting is not something to be done superficially—it is to be lodged in the heart of the people.

What is to be planted on Jerusalem's heart is that her warfare is ended, her iniquity is pardoned and she has received double from Jehovah for all her sins. This cannot have the return from the Babylonian captivity for its essential goal for the nation of Israel enjoyed only a brief respite from conflict and struggle after their restoration. Daniel predicts 490 years of "trouble" to follow the restoration from captivity in minute detail (see our commentary on *Daniel*, College Press). Daniel also predicts that Israel's iniquity will not be pardoned until the end of those 490 years (Dan. 9:24-27 in our commentary). So, the comforting or strengthening of Jerusalem is predicated on the promise of cessation of warfare and pardoning of iniquity in the great Messianic era of the future. That era will be announced by "The Voice" who was none other than John the Baptist. Jerusalem "received of Jehovah's hand double for all her sins." This may mean either her punishment was abundant or her blessing was abundant. In either case, once again, it can find its ultimate fulfillment only in the Messiah (cf. Isa. 53:1-2 for abundant punishment and Isa. 61:1-11 for abundant blessing—both in the Messiah).

v. 3-8 STRAIGHTEN: The Hebrew construction is interesting. Literally it is *qol qorea,* "voice, one crying." The first three gospel writers all confirm this found its fulfillment in John the Baptist (Mt. 3:3; Mk. 1:2-3; Lk. 3:4-6).

Certainly, all the prophets from Isaiah to Malachi were commissioned by this command to "prepare" the way for the coming of the Lord. Unquestionably, a faithful remnant needed to be continually "prepared" so that new generations of a messianic nucleus might be preserved through the centuries from Isaiah to Christ. But it was John the Baptist who had the climactic job of preparing an *immediate* nucleus for the coming of God in the flesh—Jesus Christ. It was John the Baptist who first immersed men and women in water for repentance unto the remission of sins (Mt. 3:1-2; Mk. 1:4; Lk. 3:1-3). It was the Immerser who pointed some of his principal disciples to Jesus (Jn. 1:29-51) and these men became apostles—evangelists and missionaries of the Messianic kingdom, the church. Indeed, even the Lord Himself said of John the Immerser,

". . . among those born of women there has risen no one greater than John the Baptist," (Mt. 11:11).

The Hebrew word *ba'aerabah* means "in the desert." It is the same word from which we have *Arabia.* The people are in the "wilderness" and God is going to come to them. They must prepare Him a way. The "desert" or "wilderness" was not necessarily an endless, flat sea of sand as we think of a desert today. A wilderness or desert could be any type of terrain which was uninhabited by people. The river banks of the Jordan, cluttered with reeds, brush and rocks was a wilderness. The barren mountains of southern Judea were a wilderness ("desert"). These wildernesses with their brush, mountains, valleys, rocks, and wild animals presented formidable obstacles to travel in ancient times. When kings and potentates wished to journey and it involved traversing such an unlikely territory, they sent great companies of slaves and workers on ahead of them to fill in valleys and lower hills and generally prepare a safe and easy pathway for them to travel. The desert is a figure of the obstacles and impediments that have kept God from His people. It was their sinful rebellion (Isa. 59:1-3) as depicted in the first 39 chapters that was keeping God from His people. This rebellious attitude in the majority will intensify in the days of Jeremiah and Ezekiel until God leaves them (Ezek. 10:18; 11:23). God wants to come to them in Person—Incarnate—in the flesh. He wants to reveal His glory to all mankind (v. 5). And when they have a remnant fully prepared —when some believe Him enough to remove all obstacles into their hearts—when some are willing to obey Him completely (like Mary, mother of Jesus), then He will come! Isaiah is emphatically the missionary book of the Old Testament. He begins his prophecy (2:2-3) by stating that "all the nations" shall flow to Zion. He ends it by stating that "all flesh" shall come to worship before the Lord (66:23). One has only to take a concordance and look for "peoples" and "nations" in Isaiah to observe how often the prophet predicts that people from all nations will eventually become citizens of the Messianic kingdom of God.

A Voice is saying, Cry out. The Voice of verse six is evidently the Lord calling upon His messengers to add more exhortation to the message of "strengthening." First, there is the exhortation to "prepare a way" for the Lord to come. The N.T. applies this to John the Baptist as the one who would prepare the hearts of people to receive the Messiah (Lk. 1:16-17). Further preparation to receive God is proclaiming the message that "all flesh is grass, and all the goodliness thereof is as the flower of the field": and the N.T. applies this to man's inability to save himself, the redemption that is in Christ, and man's access to that redemption through obedience to the gospel (I Pet. 1:13-24). Now the prophets from Isaiah to Malachi were charged to preach man's frailty and his inability to save himself, and the redemption of God provided by grace in some future era. And all their contemporaries who believed this and trusted in Jehovah were straightened out in their view of man and God. But only the substitutionary death of Christ and His resurrection (the gospel) validated once and for all man's lostness and God's faithfulness. Only the gospel straightens man out so God can come to him. Only the gospel demonstrated ultimately that the word of God shall stand forever. The New Testament is the fulfillment of the entire "strengthening" half of Isaiah's prophecy (ch. 40-66)!

v. 9-11 SURRENDER: The construction of the Hebrew in verse nine does not necessitate the "tidings" to be told "to" Zion. Literally translated the verse would read, "So, a mountain high go you to, you bringer of good tidings, Zion." We have indicated this in our paraphrase. In other words, Zion is the bringer of good tidings—not the one to whom good tidings are brought. Zion and Jerusalem are personified as proclaimers of good news. Isaiah predicted earlier that the law and the word of the Lord would "go forth" out of Zion and Jerusalem (Isa. 2:3). The good tidings are to be proclaimed *koakh,* powerfully, and, *tiyraaiy,* fearlessly.

What is Zion to proclaim? Behold! God is coming in mightiness! *Adonai-Yaweh,* the Lord-Jehovah is coming. *Zeroau,* arm, usually symbolizes a characteristic—power. It may also symbolize the Messiah who came as God's "Arm" to rule (cf. Isa. 51:4-5; 52:7-10; 53:1; Luke 1:51). Isaiah 52:7-10 also predicts the "good tidings" by which the covenant people are to be "comforted" involving the Lord "baring His holy arm before the eyes of all the nations." It is apparent that "arm" here and in 52:7-10 refers to the Messiah.

There could hardly be a better climax to this great Messianic prologue of the "comfort" section in Isaiah's book than verse 11. The "shepherd" can be none other than Jesus Christ, the Good Shepherd. The Messiah-shepherd is one of the greatest concepts of Old Testament prophecy (cf. Ezek. 34:20-34; Micah 5:1-4; Zech. 11:7-14; 13:7, etc.). Jesus called Himself, The Good Shepherd (Lk. 15:3-7; Jn. 10:1-30) and His audience as a "flock" that needed shepherding (Mt. 9:36-38; Jn. 10:1-30).

If Isaiah and those prophets who come after him are to prepare mankind for the coming of the Lord, they must get men to prepare their wicked, desert-like hearts like a smooth, straight highway; they must straighten out their evaluation of man's ability to save himself and decide that man is capable of abiding forever only if he abides in the eternal word of God; they must surrender to the good tidings that God is going to send His "Arm"—the tender, Good Shepherd—to rule for Him.

Isaiah was writing of the glorious future for the benefit of the people of his day. Isaiah's task was to preserve a remnant of faithful Israelites who would be able to endure the disintegration of their nation, go into captivity and return to carry on the Messianic destiny. This remnant was to pass on their faith in the prophetic promises that this destiny would be preserved by God and ultimately fulfilled—if not in their lives, in some glorious era to come. There may be an initial reference in this prologue to the restoration of the Jews to Palestine in the days of Ezra, Zerubbabel and Nehemiah.

But, unquestionably, the ultimate focus of the great redemption promised here—the coming of God to His people who are prepared—is to the Messiah and His kingdom—the church. We have inspired documentation in the New Testament that this is so!

QUIZ

1. Give as many arguments as you can that Isaiah is the author of the entire book by his name.
2. What does the word "comfort" mean?
3. Why cannot the ending of warfare, etc., be applied to the Israel returned from Babylonian captivity?
4. Who is the "voice" that was to cry, "Prepare"?
5. What does the figure of speech, "make level in the desert a highway" refer to?
6. How much emphasis does Isaiah place on a missionary task?
7. What do men need to straighten out about "all flesh"?
8. What message is Zion to proclaim as good tidings?
9. What proof do we have that these eleven verses are Messianic?

b. PERCEIVE THE NATURE OF THE LORD

TEXT: 40:12-26

12 Who hath measured the water in the hollow of his hand, and meted out heaven with the span, and comprehended the dust of the earth in a measure, and weighed the mountains in scales, and the hills in a balance?
13 Who hath directed the Spirit of Jehovah, or being his counsellor hath taught him?
14 With whom took he counsel, and who instructed him, and taught him in the path of justice, and taught him knowledge, and showed to him the way of understanding?
15 Behold, the nations are as a drop of a bucket, and are accounted as the small dust of the balance: behold, he taketh up the isles as a very little thing.
16 And Lebanon is not sufficient to burn, nor the beasts thereof

sufficient for a burnt-offering.
17 All the nations are as nothing before him; they are accounted by him as less than nothing, and vanity.
18 To whom then will ye liken God? or what likeness will ye compare unto him?
19 The image, a workman hath cast it, and the goldsmith overlayeth it with gold, and casteth for it silver chains.
20 He that is too impoverished for such an oblation chooseth a tree that will not rot; he seeketh unto him a skilful workman to set up a graven image, that shall not be moved.
21 Have ye not known? have ye not heard? hath it not been told you from the beginning? have ye not understood from the foundations of the earth?
22 It is he that sitteth above the circle of the earth, and the inhabitants thereof are as grasshoppers; that stretcheth out of the heavens as a curtain, and spreadeth them out as a tent to dwell in;
23 that bringeth princes to nothing; that maketh the judges of the earth as vanity.
24 Yea, they have not been planted; yea, they have not been sown; yea, their stock hath not taken root in the earth: moreover he bloweth upon them, and they wither, and the whirlwind taketh them away as stubble.
25 To whom then will ye liken me, that I should be equal to him? saith the Holy One.
26 Lift up your eyes on high, and see who hath created these, that bringeth out their host by number; he calleth them all by name; by the greatness of his might, and for that he is strong in power, not one is lacking.

QUERIES

a. What is meant by the mountains being "weighed"?
b. What is the "circle of the earth"?
c. What does God call "by name"?

PARAPHRASE

Who else has measured all the oceans, lakes and rivers in the infinite palm of His hand and measured off the heavens with His yardstick? Who else is able to measure the land of the earth in its proper one-third portion? Who else is able to weigh accurately the mountains and hills in the proportion needed upon the earth? Who regulated the Spirit of the Lord with rules or directions according to which all this was to be done? With whom did He consult? Who instructed Him how to create all this and who taught Him what to do with it? Who gave Him this omniscient understanding? Indeed, the great masses of people over whom the Lord rules are no more burden to Him than a drop in a bucket is a burden to the man who carries it and no more than a tiny speck of dust would tip the balance of a scale. Indeed, the islands and continents may be carried by Him as if they were an infinitesimal atom. All the wood of Lebanon's forests is not enough to provide a sacrificial fire, nor all Lebanon's animals enough to provide a sacrifice sufficient to His majesty. Compared to His greatness, the masses of humanity and the power of man's empires are as nothing—as if they did not even exist.

To whom then will you compare God? Who or what resembles Him? Will you be so foolish as to liken God to one of your man-made images? These are made by men, in the likeness of man, from earthen metals and with man-made ornamentations. Even your poor people, who cannot afford gold and silver, will not be outdone in foolishness. They select a tree they think will not rot and hire skilled artisans to carve them an idol they think will be permanent. Why do you continually refuse to acknowledge who the real God is? Why do you continually refuse to listen to His prophets tell you who the real God is? It is not because you have not had the truth about God preached to you, is it? It is not because you have not been able to understand what His creative works say about Him, is it? What you have heard and what you have seen should have taught you that it is Jehovah who is enthroned upon the zenith of the earth and upholds His creation by His almighty power. Men and their idols are as weak and powerless as grasshoppers when compared to Him. He stretches out the heavens as easily as man would a curtain and makes a tent of all the heavens for His own dwelling place. He is the One who deposes princely rulers from their thrones, and brings down high and mighty human judges to nothingness. In fact, many of these pretended potentates scarcely come to power before Jehovah sees fit to remove them. Rulers are one moment upon the throne; the next they are gone like stubble in a whirlwind.

So, there is no one to whom you may compare Me, is there? There is nothing that is equal to Me, is there? Look up into the heavens! Understand that Jehovah is Creator of all the universe. He brought every single star into being and knows exactly how many stars there are. He has named every one of them and calls the roll like a military commander. Because of His great power and mighty strength, not one of them is missing.

COMMENTS

v. 12-17 SOVEREIGN CREATOR: If God's covenant people are to be strengthened (comforted) in order to fulfill their messianic destiny they must prepare themselves to receive God's coming to them in the flesh. This is announced in 40:1-11. But they are not prepared. They have made for themselves gods of wood and metal. They do not know the God who speaks to them through the prophets because they have rejected His word for that of the "mediums and the wizards" (Isa. 8:19). They *think* they know him. But they have compared Him to their idols and pronounced Him impotent, unable to carry out His promises (cf. Isa. 5:18-20; 29:15-16; 48:1-5; Jer. 17:15, etc.). In fact, Isaiah's contemporaries have already told him *they do not want to know* the Holy One of Israel! (Isa. 30:9-11).

It is interesting that Isaiah, attempting to prepare the people for the messianic destiny, does not spend his time in elaborate plans for organization, entertainment, chicken-dinners, welfare programs, singing, or emotion-packed stories. He preached a logical, reasonable sermon on the nature and character of God. Mankind is not going to be saved by human programs but by *perceiving* the Person of God (see Special Study, "The Faith Once Delivered For All Time," *Isaiah, Vol. II,* pg. 250-257, College Press).

Who is the God whose coming the prophet has predicted? He is the Sovereign Creator. He has created the earth and its physical features in perfect proportion necessary to maintain the intricate balance of life. The fundamental principle of geophysics known as *isostasy* ("equal weights") is announced in verse 12. The waters of the earth's surface, the land-mass and the atmosphere were created with the preciseness necessary to cause the proper gravitational and hydrological functions to sustain life on this planet. The Hebrew word *shalish* is translated *measure* referring to "the dust of the earth . . ." and means literally *a third*. The surface of the earth consists of land and water. Land, the solid part, covers about 57,584,000 square miles, or about three tenths (⅓) of the earth's surface! Amazing! How did Isaiah know that "the dust of the earth" was *a third* 2700 years ago? The only accounting for it is that it was divinely revealed to him!

The God who is coming is not only omnipotent, He is omniscient. The verb translated *directed* in verse 13 is the Hebrew *tikken* and may also be translated *measured.* He who has measured the creation cannot be measured by the creation. He is unmeasurable and unsearchable (cf. Job 5:9; Psa. 145:3; Isa. 55:8-9; Rom. 11:33).

Creation required infinite, supernatural knowledge. Look wherever he will—into the vastness of outer space or into the minuteness of biological space or into the labyrinthine space of human personality—man reaches limits to his knowledge. But God knows. This was demonstrated once for all in Jesus Christ who calmed the seas, raised the dead, cast out demons, read the minds of His disciples and enemies, and predicted the future behavior of men and women. God knows—but no one taught God this knowledge, for no creature possesses such knowledge.

How did Isaiah come to such a lofty concept of God? Not by human speculation. One has only to read ancient literature of the Chaldeans, Persians, Greeks and Romans to understand that the great thinkers of history never reached such sublime heights as these in their speculations about origins and gods. Isaiah's knowlege of God came by revelation (Isa. 64:4; I Cor. 2:1-13).

Not only is Jehovah infinitely supreme to individuals, He is sovereign to and independent of nations. Powerful world empires consolidate human wisdom, human power and natural resources, and seem to be able to exercise and execute the will of man in opposition to the will of God. World empires appear at times to have the power to usurp the sovereignty of God upon the earth. But compared to the power and wisdom of God they are as infinitesimal as a "drop in a bucket." It is not that God has no concern for the nations. The Bible is His love letter to the world. But as far as their opposition to the fulfilling of His purposes, it is "less than nothing—vanity." His Being and His Sovereignty is not dependent upon them. They do not create Him—He creates them. He does not need them. If all creation were a temple, Lebanon an altar, its lordly woods the fire-wood, and its countless beasts the sacrifice, it would not be an offering sufficient to make Jehovah dependent upon man. If God were hungry He would not need to depend upon man (Psa. 50:3-15). If He needed a house He would not need to depend upon man (Isa. 66:1-2).

Perhaps Christians today need this sermon of Isaiah! Perhaps we sometimes flirt with the same arrogance of the Jews of Isaiah's day—that God could not do without us! God is not dependent upon our goodness, our offerings, our wisdom, our buildings. It is we who need His goodness. We need to make offerings to Him. The Jews were not ready for God to come to them until they perceived this. No man is ready to receive God, His Son or His Spirit, until he perceives the same thing.

v. 18-20 STUPID CREATURES: Since God is infinitely powerful, infinitely wise and unsearchable, it is sheer stupidity for the creature to attempt, in his finite limitations, to carve a likeness in wood or stone and think he has reproduced the totality of God. It is also sheer stupidity for men to devise political, ethical and philosophical systems and assume they have reproduced the totality of God. Man is limited to the experienced. God is beyond the experienced. The only possibility of man reaching beyond the experienced is that the Unexperienceable One shall reveal Himself in man's experience. This He did in Jesus Christ. God can create man in His image—but man cannot create God in his image. Edward J. Young says it succinctly, "Isaiah's question (v. 18) brings us to the heart of genuine theism. There can be no comparison between the living, eternal God (*'el*) and any man, for man is but a creature. Man is limited, finite, temporal; God is infinite, eternal, and unchangeable in all His attributes and perfections. In our thinking about God the infinite distance between God and the creature must ever be kept in mind. To break down this distinction is to fall into the sin of idolatry."

The Hebrew word *pesel* is translated *image* or *graven image* and is the thing Israel was forbidden to have in the Decalogue (Ex. 20:4). Moses was warned that God cannot be represented by any "form" (Deut. 4:12-24). Men seem to have an insatiable desire to "see" some "form" of God (Jn. 14:8-11), yet no one has ever "seen" Him (Jn. 1:18; 6:46; Col. 1:15; I Tim. 1:17; 6:16; Mt. 11:27; I Jn. 4:20). Christians are to be "conformed to the image of His Son" (Rom. 8:29; II Cor. 3:18; Col. 3:10), but this does not mean the flesh and blood body of Jesus (cf. I Cor. 15:49-50). It is therefore a dangerous practice to make statues and pictures of Jesus and depend upon them for our concept of the Son of God (besides the fact no one actually knows today the precise physical features of Jesus). It is the thinking and acting of Jesus we are to adore and recreate in us—not His human body. Perhaps this is why God saw fit to obliterate from history any exact description of Jesus. Perhaps this is why God has seen fit to erase any precise location of Jesus' birth, home, etc., lest men be more tempted than they are to worship things and places rather than the Person.

The silliness of attempting to fashion a Creator out of that which is created is best exemplified by Isaiah 44:9-20. There the idol-maker cuts down a tree and with half he builds a fire and cooks his food and with the other half he makes himself a god. How ridiculous! It is a fundamental principle of life that men take on the character of that which they worship (Psa. 115:3-8; Hosea 9:10; Rom. 1:18-32). Idolatry produces stupidity, degradation and death. Carving images of men and animals from wood and stone to adore and worship is not the only form of idolatry. Disobedience and rebellion against God's commands (I Sam. 15:23) and covetousness (Col. 3:5) are both forms of idolatry.

Even the poor people of Isaiah's day refused to be deprived of indulging in idolatry. They could not afford gold and silver so they had a craftsman carve them an idol from hard wood. Making of idols was taken seriously by those who worshipped them. Only the best craftsmen fashioned them lest the production be an unworthy representation of the god or goddess. They must be made substantially of endurable materials. The larger they were and the longer lasting, the more prestige and power the idols supposedly retained.

v. 21-26 SENSIBLE CONSIDERATION: There are two sources from which these stupid people should have perceived the sovereignty of Jehovah and prepared for His coming—the *word* of God and the *world* of God. Isaiah's questions are rhetorical. Only one answer is possible—yes! Over and over, through His spokesmen (the patriarchs and the prophets), the existence and nature of the Creator was proclaimed to Israel. Day by day Israel could see the Creator in nature and providence. Have they heard? have they known? Yes! There is no excuse for their stupidity. They could not plead ignorance as the cause for their idolatry. Their sin is deliberate and in spite of their knowledge (see Special Study, "Unbelief is Deliberate," *Isaiah Vol. II,* pg. 99, College Press).

The prophet implores his people to come back to a sensible consideration of the sovereignty of Jehovah based on more evidence from creation and history. One thing is certain from man's experience—man is not supernatural and omnipotent. Compared to the eternal, sovereign Jehovah, who sits enthroned upon the "circle" (zenith) of the earth, men are like grasshoppers. Get all the millions and millions of grasshoppers together and they cannot hold the world in its course. All the men of the world are like that. Some interpreters see in the word *hkoog* ("circle") an indication that ancient people knew the world was round. Others think it merely means the highest part of the horizon or the zenith. God is pictured as sitting over the highest part of the earth to watch over His creation. The emphasis of the context is on comparing the power of God and the weakness of man. God also stretched out the heavens as effortlessly and quickly as a man in Isaiah's day would stretch out a curtain. These vast, endless, majestic heavens are His dwelling place. Light travels at approximately 186,000 miles per second. The estimated distance to the extent of the *known* universe is 6,000,000 light *years!* Multiply the number of seconds in a year by six million and you get the estimate of the *known* universe. But there are areas beyond that!

Proud, haughty, presumptuous human potentates and rulers strut through history pretending they rule the earth. But it is Jehovah who gives and takes away (cf. Dan. 2:20-23; Jer. 27:5-11; Isa. 45:1-7). God plants and sows and lets them take root only as long as He wishes. Some men scarcely are sown and hardly take root before He takes them away like the whirlwind takes chaff away. All flesh is like grass (I Pet. 1:24-25). Our years are "soon gone and we fly away" (cf. Psa. 90:9-10; Mt. 6:27; Jas. 4:13-17), but God is forever.

The prophet repeats his challenge. There is no being to whom one may liken Jehovah. No one in all His creation is His equal. He is the Incomparable One. He has created the stars and planets. He knows how many there are and has a name for each of them. Man cannot even count the stars, let alone create one. Someone has pointed out that while God formed other animals to look downwards for pasture and prey, he made man alone erect, and told him to look at what may be regarded as his own habitation, the starry heavens. When man seriously contemplates the heavens he is pointed to the Creator (Psa. 19:1-6). Charles A. Lindbergh was 25 years old when he took off from Roosevelt Field, New York, at 7:52 a.m. on May 20, 1927. After more than 3600 miles and 33½ hours, he landed at LeBourget Field near Paris, France. When he had flown his trusted plane, "Spirit of St. Louis," midway on its transatlantic flight he began to think of the smallness of man and the deficiency of his devices, and the greatness and marvels of God's universe. He mused, "It's hard to be an agnostic here in the 'Spirit of St. Louis' when so aware of the frailty of man's devices. If one dies, all God's creation goes on existing in a plan so perfectly balanced, so wondrously simple and yet so incredibly complex that it is beyond our comprehension. There's the infinite detail, and man's consciousness of it all—a world audience to what, if not to God."

QUIZ

1. Why must Isaiah's people know about the nature of God?
2. How does Isaiah proceed to bring the people to this knowledge?
3. What is interesting about Isaiah's statement about the dust of the earth having been measured by God?
4. How did Isaiah come to such a lofty concept of God?
5. What can Christians learn from this emphasis on the nature of God?
6. Why is making graven images stupid?
7. What other forms of idolatry are there?
8. Why should the contemplation of the heavens point man to God?

c. PERSEVERE IN WAITING FOR THE LORD

TEXT: 40:27-31

27 Why sayest thou, O Jacob, and speakest, O Israel, My way is hid from Jehovah, and the justice due to me is passed away from my God?

28 Hast thou not known? hast thou not heard? The everlasting God, Jehovah, the Creator of the ends of the earth, fainteth not, neither is weary; there is no searching of his understanding.

29 He giveth power to the faint; and to him that hath no might he increaseth strength.

30 Even the youths shall faint and be weary, and the young men shall utterly fall:

31 but they that wait for Jehovah shall renew their strength; they shall mount up with wings as eagles; they shall run, and not be weary; they shall walk, and not faint.

QUERIES

a. Why did Israel have such an attitude toward Jehovah?
b. When would Jerusalem come to "renew their strength"?

PARAPHRASE

O Jacob, O Israel, how can you say, The difficult way I must travel is hidden from Jehovah, and God does not notice my trouble and take up my cause and defend my rights? You certainly have had plenty of opportunity to know this is not true of Jehovah, haven't you? You have certainly heard the truth about Jehovah, haven't you? Jehovah is the God of eternity. He was before creation and He is the Creator. He is eternal in all His attributes and eternally powerful and strong and vigilant. He never tires or grows weary. Finite men will not understand this eternality because it is impossible for men to fully comprehend the infinite. There is abundant evidence of God's eternal power so men may believe even if they cannot understand it. Jehovah is the One who gives power and strength to everyone else! All men eventually grow weak and exhaust their strength, even the young, virile athletic-type men tire and grow weary. But those who believe in Jehovah will be given fresh strength, will rise up from their difficulties as if they were eagles soaring upward to the heavens, will run upon their course of life as steadily as a racer who never tires or as one who walks for miles and miles and never grows weary. Jehovah will give those who believe in Him a measure of the divine strength that He Himself has.

COMMENTS

v. 27-28 POWER IN JEHOVAH: If the people of the Lord (in this case Israel) are to receive the comfort He offers through the promised Servant, they must prepare, perceive and persevere. The people have, either unconsciously or deliberately, mentally reduced Jehovah to the level of their idol-gods. The influence of Baalism in Judah from the days of Isaiah to the captivity grew until the people practically called Jehovah Baal, and Baal Jehovah (cf. Isa. 66:17; Jer. 2:8; 12:16; 23:13; 23:27; Hosea 9:10; 13:1-2). When one reduces his concept of God to a wooden statue or a human philosophical system, one cannot help feeling his god is powerless to help him—for his god is nothing more than a creation of his own futility and frustration! Isaiah's people, however, had abundant teaching and evidence that Jehovah was eternal (see comments 40:21, etc.). Their complaint that Jehovah was unconcerned or unaware of their struggles was inexcusable. What their problems were at this time we are not told. It may refer to the political and military pressures being felt by the whole world as a result of the life-and-death struggle between the Assyrians and the Babylonians. Judah had become a political "pawn" on the geographical chess-board of these two great world empires. So Judah was complaining that Jehovah was either incapable of protecting her rights (Heb. *mishepatyi; cause*) or impervious to her situation.

Isaiah reminds the people that historically they have had prophet after prophet teach them of Jehovah's omnipotence and omniscience. Generation after generation they have had demonstrations of His constant concern for them and His repeated miraculous deliverances. Their fault was that of so many of us—letting circumstances overwhelm us. Peter would have walked on water—until he saw the waves (Lk. 14:22-33). The people of Judah had another problem—they could not understand eternality, deity, supernaturalness. They understood (they thought) only the natural, experienceable. Like so many today, what cannot be understood or reduced to the experienceable cannot be believed. Isaiah confirms that Jehovah, being Eternal Creator, is fully understood by no human being. But that does not keep man from believing when he has sufficient evidence to believe. Man does not fully understand all the physical and material things he knows about (gravity, nuclear physics, tornados, etc.), but he forms certain fundamental beliefs from what evidence he does have and functions toward a purpose on that basis.

v. 29-31 PARTICIPATION BY FAITH: God is the source of all strength, physical and spiritual. But it is the spiritual, moral strength that is most important. God is able to fashion any kind of physical body He wishes (I Cor. 15:35-58). But the glorified, immortal body will house only a demon if the spiritual is not reborn, renewed. That renewal, though supplied by God, is participated in only by faith on the part of man.

The promise of renewal here then looks forward to the coming of the Messiah (the "consolation of Israel") (cf. Lk. 1:51-55; 2:25-32, etc.). The Hebrew word *kivvah* is translated *wait* but also means *trust, hope.* It seems paradoxical but the one who depends upon the Lord is the one who is strong (cf. II Cor. 12:9-10; Eph. 3:16; Col. 1:11; Phil. 4:13; II Tim. 4:17; I Pet. 5:10, etc.). The most perfect specimen of human strength sooner or later exhausts his human resources. But the man who waits upon the Lord is strong and unmovable even when the physical body begins to deteriorate. Of course, the Lord is calling upon the people of Judah to trust Him presently in the midst of the circumstances which have caused them to doubt. They must believe now that He will fulfill what He has promised. Although they cannot understand His ways He is cognizant of their way and will supply spiritual and moral strength to them if they will participate by faith. He will not take away their circumstances, necessarily, but will supply them the spiritual strength to conquer their difficulties.

QUIZ

1. Why did the people think Jehovah was unconcerned with their problems?
2. Did they have a right to such an attitude?
3. What was really their problem?
4. When was the promise of renewed strength to be ultimately fulfilled?
5. What is another meaning of "wait for Jehovah"?

2. CONQUEST, CHAPTER 41

a. GENTILES SILENCED

TEXT: 41:1-7

1 Keep silence before me, O islands; and let the peoples renew their strength; let them come near; then let them speak; let us come near together to judgment.

2 Who hath raised up one from the east, whom he calleth in righteousness to his foot? he giveth nations before him, and maketh him rule over kings; he giveth them as the dust to his sword, as the driven stubble to his bow.

3 He pursueth them, and passeth on safely, even by a way that
he had not gone with his feet.
4 Who hath wrought and done it, calling the generations from
the beginning? I Jehovah, the first, and with the last, I am he.
5 The isles have seen, and fear; the ends of the earth tremble;
they draw near, and come.
6 They help every one his neighbor; and every one saith to his
brother, Be of good courage.
7 So the carpenter encourageth the goldsmith, and he that
smootheth with the hammer him that smiteth the anvil,
saying of the soldering, It is good; and he fasteneth it with
nails, that it should not be moved.

QUERIES

a. Who is the one from "the east" raised up by God?
b. Which "isles" fear, tremble and encourage one another?

PARAPHRASE

Shut up and listen to Me, all you heathen enemies of Mine. I challenge all My enemies to clothe themselves in all the power they can muster and present themselves before Me. Then, when they have all the strength they can muster, let them speak and we will enter into contest together. I want to ask you ahead of time, Who do you think is raising up from the east your conqueror and My executioner of justice? It is I, Jehovah, whose sovereign providence gives you into My servant's hand. I give all your kings to be ruled over by him and I give your people to be ground into dust and smashed into pieces like stubble by the sword and bow of his warfare. He chases all My enemies away and goes wherever he wishes in safety—even through territory unfamiliar and hostile to him. Who is capable of such omnipotence? It is He who, ever since there has been a human history, has called into existence the generations of men—even Jehovah, the Eternal, Uncaused First Cause. He is, I AM! The pagan peoples see and fear. My servant will strike trembling terror into the hearts of all people. Still they will draw together with one another and unite in their opposition to him to help and encourage one another insisting he is not capable of overcoming them all. They will feverishly engage themselves in the production of new and more ornate idols. The craftsmen will urge one another saying, We are doing a good job on these idols—these will surely be great enough and permanent enough to keep us safe from him.

COMMENTS

v. 1-4 Jehovah Reigns: Just as the predicted *Comfort* of chapter 40 was to come to the Jews after their exile but realized ultimately in the Messiah, so the *Conquest* of chapter 41 is to come to the Jews (through Cyrus) but will be realized ultimately in the Messiah. Both *comfort* and *conquest* are to come to God's people through a *servant*. The *Servant* section (ch. 40-53) portrays three servants of Jehovah engaged in fulfilling His redemptive plan for mankind. *Cyrus, Israel* and the *Suffering Servant,* are the three servants of Isaiah's message. Cyrus and Israel are apparently types of the Suffering Servant—Cyrus typifying the conquering, judging aspect of the Messiah's work and Israel typifying the atoning, sanctifying aspect of the Messiah's work. Isaiah intertwines or meshes the work of all these closely together in this Servant section until it is difficult to distinguish which one he is describing. At times it appears he is describing both the type and the Antitype (e.g., Cyrus and the Messiah) in the same passage—as in our present passage.

The word *hkeriyshu* is translated *keep silence* and means literally, "to be blunted, dull, dumb, silent," or "to hold the peace." Jehovah *commands* silence. He is going to issue an omnipotent, omniscient edict. He is going to predict providential events which will alter the destinies of all men and all nations. He is about to tell the world how He is going to "run things." Mankind insists it is going to tell God how it is going to "run the world." But God, through His prophet, commands, "Shut up, I'm going to tell you how I am going to run things."

The "islands" are the islands of the Mediterranean and Aegean. The isthmus of Greece and the islands of the Aegean (known as Javan to the Hebrews) represented the remotest regions of heathendom to the Hebrews of Isaiah's day. The Lord God is challenging the world that stands in opposition to His redemptive program to come before Him having clothed (*hkeliyphu,* Heb.) themselves in renewed strength and vigor and meet Him in a contest. The outcome of this contest will determine who "runs the world." Similar challenges are made by Jehovah in Joel 3:1-15 (see our comments in *Minor Prophets,* College Press, pgs. 193-196) and Ezekiel 38-39. Joel and Ezekiel are predicting the battle of God and the world through Jesus Christ at the cross and the resurrection. We suspect that Cyrus' conquest of the world (bringing God's judgment upon it) and Cyrus' release of the Jews to return to their homeland (bringing God's redemption to them) was *typical* of the same battle at Calvary and the empty tomb.

The present passage speaks of Cyrus, emperor of Persia ("one from the east."). There can be little doubt about this when one sees the extended context of Isaiah (cf. Isa. 44:28; 45:1; 45:13; 46:11; 48:14-16). It predicts events and persons at least 100 years or more before they happened. Isaiah died about 700-690 B.C. Cyrus conquered Astyages in 550 B.C. and became sole ruler of Elam (Persia). Cyrus was probably born about 590-580 B.C.

Isaiah uses a word, *leaumiym* (root is *loam*), peculiar to his writings, which is translated *peoples.* It is less definite than either *goiym* or *'ammiym,* two other Hebrew words translated *peoples. Goiym* stands for *Gentiles; 'ammiym* refers to a people as viewed by themselves, or, *we people; loamiym* stands for *all races* of people in general. God's announcement that He is going to take another omnipotent, providential step in His program of redemption through Cyrus (bringing the world under the magisterial rule of Cyrus and return of the covenant people to their land) is not a provincial announcement—it is worldwide! Cyrus will be God's servant for all *races!*

Persia (today's Iran) was directly *east* of Palestine. In Isaiah's day it was known as Elam. The Persian empire flourished for approximately 200 years (549-332 B.C.) until Alexander the Greek conquered the world and turned it into a semi-Greek culture. "One from the east" definitely means Cyrus but probably includes all succeeding Persian emperors since the restoration of the Jewish people proceeded under Cyrus' successors (see our comments *Daniel,* College Press, pages 347-349). *Tsedeq* (translated *righteousness*) would be better translated *justice.* It may refer to the justice of God upon His enemies accomplished through Cyrus as a secondary agent, or, it may refer to the personal character of Cyrus. Both would be appropriate since God uses secondary agents to govern the world and administer justice and Cyrus (as well as most of his successors) was known for fair, honest and just treatment of his subjects. The Jews, especially, held the Persians in high esteem for the treatment they received at their hand.

God's challenge to the races is: Which god of the races is able to withstand the one from the east whom I will send to execute My justice? Jehovah, the God of Israel, gives temporary rule of His world to whomever He pleases (cf. Isa. 10:5-19; Jer. 27:1-11; Dan. 7:6; 9:24, etc.). When God's providence is decreed and predicted, nothing can thwart it! Cyrus shall, as God's servant, pound those who resist into dust and stubble with his weapons of war (sword and bow). Cyrus and his successors will conquer Asia Minor, Egypt, into India, and cross the Aegean and, for a time, occupy European soil in Greece. This is Cyrus II, or Cyrus The Great and few world conquerors have been regarded as highly as Cyrus. The Persians called him father. The Greeks regarded him as a master and lawgiver. When Alexander the Great found that Cyrus' tomb had been rifled (by Greek soldiers and grave robbers), he ordered that the body be replaced and the contents of the tomb be restored as far as possible. To the Jews he was the Lord's anointed who ended the Babylonian exile and opened a new era in the history of Israel. Cyrus did not force Persian ideas on his subjects, but rather formed a synthesis of the ancient cultures of Mesopotamia, Syria, Asia Minor, the Greek cities, and parts of India. It is reported by some historians that he was a monotheist, which would have exalted his image in the eyes of the Jews.

Cyrus marched on and on in *shalom* (safety), into the far reaches of civilization unfamiliar and hostile to him, until he met his death in battle about 530 B.C. His body was carried back to Pasargadae, one of his capital cities. There his body was covered with wax, according to Persian custom, and placed in a stately, dignified tomb which was guarded by faithful priests for 200 years. The tomb is still standing, but its contents have long since been removed.

Who has wrought this? Are the passing events of history, the births of nations and their deaths, merely the results of chance arrangements of atoms? Is the governing of the world left to the whims of tyrants and anarchists? Is history cyclical and doomed to repeat itself forever—doomed never to reach the perfection it longs for? No! No nation exists apart from God. He calls the generations into existence. He makes rulers His servants. All of history, in one way or another, serves God's purpose. His purpose is to create out of mankind a kingdom of His own, trusting in His sovereignty, depending upon His grace, sanctifying itself in His holiness. The majority of men and women are in rebellion against God's purposes. The establishment of the kingdom of God (Christ as King, the church as the kingdom) began in a family (Seth, Noah and Abraham), expanded to a nation (the Israelites), then encompassed the world (the church). The very fact of the establishment of the kingdom program on earth, through men, pronounced the *judgment* of God upon all human governments and efforts to usurp God's sovereignty over man. Our text is simply another announcement by God that He is going to act through Cyrus to preserve His covenant people and His work of establishing His kingdom. Thus, *all races* are called together for a demonstration of His sovereignty by the very fact that God is able, through His prophet, to predict the conquest of Cyrus one hundred years before Cyrus was born!

Delitzsch says of verse four, "It is the full meaning of the name Jehovah (*Yaweh*) which is unfolded here; for God is called Jehovah as the absolute I, the absolutely free Being, pervading all history, and yet above all history, as He who is Lord of His own absolute being, in revealing which He is purely self-determined; in a word, as the unconditionally free and unchangeably eternal personality."

v. 5-7 JAVAN REELS: One has only to read the history of Persian conquests to see the fulfillment of these verses. The isles of the Mediterranean and the Aegean reeled and trembled under the warfare of Persian armies. They formed alliances and coalitions against the Persians. By the summer of 539 B.C. the Persian armies were ready to attack Babylon. Nabonidus, sensing the situation, brought the gods of the outlying regions into his capital, trusting that they would aid him in his time of need. This antagonized the people whose gods were displaced and brought further resentment to the priests of Babylon. This appears to be a direct fulfillment of verses 5-7.

All during the Persian rule there were those segments of the empire resisting Persian friendship to the Hebrews (cf. Ezra 4:3-16). After the Persian empire, the Syrians (under the Seleucids) and the Egyptians (under the Ptolemies) opposed the work of God by persecuting the Hebrew people. Daniel predicts all these "times of trouble."

What Isaiah is predicting in verses 5-7 is that although Cyrus and the Persians shall be raised up by God to execute His judgment upon the heathen opposition to God's kingdom work, the heathen will tremble but they will not repent. They will unite, encourage one another, and continue to trust in gods of gold and wood. They will make newer and more gods, complimenting themselves that they have done a good job and that they have made gods that will survive the Servant of Jehovah.

Of course, new and better gods did not stop Cyrus. The Lord used him to fulfill that portion of the plan of divine redemption for which Cyrus was needed. Then, when the Lord needed Alexander the Great and all that his hellenization of the world could contribute to that redemptive plan, He permitted the Greeks to serve Him. Jehovah "runs the world" and there are not any gods of any race to usurp His sovereignty. Jehovah has silenced them all! Ultimately God silenced all His opposition at the cross and the empty tomb. Perhaps, in type, His work through Cyrus points to that ultimate moment!

QUIZ

1. Who are the three Servants of this section?
2. Why does God command the peoples to be silent?
3. Where else does God challenge the world to meet Him in contest?
4. How does God call Cyrus "in righteousness"?
5. How "great" was Cyrus?
6. What is the point in God predicting through Isaiah, 100 years before, these events concerning Cyrus?
7. Did the people of the "isles" actually try to make new and better gods to stop Cyrus? When?

b. GOD'S PEOPLE SAVED

TEXT: 41:8-13

8 But thou, Israel, my servant, Jacob whom I have chosen, the seed of Abraham my friend,
9 thou whom I have taken hold of from the ends of the earth, and called from the corners thereof, and said unto thee, Thou art my servant, I have chosen thee and not cast thee away;
10 fear thou not, for I am with thee; be not dismayed, for

I am thy God; I will strengthen thee; yea, I will help thee; yea, I will uphold thee with the right hand of my righteousness.

11 Behold, all they that are incensed against thee shall be put to shame and confounded: they that strive with thee shall be as nothing, and shall perish.

12 Thou shalt seek them, and shalt not find them, even them that contend with thee: they that war against thee shall be as nothing, and as a thing of nought.

13 For I Jehovah thy God will hold thy right hand, saying unto thee, Fear not; I will help thee.

QUERIES

a. Why is Israel reminded of her servanthood?

b. When did God bring to nothing those who made war against Israel?

PARAPHRASE

But you, Israel, you are my chosen servant. You have a special heritage to fulfill because you are the descendants of Abraham whom I knew as My friend. Through him I fashioned you as a nation to serve me from out of the midst of heathendom. If I have done all this especially for you I certainly will not desert you if you will carry out your mission of service to Me. Therefore do not fear any of your enemies because I am with you. There is no reason for you to despair. I, Jehovah, am your God and I will give you divine strength and help. Yes, indeed, I will cause you to stand with My righteous and powerful right hand. Wait and see—all those who hate you will be confounded, humiliated and destroyed. Those who oppose you will be annihilated. Even if you go around looking for your enemies you will not be able to find any. I repeat, those who make war against you will be utterly obliterated.

It is I, the Lord your Great God, holding on to your right hand. And I say to you I will not let you go so do not be afraid.

COMMENTS

v. 8-10 SERVANTHOOD OF ISRAEL: God chose the Hebrews for special servanthood. They were to serve Him as a consecrated, holy priesthood. (cf. Ex. 19:5-6; Lev. 25:55; Deut. 4:5-7; 7:6-8; 14:2; 26:18-19) By their consecration to His commandments they would be the human agency through which God could send the Redeemer in human flesh. They would also serve as witnesses to the glory of Jehovah to the nations round about them. The Lord did not choose Israel according to human standards, i.e., Israel was not large in population or wealth (Deut. 7:7). He chose Israel by His sovereign grace—because He loved her (Deut. 7:8; 10:12-22).

The point of this passage, however, is to allay the fears of the people of Isaiah's day. Isaiah's contemporaries were filled with terror at the threats of Assyria and Babylon. They began to despair that God would ever be able to fulfill His covenant to them. So Isaiah reminds them that if God could take a man like Abraham from a background of heathen idolatry, make him a friend of God and protect, sustain and multiply him into a nation, God can protect His people in Isaiah's day! If God can take that nation, from Abraham's loins, and deliver them from the power and temptations of Egypt, He can certainly deliver Isaiah's Judah from the threats of Assyria and Babylon. And if Isaiah's people will serve God and trust Him, He will fulfill His covenant with them. He is the same God who was with them in Egypt, in the wilderness, in the day of the Judges and in David's day.

v. 11-13 SUBJUGATION OF ISRAEL'S ENEMIES: Now the process by which God fulfills His covenant involves the preparation of a people to make them capable of receiving its fulness! This preparation involves discipline, repentance and holiness. The Lord did not take Moses and his people directly from

Egypt to Canaan. They demonstrated they were not mature enough for that, so they were disciplined forty years in the wilderness. In Isaiah's day it was apparent God's covenant people needed some severe discipline and serious penitence. Isaiah is attempting to prepare his people spiritually for the coming captivity. He is trying to reorient their thinking about who God is and what He does that they may have faith in Him in spite of the circumstances of the imminent exile.

The troubles of the Jews (called "indignation" by Daniel) did not cease with the Babylonian exile. Great and powerful enemies opposed the Jews ever after (Babylon, Persia, Greece, Syria, Egypt, Rome, etc.). So, this passage has its fulfillment, not in genetic, national, Israel, but in the children of Abraham according to faith (Rom. 4:1-25; Gal. 3:6-9; 3:15-29). It is readily apparent from the New Testament that God's deliverance of His covenant people from their enemies was not intended to be fulfilled physically, but spiritually (which is more important) (cf. Lk. 1:46-55; 1:68-79; Eph. 6:10-18; Col. 2:12-15, etc.). It is true, God preserved a physical nation, the Jews, until about 70 A.D. when they were scattered all over the world by the Romans. They are still a dispersed and dispossessed people today (in spite of the fact that a very small percentage of Jews maintain a very tenuous occupation of a portion of Palestine). But even this preservation of a physical nation until 70 A.D. was possible only because a small minority (remnant) of that nation trusted God and hoped in the messianic promises. Now that the Messiah's kingdom has been established physical, national relationship is no longer efficacious with God. Within the Messiah's kingdom there is neither Jew nor Gentile. God has always been interested in the spiritual man (Rom. 2:28-29), not just his nationality. The true Israel of God walks by the rule that neither circumcision (Jew) nor uncircumcision (Gentile) counts for anything, but a new creation (Gal. 6:15-16).

If Israel of Isaiah's day will serve the Lord by believing and obeying, He will deliver them from those who would oppose the redemptive work of God in the world. God will deliver the Jews from Assyria, Babylon, Persia, Syria, Egypt and, in the days of the Roman empire He will fulfill His covenant through the Messiah. The Messiah will defeat once and for all the power of the devil. The Messiah will demonstrate historically that God is able to defeat even death. All the promises of God find their Yea! in Christ (II Cor. 1:20).

QUIZ

1. What service was Israel to render as God's servant?
2. What was the basis upon which God chose Israel as His servant?
3. What is the point of emphasizing Israel's servanthood?
4. What enemies will God destroy?
5. What is the long-range fulfillment of this passage?

c. GLORY TO GOD

TEXT: 41:14-20

14 Fear not, thou worm Jacob, and ye men of Israel; I will help thee, saith Jehovah, and thy Redeemer is the Holy One of Israel.
15 Behold, I have made thee to be a new sharp threshing instrument having teeth; thou shalt thresh the mountains, and beat them small, and shalt make the hills as chaff.
16 Thou shalt winnow them, and the wind shall carry them away, and the whirlwind shall scatter them; and thou shalt rejoice in Jehovah, thou shalt glory in the Holy One of Israel.
17 The poor and needy seek water, and there is none, and their tongue faileth for thirst; I Jehovah will answer them, I the God of Israel will not forsake them.
18 I will open rivers on the bare heights, and fountains in the

midst of the valleys; I will make the wilderness a pool of water, and the dry land springs of water.
19 I will put in the wilderness the cedar, the acacia, and the
myrtle, and the oil-tree; I will set in the desert the fir-tree, the pine, and the box-tree together:
20 that they may see, and know, and consider, and under-
stand together, that the hand of Jehovah hath done this, and the Holy One of Israel hath created it.

QUERIES

a. Why is Jacob called a "worm"?
b. Did God ever make such physical changes to Palestine as are described in verses 18 and 19?

PARAPHRASE

Do not be afraid Israel. Although you are as despised as a worm, I will help you, says Jehovah. Your Savior is the Eternal Holy One of Israel. I am going to make you grind your enemies into pieces like a new threshing sledge grinds wheat into chaff. Even though those who oppose you may be as formidable as great mountains, you will grind them down and blow them away into nothingness. Then you will give praise and glory to Jehovah and be filled with joy because the Holy One of Israel has delivered you. Right now you are spiritually destitute and in need of the living water and there is none. But I, Jehovah, will answer those who recognize their need and call upon Me. I will not forsake any of My faithful ones. In the midst of the thirst of My people for life I will open a river. I will completely reverse these conditions of spiritual aridness. The change will be miraculous. Those who remain faithful to Me will partake of life-giving water everywhere and will grow and produce fruit and will be like an oasis of trees and pools in a desert wilderness. The objective is that man may see, know, consider, and understand together that the Lord, not man, created this miraculous change.

COMMENTS

v. 14-16 WORM WINS: The Hebrew word *tola'ath* is translated worm and is the name of the *coccus worm* which was the worm used in making scarlet dye. It is the same word used in Psa. 22:6 in reference to the scorn and despite men will show the Messiah. Jacob (Israel) is called a worm by Isaiah to describe the scorn with which the nation is looked upon by its enemies. Assyria considers Judah with contempt (see comments Isaiah 36:8-9). It is interesting that God's covenant people are called "worm" and the Messiah calls Himself "worm" (Psa. 22:6). God is going to give the covenant people victory over their adversaries. They may go into captivity but eventually they will return, by the Spirit of God, to resume their service of messianic destiny. Their enemies will, one by one (Assyria, Babylon, Persia, Greece, Rome) be ground to chaff (cf. Dan. 2:31-45, esp. 2:35), and blown away. A threshing sledge was a flat plank or planks of wood with rollers underneath studded with metal spikes for threshing wheat. They were sometimes put to use by armies to torture and execute prisoners of war. This prediction of covenant victory over enemies ultimately was fulfilled in the Messiah. The Messiah's victory will usher in a universal kingdom of God (the church) and men of all nations will rejoice and give glory to the Holy One of Israel who accomplished it all (cf. Isa. 2:1-5; 19:16-25; Zech. 14:16-21, etc.).

v. 17-20 WATER IN THE WILDERNESS: Isaiah describes the destitution of the covenant people under another figure. They are "poor and needy" seeking water and there is none. They appear to be helpless and hopeless. We think this applies to their spiritual destitution. At no time has God ever physically watered all the wastelands of Palestine. This passage undoubtedly refers to the spiritual water of life to be supplied by the Messiah (cf. John 4 and John 7). This passage is parallel to Isaiah, chapter 35 (see our comments there). The point is that God is going to completely reverse their spiritual situation from destitution to abundance. Edward J. Young comments: "The emphasis upon water and trees had also been found in the account of Eden in Genesis 3. Through the entrance of sin into the world, however, the garden was forfeited, and man entered a world where thorns and thistles would grow and he would labor by the sweat of his brow. In picturing the future age of blessing, the eschatological period when the restoration will occur, Isaiah uses the combined figures of water and trees. It is as though a bit of heaven had come down to earth; and indeed, those who one day will be blessed of these rivers and these trees are in the heavenlies in Christ Jesus." And the objective for all this spiritual regeneration is to bring glory to the Holy One of Israel who shall do it. Israel, the worm, the poor and needy, is incapable of changing its despicable condition. God will, by His grace, send His Servant the Messiah to create the new order. Isaiah's contemporaries are called upon to believe the Lord's promise and wait upon Him in faith.

QUIZ

1. What connection does "worm" have with the Messiah?
2. Who will rejoice in the victory of God's people over their enemies?
3. Why call Israel "poor and needy"?
4. What parallel passage in Isaiah helps understand the figures of water and trees?
5. What is the object of this great reversal of Israel's circumstances?

d. GOOD TIDINGS

TEXT: 41:21-29

21 Produce your cause, saith Jehovah; bring forth your strong
reasons, saith the King of Jacob.
22 Let them bring them forth, and declare unto us what shall
happen: declare ye the former things, what they are, that
we may consider them, and know the latter end of them;
or show us things to come.
23 Declare the things that are to come hereafter, that we may
know that ye are gods: yea, do good, or do evil, that we
may be dismayed, and behold it together.
24 Behold, ye are of nothing, and your work is of nought; an
abomination is he that chooseth you.
25 I have raised up one from the north, and he is come; from
the rising of the sun one that calleth upon my name: and
he shall come upon rulers as upon mortar, and as the potter
treadeth clay.
26 Who hath declared it from the beginning, that we may
know? and beforetime, that we may say, He is right? yea,
there is none that declareth, yea, there is none that showeth,
yea, there is none that heareth your words.
27 I am the first that saith unto Zion, Behold, behold them;
and I will give to Jerusalem one that bringeth good tidings.
28 And when I look, there is no man; even among them there
is no counsellor, that, when I ask of them, can answer a
word.
29 Behold, all of them, their works are vanity and nought;
their molten images are wind and confusion.

QUERIES

a. Who is Jehovah challenging to "produce cause"?
b. Who is being "raised up from the north"?
c. Who is the "one that bringeth good tidings"?

PARAPHRASE

All you who have put your trust in idols, I, Jehovah challenge you to demonstrate causes and reasons for such trust. Bring forth your idols and let them declare what is going to happen. I challenge them to tell what has occurred in years gone by and what it all means; and I challenge them to tell what is yet to come—predict the future. Indeed, your idols may prove they are deities if they are able to predict the future and do supernatural works of deliverance and judgment which will astound us. As a matter of fact, your idols are less than nothing and they can do nothing at all. Men and women who choose to worship idols are disgusting and detestable. I, the Lord, am going to raise up one (Cyrus) to deliver My people from their enemies. He will come from the east by way of the north and he will do My will. He will tear down rulers and kingdoms as easily as he does mortared walls. As the potter is able to trample upon the clay with which he works, so will this deliverer trample under foot his opposition. Which of the pagan deities have predicted this so that when it comes to pass we may know they are gods? Not a one! No other god known has said anything at all about it! I, Jehovah, was the first and only One to tell My covenant people, Look! Look! Your deliverers. Furthermore, I will give to Jerusalem a prophet to announce this good news of deliverance. But when I look among all the pagan deities there is not a single one who can give any kind of counsel—not a one of them answers My challenge. You see? they are all foolish, worthless things; these idols are all as empty as the wind.

COMMENTS

v. 21-24 Challenge: Now Jehovah is going to prove His previous claims that His covenant people need not fear the threats of their enemies (Assyria and Babylon). There were many in Israel and Judah listening to the alleged prophecies of false prophets and the oracles of pagan gods. These false prophecies predicted the obliteration of the Jews and the downfall of the Jewish God, Jehovah. It seems astonishing that the Jews, with all their history of miraculous deliverances from the Egyptians, Canaanites, Philistines, etc., could ever doubt Jehovah's power. They had become so engrossed in politics, economics, pagan philosophies and just plain sensuality, they had no time for God and His Word. As a result when it became apparent they were going to be invaded by the awesome, terrifying hordes of Assyria and Babylon, they could not turn to Jehovah. They did not know Him! Most of the Jews turned to pagan soothsayers and idol-priests (cf. Isa. 8:16-22, etc.). But God, through the prophet Isaiah, is revealing that He will deliver His people from these terrible enemies. Positive, empirical, proof that Jehovah is their only Deliverer is demonstrated once and for all in fulfillment of prophecy. When history is predicted before it happens it is a claim to omniscience and omnipotence. When that prediction comes to pass it demonstrates deity. The authority of a prophet was proved by the fulfillment of his predictions (Deut. 18:21-22). Jehovah challenges all the pagan gods to give proof of their divine power by divulging the future. Jehovah challenges the idols and their priests to "declare the former things" which is a call to interpret past history. They cannot even do this! Then He calls them to "show us things to come." God does not want credulous worshipers. Preaching without proof and evidence is scarcely preaching at all. It encourages naked credulity and shallow conviction. So, when God sent Isaiah to produce faith in His deliverance, He gave proof and evidence of His power. That proof was that Jehovah could foretell, through His prophet, the future. Pagan deities could not. This same confrontation (between God's prophets and pagan idols) recurs over and over again in history (Moses, Elijah, Jeremiah, Daniel, Paul). God does not shrink from the demand of authenticating credentials for His Word. What Jehovah predicts has already been recorded in 41:2ff in the "one from the east." The prediction is repeated in 41:25ff. But for now, Jehovah's challenge goes unanswered and the conclusion is inevitable—idols are not gods! As a matter of fact, idols are less than nothing. The verdict is: idols are a total minus-quantity and so is their work. They cannot do good nor can they do evil. Missionaries have found in modern pagan tribes demonstrations of the power the mind has over the body when the mind is "psyched" or hypnotized by superstition and fear. But they have also found that once the idol-worshipper sees a demonstration that their idol is "nothing" he is at once healed of his physical malady. Abomination is from the Hebrew word *tuaivah* which means abhorrent, disgusting, detestable, repugnant. Those who deliberately choose to worship idols soon become like the thing they worship (cf. Hosea 9:10; Psa. 115:3-8).

v. 25-29 CONFUTATION: The "one from the north . . . from the rising of the sun" is the same one from "the east" in 41:2, Cyrus, king of Persia (cf. comments 41:2ff). The massive armies of the great Mesopotamian empires (Assyria, Babylon, Persia) all swooped down on Palestine from "the north." One only has to look at a map of the Near East to see that ancient armies could not march west over the Arabian desert since they had to sustain themselves by daily forage for food and water. So they marched north and came across the "fertile crescent" and entered Palestine from the north. Cyrus will be irresistible. He will do with the enemies of God's people what a potter does with his clay. Now, says Jehovah, which pagan idol or pagan prophet foreknew any events to show they knew Israel's destiny or the future history of Mesopotamian empires? Have any of their words ever been fulfilled so that men were obliged to say, "That idol was right"? Not a one! Not one word about Israel's deliverance through the "one from the east" ever came from the heathen oracles. Jehovah, through His prophets, was first and only to make such a declaration. He announced that the Deliverer would come to Zion. Even in the midst of all His announcements of the future captivity He announces deliverance from it by the "one from the east." This would be good news to Jerusalem. Of course, it would be good news only to those who believed. That was always a minority.

The majority of the people never even recognized the promises of deliverance because they refused to believe the predictions of judgment in the first place. And when one looked toward the pagan gods and prophets one could find no intimation whatsoever of this great deliverance. There is only stupid silence. They do not know the future. So they are nothing. They are powerless. They are just wind. Finis! The contest is over—God is victor. Jehovah conquers all for His people.

QUIZ

1. Why did the Jews listen to pagan prophets?
2. Why does God give proof and evidence for His omniscience?
3. Why are those who choose idols an "abomination"?
4. Why did the Mesopotamian armies come from the north?
5. How much did the pagan oracles say about Israel's deliverance?
6. What is the conclusion of the contest between God and idols?

3. COVENANT, CHAPTER 42

a. SEE MY SERVANT

TEXT: 42:1-9

1 Behold, my servant, whom I uphold; my chosen, in whom my soul delighteth: I have put my Spirit upon him; he will bring forth justice to the Gentiles.
2 He will not cry, nor lift up his voice, nor cause it to be heard in the street.
3 A bruised reed will he not break, and a dimly burning wick will he not quench: he will bring forth justice in truth.
4 He will not fail nor be discouraged, till he have set justice in the earth; and the isles shall wait for his law.

5 Thus saith God Jehovah, he that created the heavens, and
stretched them forth; he that spread abroad the earth and
that which cometh out of it; he that giveth breath unto the
people upon it, and spirit to them that walk therein:
6 I Jehovah have called thee in righteousness, and will hold
thy hand, and will keep thee, and give thee for a covenant
of the people, for a light of the Gentiles;
7 to open the blind eyes, to bring out the prisoners from the
dungeon, and them that sit in darkness out of the prison-
house.
8 I am Jehovah, that is my name; and my glory will I not
give to another, neither my praise unto graven images.
9 Behold, the former things are come to pass, and the new
things do I declare; before they spring forth I tell you of
them.

QUERIES

a. Who is the "servant"?
b. What is meant by "he will not cry, nor lift up his voice . . ." etc.?
c. What does the name "Jehovah" mean?

PARAPHRASE

Look! by faith see My Servant-Messiah whom I shall give My full support. He shall be sent as My chosen One, and My delight in Him shall be made manifest. I will demonstrate that I have put My Spirit upon Him. He will accomplish justice for the people of all nations. He will not be loud and boisterous. He will be gentle, meek and humble and will not practice self-seeking methods. He will not crush and exploit the helpless nor extinguish hope and faith. He will establish real justice and real truth. He Himself will not be quenched or bruised until He accomplishes His mission to establish justice for all mankind. All mankind waits for His truth. This is what Almighty God, Creator of the heavens, Creator of the earth and the green grass, Creator of life, breath and spirit in all men who live upon the earth affirms: I Am Jehovah, Covenant-God, and I have called You, My Servant, to a covenant of righteousness. I have made solemn promise to You to clasp Your hand in Mine and to protect You. It is My purpose to give You for a covenant of Mine for all peoples—even a light to the pagans. I, Jehovah, am giving you to open the "eyes" of men's minds which have been blinded by sin, to deliver all men who are imprisoned and enslaved in the dungeon of unbelief. I am Jehovah, Faithful-Promiser, that is My express nature; I share this glory with no other, least of all gods of wood and stone. Everything I, Jehovah, foretold in the past came to pass just as I said it would. These new things I tell you about My Servant will just as surely come to pass even though I tell you before they happen.

COMMENTS

v. 1-4 CHARACTER OF THE SERVANT: The word *'avediy* is the Hebrew word for bond servant. There is another word, *sakiyr,* meaning hired servant. This is the Messiah! That is evident from Matthew 12:17-21. When the Incarnate God came to man, He came as a servant—the lowliest of servants—a slave (cf. Phil. 2:7 *doulou,* Gr. for slave). *Bekhiyriy* means "choice one" and *ratsethah* means "willing acceptance" (or "delight"). Of all the servants at Jehovah's disposal, this One was the only acceptable One and so God chose Him. This Servant stands in peculiar relationship to Jehovah, He is the Son (cf. Jn. 1:18, etc.). This makes His servanthood astounding. Many servants have been elevated to sonship—but no father wants his son to suffer the indignities of servanthood (cf. Phil 2:5ff; Lk. 15:19ff). This Servant will be sustained by the Spirit of the Living God upon Him. He will have God's Spirit without measure (Jn. 3:31-36) and in Him will all the fulness of God dwell (Col. 1:19; 2:9). The Son is the only servant fit to establish the Father's covenant. He will come with all authority and faithfulness of the Father to deliver judgment, *mishphat,* in this instance meaning justice, to the *goiym* (Gentiles).

The nature of the Servant of Jehovah will be diametrically opposed to all human concepts of saviourhood or messiahship. He will not put on a huge show and make a lot of noise. He will not advertise nor hire a public relations man to create for Him a popular image. He will not call attention to Himself merely for His own satisfaction. He will not seek His own glory (cf. Jn. 5:41; 8:50). He comes humbly (cf. Zech. 9:9). He comes to save, not to win the acclaim of men. He comes to serve, not to be served. Most human saviours and deliverers reach their positions of power by exploitation, to one degree or another, of those less talented, poorer, or weaker than they. The world expects its messiahs to be ruthless, proud, indulgent and patronizing. Nietzsche's "Superman" was to be the result of elimination of all the weak people of the world. Nietzsche advocated breaking and crushing all the "bruised reeds" and quenching all the "dimly burning wicks." His philosophy declared all Jews and Christians weak. Adolph Hitler believed Nietzsche. Hitler was the self-acclaimed messiah of the German people. There have been politicians in our own country subscribing to the same philosophy. Their idea is that the masses are too ignorant to know what is best for them; break them, quench them; then patronize them with all-encompassing government. But the Servant of Jehovah comes to be a servant of the bruised and dimly-burning. He comes to heal and help. He will be a King who serves His subjects—even to die for them. He will search their hearts and personalities and find any spark of good and fan it, if possible, into a flame of faith and holiness. He will pour Himself into them to give them a power to reach their highest potential. He does not befriend them to take from them, but to give to them. This servant will be a suffering Servant (Isa. 53:1-12); He will be a shepherding Servant who tenderly feeds the sheep, not one who devours the flock (Ezek. 34:1-31). The Servant of Jehovah will establish what is right (justice) by what is true (in truth). He will not be fooled by appearances; He will not judge by partiality; He will not accept or practice falsehood. He will personify absolute truth.

There is an interesting play-on-words between verses 4 and 3. In verse 3 the verbs *ratsuts* (bruised) and *kehah* (growing dim) are used again in different form *yikeheh* (He will not *grow dim*) and *yaruts* (He will not be crushed) in verse 4. He will, in the flesh, in servant-form, be victorious and able to help the crushed and quenched! (cf. Heb. 4:14-16).

v. 5-9 Commission of The Servant: God's Servant will come (a) with all the power of the Almighty Creator, (b) in divine righteousness, (c) in divine fellowship, (d) as the covenant of God personified, (e) to deliver, (f) and to fulfill the promises of Jehovah and thus to glorify Him.

This Servant will be sent with all the authority and power of Jehovah. He will have creative power resident in Him. He will do the work of the One and Only True God. The implication of verses 5 and 6 are that the Servant will have all the power to create matter and life that Jehovah has. But the most important mission of the Servant will be "righteousness" and "for a covenant." The Servant's primary objective will be to involve the Gentiles! This is no covenant of commandments, only, but a covenant whose terms and relationships are in a Person, a Life, the Son of God. The Servant Himself will come as Man to accomplish and earn the covenant relationship with Jehovah by suffering the penalty of man's breaking covenant (cf. Mt. 26:26-29; Mt. 20:28; Lk. 24:44-49; Heb. 10:1-25, etc.). Men may enter into that covenant by a relationship of personal faith in Him and His redemptive work, allowing that faith to produce His character in them. The Servant furnishes the righteousness—the covenant-members receive it by faith and obedience. The main thrust of Jesus' ministry was to persuade His people that He was equal with the Creator and that the Covenant of Jehovah was to be Personified in Him. Both of these concepts were rejected and despised by the main body of Jewish people in Jesus' day, not because Jesus failed to demonstrate evidence to substantiate His claims, but because they did not have the love of God in their hearts (cf. John, ch. 7, 8, 9).

To understand the primary meaning of the prediction that the Servant will "open the blind eyes," and "bring out the prisoners," etc., one must compare Isaiah 61:1-2 with Luke 4:16f. Jesus did not do many mighty works in Nazareth, and yet He declared the "release of captives," and "recovering of sight to the blind," was being fulfilled in the very act of "preaching the good news to the poor" there in Nazareth. So, this mission of the Messiah-Servant is not to find its ultimate fulfillment in physical healing alone.

The people of Isaiah's day may as well stop worshipping idols for the glory of Jehovah will be manifested in only one, Himself, Incarnate in the Servant-Son. This is final, absolute and certain to come to pass. Just as surely as the former things God predicted through previous prophets (Moses, Joshua, Samuel, David, Elijah, et al.) so these "new things" which Jehovah predicts through Isaiah, as incredible as they are, will certainly come to pass. The indication is that the people must surrender to the will of God that their salvation is not in national or ethnic relationship but relationship to Him and the Servant whom He shall send, (cf. Jn. 5:23, 38; 6:29).

QUIZ

1. This Servant is the Messiah. Does the N.T. substantiate Jesus as the Servant of Jehovah? Where?
2. What is to be the nature of this Servant?
3. How does this nature compare with that of human saviorhood?
4. How does the Servant become Jehovah's covenant?
5. What is the primary fulfillment of the Servant's opening the eyes of the blind?
6. Why the warning that Jehovah will not give His glory to another?

b. SING A SONG OF PRAISE

TEXT: 42:10-17

10 Sing unto Jehovah a new song, and his praise from the end of the earth; ye that go down to the sea, and all that is therein, the isles, and the inhabitants thereof.
11 Let the wilderness and the cities thereof lift up their voice, the villages that Kedar doth inhabit; let the inhabitants of Sela sing, let them shout from the top of the mountains.
12 Let them give glory unto Jehovah, and declare his praise in the islands.
13 Jehovah will go forth as a mighty man; he will stir up his zeal like a man of war: he will cry, yea, he will shout aloud; he will do mightily against his enemies.
14 I have long time holden my peace; I have been still, and refrained myself: now will I cry out like a travailing woman; I will gasp and pant together.
15 I will lay waste mountains and hills, and dry up all their herbs; and I will make the rivers islands, and will dry up the pools.
16 And I will bring the blind by a way that they know not; in paths that they know not will I lead them; I will make darkness light before them, and crooked places straight. These things will I do, and I will not forsake them.
17 They shall be turned back, they shall be utterly put to shame, that trust in graven images, that say unto molten images, Ye are our gods.

QUERIES

a. Who is to sing to Jehovah?
b. Why a "new" song?

PARAPHRASE

Sing to Jehovah a new song appropriate to the new thing He will do. Sing His praises all over the whole earth. Let all who travel over the world by sea and every creature in the sea sing to Jehovah. Let all the coastlands around the sea, the islands, and all who inhabit them sing to the Lord. Let the inhabitants of the desert cities and villages of Arabia and Edom shout loud praises from their mountain tops. Let all the Gentiles in the far off western islands praise and glorify Jehovah as God. The reason the whole earth should sing and shout the praises of Jehovah is that Jehovah is going forth as a mighty warrior to win a decisive and complete victory over His enemies and all who oppose His redemptive work for man. Jehovah says He has held Himself in restraint against His enemies long enough. Now, like the great inhalations and expirations of a woman gasping in child-delivery, that which I have so long concealed in Myself shall be accomplished. I will make the land of My enemies a waste land; its hills and mountains I will level; its vegetation I will kill with drought; I will dry up its rivers and pools until they are dry land. I am going to devastate My enemies. The ones My enemies have captured and made blind I will deliver by a deliverance known only to Me. I will lead them along a Way they can never discover. I will turn their darkness into light and all the rugged hindrances and crooked places will be straightened out by Me. These are the things I will do, says Jehovah, and I will not forsake all these blind ones. When I accomplish this great, magnificent victory, it will reveal the utter shame of idolatry and cause those who worship idols to recognize the impotence of idols.

COMMENTS

v. 10-12 SING TO JEHOVAH: God's people are invited to sing. The motive for this is the promise of the coming Servant and the great victory He will win and the deliverance He will accomplish. The work of the Servant will be so unique (spiritual deliverance) that it will be a *NEW* song. The subject matter for the lyrics of this song has never been available before (the redemption of the Christ). God's people have always been able to sing praises for God's love, power, deliverance (cf. Ps. 40:3; 42:8; 96:1; 98:1; 149:1; Isa. 30:29, etc.). But this *new* song will be one unknown to angels for it will be known only to the redeemed (cf. Rev. 14:3; 15:3-4). It will be a song to be sung by the universal kingdom of God—people from the western isles (Gentile regions) will sing it (Eph. 5:18-20; Col. 3:12-17). No area is to be excluded from the invitation to sing this new song—not even those who dwell in wilderness (sparsely inhabited) regions. Of course, one must believe and appropriate the Life the Servant provides before one may sing the song—but all are invited.

This passage, and the many others about songs of believers, would lead us to think that the lyrics of Christian music should be restricted primarily to the objective deeds of God and Christ in the great work of redemption and much less (than in the current fad) to the subjective experience of the song writers. The great redemptive acts of God do not vary and are not dependent upon the vascillating fickleness of human emotions and feelings for their apologetic or persuasive value. Human "religious experiences" are dependent upon feelings. Not everyone feels the same way all the time. But God's deeds are always true, no matter how anyone feels. "Let them give glory unto Jehovah . . ."

v. 13-17 SONG OF JUSTICE: The song will be about God's long awaited defeat of His enemies having finally been completed. God has, for good reasons of his own, held back in sending the Servant to defeat His enemies once and for all. It has not even been easy for Jehovah to refrain from doing battle and winning the victory. Many prophets and godly men have questioned and will continue (e.g., Habakkuk; the apostles, Acts 1:6) to question God's time-table of kingdom establishment. But God will do things when the time is right (cf. Gal. 4:4; Heb. 1:1, etc.). And so the time came for God to "disarm the principalities and powers and make a public example of them, triumphing over them in him" (Col. 2:15). That was when He destroyed the power of the devil (Heb. 2:14-18). All this will cost God pain and travail. The great Creator will agonize and hurt because in accomplishing the work of redemption He will make Himself vulnerable by loving through the Incarnate Son as He has never loved before. The agony and pain of God will be manifested physically in the Son and His blood-stained cross.

All the things men have depended upon before will be "dried up" and the "blind" will be delivered from the enemies of Jehovah by the Servant's leading in a way no one knows. It was very apparent when Jesus began to teach concerning the Kingdom of God that no one knew God's way. Men had to have it revealed to them. So Jesus revealed it—in the Sermon on the Mount, in the Sermon on Parables. Only the humble and penitent were able to recognize the Way (cf. Harold Fowler's comments, *Matthew, Vol. I & II,* College Press, on the above sermons). The blind in the passage before us refers to the spiritually blind (cf. Isa. 9:2; 61:1-2; Mt. 4:12-17; Lk. 4:16-30; Jn. 9:35-41; Rev. 3:15f).

But while the blind will be led to the light, those who think they see through idolatry (vain philosophies of worldly-minded) will be turned back and utterly put to shame. As a matter of fact, what becomes deliverance for the true Israel of God (the redemptive work of the Servant—death and resurrection), becomes a complete defeat for God's enemies (idolatry and all other human ideologies). If idolatry and human philosophy's attempts to deal with the human predicament (sin) are ever to be put to shame it is through the historically accomplished and historically eyewitnessed bodily resurrection of Jesus Christ. In the light of what God did through this great event, it is the shame of all shames to worship gods of human origin—be they of stone and wood or philosopher's minds.

QUIZ

1. What is the motive for the song that is to be sung by believers?
2. Why is it a *new* song?
3. Who can know this song?
4. What should be the lyrics of Christian songs?
5. When did God finally stop refraining from His long awaited defeat of His enemies?
6. Who are the blind?
7. What is the shame of all shames?

c. SIGHTLESS SERVANTS

TEXT: 42:18-25

18 Hear, ye deaf; and look, ye blind, that ye may see.

19 Who is blind, but my servant? or deaf, as my messenger that I send? who is blind as he that is at peace with me, and blind as Jehovah's servant?

20 Thou seest many things, but thou observest not; his ears are open, but he heareth not.

21 It pleased Jehovah, for his righteousness sake, to magnify the law, and make it honorable.

22 But this is a people robbed and plundered; they are all of them snared in holes, and they are hid in prison-houses: they are for a prey, and none delivereth; for a spoil, and none saith, Restore.

23 Who is there among you that will give ear to this? that will hearken and hear for the time to come?

24 Who gave Jacob for a spoil, and Israel to the robbers? did not Jehovah? he against whom we have sinned, and in whose ways they would not walk, neither were they obedient unto his law.

25 Therefore he poured upon him the fierceness of his anger, and the strength of battle; and it set him on fire round

about, yet he knew not; and it burned him, yet he laid it not to heart.

QUERIES

a. Who are the "blind" of verses 18 and 19?
b. How did Jehovah make the law "honorable"?

PARAPHRASE

People of God, servants of Jehovah, open your ears and listen; open your blind eyes and see what I am showing you. But then, who in all the world is as blind as My servant Israel or as deaf as Israel who was sent as My messenger in the earth? I repeat, the blindness of Israel who is supposed to be allied to Me in friendship and peace, supposed to be My confidant, is incredible! You see much but you do not keep what you see; you listen to many things but you do not obey them. To display His own righteousness, Jehovah was glad to give to Israel a great and glorious revelation of Himself in His law. And yet, His greatness and gloriousness is not reflected in this people of the law for they are a people robbed, enslaved, imprisoned, trapped, fair game for all their enemies and, having refused Him, there is no one to protect them. Oh, isn't there just one of you who will listen to Me and My prophet? Isn't there one who will learn from all the instruction and experience of this nation and obey and avert the ruin that awaits disobedience? Don't you know Who let Israel be robbed and hurt? Was it not plain to you that it was Jehovah? It was the Lord this people sinned against when they refused to walk in His ways and did not obey His law. On account of this disobedience God poured out upon Israel His divine fury in war and other calamities—still Israel refused to recognize that this was chastening from Jehovah.

COMMENTS

v. 18-22 INCREDIBLE: That the "servant" in this section is Israel cannot be denied when the reader sees the context. The servant could not possibly be the Messiah for it is said of the servant here that he is blind, deaf, observes not, hears not, is robbed, plundered, none delivers, etc. In verse 19 the servant is *meshullam,* the Hebrew word translated "at peace," a derivative of *shallom.* Keil and Delitzsch say "it is the passive of the Arabic *muslim,* one who trusts in God," or the surrendered one. This characterization of what God intended Israel to be in servanthood intensifies the contrast with what Israel is portrayed as being. That Israel should be so blind is incredible. Jehovah has the prophet repeat the rhetorical question for emphasis! (see Jer. 18:12-13; Amos 3:9-10).

Israel had been privileged to "see" many things. Israel had the law of God revealed in human language to read and study; he had the record of the historical deeds of God's miraculous deliverances and chastenings upon his nation. But Israel's response did not match his opportunity. Israel did not keep what he saw and heard. In verse 20 two fundamental Hebrew words are used; *shemor* (from *shemar*) meaning to *keep,* and *shama,* meaning to *obey* or *hear.* To the Hebrew, hearing was equivalent to obeying. When a person did not obey, he had not heard!

It was Jehovah's good pleasure to magnify the manifestation of His character and demonstrate the gloriousness of His nature through His holy law. This was the sovereign way God chose to exhibit His holiness to man providing man with a motive and means of partaking, through faith, in that holiness. The law of God was holy and good (cf. Rom. 7:12), it was the free rebellion of man against what he knew to be holy that was wrong, not the law (cf. Rom. 7:13-14; 8:3). The law of God, humbly believed and obeyed, would have driven the Israelites to trust in the promised and typified mercy of God to come—and that is just where God could have saved them and used them as servants. But, incredible as it was, they chose to trust in alliances with Egypt and Assyria, to worship heathen gods, and as a result enslaved themselves under Assyrian tribute (see comments chapter 7). They would, in another generation or two of rebellion against the law of God, make themselves easy prey for the Babylonian captivity.

v. 23-25 INCORRIGIBLE: The question of verse 23 is a wish that *one* might be found among the nation (cf. Jer. 5:1-2) who will hear and obey. Is there not one who will learn from history and prepare themselves for the judgment that is to come upon this nation? Have they all forgotten that it was Jehovah who gave their forefathers over to judgment and chastening (cf. Amos 4:6-12). It is interesting to note that the Hebrew word *shama* is translated *obedient* in our English version of verse 24. The Hebrew word translated *law,* is *torah.* The nation, for the most part, was incorrigible. They deliberately and obstinantly chose not to walk in the ways of Jehovah (cf. Jer. 6:16-19). They refused to learn from the history of their rebellious ancestors in the wilderness wanderings and the days of the Judges. Time and time again God chastened Israel by slaughter of war, destruction of her cities, drought, pestilence—still Israel knew it not. It was not a lack of an authentic historical record of God's divine deeds—it was a moral unwillingness to accept it.

QUIZ

1. What are the reasons the "servant" of these verses cannot be the Messiah?
2. How is Israel characterized in verse 19?
3. What did Israel do with the many things he had been privileged to "see" and "hear"?
4. What did the law manifest?
5. Did Israel's rejection of the law mean the law was not good?
6. Did Israel's incorrigibleness stem from lack of ability to know about God's chastening?

4. CALL, CHAPTER 43

a. TO BE A POSSESSION

TEXT: 43:1-7

1 But now thus saith Jehovah that created thee, O Jacob, and
he that formed thee, O Israel: Fear not, for I have redeemed
thee; I have called thee by thy name, thou art mine.
2 When thou passest through the waters, I will be with thee;
and through the rivers, they shall not overflow thee: when
thou walkest through the fire, thou shalt not be burned,
neither shall the flame kindle upon thee.
3 For I am Jehovah thy God, the Holy One of Israel, thy
Saviour; I have given Egypt as thy ransom, Ethiopia and
Seba in thy stead.
4 Since thou hast been precious in my sight, and honorable,
and I have loved thee; therefore will I give men in thy stead,
and peoples instead of thy life.
5 Fear not; for I am with thee: I will bring thy seed from the
east, and gather thee from the west;
6 I will say to the north, Give up; and to the south, Keep not
back; bring my sons from far, and my daughters from the
end of the earth;
7 every one that is called by my name, and whom I have created
for my glory, whom I have formed, yea, whom I have made.

QUERIES

a. Why remind Israel she belongs to God?
b. When will Israel walk through waters?
c. When will the great "gathering" take place?

PARAPHRASE

And now, in light of the foregoing, Jehovah says, I am your Creator and your Former, O Israel, so you need have no fear. I have redeemed you in the past and will do so in the future. You are mine; I have special claim on you. You did not even name yourself—I did. You were singled out by Me for a special purpose. So, when you have to pass through dangerous waters and flooded rivers you need not fear they will overcome you; when you have to walk through fires of your oppressors you will not be burned—you will not even be touched by the flames. You know who I Am, I Am Jehovah, Covenant God, the Holy One of Israel, your Saviour. I have paid a high price for you giving up whole continents like Egypt, Ethiopia and Seba as a ransom for you. Ever since the time you became My precious possession I have honored you and loved you dearly. And on account of My love for you I will continue to exchange the lives of other peoples to keep you as My special people. Do not be afraid of your enemies, for I, Your Covenant-God, Am with you always. Even if you are scattered all over the world, I promise to gather my sons and daughters from the east, west, north and south. Yes, every one who will surrender to be called by My name, I will have produced as a new creation, will have shaped him and perfected and completed him for My glory.

COMMENTS

v. 1-4 Redemption: This chapter forms the climactic statement of God's *Purpose* for Israel's servanthood—to be God's Called. This chapter also forms the conclusion to the preceding discussion of the interrelation of national Israel—covenant Israel—to the Messiah. This whole section of *Salvation Through God's Servant* (chapters 40-53), is a kaleidoscopic view of the correlation of Israel and the Messiah. Israel was called for the messianic purpose, but she sinned. God must chasten her to purify her. After her purification she will be redeemed and from her will come the Messiah and His kingdom in which only the regenerated shall dwell.

Two words are used in verse one to emphasize Jehovah's claim upon Israel; *bara,* create and *yatzar,* form, shape, are the distinctive Hebrew words showing God's unique relationship to Israel. She is His possession by right of His having brought her into existence and having molded her into what He wants her to be. The Hebrew word for *redeemed* is *goael* and a derivitive of the same word is sometimes translated *kinsman* (cf. Ruth 3:2, etc.). Israel is kin to God by creation and redemption. Israel is God's child, His son, His bride (cf. Ezek. 16:1f; Hosea 11:1f; Isa. 49:14-18; 62:1f, etc.). Israel is God's precious possession. The placing of the two names of verse one are interesting. *Yaakoov, Jacob,* means "defraud, circumvent, crooked, deceitful," while *Yisrael,* Israel, means "prevail, prince or ruler of God, or perhaps, God will rule." *Israel* is the name God gave Jacob after Jacob wrestled with the angel of the Lord and prevailed. Hosea appeals to the spineless, compromising Israel of his day to take again the character of its forefather who was so singleminded about striving for the spiritual birthright (cf. Hosea 12:2-6). So, Israel was what God named this nation because He redeemed it or purchased it, not only through the change made in Jacob's character, but also throughout her history. This is what God calls Israel—mine!

Not only has God redeemed Israel, He will continue to do so. He will *protect* her. When she is forced to go through waters (probably when being taken captive, for there were hardly any bridges over rivers then) God will keep her from being swept away. When they were forced to walk through fire, God would not allow the flame to consume them. A literal fulfillment of protection from fire is recorded in the event with the three Hebrew men (Daniel 3:1-30) in the fiery furnace of Nebuchadnezzar. The point is Israel need not fear extinction for God is powerful and mighty to save from any thing. God could even save them from lions (Daniel), hangmen (Esther) and their own countrymen (Jeremiah).

Jehovah, Creator of all mankind, is jealous enough for Israel, His precious servant, called to glorify His name in all the earth, He is willing to give up other nations and peoples as a substitutionary ransom to keep Israel. God is ready to sacrifice practically the whole African continent (as was then known, Egypt, Ethiopia, and Seba) if need be to keep Israel free to fulfill her messianic destiny. Some think this is a prediction that God is willing to, and did, assign Egypt, Ethiopia and Seba to Persia as compensation for their letting Israel return to Palestine by the edict of Cyrus (cf. II Chron. 36; Ezra 1). Egypt and Ethiopia did submit to the Persian yoke in the days of Cambyses (cir. 527-526 B.C.), about 10 years after the return of the exiled Jews to Palestine.

From the time the promise was given to Jacob (Gen. 28:14), Israel became precious to Jehovah. From that time on God placed the interests of Israel above those of other peoples. Young says, "Perhaps the general thought is simply that in choosing Israel God passed by other nations and thus they were sacrificed (i.e., were the ransom price) in its place." The point, of course, is not that Israel of itself merits this evaluation of preciousness; the point is God's grace. Paul makes this matter clear in Romans, chapters 9-10-11. Israel's preciousness consists solely in God's sovereign choice of her to be His servant. The same is true of the new Israel, the church. The church is precious not because of the merit of the human beings in her membership but because of God's sovereign redemption by grace to the church in the unique work of Christ, offered through belief and obedience of the Gospel. The preciousness of the church is shown in that God was willing to offer His *monogenes,* "only, unique" Son as a ransom.

v. 5-7 REGENERATION: The captivity, which was certain to come, was symbolic of the estrangement between Israel and God. Israel willfully and deliberately separated themselves from His holiness (cf. Isa. 30:1-14, etc.). The separation was not God's choosing. However, in order to demonstrate vividly Israel's need for God's holy fellowship, God delivered her to captivity. But Israel is not to fear. Because a remnant has believed the prophets and remain true to Jehovah, He will bring them back from all over the earth to their land again and to their appointment with destiny. That return from the exile, however, is only a first step. The meaning of these verses is by no means restricted to the return from the captivity. As Young says, "In a far deeper sense it is addressed to all those who are afar off, who can be brought to the true Mount Zion only by the gracious working of the Lord . . . The reference is to the spiritual gathering of lost sinners in Jesus Christ." The "seed" refers to the spiritual descendants of Jacob. There are plenty of references in Isaiah to demonstrate this principle (cf. comments on Isa. 19:16-25, etc.).

Verse seven indicates that God is referring to His spiritual people and not just physical Israel, when it says "every one that is called by my name." Jesus made plain who God's sons were in John 8. Not all descended from Israel belong to Israel (cf. Rom. 9:6; Rom. 2:25-29; Gal. 6:13-16, etc.). Anyone who does not come to God through Jesus Christ is not called by God's name. The arrangement of the words, *created, formed,* and *made,* seem to be in an ascending scale depicting the work of God in the redemption of those called by His name. First there is the *new creation* (the initial new birth, becoming a Christian), then the *shaping* or *molding* of that life into the image of Christ from one degree of glory to another and last the *perfecting* or *consummating* work of glorifying the child of God. Isaiah is talking about a regeneration. He is depicting the bringing from an Israel that was one only in name, to Israel that is one in truth!

QUIZ

1. In how many ways did Israel belong to God?
2. What is significant about the arrangement of the names Jacob and Israel?
3. When did some Israelites literally experience salvation from fire?

4. How did God ransom Israel by using other nations and peoples?
5. What makes the new Israel, the church, so precious to God?
6. What evidence is there that verses 5-7 probably refer to messianic times?

b. TO BE A PROCLAIMER

TEXT: 43:8-13

8 Bring forth the blind people that have eyes, and the deaf that have ears.
9 Let all the nations be gathered together, and let the peoples be assembled; who among them can declare this, and show us former things? let them bring their witnesses, that they may be justified; or let them hear, and say, It is truth.
10 Ye are my witnesses, saith Jehovah, and my servant whom I have chosen; that ye may know and believe me, and understand that I am he: before me there was no God formed, neither shall there be after me.
11 I, even I, am Jehovah; and besides me there is no saviour.
12 I have declared, and I have saved, and I have showed; and there was no strange god among you: therefore ye are my witnesses, saith Jehovah, and I am God.
13 Yea, since the day was I am he; and there is none that can deliver out of my hand: I will work, and who can hinder it?

QUERIES

a. Who are the "blind" and "deaf" challenged in verse eight?
b. Why is God so concerned about Israel's witnessing?

PARAPHRASE

I, Jehovah, challenge the blind heathen to bring forth their gods and their soothsayers who claim they can see and hear supernatural things. Gather all the heathen nations as one; who among their gods can proclaim anything like My present prediction of the restoration of My people Israel? To prove that they can, let them cite former events which they predicted and which had really taken place. Let them present their eyewitnesses of such earlier prophecies and so prove themselves to be gods by substantiating the truthfulness of their claims. But I call you, Israel, as witness of the historical facts concerning My infallible knowledge of the future, says Jehovah. You have been Mine in a special, miraculous relationship and you can certainly testify to that experience of service. You, Israel, have enough evidence to know and believe that I Am the only God there is. There was no god before Me and there shall be none after Me. I, indeed I, am Jehovah; there is no other saviour. I have declared My power and have shown you My power by My great saving acts among you. This demonstrated to you that there was no foreign god who could claim to be a god. You have seen My deeds, you know that I am God, and therefore, you, Israel, are My witnesses. As long as time has existed, from the first day of time and before that, I Am; there are no other gods anywhere; there is no one to stop what I wish to do.

COMMENTS

v. 8-10 MESSENGER: Israel was called by God to be His servant as a testimony among the nations of Jehovah's sovereignty (cf. Ex. 19:5; Deut. 4:6-7; 14:2; 26:18; 28:10; Psa. 135:4; Lev. 20:24-26; Deut. 7:6). The passage before us deals with God's call to this servanthood. Israel had not fulfilled her purpose (cf. Amos 3:9-11; Jer. 2:9-13; 18:13), she "out-heathened the heathen." She was given the land of Canaan to show the heathen nations the holiness of God, but she became more unholy than the heathen around her! Now, Isaiah, speaking for Jehovah, is calling for a remnant of Israel to turn again to this God-oriented purpose.

The "blind" and the "deaf" are the Gentiles who claim they have "eyes" and "ears" to see and hear what is truth through their idols and diviners. But Jehovah challenges them to gather all the idols and soothsayers of all the nations on the earth and bring forth evidence of their abilities. God has challenged the heathen gods many times before (Moses and the Egyptian magicians; Elijah and the prophets of Baal) and He makes the challenge many times after this (Isa. 44:9f; Daniel 1-6, etc.). God is predicting, through His prophet Isaiah, the captivity and restoration of Israel. Which one of the heathen gods Israel has adopted is able to infallibly foretell the future like Jehovah? The false prophets of Israel are continually insisting that no captivity will come to them (cf. Micah 3:9-12). If the heathen gods Israel worships are gods, let them bring a record of their prophetic successes of the past. How many historical events have they foretold and seen fulfilled? Jehovah is not afraid of such a challenge for He knows they are not gods (Jeremiah demonstrated the impotence of the false prophets when he challenged the predictions of Hananiah, Jer. 28:1-17). The god of Israel is the only God of truth. He alone has the truth. He alone knows righteousness and holiness. Israel is the only messenger of truth and righteousness, but they have rejected this servanthood for false gods. The challenge to the nations to amalgamate all their powers and present the best opposition they can to the sovereignty of Jehovah is much like the challenge in Joel 2:30—3:21 (see our comments there in *Minor Prophets*, by Butler, College Press).

The heathen opposition has no witnesses and no evidence. But Jehovah has. Israel is God's witness. In fact, this is their destiny. Israel is not called to be a mighty worldly power dominating other nations and exercising world-empire. That never was Israel's destiny and never shall be. The new Israel, the church, is not of this world. Israel testified by her very existence and was called to testify by her deeds and words that Jehovah is the only God. Leupold says, "Monotheism is Israel's most precious insight. Whatever indications along this line had begun to glimmer here and there in divine revelation, all this now comes to clear expression and is finalized by our prophet." God had chosen Israel to be His servant, to be the instrument through which He could manifest His power and glory and holiness to all the earth. Israel had plenty of empirical proof of Jehovah's sovereignty. There was no reason for Israel not to know and believe there was only One God! But Israel set aside reason in favor of greed, lust and pride. For this the prophets often characterized their countrymen as irrational, stupid, perverse, self-willed, stubborn (cf. Ezek. ch. 2 & 3, etc.). The prophets did preserve a small remnant of faithful who did become witnesses in all the earth to the sovereignty of Jehovah. The dispersion of these faithful by the Persians, Greeks and Romans prepared the way for the preaching of the gospel all over the world in the first century A.D.

v. 11-13 MESSAGE: The absolute sovereignty of Jehovah is the message Israel is to proclaim. They are witnesses to it. They have seen and heard first-hand—for that is what a witness is. A witness does not tell what he thinks or feels—he tells what he has seen and heard. What Israel has seen is only Jehovah can save. Jehovah demonstrated to the sensory organs of man (eyes, ears, touch, etc.) that He alone saves. Jehovah did not reveal His saving power to Israel in a systematic philosophy—He revealed it in deeds, events, in the historical, human frame-of-reference. He also demonstrated experientially that none of the gods of man, none of the pagan idols, could save. Therefore, Israel *must* be God's witness. God has not revealed Himself so precisely and extensively to any other people. God has no other witnesses. Isaiah knows about such a "manifest destiny." When Isaiah was in the temple, God asked, "Who will go for us, whom shall I send?" (cf. Isa. 6).

There cannot be another witness and there cannot be another God. There is only one God. He is from everlasting to everlasting.

He had no beginning and has no end. Where is there one who can gainsay that!? God may be morally rejected and disobeyed, but His eternal power and deity cannot rationally be denied (cf. Rom. 1:16f). Philosophy, science or psychology can never *disprove* the existence of God. Men would have to know everything there is to know, have existed everywhere there is existence in order to absolutely disprove God. So far, all the evidence proves beyond any *reasonable* doubt, that Jehovah does exist and none can deliver out of His hand and none can hinder whatever He wants to do!

QUIZ

1. What does the Bible say in other books about Israel's call?
2. What is God's challenge to the heathen concerning their gods?
3. Where has another challenge to pagan powers like this been issued in the prophets?
4. If there was plenty of evidence for Israel to witness the sovereignty of God, why didn't she?
5. What is a witness?
6. How did Israel qualify as a witness?
7. Why *must* Israel be God's witness?

c. TO BE A PROTOTYPE

TEXT: 43:14-21

14 Thus saith Jehovah, your Redeemer, the Holy One of Israel: For your sake I have sent to Babylon, and I will bring down all of them as fugitives, even the Chaldeans, in the ships of their rejoicing.
15 I am Jehovah, your Holy One, the Creator of Israel, your King.
16 Thus saith Jehovah. who maketh a way in the sea, and a

path in the mighty waters;
17 who bringeth forth the chariot and horse, the army and the
mighty man (they lie down together, they shall not rise;
they are extinct, they are quenched as a wick):
18 Remember ye not the former things, neither consider the
things of old.
19 Behold, I will do a new thing; now shall it spring forth;
shall ye not know it? I will even make a way in the wilderness, and rivers in the desert.
20 The beasts of the field shall honor me, the jackals and the
ostriches; because I give waters in the wilderness, and rivers
in the desert, to give drink to my people, my chosen,
21 the people which I formed for myself, that they might set
forth my praise.

QUERIES

a. How does Babylon enter into the picture here?
b. What "way" does Jehovah make in the sea?
c. What are the "rivers in the desert"?

PARAPHRASE

A prediction! Your Covenant-God, your Redeemer, the Holy One of Israel, says, For you I have decreed the doom of Babylon. I have determined to send an army to Babylon to execute My decree and I will defeat them and send them all fleeing like fugitives in the merchant ships and battle ships they are so proud of now. Though you are about to go into captivity and be without a human king, I want you to know I am Jehovah, your Holy One, the Creator of Israel, your only real and everlasting King. It is Jehovah who says all this; the God who makes pathways in the seas as He did through the Red Sea when He delivered your forefathers from Egypt. Jehovah was the One who brought that great Egyptian army with its horses and chariots to its grave in the sea. Jehovah literally extinguished the enemies of His people there, like a man blows out a lamp. But, do not let your minds dwell on the past to the point that you wish you could go back to those days. Look! That is nothing compared with what I am going to do! I am going to do something completely new; in fact, I have already begun it. Do you not recognize what I am starting to do? I am beginning to make drastic changes that will affect the whole world. I am going to give living water to a desert-type world of humanity through my servant-people, my chosen, as they testify to My redemptive acts.

COMMENTS

v. 14-17 OPPRESSOR DEFEATED: God makes a prophetic decree. He dooms Babylon, the oppressor of His covenant remnant, *before* Judah is taken captive. Babylon is already looming on the political horizon as a pagan world power standing in opposition to God's redemptive people (cf. comments on chapter 39, Vol. II). How does Jehovah "send" to Babylon and bring them down? Apparently this is a prophecy of the Persian conquest of Babylon. It was the Persians who after conquering Babylon, decreed and financed the return of the Jews to Palestine (see our comments, *Daniel,* College Press, chapters 7-9). The Persians served as God's instrument to execute His deliverance of Judah. There is a great deal of irony in the predicted Babylonian fall. They will flee like fugitives. Once proud, secure, self-sufficient, powerful Babylon who made so many flee their homelands as fugitives will suffer the same fate (see Habakkuk's description of the fall of Babylon). Even more ironic, the great fleet of merchant ships and navy vessels which made Babylon so rich and powerful, and which brought so much gladness to the hearts of the Babylonians, will be jammed full of terrified, fleeing fugitives. The Chaldeans, like the Assyrians, had mighty warrior kings. They were rich, powerful and pompous. They were feared and idolized by all the world. But Israel's king is *King of kings!* He is Jehovah, Creator, Judge, Holy One and Redeemer. Though Israel might appear to be without a king during the captivity in Babylon, her King would demonstrate His power time and time again (cf. Dan. 2:47; 3:28; 4:37; 6:25-27). Finally, He would demonstrate His sovereignty in the restoration of the nation under Ezra, Zerubbabel and Nehemiah (cf. II Chron. 36:22-23; Ezra 1:1-4). The "way in the sea" in verses 16 and 17 is a metaphorical allusion to Jehovah's deliverance of the children of Israel through the Red Sea under the leadership of Moses. Just as Jehovah overcame natural obstacles and powerful, wicked human oppressors when He delivered Israel from Egypt, so He will deliver Israel from her captivities under Assyria and Babylon. That mighty Egyptian army with its chariots of war, before which Israel trembled and cringed, lay extinct at the bottom of the Red Sea. So, Jehovah will snuff out the mighty Babylonian empire in one night! (cf. Dan. 5:1-30).

v. 18-21 OPPRESSED DELIVERED: But, as grand and glorious as these great national deliverances are, they are warned they should not let their hopes rest on them. God is going to do a new thing much more glorious. The "new" thing is apparently not just the deliverance from the Babylonian captivity, though that is its starting place. It must be more than that for the deliverance from captivity is not any more glorious than the exodus from Egypt. The "new" thing in itself is the wondrous new redemption accomplished in the death and resurrection of the Messiah (cf. Isa. 42:9-10; 48:6; 62:2; 65:17; 66:22; Ezek. 11:19; 36:26; 18:31, for the *new* thing God is going to do in the messianic kingdom). Even "now" it was beginning to be apparent to those who had the faith to see it. The revelations of Ezekiel (40-48) and Daniel (7-12) graphically outlined the mission of Israel as prototypical of the redemption for all mankind from their captivity in sin. Men of faith, like Daniel, recognized that God was already beginning to do this "new" thing. They anxiously desired to know when it would come to its completion (cf. Dan. 12:5f; I Pet. 1:10-12). The figurative language describing "a way in the wilderness, and rivers in the desert," is a favorite vehicle of prophetic literature to describe the messianic blessedness (cf. Isa. 19:23; 35:1-10; 51:3, etc.). When God shall have finally and fully regenerated men, nature itself shall also be redeemed (cf. Rom. 8:18-25). This, too, is a much used expression of the prophets to show that, as Keil and Delitzsch say, "when the sufferings of the people of God shall be brought to an end, the sufferings of creation will also terminate; for humanity is the heart of the universe, and the people of God (understanding by this the people of God according to the Spirit) are the heart of humanity." In other words, the consummation of God's redemptive work will result in the reclamation of men and nature which were cursed in the garden of Eden because of sin. God is working in regenerate men by the power of the gospel received and lived by faith. Regenerated man will then be at harmony with his God, himself and God's creation. At this point, God will redeem his natural creation and create a new heaven and a new earth (II Pet. 3:13). Thus, Paradise will be restored. But it is not the surroundings, the natural environment that is significant. God can make that over by sheer force. He has made man with a free will to choose his own destiny. The remaking of man is all important. Heaven will not be heaven so much for that natural place in which we find ourselves as that nature which is found in us. No better commentary on verse 21 can be found than that in I Peter 2:9: "But you are a chosen race, a royal priesthood, a holy nation, God's own people, that you may declare the wonderful deeds of him who called you out of darkness into his marvelous light."

QUIZ

1. How did God send to Babylon and bring them down?
2. What is the irony in the prediction of Babylon's fall?
3. Why tell Israel not to remember the former things?
4. What is the "new" thing?

5. Why mention the "beasts" of the field honoring Jehovah?
6. When did Israel finally fulfill its purpose to "set forth" the praise of Jehovah?

d. TO BE PERFECTED

TEXT: 43:22-28

22 Yet thou hast not called upon me, O Jacob; but thou hast been weary of me, O Israel.
23 Thou hast not brought me of thy sheep for burnt-offerings; neither hast thou honored me with thy sacrifices. I have not burdened thee with offerings, nor wearied thee with frankincense.
24 Thou hast bought me no sweet cane with money, neither hast thou filled me with the fat of thy sacrifices; but thou hast burdened me with thy sins, thou hast wearied me with thine iniquities.
25 I, even I, am he that blotteth out thy transgressions for mine own sake; and I will not remember thy sins.
26 Put me in remembrance; let us plead together: set thou forth thy cause, that thou mayest be justified.
27 Thy first father sinned, and thy teachers have transgressed against me.
28 Therefore I will profane the princes of the sanctuary; and I will make Jacob a curse, and Israel a reviling.

QUERIES

a. Did the people of Israel consider God's offerings a burden?
b. What is the "sweet cane" they should have bought?
c. How are they to put God in "remembrance"?

PARAPHRASE

In spite of all My graciousness in calling you to the honored place of servant of the living God, you have not honored that call by seeking after Me, O Jacob. As a matter of record, you have said, We're tired of Jehovah, and of doing things His way! All the offerings of sheep and all the other sacrifices you have brought are not really because you love Me, but are dedicated to your own self-righteousness. The offerings and sacrifices I commanded in My law were intended to give you a way to express your joy for My grace and goodness to you, never did I think they would be considered insufferable by you. You never did anything special for Me like buying expensive sweet cane to make the sacred incense and anointing oil. You did not drench My altar with the choicest fat of your sacrifices. But you have gone out of your way to load Me down with your insults and rebellions. I am sick and tired of your disobedience. When I blot out your transgressions and forget your sins, it will be for My own sake and out of grace—not from any perfect goodness on your part. Remember who I am. I am God and you receive forgiveness on My terms—not yours. If you think you can justify yourself without My grace, then plead your case! The father of your nation was a sinner, and all those who have been sent to teach you not to sin have sinned. Because of this continual increase in rebellion and sin I will take Israel and her spiritual leaders and profane them in a pagan land. There they will be like outlaws and mocked as fugitives.

COMMENTS

v. 22-24 To Praise: Israel was called to praise and exalt the name of Jehovah by worshipping Him and keeping His commandments. By worship and obedience to Jehovah's Law, Israel would thus "call" upon Him in faith and show her dependence on His grace. However, Israel did *not* call upon

Him. Israel did not obey Jehovah's Law. Israel considered the Law of Jehovah insufferable, restrictive, boring, and she tired of its discipline, (cf. Isa. 7:13; Jer. 9:5; Micah 6:3; Hab. 3:2; Malachi 2:17, etc.). Israel tired of God as lustful men tire of their wives (Jer. 3:19-20; Hosea 1 & 2; Ezek. 16:1f). The word of the Lord became to Israel an object of scorn (Jer. 6:10, 16). To be sure, Israel had trampled God's courts with multitudes of sacrifices and offerings (Isa. 1:10-17). But, the prophet speaks with sarcasm. Israel was not really bringing all those sacrifices to honor Jehovah. They were doing it to honor themselves. They were more than willing to bring ten thousand offerings as a substitute for putting to practice the Law of God in personal godliness (Micah 6:6-8). They were willing to earn religious merit from sacrifices as long as the Holy One of Israel did not demand moral holiness from them. It was not the number of offerings that burdened the Israelites, it was the moral "strings" attached to a humble relationship of faith and obedience to a Holy God that "wearied" Israel. The astonishing thing is Jehovah's law was always a refreshing, regenerating, pleasurable experience every time Israel obeyed it—individually and nationally (cf. Psa. 119, etc.). Jehovah intended only blessing in His Law (Deut. 28:1f). History proved it!

The "sweet cane" (Heb. *kaneh*) of verse 24 was probably the scented calamus (reed) or some kind of aromatic bark. It was an ingredient of the holy oil (Ex. 30:23); imported from a distance (Jer. 6:20; Ezek. 27:19) and was thus rare and costly. Its sweetness refers to the scent, not the taste. Another Hebrew word in this verse is significant (*kaniytha*) because it is from the same root as the word translated "sweet cane" but means "bought" or "purchased." There appears to be a definite play upon words here emphasizing the preciousness of the offering of cane. *Reviythaniy* is translated "filled" in the same verse but literally means "moisten, satiate," or "drench." The point of this verse is simply this: the people of Israel had not really extended themselves in giving offerings of quality or quantity. They probably skimped on their offerings much the same as their descendents did after the return from the captivity (cf. Malachi 1:6-14; 3:6-12, etc.). On the contrary, Israel had gone out of its way to load Jehovah down with its insulting rebellion. The word "burdened" in this verse is from the Hebrew root *'avad* meaning "servile labor." The guiltiness of Israel pressed upon The Holy One of Israel, as a burden does upon a servant. The other word, "wearied," is from the Hebrew root *vaga'* which means literally, "fatigued" or "exhausted." Instead of Israel fulfilling its calling to *praise* Jehovah, it was a *pain* to Him. But the Lord is going to create for Himself an Israel (a new Israel, ruled by His new David) that will fulfill its calling of praise. And He is beginning the work with the prophets and the captivity (cf. Isa. 43:19).

v. 25-28 To Pardon: Jehovah is going to perfect (bring to fruition or completion) from the Israel of Isaiah's day, a *pardoned* Israel. There is a very interesting three-fold repetition of the personal pronoun "I, I, I am," in the Hebrew construction of verse 25, translated "I, even I, am he . . ." It means emphatically that Jehovah *alone* is responsible for any blotting (*makhah,* taking away even down to the very core or marrow) out of transgressions. Jehovah does it exclusively from His own graciousness, for His own name's sake. He does it because of Who He Is—not from any merit of man's person. The rest of the context indicates this is the emphasis. Jehovah wills to pardon man and Jehovah accomplishes man's pardon by His work and Jehovah decrees the terms of acceptance. Man is left free to accept or reject the divinely procured pardon according to man's willingness to obey the divinely decreed terms. One thing is certain; standing before the tribunal of God, no man can claim self-justification. Jehovah warns Israel to "remember" Who He Is! He knows their sins (cf. Amos. 5:12; 5:8; Ezek. 8:12; 9:9, etc.). The first "father" of Israel, Abraham, called "father of the faithful and friend of God," sinned. All the "teachers" (prophets, priests and kings) of Israel sinned (Isa. 53:6; Psa. 14:2-3; 53:3)—all have sinned. Therefore, Jehovah would have to take away

Israel's priests (because they were leading Israel to sin) into captivity. Israel's access to God through its priesthood and its sanctuary would be suspended until she repented. Jacob (Israel) was to be made a "curse" (*kherem* in Hebrew, literally, *devoted* or *banned,* or *outlawed*). Israel was to suffer the *ban* of God and become an outlaw (read Deut. ch. 28:15f), and instead of being respected by vile pagan nations, Israel would be reviled. God called her from the beginning to show forth His wonderful grace and forgiveness through covenant relationship, but she rejected His covenant and His grace. Now she must be "allured" back to pardon in a new covenant relationship, but through "trouble" (see our comments, *Minor Prophets,* Hosea 2:14-15, College Press). Israel's pardon will be perfected when she brings forth her Messiah, but she must be prepared for that by chastening.

QUIZ

1. How did Israel express its weariness of Jehovah?
2. Why did God say He had not wearied them with offerings?
3. How did Israel burden God?
4. Why call Israel to remember Jehovah?
5. What perfection is Jehovah calling Israel to in this section?
6. What curse was placed upon Israel?

EXAMINATION

CHAPTERS FORTY THROUGH FORTY-THREE

DEFINITION

(Define the following words or phrases as they were discussed in the comments.)

1. speak *comfortably*
2. *voice* of one crying
3. *wilderness*
4. *measured* the waters

5. *wait*
6. keep *silence*
7. *worm*
8. *servant*
9. my *chosen*
10. *hear*
11. *created*
12. *formed*
13. *redeemed*
14. *blind* or *deaf*
15. *new* thing
16. *sweet cane*

MEMORIZATION

The ______ of one that crieth, ______ ye in the wilderness the ______ of Jehovah; make level in the ______ a highway for our God. Every ______ shall be exalted, and every ______ and hill shall be made______; and the uneven shall be made ______, and the rough places a plain: and the ______ of Jehovah shall be revealed, and all ______ shall see it together; for the mouth of Jehovah hath spoken it. (40:3-5)

EXPLANATION

1. Explain the connection between man's strengthening and Isaiah's focus on the nature of Jehovah.
2. Explain why men find such fascination with idols and images.
3. Explain Isaiah's command that the "islands" keep "silent."
4. Explain why the Servant who will not cry or lift up his voice was such a contrast in character to the common Jewish concept of Jehovah's Servant.
5. Explain who the servant of Jehovah is who comes from the "north."
6. Explain Isaiah's use of three different servants in these chapters.

APPLICATION

(In its context every scripture has one meaning—the author's intended meaning. How may the following be applied in the believer's life?)

1. Why do we need applied to our lives Isaiah's teaching on the transcendence or independence of God?
2. May we use Isaiah's repeated references to the wonders of creation in any application for today's world?
3. What application of Israel's servanthood to God can we make in the church's relationship to Christ today?
4. Is there an application (besides the fulfillment of prophecy) for us in the task God gave to the prophet when He said, "comfort ye my people"?
5. May we learn from the symptoms of unbelief in the people of Isaiah's day, something to be applied to the society in which we live?
6. Does God still use men and natural forces as His agents in history today? Can we apply principles to understand history today from the inspired revelation of history in Isaiah's day?
7. Is there some application that may be made about religious music from this section of Isaiah (esp. 42:10-17)?

B. POWER OF THE LORD'S SERVANT
CHAPTERS 44-49

1. SOVEREIGN OVER ALL GODS, CHAPTER 44

a. SHOWS FAVOR TO THE FAITHFUL

TEXT: 44:1-8

1 Yet now hear, O Jacob my servant; and Israel, whom I have chosen:

2 thus saith Jehovah that made thee, and formed thee from
the womb, who will help thee: Fear not, O Jacob my servant;
and thou, Jeshurun, whom I have chosen.
3 For I will pour water upon him that is thirsty, and streams
upon the dry ground; I will pour my Spirit upon thy seed,
and my blessing upon thine offspring:
4 and they shall spring up among the grass, as willows by the
watercourses.
5 One shall say, I am Jehovah's; and another shall call himself by the name of Jacob; and another shall subscribe with
his hand unto Jehovah, and surname himself by the name of
Israel.
6 Thus saith Jehovah, the King of Israel, and his Redeemer,
Jehovah of hosts; I am the first, and I am the last; and besides me there is no God.
7 And who, as I, shall call and shall declare it, and set it in
order for me, since I established the ancient people? and the
things that are coming, and that shall come to pass, let them
declare.
8 Fear ye not, neither be afraid: have I not declared unto thee
of old, and showed it? and ye are my witnesses. Is there a
God besides me? yea, there is no Rock; I know not any.

QUERIES

a. Who is "Jeshurun"?
b. When is this promise of the Spirit to be fulfilled?
c. Why the different names in verse five?

PARAPHRASE

Although chastisement is sure to come to you, O Jacob my servant, I want you to know I called you Israel because I have chosen you for something better which will surely result from your chastening if you will listen and obey Me. First of all, remember, I, Jehovah, created you as a nation; your birth as a people was My doing. Surely you know I will help you. Do not be afraid Jacob my servant, Jeshurun, my chosen, for your offspring who are faithful and the messianic seed among you will have My Spirit poured out upon them and they will spring up and grow a harvest like the dry ground produces when streams of water are poured upon it. They will thrive like the abundant grass and trees that grow by the river banks. One by one they will proclaim that they belong to Jehovah. Some will bear witness that they belong to Jehovah by writing it down, counting it an honor to be called "Jehovah's." Secondly, need I remind you that I am the King of Israel; I am Israel's Redeemer; I am Jehovah, Lord of all the heavenly hosts; I am before all that begins and after all that ends—First and Last; there is no other God besides Me. If there is any man or god like Me, let him stand forth and declare it and prove his claim by ordering the course of history like I have from the very beginning. If there is anyone like Me let him prove it by predicting what will happen in the future. No, Israel, you have nothing to fear from these others who claim they are gods and have omnipotent power. I have proved to you long ago that I am the only God there is haven't I? By the prophecies I have declared and their fulfillments which you have experienced, you are witnesses to the fact that I am the only God. Is there any other God? No! None that I know about! There is no other Rock!

COMMENTS

v. 1-5 Invigorates: Although the chastening judgment of Jehovah is predicted with absolute certainty (chapter 43) upon Israel, still Israel is the chosen of the Lord. They were not even a nation when God chose them. He took them as nomadic sheepherders and formed them as an instrument of His from nothing! God molded them from useless clay into a vessel for His purpose (cf. Rom. 9:19f). They should surely know that

God desired with all His heart to help them and favor them. But God could not help them become the vessel they were chosen to be because they did *not want* to be that vessel! The Lord knew, and predicted through His prophet here, there would be a remnant formed from the chastening captivity which would believe and surrender to its chosen purpose. This remnant, even now being formed by Isaiah's preaching, need not fear the impending judgment. God's purpose will survive through this remnant called Jeshurun (the name means: right, upright, esteemed, righteous). The prophet suddenly makes a dramatic shortening of perspective in verse three. From the promise of help to the remnant of Israel formed from the chastening captivity Isaiah focuses his prophetic telescope down on the time when God will "pour my Spirit upon thy seed . . . and thine offspring." God's redemptive purpose will be accomplished ultimately in the "seed" and "offspring" of Israel. What is this pouring out of the Spirit? Is it the special, miraculous Spirit on the apostles at Pentecost (cf. Joel 2:28f; Acts 2:14f), or is it the promise of the Holy Spirit to all obedient believers (Isa. 32:14; Acts 2:38-39)? Isaiah could be making a general prophecy in which both were intended since without the miraculous revelation of the gospel covenant terms of salvation through the Spirit to the apostles there could have been no indwelling presence of the Spirit. Whatever the case, we feel certain Isaiah's prophecy of the Spirit here is intended to be fulfilled in the new covenant believer. Christ is the "seed" and "offspring" (cf. Gal. 3:15-29) and Christians are "offspring" by being in Him. So, Isaiah has skipped from the Captivity to the New Covenant without any mention of the centuries between. Keil and Delitzsch think "the threefold *zeh*" (demonstrative pronoun) (*one . . . another . . . another*) indicates verse five is speaking of the heathen (cf. Psa. 87:4-5). Gentiles will take pride in belonging to Jehovah. They will confess their allegiance orally and *yiketov* (from *kathav,* to subscribe) in writing. The emphatic willingness of the Gentile to allow himself to be "surnamed" Israel is an astounding prophecy in view of the contempt most of the heathen world had for the

Hebrew and his God. Nothing short of conversion and rebirth could fulfill this prophecy!

v. 6-8 INFORMS: Man thinks in terms of beginnings and endings. Timelessness is outside man's experience. God condescends to man's limited experience and calls Himself, the first, and the last. When time began, God was already there; when time shall end, God will still be there. Many heathen people claimed such eternal existence for their gods, but they could not prove it. Jehovah demonstrated His eternal deity, not only in the things He made (cf. Rom. 1:18f), but also in the predictions and revelations He gave through His prophets. Jehovah challenged and defeated scores of false prophets and false priests (scoffers of the days of Noah; magicians of Pharaoh in Moses' day; false prophets of Baal in the days of Elijah; the witch of Endor in King Saul's day; the false prophet Hananiah in Jeremiah's day). None of these were able to meet the challenge of Jehovah. In every instance Jehovah demonstrated that only He has absolute knowledge and power. Now, Isaiah is emphatically reminding his generation that as the Lord's servant the power of Almighty God is available to them in the supernatural revelation of Jehovah through His prophets. He knows their future and their destiny—they do not need to be afraid—they simply need to trust Him. Has He not from of old proven His omniscience? And are they not witnesses to it? There is no other god they need to fear.

QUIZ

1. Who is the seed and offspring of verse three?
2. Why is the prediction of verse five such an astounding one?
3. When had God proved He was the only God?
4. Why should Israel not be afraid?

b. SHOWS THE FRAUDULENCE OF FALSE GODS

TEXT: 44:9-20

9 They that fashion a graven image are all of them vanity;
and the things that they delight in shall not profit; and their
own witnesses see not, nor know: that they may be put to
shame.
10 Who hath fashioned a god, or molten an image that is
profitable for nothing?
11 Behold, all his fellows shall be put to shame; and the workmen, they are of men: let them all be gathered together,
let them stand up; they shall fear, they shall be put to shame
together.
12 The smith maketh an axe, and worketh in the coals, and
fashioneth it with hammers, and worketh it with his strong
arm: yea, he is hungry, and his strength faileth; he drinketh
no water, and is faint.
13 The carpenter stretcheth out a line; he marketh it out with a
pencil; he shapeth it with planes, and he marketh it out
with the compasses, and shapeth it after the figure of a
man, according to the beauty of a man, to dwell in a house.
14 He heweth him down cedars, and taketh the holm-tree and
the oak, and strengtheneth for himself one among the
trees of the forest: he planteth a fir-tree, and the rain doth
nourish it.
15 Then shall it be for a man to burn; and he taketh thereof,
and warmeth himself; yea, he kindleth it, and baketh bread:
yea, he maketh a god, and worshippeth it; he maketh it a
graven image, and falleth down thereto.
16 He burneth part thereof in the fire; with part thereof he
eateth flesh; he roasteth roast, and is satisfied; yea, he
warmeth himself, and saith, Aha, I am warm, I have seen
the fire:
17 and the residue thereof he maketh a god, even his graven
image; he falleth down unto it and worshippeth, and prayeth
unto it, and saith, Deliver me; for thou art my god.

18 They know not, neither do they consider: for he hath shut their eyes, that they cannot see; and their hearts, that they cannot understand.

19 And none calleth to mind, neither is there knowledge nor understanding to say, I have burned part of it in the fire; yea, also I have baked bread upon the coals thereof; I have roasted flesh and eaten it: and shall I make the residue thereof an abomination? shall I fall down to the stock of a tree?

20 He feedeth on ashes; a deceived heart hath turned him aside; and he cannot deliver his soul, nor say, Is there not a lie in my right hand?

QUERIES

a. Why the question of verse ten?
b. Why the detailed description of the work?
c. How have their eyes been shut?

PARAPHRASE

Those who carve out graven images and call them gods are all fools. These idols which they are so proud of are worthless. All those who make testimonies to idols are as dumb as the idols because they have blinded themselves to the truth about their gods. Who but a fool would create something with his own hands and call it a god when he knows it cannot be greater than himself. All those who join with this fool who has made his own god will also be shown to be fools. Yes, and included in this group of fools are the workmen who manufactured the idol—they stand right alongside the other fools. The foolishness of the making of idols is seen in the exhaustive amounts of energy craftsmen waste in manufacturing gods which cannot see or know. The iron-smith has had to first make his tools to work the metal which covers the wooden image. Then he uses these tools, working long, hard, exhaustive hours working and reworking the metal. He foolishly works himself so long over the forge he gets weak and almost faints. Before he wastes this much energy, the carpenter has gone to great lengths to sketch the image on a block of wood, shape it with his tools, sketch some more, work it some more, and what does he end up with—something in the image of man. Even if it is in the image of the most masculine of men, it is still a man-image and then it is put into a man-made temple. But before the carpenter has wasted all his energies in producing the mere image of a man to call his god, the woodsman has wasted time, energy and money planting trees, cultivating them, selecting just the right one. Then he cuts it down and half of it may be used to make an idol and half of it may be used to fire an oven for cooking meals. Yes, as stupid as it may sound, a man will take a tree and with half of it he will build a fire and warm himself and cook his meals and with the other half of it he will carve himself an image of man and fall down before it and worship it. Incredible as it may sound, a man takes half a tree and builds a fire, cooks his meal, stands right there in front of the fire and says, Oh, that feels good, I feel that heat warming me; then, with what is left of that same tree, he carves an idol and falls down and worships, praying to it, Deliver me, oh my god! Such idiocy—they act like they do not have any brains at all. Apparently they have never reflected a moment on how stupid such an action is! They have plastered shut their own eyes so they cannot see and they have plastered shut their hearts so they cannot understand. These fools never stop to really think all this out with any perception. They never reason this way: Now, part of this tree I have burned in the fire and cooked my meal on! Does it make sense to take the other half of a piece of fuel and make it into something as deprecating and shaming to good sense as an idol? They never stop to think: Shall I, a living, thinking, feeling being, fall down to a chunk of wood and call it a god? The fool who makes idols, so easily reduced to ashes, has been deluded by his own choice. He really does not want spiritual deliverance and so finds none and it never occurs to him to say, Isn't this all a big lie?

COMMENTS

v. 9-17 GRAVEN IMAGES: There are a number of Hebrew words for *idol; 'alilim* (a thing of nought); *atsabbim* (an image of grief); *gilulim* (a filthy image); *tsirim* (images of stone); *teraphim* (images) and others. The word used in verse nine is *pesel* which means specifically "graven thing" or sculpture. The object of the *pesel* or sculpture was to make some material into a representation of the invisible God to be worshipped and thus it was an idol. The word translated *delight* is also interesting; it is *hkamudyehem* which means *desirable, delectable, precious, darling.* Their graven images were more than ornaments! They venerated, pampered and worshiped those pieces of stone and chunks of wood much like the ignorant masses of India worship cows and the Buddhists of Japan worship statues of bronze and gold.

Isaiah is shaming the foolishness of the people who make and worship idols as much as he is the idols themselves! Those who make them are *tohu,* "void, empty, vain" people. Their "witnesses" is reference to the idolaters who are the only witnesses the idols could have. The idols are dumb and so are those idolaters (the people) who testify to them. It must have taken a great deal of courage for Isaiah to make such scathing public rebuke of idolatry. It had been instigated and approved by Ahaz and was practiced by the majority of the population. The prophet presents a sarcastic question: Who but a fool would fashion something with his own hands and call it a god when it cannot ever be more than it is—a piece of wood or stone? In verse 11 Isaiah offers both a prediction and a challenge. He predicts that idolaters will someday be acknowledged as the fools they really are. His prediction has come true. Idolatry stands discredited as utter folly in most of the world today. The discrediting of idolatry is due fundamentally to Christianity, not science! Science is due to Christianity! Isaiah challenges that if all the idolaters and idols could be gathered together in one great mass meeting to substantiate the truthfulness of idols, they could present no evidence or verification. Their images would still remain dumb, unable to speak, hear or see and unable to deliver, save or act at all!

Our author now begins (v. 12-17) one of the most satirical, comical passages of the Bible! This is the graphic, ludicrous picture of the idol-smith as seen from God's perspective. We must understand that most idols were composites of wood and metal. First, a wooden image was carved with the desired features. Then molten metal (gold, silver, bronze, etc.) was poured over the wooden image and the metal is then polished and worked again into the desired product. All this craftsmanship required proper tools and so Isaiah begins his picture describing the hot, exhausting, famishing work invested by human beings in just the tools to make idols. All that human energy to make tools to make something that is nothing! Then the craftsman *hkarash* (*artificer, engraver,* probably from the root, *to scratch*), spends long hours sketching, measuring, shaping, remeasuring, shaping again and the end product is the image of a man! Perhaps it would be the most masculine man with the most perfect features the craftsman could fashion, but still the image of man. Water cannot rise above its level. So, the human cannot produce the divine—not even an *image* of the divine! And the *image* of man is not alive. It is only an image of the features of man—not man! Most idols are much more decadent than that because they are images of beasts and creeping things!

The prophet has described the process of idol-making in reverse order. In verses 14-17 he describes the initial steps in the formation of a graven image. Even before the craftsmen begin there is much human energy exerted on a project of "nothingness." The woodsman must spend time deciding on the proper tree (only the best will do for one's god). Then much energy and time is invested in hewing down the tree, sectioning it and hauling it to the craftsman. But before all this long years of time has been invested in planting, nourishing and protecting the sapling until it was time to harvest it for idol-making. The destiny and existence of this "god" was totally dependent upon the circumstances of weather and growth and man's whims of selection and harvesting it should appear absolutely idiotic to think the thing formed was a "god"! But that isn't all! After planting a sprout, watching it grow into a sapling, then a tree, then taking all the pains to select, harvest, transport, and sell to the craftsman, one watches as the craftsman takes half of the log for a "god" and casts the other half aside for cook-wood! How utterly incredible! Out of the same log a man makes a god and fuels a fire to cook his meal or warm his body! What supernatural guidance did the craftsman use to decide from which half to make a god and which to burn in the fire? Why couldn't the half in the fire have made a god equally as well as the other half? There is an interesting use of the word *raiyth* from the root *raah to see.* The Hebrews used *see* often to mean *feel, experience.* The idea is the contrast between *feeling* the warmth of the fire made by the same wood the man falls down before to worship as a god! How senseless! He has just felt the warmth from the fire of the wood and now he cries out, Deliver me, to part of the same wood! How can men and women be so stupid?

v. 18-20 GULLIBLE IDOLATERS: Lange says the *tahk* (shut, plastered shut) of verse 18 should be considered as the nominal form and take as its nearest qualification the word *'aeyneyhem* which is 3 pers. pl. masc. In other words, *they* plastered their eyes shut—not God. It is apparent from the context that the idolater exercised his own choice in knowing or not knowing the utter stupidity of idolatry. The Hebrew *lo-yashyiv el-libbo* means literally, "carry not back into the heart," and is translated in the ASV "none calleth to mind." Evidently these idolaters once had understanding about the vanity of idols, but they did not "carry it back into their hearts." They rejected any willing reflection or investigation of their practices. They refused to come to the light lest their deeds be exposed (cf. Jn. 3:18-20). It certainly was not because they were incapable of understanding the stupidity of their practice—they simply did not want to "carry it back into their minds." *To'evah* is "an abhorrence" or an "abomination." Its evaluation comes from God, not from man. Men who make them think them darling—God calls them abominations! Idols insult God and degrade and eventually destroy men whom God made in His own image.

The man who makes idols of wood and metal which are so easily reduced to ashes has been led astray from truth by a heart overpowered with self-delusion and cannot be saved nor does it ever occur to him to say, Isn't all this a big lie? The most enslaving delusion is self-delusion, because it has to do with selfish feelings—not objective truth. There does not seem to be any hope for these idolaters of Isaiah's people unless they are willing to investigate what is outside their own feelings and desires. As long as men accept only what agrees with their feelings and desires, and are unwilling to accept that something may be valid truth outside their own autonomous selves, they cannot be saved. God is transcendent. He is the objective Object. He is the eternal Person. He is truth, outside of and beyond man. His being, objectivity and truthfulness must be validated by His revelation of Himself. Man cannot reduce Him to man's limited experience for man can rise no higher than himself (as evidenced by his idols)!

QUIZ

1. What is a "graven image"?
2. How would you characterize Isaiah's mood in this dissertation against idol-making?
3. What is a "carpenter"?
4. How does the idol-maker "see" the fire?
5. What is the meaning of "none calleth to mind"?
6. Why is the idol-maker unable to evaluate idolatry as a lie?

c. SHOWS THE FRUSTRATION OF FOOLISH COUNSEL

TEXT: 44:21-28

21 Remember these things, O Jacob, and Israel; for thou art
my servant: I have found thee; thou art my servant: O Israel,
thou shalt not be forgotten of me.
22 I have blotted out, as a thick cloud, thy transgressions,
and, as a cloud, thy sins: return unto me; for I have redeemed thee.
23 Sing, O Ye heavens, for Jehovah hath done it; shout, ye
lower parts of the earth; break forth into singing, ye mountains, O forest, and every tree therein: for Jehovah hath
redeemed Jacob, and will glorify himself in Israel.
24 Thus saith Jehovah, thy Redeemer, and he that formed
thee from the womb: I am Jehovah, that maketh all things;
that stretcheth forth the heavens alone: that spreadeth
abroad the earth (who is with me?);
25 that frustrateth the signs of the liars, and maketh diviners
mad; that turneth wise men backward, and maketh their
knowledge foolish;
26 that confirmeth the word of his servant, and performeth
the counsel of his messengers; that saith of Jerusalem, She
shall be inhabited; and of the cities of Judah, They shall
be built, and I will raise up the waste places thereof;
27 that saith to the deep, Be dry, and I will dry up thy rivers;
28 that saith of Cyrus, He is my shepherd, and shall perform
all my pleasure, even saying of Jerusalem, She shall be built;
and of the temple, Thy foundation shall be laid.

QUERIES

a. What "things" are to be "remembered" by Israel?
b. Who are the "liars" of verse 25?
c. Why mention Cyrus again?

PARAPHRASE

As you contemplate the idiocy of idolatry, remember the following things too, O Jacob, and Israel. First, you are mine. I chose you and I created you as a people, to be My servant in a divine destiny. Second, I could never forget you Israel, for it was I who blotted out your transgressions and sins. You must return to Me and never forget Me, Israel, for I purchase you with the price of redemption. Indeed, your redemption is so glorious it involves the heavens, mountains, and the forests. The whole universe will sing and shout Jehovah's praise. Jehovah's redemption of Israel will, in its completion, redound to His glory in Israel. This is what Jehovah, your Redeemer and Progenitor says: I am Jehovah-the-Faithful. I am Jehovah, Creator of all things. I alone formed the heavens and the earth. Who could say they helped Me? I frustrate the fulfillments of the false prophets and expose them as liars and make the soothsayers appear to be mad men. I refute the wisdom of unbelieving counselors and demonstrate it to be foolishness. But when My servants, the prophets, predict that Jerusalem shall be inhabited and the cities of Judah shall be built and that the waste places shall be populated, I make their predictions come to pass! When I say to what opposes My redemptive people, Be gone! it shall be gone! And when I say Cyrus shall be My shepherd to fulfill My purposes by giving permission for the building of Jerusalem and the Temple, that is exactly what shall come to pass.

COMMENTS

v. 21-23 FORGIVENESS IS IN JEHOVAH: The message of this section is that Israel is to *remember* (Heb. *zekar*) who Jehovah is. We remind the reader, this is the very essence of biblical religion—the realization of the objective Personhood of God. Biblical religion is not how man feels, but what man acknowledges about who God is and what God has said. Especially

Israel is admonished to remember who Jehovah is in view of the foregoing expose of the idiocy of idolatry. All men are vulnerable to idolatry if they do not acknowledge the objective reality of the eternal, supernatural Personhood of Jehovah. Man must have a god. He will make one of wood or stone, of science or government, of fame or fortune—or even of himself. Israel must remember that Jehovah chose her and created her for Himself. He evidenced His special claim upon her in ages past by miraculous powers of deliverance, sustenance, subjugations and revelations. He demonstrated that He was a living God, capable and willing to guide and guard Israel over thousands of years. He never forgot her!

The blotting out of Israel's sin is apparently in promise here. We know from the New Testament that the actual, historical event which blotted out sin and *accomplished* redemption was the atoning death of Jesus Christ (cf. Heb. 10:1-18). The blood of bulls and goats could not take away sin. The Hebrew who offered his sacrificial lamb lived in faith that God would, someday, accomplish the act which would atone for his sins and thus fulfill His promises. The point being stressed in verse 22 is willingness and mercifulness of God in promising to blot out Israel's sin and offering her, even then, a way to believe in that promise. The redemption spoken of in verses 22 and 23 cannot refer to the return from the exile, for there was no permanence to that. The Hebrew word *goal* is repeated in this text and it implies more than forgiveness of sins; it implies that a price has been paid to purchase Israel. That price was God's dear Son on Calvary. Certainly, the redemptive plan included God's deliverance of Israel from her captivity so she might bring forth the Suffering Servant. And this is exactly what Israel needed to *remember* now—her redemptive servanthood. She needed to remember that God had called her and promised her (in type and prophecy) redemption. God's promises are as good as done! God can direct His prophets to predict the future as if it were accomplished!

All nature is bound up with the destiny of mankind. When man sinned, God cursed nature so man would not, in his sinful state, fall in love with this earth. When Christ died on the cross suffering the curse upon man and earning man's redemption, He also suffered the curse upon nature and earned nature's redemption. Therefore, in view of the certainty of God's redemption of Israel, all of God's creation can rejoice and sing and shout because all of God's creation is equally certain of its redemption. The true Israel of God is destined for dominion over a redeemed and recreated Eden (cf. Rom. 8:18-25; Heb. 2:5-9; II Pet. 3:13). Israel must remember that and repent of idolatry!

v. 24-28 FAITHFULNESS IS IN JEHOVAH: Another aspect of Jehovah's nature Israel is to *remember* is His absolute faithfulness. He alone is sovereign. He alone knows the future. He alone speaks and it comes to pass. Who dares challenge His claim that He created everything? Who can bring forth evidence to dispute His claim? Job learned a lesson he probably never forgot (Job 38-40) about challenging the sovereign wisdom of God. Many alleged "scientific" explanations of the formation of the universe are posited today but they are moral evasions, not verifiable scientific demonstrations.

Jehovah demonstrates His omnipotence and omniscience over and over again by frustrating the alleged "signs" of the liars (Heb. *baddim*, feigners, fakers, false prophets). The Lord may expose the false prophet immediately or He may take a long time to do so, but eventually the false prophet is exposed and the Lord's Word is vindicated. Isaiah was one of those prophets of the Lord whose word was confirmed publicly (cf. Isa. 36-38). Jeremiah (Jer. 28:5-17) was another! The list goes on and on. The Lord is still frustrating the fakers and confirming the veracity of His Word today! But this text is directed especially to Israel. She must remind herself of God's omniscience and not listen to the oracles of the idolatrous false-prophets. When God says Jerusalem would be inhabited and the cities of Judah (although many of them had been made desolate by the Assyrian armies) would be built, Isaiah's contemporaries must believe it will surely come to pass. Ultimately, Jehovah is going to confound the wisdom of the wise in His

Suffering Servant. God will use the "Foolishness" of the cross to save those who believe (I Cor. 1:18f). The idea of a crucified Messiah was utterly foreign to the Jewish concept. Isaiah predicted that (Isa. 53:1-9)! Peter confirms the Jewish revulsion at the concept of a dying Messiah (cf. Mt. 16:21-23, etc.). The total absence of any specific reference to a personal, dying Messiah in the Jewish apocrypha confirms this.

The point of these verses is the way in which Jehovah confirms His sovereign will. He confounds and frustrates the vain predictions and philosophies of men and fulfills the predictions of His commissioned prophets. Many said Jehovah's program to redeem mankind and form a redeemed people on earth would not survive. Great empires and powerful emperors opposed it. They overran Jerusalem, tore down His temple and slaughtered His people, but God preserved a remnant through the centuries. Out of that remnant (Jerusalem and Judah) God produced Jesus Christ and His church. No river was "deep" enough to stop God from keeping His promise of redemption. No empire was large enough, cruel enough, rich enough to keep God from preserving those who remained faithful to Him. God was able even to use Cyrus, a pagan ruler of Persia, to "shepherd" His people and send them back to Jerusalem to rebuild the temple. God used Nebuchadnezzar and many others to fulfill His purposes (cf. our comments in *Daniel,* College Press, chapters 7-12). We will have much more to say of Cyrus in the next chapter.

Israel is to renew its divine destiny as the servant of Jehovah on the basis of Jehovah's faithfulness. Jehovah will keep His promises, and no amount of opposition will stand in His way. As a matter of fact, Jehovah will use His opposition as servants and shepherds to carry out His plan. Israel is more than a conqueror through Him who loves her! The church must daily renew its divine destiny as God's Zion in the world today on the basis of Christ's faithfulness to keep His promises. Let the church focus its preaching on the nature of Christ—who He is and what He promises, and this will build the kingdom of God. Man has many questions, but Jesus cuts through all our irrelevancies and goes to the very heart of our problem when He asks, "Whom do you say that I am?" (Mt. 16:15). For in this question He asks for conviction, confession and commitment to the only thing that matters—the deity of Jesus of Nazareth. Once that is settled, all else falls into proper place.

QUIZ

1. Why is it important to remember *who* God is?
2. How was Israel's sin blotted out?
3. Why is God able to direct His prophets to predict the future as if it were already accomplished?
4. Why direct the heavens to sing?
5. How does God frustrate the signs of the liars?
6. In what or whom did God ultimately confound the wisdom of the wise?

SPECIAL STUDY

THE TRANSCENDENT GOD REVEALED HIMSELF

John 1:18

by Paul T. Butler

INTRODUCTION

I. THE POSSIBILITY OF GOD REVEALING HIMSELF

   A. Once established from Theism (natural revelation) that God exists and that He is the Uncaused, First Cause, with eternal power and deity (Rom. 1:20), the Purposing Designer of the universe—

      1. then unless that which He created is greater than He . . . and
      2. unless the laws He created are greater than the Lawgiver . . .

3. There is no escaping the conclusion that He can, if He wishes, intervene in the universe to reveal Himself, to accomplish His omnipotent will and purpose.

B. Uniformitarianism (dogma of the so-called "immutable laws of nature") does not preclude the possibility of supernatural intervention
   1. The "uniformity of nature" is not a force, it is a mere abstract designation of the force that is observed to be working.
   2. Both Heisenberg's principle of "indeterminacy" and Einstein's principle of relativity show that natural law is not "immutable."
   3. The absolute uniformity of nature depends upon human *observation of all time and all experience*—human observation has not been long enough into the past to say that these laws have always acted uniformily—nor can human observation say with any absoluteness what these laws will do in the immediate future!
   4. The question whether God has revealed Himself or not must be decided on the basis of evidence. Is there any evidence of supernatural intervention or revelation?

II. THE PROBABILITY OF GOD REVEALING HIMSELF

A. Would God create man and leave him all alone? All reason cries NO!
   1. A man given a free will might do things contrary to the will of his Creator and be in danger, so the Creator would want to warn the creature.
   2. The Creator is a Being of Purpose. There must be some purpose for man. There is no way for man to find the Purposer's purpose for him unless the Purposer tells it!

B. All religions, however pagan, have some form of revelation from their gods. Where did this idea of the higher being revealing himself come from if God did not put it there and if such a revelation had not, in fact, occurred?

III. THE PROGRAM OF GOD'S REVELATION OF HIMSELF

A. In History (events and deeds)
B. In Words (directly and through human agents in human language)
C. In Person (Jesus Christ)

DISCUSSION

I. GOD REVEALED HIMSELF IN HISTORY—IN EVENTS, DEEDS OR IN NATURE

A. In Acts 14:15-18, Paul told the citizens of pagan Lystra that the Creator-God *"did not leave himself without witness,* for he did good and gave you from heaven rains and fruitful seasons . . ."
B. In Acts 17:22-30, Paul told the Athenian philosophers that what they and their poets had been led (by a revelation they had of God through nature and reason) to worship was a Person, not a thing of stone or wood. The Athenians should have known this and deduced it from the nature of their own being!
C. In Romans 1:19-20, Paul writes that the Gentiles had a revelation of the wrath, the eternal power and deity of God in that which had been created (nature); cf. Psa. 19:1-4.
D. God has revealed Himself through supernatural events (we call them miracles) which have taken place historically. Such events cannot be explained as natural phenomena (parting of the Red Sea; Noachian Flood, etc.) except by men who choose to deliberately ignore the facts (cf. II Pet. 3:5).
   1. As a result of such supernatural events, having been

empirically demonstrated, God expects man to reason to the Uncaused Cause (cf. Ex. 14:10-18; Psa. 44:1-3; 67:7-10; 78:1-72; 105:1ff; 106:1ff; 136:1ff).

2. Compare these references also: Dan. 4:34-37; Heb. 2:2-4; Jn. 5:19-23; 10:31-39; 14:8-11.

E. Some still refuse to admit, even in the face of demonstrable, historical evidence, that miracles have occurred. C. S. Lewis puts it this way in "Miracles" . . . "Because such an admission would force them to admit there is a living God! Men exclude miracles from the realm of possibility today because in so doing they fashion for themselves a God who would not do miracles, or indeed anything else. Men are reluctant to pass over from the notion of an abstract and negative deity to the living God. An abstract and negative deity does nothing, demands nothing. He is there if you wish for Him, like a book on a shelf. He will not pursue you. It is with a shock that we discover a "living God." You have had a shock like that before, in connection with smaller matters—when the line pulls at your hand, when something breathes beside you in the darkness. So here; the shock comes at the precise moment when the thrill of *life* is communicated to us along the clue we have been following. It is always shocking to meet life where we thought we were alone. 'Look out,' we cry, 'it's alive!' An impersonal God—well and good. A subjective God of beauty, truth and goodness, inside our own heads—better still. A formless life-force surging through us, a vast power which we can tap—best of all. BUT GOD HIMSELF, ALIVE, PULLING AT THE OTHER END OF THE CORD, PERHAPS APPROACHING AT AN INFINITE SPEED, THE HUNTER, KING, HUSBAND, THAT IS QUITE ANOTHER MATTER! There comes a moment when the children who have been playing cops and robbers hush suddenly: was that a real footstep in the hall? There comes a moment when people who have been dabbling in religion ('Man's search for God') suddenly draw back. Supposing we really found Him? We never meant it to come to *that!* Worse still, supposing He had found us?"

THIS IS WHY PEOPLE DENY THAT GOD HAS REVEALED HIMSELF HISTORICALLY IN EMPIRICALLY WITNESSED DEEDS . . . OR PERSONALLY IN JESUS CHRIST . . . HE IS, THEN, THE LIVING GOD!

II. GOD REVEALED HIMSELF IN WORDS—IN HUMAN LANGUAGE

A. A verbal revelation is necessary

1. Some historical events lend themselves to interpretation by the innate capabilities of the mind of man alone (Rom. 1, etc.)
2. Most events, however, must be interpreted by God to man in a verbal communication if man is to understand their revelatory nature.
3. Revelation then consists of event and interpretation. God acts in history and discloses by words the meaning of His acts.
4. The interpretation of the prophets, of Jesus Christ and of the apostles of what God has done in History is itself a part of the revelatory situation.
5. God communicated in words to Adam even before Eve was created (Gen. 2:15-17)—God gave Adam the ability to use language and name the animals before Eve was created (Gen. 2:20).

B. The nature of language as a medium of revelation

1. Written words have the same validity as the actual words of the speaker and this is shown by the fact that written words are admissible as evidence in a court of law, carrying the same weight as those of a living and present witness.
2. Speech, as defined by Wm. J. Martin, "is the act by which the speaker provides with perceptible garments the invisible offspring (thoughts) of his mind."
3. Language makes the communication of thoughts possible by providing verbal "deputies" for the

ingredients of many situations.

4. By language it is possible also for a speaker to superimpose his will on another, and thus it becomes possible for the Holy Spirit to superimpose His will upon us and within us through a verbal revelation.
5. Language makes possible even the communication of inaccessible matter (the supernatural wisdom and plan of God, which would be inaccessible if He did not speak it to us in language).
6. Language is necessary even for the mind of man to communicate with itself, for the mind is never completely happy until it has reduced its problems to linguistic terms.

C. Existential theology denies that God can or will reveal Himself propositionally (that is, they affirm that God does not reveal Himself verbally, through words, but by direct confrontation, subjectively) —BUT
1. We cannot have the knowledge of God without the knowledge *about* God!! anymore than we can have a knowledge of our wives or children without a knowledge *about* them!
2. We cannot claim the transcendent experience, the oneness of the soul with God, without the truth that God gives of Himself in the saving events of history, the truth of which comes to us by historical media.
3. Christian faith is not hung on a sky-hook but is founded securely in fact. One senses that the writers of the N.T. were terribly empirically minded. The fact-basis of faith is everywhere apparent in Scripture.
4. Faith without truth is impossible! and that truth is not some ether that haunts the atmosphere or the brain but something that is the function of statements and that grasps us when there is conveyed that which is actually the case.
5. To be personal means to be a self, a rational self, a moral self, and a purposing self. Man is both intellectual and moral. The one cannot be separated from

the other. Response to the truth is moral as well as intellectual. Therefore there must be propositional truth in verbal form before there can be either an intellectual or moral confrontation with God!!

6. Confrontation involves the meeting of minds, of common response to one another—in the truth. The confrontation of persons involves the communication of truth. Truth is a function of language!

D. Language and Personal Encounter

1. Events (nature, history) cannot bring about the personal encounter which the genius of language alone can accomplish.
2. By means of the sense of hearing, as the receiver of verbal communication, one mind can make contact with the mental world of another mind and can influence that inaccessible and mysterious realm of thought.
3. Further, with the voluntary cooperation of the recipient, one may learn in turn something about the contents of that other mind.
4. Without such voluntary cooperation and without communication THERE IS AN IMPENETRABLE BOUNDARY TO PERSONAL ENCOUNTER . . . this is exactly what Paul says in I Cor. 2:11 . . . "For what person knows a man's thought except the spirit of the man which is in him?" The mind of the man sitting next to you may be quite inaccessible to you, while at that very moment a friend a 1000 miles away may be allowing you, by means of a letter, to learn something of what is beyond this boundary . . . the act of crossing this boundary is one of the most remarkable phenomena of our experience.
5. If God willed to cross this boundary, He could surely do so by the existing means so extensively used between man and man. This is what the Psalmist infers in Psa. 94:8ff . . . If God made the eye, He can see . . ." AND IF GOD MADE THE TONGUE, HE CAN TALK!

E. The Bible leaves us in no doubt whatever that the vehicle of revelation is language (words).

1. Language is versatile: it is unique in the reception and transmission of knowledge; it is the only means which possesses such potentiality.
2. Mystical communication, in which the intellect is in abeyance and the object of the participant is to merge himself by a non-verbal process in the Godhead, is excluded by a word often on the lips of the writers of the O.T. The word is translated "to hear," and signifies not only to hear, but "to understand" and even "to respond" to what is said.
3. There are literally thousands of references in both O.T. and N.T. representing God as "speaking" *words* (cf. Ex. 20:1; Deut. 1:6; Psa. 33:9; Jer. 7:13; 14:14; Jn. 6:63; Mt. 24:35; Jn. 17:14, 17).
4. Language is the only conceivable means of communicating non-empirical places, things or concepts (heaven, hell, remission of sins). It has the ability to cross dimensional limits of time, space, etc., and communicate by verbal deputies (figures of speech, analogies, etc.) the non-experienceable. It has the ability to bring about PERSONAL ENCOUNTER, I Cor. 2:13.
5. Yet language is inadequate to describe the ultimate realities of such things as heaven, hell, etc. ON THE OTHER HAND, INADEQUACY DOES NOT MEAN ERRONEOUSNESS. Paul was "caught up into the third heaven and heard things it was impossible for him to utter." (II Cor. 12:1-4) We do not believe the book of Revelation's description of heaven is in any ultimate sense, adequate, yet it is adequate enough in its relative sense to engender love, faith and purpose in the believer's heart.

III. GOD REVEALED HIMSELF IN A PERSON, HIS UNIQUE SON, JESUS CHRIST

A. Because God is personal, the final revelation of Himself was a Person.
   1. Heb. 1:1-4, In times past God revealed Himself in many ways, and through many servants (prophets), but in the last dispensation He has revealed Himself in the Son. This Son is: Heir, Co-Creator, Glory of God, Express Image of His Person, Sustainer, Majesty on High.
   2. John 1:1-18, The Third Person of the God-head became Incarnate and "tabernacled" among men. Men beheld His glory as of the only unique Son from the face-to-face presence with the Father. No man has seen God at any time, but the Son has declared Him (exegesatos) "exegeted" Him.
   3. Phil. 2:5-10, God took upon Himself the form of a man and suffered the death of the cross, revealing the love of God.
   4. II Cor. 5:19, God was in Christ, reconciling the world unto Himself.
   5. Heb. 10:4-10, He came in a body prepared for Him to do the will of God willingly, and by that will we are sanctified.
   6. His name is Immanuel ("God with us"), Matt. 1:23.

B. The Son of God became Incarnate and *acted* in history and *spoke* exactly and exclusively the very words God willed Him to speak!! Luke says his gospel document is a "treatise . . . of all that Jesus began both to do and teach . . ." Acts 1:1.
   1. Jesus lived and taught the love of God perfectly.
   2. Jesus lived and taught the compassion of God perfectly.
   3. Jesus lived and taught the righteousness of God perfectly.

C. The most important statement of Jesus concerning His personal revelation of the Father is found in John 14:7-11.

   "If ye had known me, ye should have known my

Father also: and from henceforth ye know him, and have seen him. Philip saith unto him, Lord, show us the Father, and it sufficeth us. Jesus saith unto him, Have I been so long time with you, and yet hast thou not known me, Philip? he that hath seen me hath seen the Father; and how sayest thou then, Show us the Father? Believest thou not that I am in the Father, and the Father in me? the words that I speak unto you I speak not of myself: but the Father that dwelleth in me, he doeth the works. Believe me that I am in the Father, and the Father in me: or else believe me for the very works' sake."

CONCLUSION

I. PERSONAL REVELATION INVOLVES DECISION, RESPONSE TO THE PERSONAL GOD

A. God meets man in the act of revelation not as an Idea, an Unmoved Mover, but as a PERSON who speaks to man and requires a response from man.

B. To say that revelation is historical, verbal and personal means, in brief, that God has come into our midst and because He has so come, we can never remain the same as we were before.

II. JESUS CHRIST IS GOD IN THE FLESH, "HEAR YE HIM!"

A. "In Him dwelleth all the fullness of the Godhead bodily." Col. 2:9

B. Do you want to know what God thinks? Read the words of Jesus and the apostles.

C. Do you want to know how God acts? Look at the life Jesus lived.

D. Do you want to know what God thinks of man? Read the Bible.

E. Do you want to know what God promises to men of faith and obedience? Read the New Testament!
F. Do you want to know what God commands man to do? Read the New Testament!

III. AT THE END OF THIS AGE GOD IS GOING TO REVEAL HIMSELF ONCE AGAIN

A. Historically, Verbally, Personally
B. I Thess. 4:16ff; II Thess. 1:7-10; Titus 2:13; I Jn. 3:1-3; Jn. 14:1-6; Acts 1:9-11

IV. WHAT IS YOUR DECISION? GOD HAS REVEALED HIMSELF TO YOU PERSONALLY, VERBALLY, YOU HAVE HAD A PERSONAL ENCOUNTER WITH GOD HERE, NOW!

HIS PERSONAL INVITATION TO YOU IS COME, RECEIVE, OBEY, TRUST.

THE BIBLE IS HIS LOVE LETTER TO YOU.

2. SOVEREIGN IN SALVATION, CHAPTER 45

a. OMNIPOTENCE

TEXT: 45:1-8

1 Thus saith Jehovah to his anointed, to Cyrus, whose right
hand I have holden, to subdue nations before him, and I
will loose the loins of kings; to open the doors before him,
and the gates shall not be shut:
2 I will go before thee, and make the rough places smooth;
I will break in pieces the doors of brass, and cut in sunder
the bars of iron;
3 and I will give thee the treasures of darkness, and hidden
riches of secret places, that thou mayest know that it is I,
Jehovah, who call thee by thy name, even the God of Israel.
4 For Jacob my servant's sake, and Israel my chosen, I have
called thee by thy name: I have surnamed thee, though thou

hast not known me.
5 I am Jehovah, and there is none else; besides me there is no
God. I will gird thee, though thou hast not known me;
6 that they may know from the rising of the sun, and from
the west, that there is none besides me: I am Jehovah, and
there is none else.
7 I form the light, and create darkness; I make peace, and
create evil; I am Jehovah, that doeth all these things.
8 Distil, ye heavens, from above, and let the skies pour down
righteousness: let the earth open, that it may bring forth
salvation, and let it cause righteousness to spring up together;
I Jehovah have created it.

QUERIES

a. How will Jehovah loose the loins of kings before Cyrus?
b. Why did God surname Cyrus for Jacob's sake?
c. How may the "skies pour down righteousness"?

PARAPHRASE

This is what Jehovah says to Cyrus the man He has especially chosen and whose career of conquest and government Jehovah will guide and sustain. The Lord will subdue great world powers and strip emperors of their strength for him; He will open city gates and no one will be able to shut them against Cyrus. Jehovah says, I will be the One preparing your path of conquest. All obstacles will be removed. Doors of brass, barred with iron will not stand in your way. Secret treasures which these kings assume cannot be found will be given to you to the end that you may know that I am God and that it is I, the God of Israel, who called you by your name many years before you were born. I have called you primarily for the sake of My servant, Israel, My chosen people. I have prophecied your name long before your birth, even though you do not acknowledge

Me as the Only God. There is no other god. I, Jehovah, am sovereign in the affairs of all men. It is I, Jehovah, who will empower you in your conquests Cyrus, although you do not acknowledge Me. I will do this so that the whole world will have opportunity to know there is no god besides Me. I am Jehovah, and there is no other god. I create both light and darkness; I send both blessing and woe; I, Jehovah, am the creator of everything. I, Jehovah, have created all of heaven and earth and I will command it and use all My creation to bring about the blessings of salvation and righteousness which I have promised to Israel, My chosen.

COMMENTS

v. 1-4 ANOINTED: The word translated *anointed* is the Hebrew word *meshikho* a form of the word *messiah.* It is astounding to learn that Jehovah has "anointed" a pagan emperor to become a "messiah" for His people. Yet, the Lord has used many "servants" from among the heathen (see Daniel 7 & 8, Jer. 27:1-11) to fulfill His redemptive plan. It is apparent that Cyrus, in his deliverance of Israel, served as a type of the Messiah-Servant to come, Jesus Christ (see special study on Types in this volume). Cyrus was not born for more than a hundred years after this prophecy. Cyrus was born in a little province in north-western Elam and just south of Media. He came to power in about 559 B.C. He was actually Cyrus II, a descendant of Achaemenes (700-675 B.C.). Cyrus' own cylinder indicates he was thoroughly imbued with the idea that he was *the* man of destiny: (the opening lines are quoted here)

> "Through all the lands he (Marduk) searched, he saw him (Cyrus), and he sought the righteous prince, after his own heart, whom he took by the hand. Cyrus, king of Anshan, he called by name; to sovereignty over the whole world he appointed him."

The rule of Cyrus meant for all the conquered world a renewed and continuous political prosperity and a religious liberty unknown in the annals of other rulers. He was the protector and the bounteous promoter of the welfare of his subjects. Their deities and their methods of worship were graciously restored, and dignified by elevating them to their former positions. The peoples, also, who had been forcibly deported from their native lands, were restored by the king's decrees. This generous policy, in contrast with that of preceding rulers, gave Cyrus great influence and power over his subjects. Part of his popularity may have been due to the fact that he was an Aryan (Caucasian), with newer and freer ideas than those of Semitic potentates.

There is an interesting statement in Josephus to the effect that Cyrus read Isaiah's prophecy and was influenced by it to free the Jews (*Antiq.* XI.1.2.). It is not impossible! Cyrus was a man interested in the religion, culture, and history of all his subjects. In his proclamation (Ezra 1:1f; II Chron. 36:22f) Cyrus attributes his actions to a knowledge of what Jehovah "commanded" him to do. There were, as we have mentioned, other reasons for Cyrus' actions; (1) it was national policy to "restore peoples to their own dwelling places." (2) Palestine had been from time immemorial a buffer state between southwestern Asia and Egypt. To occupy and hold the strong fortress of Jerusalem was the first step toward the conquest of the rival power. If Cyrus could secure that advantage by aiding the Jews to rebuild and hold it, he would be setting up one battlement in the face of Egypt's army. For one of his next strokes, after Babylon, would be at the rival imperial power on the Nile. For more on Cyrus and the Medo-Persian Empire see *Daniel*, by Butler, College Press, pages 223-233 and 296-298.

There are three distinct reasons God uses Cyrus and speaks so intimately to him nearly 200 years before his birth:

(a) Cyrus is to know that the God of Israel is the only God there is, (v. 3).
(b) Cyrus is to serve Jehovah for the sake of Israel, (v. 4).
(c) Cyrus is to serve Jehovah in order that all men may know Jehovah is the only God there is, (v. 6).

It is apparent that Cyrus was never converted to monotheism or the worship of Jehovah as the only God, for in many of his proclamations, he acknowledges Marduk as god. Whatever Cyrus accomplished, it was because Jehovah, sovereign Lord of all creation, permitted him to do it. Not only did Jehovah permit it, He assisted Cyrus in its accomplishment (cf. Jer. 27:1-11).

v. 5-8 ALMIGHTY: This is one of the great passages of the Bible teaching that God is immanent in His creation. God has not created the universe and wound it like a clock, only to go off somewhere and let it run itself. He is personally and directly involved in its day-by-day operation.

a. In Christ, all things consist, or hold together, Col. 1:17
b. He upholds all things by the word of His power, Heb. 1:3
c. He makes his sun rise on the evil and on the good, Mt. 5:45
d. He gives rain from heaven and fruitful seasons, Acts 14:17
e. His wrath is revealed from heaven, Rom. 1:18-32, "in the things that have been made."
f. In everything God works for good with those who love him, Rom. 8:28-29
g. All that happens in history and nature is under the sovereign Throne of God and the Lamb (cf. Rev. 4-9).

If there is one thing made abundantly clear from the prophets (and confirmed by the New Testament) it is that God is sovereign of both weal and woe. Is God in the whirlwind? Yes! (Nahum 1:3; Zech. 9:14). Is God in the earthquake? Yes! (Isa. 29:6; Acts 16:26; Mt. 24:7; Rev. 6:12; 8:5, etc.). God is in locust plagues, fires, floods, famines, droughts, plagues. "Does evil befall a city except the Lord hath done it?" (Amos 3:6). When some "good" comes everyone is agreed it is *directly* from the Lord. When some "woe" comes let us be equally assured it is from the Lord. Do tornadoes, earthquakes and famines mean those who are "victimized" are worse sinners than others? No! Jesus cleared that up in Luke 13. Whatever happens, wherever it happens, it is God's message to a cursed and doomed universe to repent! All who do not repent will likewise perish! What of those who are repenting and yet perish? They "come out of their great tribulation" (Rev. 7:13-17); they are "rested from their labors" (Rev. 14:13); and their works follow after them. They are blessed! There is only one part of God's creation granted the sovereign exercise of free will—man! All the rest of His creation is under His *direct operation.* "Nature" is simply a word used by man to evade this fundamental issue that it is *God* who is Creator and *Sustainer.* But both good and evil, no matter with whom they originate, are never out of God's control. Even Satan's deliberate evil and the freely chosen evil deeds of men are under His control and are being used (and will be ultimately used) to serve His sovereign purposes and redound to His Absolute glory! Both the weal and woe of God is designed to lead man to repentance (cf. Rom. 1:18 with Rom. 2:4); see Isa. 14:24-27; 44:24-28; Jer. 27:1-11; Job 2:1-6; II Cor. 12:1-10; Dan. 2:20-23. Do men still rule by God's sovereign permission? Does God still send famines, earthquakes, fires, floods, whirlwinds, sun and rain, fruit and harvest season? Yes! He is the same God today He was thousands of years ago! Men still choose sin and evil rebellion because God has granted them the freedom to make that choice, and God is in no way to blame for their choice nor is He the author of their evil. But rest assured their evil will in no way triumph over the sovereign will of God. It is His will that their impenitent, unforgiven evil shall be punished forever—and so it will be! Furthermore, their evil in this life is permitted by Him and used as chastening, warning, perfecting, strengthening agents upon all who will put their trust in Him.

Verse eight appears to be Isaiah's own surrender to the expressed sovereignty of God just proclaimed. It is, as it were, a prayer of Isaiah looking forward to the prospective mission of Cyrus and its salvation for the people of God. Isaiah prays that God's whole universe join in with God's program of redemption for Israel and the nations. Let all of God's creation bring forth and pour down spiritual blessings in heavenly gifts, according to the will and in the power of Jehovah, whose ultimate purpose is a new spiritual creation. Any man who believes and contemplates the absolute sovereignty of Jehovah as expressed by Isaiah here must be led to the same adoring prayer!

QUIZ

1. Why would God use the term *anointed* to refer to Cyrus?
2. Is it possible that Cyrus might have known about this prophecy?
3. How did Cyrus fulfill this prophecy?
4. To what extent does God exercise control over the universe today?
5. Is God the author of evil?

b. OBEDIENCE

TEXT: 45:9-13

9 Woe unto him that striveth with his Maker! a potsherd among the potsherds of the earth! Shall the clay say to him that fashioneth it, What makest thou? or thy work, He hath no hands?

10 Woe unto him that saith unto a father, What begettest thou? or to a woman, with what travailest thou?

11 Thus saith Jehovah, the Holy One of Israel, and his Maker: Ask me of the things that are to come; concerning my sons, and concerning the work of my hands, command ye me.

12 I have made the earth, and created man upon it: I, even my hands, have stretched out the heavens; and all their host have I commanded.

13 I have raised him up in righteousness, and I will make straight all his ways: he shall build my city, and he shall

let my exiles go free, not for price nor reward, saith Jehovah of hosts.

QUERIES

a. Who is God warning not to strive with his Maker?
b. Why does God challenge, "ask me of the things that are to come"?

PARAPHRASE

Cursed is the man who contends with Me about what I have just predicted! Men are creatures, not Creators—they are like earthenware pots and have been formed. They are not Formers! Now, shall the clay (man) say to him that fashions it (God), What do you think you are doing—You can't do that!? For man to tell God He cannot do what He says He will do is as foolish as an unborn son telling his father and mother they cannot bring him forth in birth. This is what Jehovah, the Holy One of Israel, Sovereign Creator says: Will you dare to question Me about what I intend to do in the future? Do you presume to tell Me what I can and cannot do with My covenant children? I am the Omnipotent Creator of everything that is! I created the earth and I created man; I created the heavens and all the heavenly beings, and everything that exists is at My command. As I predicted, because of My own righteous purpose, I raise up Cyrus and I will personally make all his ways successful. He will build My city, Jerusalem, and he will free My people from their captivity. He will not do it because he has been paid to do so; he will do it because the Lord Jehovah of hosts has spoken!

COMMENTS

v. 9-11 PRESUMPTION: God knows His former prophecy that Cyrus, a pagan emperor, is to be His anointed servant to deliver God's people, will meet with incredulity. It would not be easy for a Jew to accept the idea that a pagan monarch could be God's "anointed"! That Jehovah, God of Israel, would ever give success to *goyim* (Gentiles) was unacceptable (cf. Hab. 1:12—2:5; Lk. 4:16-30). But the rejection of God's word is moral rebellion and inexcusable. God has demonstrated in the past that He may do anything He wishes to do. He has demonstrated that when He speaks it comes to pass. Those who thus "contend" with Him are like *kheres* (earthenware pots) talking back to their *yatsar* (former) (cf. Isa. 29:16; Jer. 18:1ff; Rom. 9:20; Isa. 10:15). God pronounces *woe* on such presumption. It is insolent disobedience to question God's word as if to say, God, what do you think you are doing by anointing a Gentile—you can't do that! The phrase, "He hath no hands" implies the skeptic is charging God with ineptitude, as if God is going to make a mess of things by anointing Cyrus. Actually, it is the skeptic who is absurd. For a man to advise God is as ridiculous as an unborn child telling its parents they cannot conceive it or bring it to birth. The two verbs *shealvuni* (ask) and *tetsavvuni* (command) are imperatives. This may be translated as either command or question. We have chosen to understand it as a rhetorically satirical question from God to the skeptic. "You dare to question Me about My prophecies? You presume to command Me what to do about My redemptive program for My covenant people?" And all this presumptive meddling in God's preannounced program is an attempted remonstrance with God about things that have not yet come to pass!

v. 12-13 PROCLAMATION: God reiterates His sovereignty. He is omnipotent and omniscient. He is so by right of His Creatorship. He made earth, man, heaven, angels and everything that exists. Everything that exists is at His command—even a Gentile emperor! But more significantly, Israel is His to command. God's prophecy of deliverance by Cyrus is a command to Israel. Her proper response is obedience—not presumptive skepticism. What God is going to do with Cyrus is on account of God's righteousness—not Cyrus' goodness. The Lord plainly states that Cyrus shall be His servant to rebuild Jerusalem and to free the captive Jews. There were four decrees by Persian rulers authorizing the Jews to return, rebuild and reinstitute their commonwealth (see our comments in *Daniel*, College Press, pgs. 347-348). Cyrus made the first decree in 536 B.C. and it is recorded in Ezra 1:2-4. The astounding thing about this statement of Isaiah (v. 13) is that it was made approximately 150 years before the fact! This is proof positive of the supernatural character of the book of Isaiah! It is also of great significance that Isaiah predicts the motivation for Cyrus' freeing of the Jews and his part in rebuilding their nation will not be for "price nor reward." Cyrus will not have to be "paid off," or "bribed." The Jews will not be released for ransom. Zechariah's prophecy reveals that God will keep the world at peace so the Jews may rebuild their temple and their cities—"not by power, nor by might, but by my Spirit, saith the Lord," (cf. Zech. 4:5-14). It is nothing short of amazing that a powerful emperor like Cyrus would free his captives without a struggle and by his own imperial edict. It would be totally unexpected behavior in a world ruler of those days. To allow some 100,000 people, who in 70 years had become an integral part of the economic, political and social system of the empire, to pick up and leave suddenly would cause unimaginable problems. But as uncommon and unimaginable as it may have seemed then, it happened—just as it was predicted. God "stirred up the spirit" of Cyrus and the Jews were returned to Palestine. No great army overpowered Persia; no exchange of money took place; there was not even a "summit meeting" of diplomats working out a release of the captives. Only the amazing *power* of the fulfillment of the Word of God being demonstrated!

Note the following things about the return from the captivity:

a. It was begun in 536 B.C., exactly 70 years after the first captivity of Judah in 606 B.C. This exact 70 years was predicted by God's prophets (cf. Jer. 25:11-12; Dan. 9:2)!
b. It was instituted by Cyrus, emperor of Persia; He was predicted to be the instigator of the return 150 years before he was born, (Isa. 45:1-13)!
c. The release of the Jews from Persia would in no way profit the emperor Cyrus. There would be no "pay-off." As a matter of fact, Cyrus decreed that people of his realm should contribute to the financial needs of the Jews to help them rebuild their nation (cf. Ezra 1:1-4)!
d. Not only were the Jews released from captivity, they were charged by the Persian emperor to reinstitue their commonwealth. This meant they were to return to self-governing nationhood (cf. Ezra 7:11-26)!

When Isaiah was making this prophecy of the release of the exiles by the hand of Cyrus, the people of Judah had not yet been taken captive! In fact, their captivity was yet some 50 years away! The point is that Isaiah's people are refusing to believe they are going away into captivity. How much more incredible to believe they will someday be released and returned to their land by an unborn, uncrowned emperor of an unformed empire. Onc only has to read the book of Jeremiah (esp. Jer. 27-28) to understand the stubborn incredulity of the people of Judah about their subjugation to Babylon. The prediction of the prophets that God's covenant people would be taken into exile was almost totally unacceptable to the populace. The prophets who told God's truth were considered traitors!

Mankind, on the whole, changes little in its attitude toward God's promises that the kingdoms of this world are doomed. Few believed Jesus when He predicted the destruction of Jerusalem—not even the disciples (cf. Mt. 23:37—24:28); not many believed the predictions of John the apostle that Rome would fall (cf. Rev. 6-20; esp. ch. 17-18); and there will continue to be "scoffers, following their own passions and saying,

'Where is the promise of his coming?' . . ." (cf. II Pet. 3:1-13). But the word of the Lord is sure! The return of the Jews by Cyrus proves it! Let us heed Isaiah, "Will you question me about my children, or command me concerning the work of my hands?" (Isa. 45:11). God will do as He has said, and no one (not even Cyrus) will deter Him! God has spoken! Man's only intelligent, hopeful response is obedience. Even when God's declarations are prophetic and, as yet, non-existent man must *believe and act* accordingly!

QUIZ

1. Why the emphasis on the sovereignty of God's predictive word here?
2. How are the scoffers characterized in this passage?
3. When did Cyrus let Israel return to its homeland?
4. Why is the return of the Jews so amazing? (name four features).
5. How is God's prophecy of deliverance by Cyrus a command to the Jews?
6. Is there a lesson to be learned today from this prediction of the return?

c. ORDER

TEXT: 45:14-19

14 Thus saith Jehovah, The labor of Egypt, and the merchandise of Ethiopia, and the Sabeans, men of stature, shall come over unto thee, and they shall be thine: they shall go after thee; in chains they shall come over; and they shall fall down unto thee, they shall make supplication unto thee, saying, Surely God is in thee; and there is none else, there is no God.

15 Verily thou art a God that hidest thyself, O God of Israel,

the Saviour.
16 They shall be put to shame, yea, confounded, all of them; they shall go into confusion together that are makers of idols.
17 But Israel shall be saved by Jehovah with an everlasting salvation; ye shall not be put to shame nor confounded world without end.
18 For thus saith Jehovah that created the heavens, the God that formed the earth and made it, that established it and created it not a waste, that formed it to be inhabited: I am Jehovah; and there is none else.
19 I have not spoken in secret, in a place of the land of darkness; I said not unto the seed of Jacob, Seek ye me in vain: I, Jehovah, speak righteousness, I declare things that are right.

QUERIES

a. How would the wealth of the Egyptians come to the Jews?
b. Why say God "hides" himself?
c. What is the point of reminding of Jehovah's creative power?

PARAPHRASE

As a result of what I am going to do with Cyrus, says the Lord, Israel will eventually inherit the wealth of those who once opposed her, like Egypt, Ethiopia and the Sabeans. That wealth will be the best of mankind putting itself in willing servitude to follow the leadership of Israel. Men from all over the world will bow down and confess that the True God is in this new Israel, beseeching her, Let us join you for we believe there is no God except your God. Of a truth, O God of Israel, you are a Saviour who works mysteriously and incomprehensibly to the finite mind of man. At that time, the great contrast between the futility of worshipping idols and the complete and eternal salvation Jehovah gives will be made manifest. The idol worshippers will be shown to be confused and the worshippers of Jehovah will never be confused. This is what Jehovah, the One who does everything for a purpose, says. Jehovah is the God of Order and Design. Everything He does has as its goal the exaltation of His name and the salvation of man—even the captivity and return of His children. He is Creator, and there is no other! He is Sovereign, and there is no other! All of this concerning His sovereignty and His purposefulness He has made known by revelation. He has even revealed His intention to redeem mankind. He has not, like the false gods, made Himself inaccessible or unknowable. I have never said to Israel, You may look for Me but I will not let you find Me. I am Jehovah, and I speak the truth openly; whatever I say is right, and it will come to pass!

COMMENTS

v. 14 CONVERSION: What is predicted in this verse will come as a consequence of what has been said about believing and obeying the promise of deliverance from the captivity through Cryus. God is going to form a *new* Israel by the process of judgment (captivity) and redemption (return). He is going to prepare a remnant of faithful believers through which He may bring the Messiah and redeem the whole world. This messianic advent is not going to occur immediately after the return from captivity. There is no necessity to force the passage to say that. But the release of the captives and the restoration of the Jewish commonwealth will be the beginning of that total process which culminates in the first coming of Christ (cf. our comments, *Daniel,* College Press, 9:24-27, pgs. 343-356). The figurative picture of many nations coming to Israel with their treasures is a favorite expression of Isaiah to predict the messianic age (cf. Isa. 2:2-4; 18:7; 19:16-25; 23:18; 60:5-22; 61:5-11, etc.). It would demand too much to force this passage to a literal meaning. We have here a prediction that the inveterate enemies of Israel will, as a result of Israel's return to her homeland, *willingly* turn over to Israel their wealth, *willingly* surrender to Israel "in chains," and *willingly* beseech Israel to be allowed to join in the worship of Israel's God. Such action has certainly never occurred by political or military persuasion. It could only be the result of conversion. Isaiah is predicting that the "new" Israel, resulting from the restored and repenting messianic remnant, will one day see the "wealth" of its enemies willingly surrendered to it. This "new" Israel will also see men of all nations, Gentiles, becoming bond-servants to Jehovah and His kingdom. Gentiles will one day recognize that there is only One true God, and He is Jehovah, and they will beg to be joined to His people. Cyrus' release of the exiles will serve this purpose. Isaiah does not tell us all the events of history that will transpire between Cyrus and the conversion of the Gentiles to the "new" Israel. That is not relevant here. The point of Isaiah's message here is that Jehovah is sovereign—He is supreme. Jehovah is a God of purpose and order, the prophet affirms and Jehovah's ultimate purpose is the redemption, not just of a 100,000 exiles from Mesopotamia, but of the whole world.

v. 15-17 CERTITUDE: Isaiah now moves to an expression of awe and praise for the unsearchableness of God's ways. The Hebrew word *misettatter* is translated "hidest thyself," and is similar to the Greek word *musterion* ("mystery") which means simply, *unknown,* or *unrevealed.* God is knowable when He reveals Himself. But there are depths to the character and mind of God that finite man could never know even if they were revealed to him. Man, living in a physical, time-space, temporal capsule is incapable of comprehending a non-physical, non-time-space, non-temporary existence. God reveals as much of Himself as man needs and is able to assimilate for the purpose of redemption and salvation and sanctification. Beyond that man is at a loss to know, not because God is unwilling, but because man is incapable (cf. Isa. 55:6-11; John 16:12; Rom. 11:33; I Cor. 2:6-13). God's predictions that He will work through a pagan ruler (Cyrus) to return the exiles and that from this will come a "new" Israel which will incorporate "slaves" who have willingly surrendered from Egypt, Ethiopia, etc., is "unsearchable" and "inscrutable." God works in His plan of redemption according to His sovereign will (this is the message of Romans 9-11). Man may understand enough of God's nature to know He is sovereign. But what man needs more than understanding is belief and obedience.

Incomprehensible as it may seem, the work of God through the *new* Israel, begun with the return of the exiles by Cyrus, will result in a great demonstration of the futility of idolatry. It seems altogether incongruous that a great pagan emperor who worships idols would begin a work that would ultimately expose the shamefulness of idolatry, but that is the meaning of verse 16. In contrast with the chaos and hopelessness of idolatry, the *new* Israel will know the orderliness and salvation of the One True God. The Israel of God will *never* know shame or confusion—her salvation and hope will outlast time. The Israel of Isaiah's day was to put its hope in this as a certitude because Jehovah is the God of order and purpose. His ways are not reducible to human reasoning or human experience, but He has revealed His nature sufficiently that human beings may trust Him completely to have their redemption and glorification as His purpose in everything He does and says. Faith in the certitude of God's purpose would be the only thing that would sustain Isaiah's people through Babylonian captivity and the long centuries of "indignation" until the coming of the Messiah.

v. 18-19 COHERENCE: Isaiah continues the theme of purposefulness. God made the world for order and purpose. He did not intend it to be perverted and turned into chaos by rebellion and sin. But man made "waste" of God's creation when he believed Satan and disobeyed God. This is Isaiah's message in verse 18. The implication is that God will, through the work begun by Cyrus and the returned exiles, proceed to restore order and purpose to His creation. Restoration of *order* is the message of Romans 1-8; it is the message of Hebrews 2:5-18.

Man once had dominion over an ordered, purposeful, paradise; he forfeited it by sin and his paradise became a "futility" (cf. Rom. 8:20); Christ's meritorious work paid the redemptive price for man and his planet and one day this redemption will be consummated (Heb. 2:5-18), and man redeemed by covenant relationship to his Maker will once again have dominion over Paradise. This is the ultimate purpose of Jehovah and the goal of the work of Cyrus and the returned exiles! The coherent reunion of man with his Maker and man with his surroundings is the goal of God. Man in oneness with his God and with his fellow man is what Jesus fervently prayed for and died for (cf. Jn. 17:1ff). Only God could accomplish that. And He would accomplish it through things unsearchable and inscrutable to the wisdom of men—the gospel of the cross (cf. I Cor. 1:10-31). All the philosophies and political schemes of men put together will never accomplish what God can do through the "foolishness" of the message of the cross of Christ—that is, reunite man in a divine coherence with his Maker!

Although the ways and means by which God does this may not be fully understood, the fact that He is going to do it is no secret! This is what the prophet says in verse 19. Jehovah makes every possible effort to reveal Himself. He wants men to trust Him and love Him and obey Him. He is not like the pagan gods and their devotees whose one aim seems to be to conceal. Those who worshiped idols and practiced sorcery found themselves being told their gods could only be discovered by secret rituals and then only a select few could know the rituals. Most Gentiles understood clearly that their gods were simply creatures of mythology and fantasy. Most were skeptical of any reality connected with religion. Jehovah is not like that! When He speaks He speaks truth. When He acts, what He does is right and real. He spoke in revelation to man. "In many and various ways God spoke of old to our fathers by the prophets . . ." (Heb. 1:1). There was no dearth of communication from Jehovah, both in word and deed, even to the day of Isaiah. He declared His purposefulness and faithfulness over and over. Now, Isaiah is calling upon his contemporaries to believe Jehovah is speaking again, openly, plainly and purposefully.

QUIZ

1. What connection does this text have with what has been said before about Cyrus and the exiles?
2. Why is the statement about the "labor of Egypt" etc. to be understood figuratively?
3. How may God "hide" Himself and "reveal" Himself at the same time?
4. How will Cyrus' work result in demonstrating the futility of idolatry?
5. What kind of coherence does God seek in His creation?
6. How will God bring about that coherence?

d. OUTREACH

TEXT: 45:20-25

20 Assemble yourselves and come; draw near together, ye that are escaped of the nations: they have no knowledge that carry the wood of their graven image, and pray unto a god that cannot save.

21 Declare ye, and bring it forth; yea, let them take counsel together: who hath showed this from ancient time? who hath declared it of old? have not I, Jehovah? and there is no God else besides me, a just God and a Saviour; there is none besides me.

22 Look unto me, and be ye saved, all the ends of the earth; for I am God, and there is none else.

23 By myself have I sworn, the word is gone forth from my mouth in righteousness, and shall not return, that unto me every knee shall bow, every tongue shall swear.

24 Only in Jehovah, it is said of me, is righteousness and

strength; even to him shall men come; and all they that were incensed against him shall be put to shame.
25 In Jehovah shall all the seed of Israel be justified, and shall glory.

QUERIES

a. Why direct the "escaped of the nations" to gather?
b. When shall every "knee bow," etc.?
c. Who is "incensed" against Jehovah?

PARAPHRASE

When this work, begun by Cyrus, resulting in a new Israel shall have culminated, all you Gentiles who wish to escape the judgment of Jehovah gather yourselves together and draw near. Those who worship idols are ignorant and lost; they pray to gods that are unable to save. Let all idol-worshippers who wish to contest My sovereignty combine all their wisdom and power and try to keep My predictions from coming to pass! After all, who has made such prophecies and had them come to pass—one of your idol-gods? No! Only Jehovah knows the future with certainty. I am the Only God there is! I am absolutely just and faithful to keep My word and I am the only Saviour there is; Let all the world turn to Me and be saved, for I am the only God there is; there is no other Savior! Since I am the only Absolute, I have sworn by My absolute sovereignty. I have spoken in these prophecies on the basis of My absolute faithfulness; they will come to pass! Indeed, every human being will ultimately acknowledge My sovereignty; every knee will bow and every tongue will confess some day that I am Lord. Some, who say, Only in Jehovah may we have real righteousness and strength, will come to Me and be saved. Those who continue to hate Jehovah will eventually acknowledge His sovereignty, but in disgrace. Through Jehovah's grace and power all the spiritual offspring of true Israel will be vindicated and justified because they have put their trust in Him, and Jehovah will give them of His glory.

COMMENTS

v. 20-21 Indictment: These verses continue and amplify the train of thought that has gone before concerning the long-range, culminating result of Jehovah's redemptive work begun with Cyrus' freeing of the Jewish exiles. This redemptive work of God will have a world-wide outreach. All those Gentiles who repent of their idolatry and acknowledge, in faith, the sovereignty of Jehovah will be saved. The Hebrew word *hikavetzu,* translated "assemble yourselves," is stronger than merely "assemble." It means "form yourselves into a specific group." Those that are "escaped" among the *goiyim* (Gentiles) are the future people from all nations who will have seen the culmination of the work begun in the return from the captivities (the institution of the messianic kingdom through Jesus Christ), recognize the sovereignty of the God of Israel, wish to escape His judgment and choose to accept His offer of salvation. In other words, it is the church of the New Testament. Isaiah is affirming (in predictive-present) that a specific group of *goiyim* will thus choose to escape the judgment upon all religions except that of Jehovah which will be made apparent to honest-minded believers through the crucifixion and resurrection of Jesus Christ. There is salvation in no one else (Acts 4:12) and this will be confirmed and affirmed centuries after Isaiah predicts it here. Many of the Gentiles would, when the new Israel (the church) began to proclaim its gospel, acknowledge the futility of their pagan religions and their own lostness (cf. Acts 19:11-20). The indictment of Jehovah is that idols cannot save and those who worship them are without knowledge of the truth.

Many of the *goiyim* would challenge that last statement! Even some of the Jews of Isaiah's day would find it objectionable.

Through the centuries from Isaiah until Christ, the whole Gentile world remained in ignorance and superstition and idolatry. Even after the resurrection of Christ men continued to cling to their idols and human philosophies (cf. Acts 17:16-33). Hundreds of millions of people today worship gods of wood and stone that cannot save them. But the sovereignty of God is demonstrated, as verse 21 states, through the fulfillment of God's prophetic word (cf. II Pet. 1:16-21). Jehovah offers the *goiyim* an opportunity to "state their case" and even invites them to pool their "counsel" and see if they can gainsay the predictions of Jehovah through His prophets. Jehovah alone knows the future and He has demonstrated it from the beginning of time by predicting events great and small in minute detail, thousands of years before their fulfillment. Much of this was prior to Isaiah's time! There was plenty of evidence even in Isaiah's day that Jehovah's word always came to pass. Isaiah himself was able to believe in the Christ as the culminating work of Jehovah (cf. Jn. 12:36-43); Abraham saw the day of Christ by faith and rejoiced (Jn. 8:56-59). But most certainly, when the prophecies Jehovah made by Isaiah gained their fulfillment, the Gentiles would have every possible proof that Jehovah is God and there is no other!

v. 22-25 INVITATION: The Hebrew word *peneu* means *turn*, thus v. 22 should read, "Turn unto me, and be ye saved." There are two other Hebrew words also used to mean turn—*shuv* and *nacham*. *Peneu* means more literally, "turn to or towards; follow; turn to face something or someone." *Peneu* is the imperative of *panah*, so it is Jehovah's command that all the world turn to Him for salvation. The word translated "be ye saved" is *heuashe'u*, the imperative of *yasha'*, and so the Lord is here expressing His deep desire that all men be saved (I Tim. 2:3; II Pet. 3:9). It is really Jehovah's tender insistence that all the world face up to the fact that He is the only God and Savior of mankind there is! Isaiah is truly the spokesman of the Old Testament for the universality of the gospel. God's outreach is to the ends of the earth. The Lord's hand is not shortened that it cannot save (cf. Isa. 59:1-3), it is man's sin (rebellion) that keeps him from being saved. In other words, man's salvation is complete and readily available but in the final analysis, it is up to man. He must choose. He must accept the covenant terms.

The salvation of all mankind. is of great significance. It is what all of history functions for; it is that for which God has stirred up the spirit of Cyrus to return the exiles. Man's redemption and regeneration is that for which God longs, plans, works and sacrifices (even His own Son). It is His total goal. So He supports His invitation to all the world with an oath. He swears by Himself. There is nothing greater to swear by (cf. Heb. 6:13-20) He swears on His eternality (cf. Gen. 22:16; Rom. 14:11). The crucifixion and resurrection of Christ was the greatest, most specific and thoroughly confirmed oath of God ever made. It was there, in history, God validated the certainty of all His promises and the faithfulness of His own nature (cf. II Cor. 1:19-21; Heb. 6:17f) when He "interposed" *Himself* with an oath. God, in the flesh, dying and coming to life again by His own power! Once and for all God proved through the empty tomb that He is the resurrection and the life. He proved that no one comes to the Father but by Jesus Christ. With absolute historic certainty God proved there that every word of His comes to pass in righteousness. He also proved that eventually every knee must bow and every tongue confess that He is God (cf. Rom. 14:11; Phil. 2:10f.). While time lasts, men are free to acknowledge His sovereignty or deny it. But when time ceases to be and men inhabit the eternal destinies they have freely chosen, they will all acknowledge His sovereignty. Eventually every thing created must acknowledge His Lordship. Some, as verse 24 points out, will confess His righteousness and strength and come to Him (for salvation). Others, incensed, hateful and rebellious to the end will know and acknowledge His sovereignty but will be "put to shame."

Jehovah will justify (vindicate) all the seed of Israel and glorify them. In our context (the work of God, begun with Cyrus, culminating in redemption for the whole world) this "seed" must refer to the spiritual Israel (cf. Rom. 2:28-29;

4:13-25; Gal. 3:6-9; 3:27-29; 6:14-16). All, both Jew and Gentile, who "turn" to Jehovah for salvation by faith will have that faith vindicated when God, "bringing many sons to glory" (Heb. 2:10), finishes His work at the consummation of it all. Right now we are being changed, by faith, from one degree of glory to another (II Cor. 3:18). One day, when time ceases to be, we shall have all the glory our Great God has prepared for us—then our faith will be vindicated! God is sovereign in salvation!

QUIZ

1. What is the nature of the "assembly" the nations are to make?
2. Who are the "escaped"?
3. What is God's challenge to the Gentiles who will not accept His sovereignty?
4. How insistent is God that the whole world "look" to Him for salvation?
5. What demonstration do we have that God's good news was universally intended?
6. What was God's greatest "oath" to the world of His faithfulness to keep His promises?
7. Who are the "seed" of Israel?

SPECIAL STUDY

TYPOLOGY

Definition: From *tupos* meaning literally "to strike"; "the mark or impression of something; stamp; impressed sign; emblem." Rom. 5:14; I Cor. 10:6, 11; Jn. 20:25 "Print" of nail (lit. usage) Webster: "A figure or representation of something to come; a token; a sign; a symbol; correlative to antitype."

Synonyms: *skia* (shadow), Col. 2:17; Heb. 8:5; 10:1
hypodeigma (copy), Heb. 8:5; 9:23
semeion (sign), Mt. 12:39
parabole (parable), or (figure), Heb. 9:9; 11:19
antitypos (antitype), Heb. 9:24; I Pet. 3:21

Characteristics of types:

1. *They are thoroughly rooted in history.* They are not myths or allegories. This is where they differ from symbols. Symbols do not necessarily have to be historical realities (such as the dreams and visions of Daniel and John in Revelation). Types are actual, historical persons, events, institutions.

2. *They are prophetic in nature.* Again they differ from symbols in this aspect. Symbols may or may not be figurative of future things. Types must always predict.

3. *They are definite, integral part of redemptive history.* They were intended to be part of God's plan of redemption. They are not afterthoughts read back into the O.T. story. They retain their typical significance even after the antitype has appeared (I Cor. 10:1-11) (Rom. 15:4).

4. *They are Christocentric.* They all point to Christ in one way or another (Lk. 24:24-44; Acts 3:32ff).

5. *They are edificatory.* They have spiritual meaning for God's people in both dispensations. The OT saint was undoubtedly edified by the typical significance of such things as circumcision (Dt. 30:6), the sacrifices (Hos. 14:2) and the coronation of Joshua (Zech. 6:9-15); also the tabernacle, etc.

   We must be careful not to think the OT saints perfectly understood all the type taught about Christ (I Pet. 1:10-12). If they understood all, it would take away the type's prophetic nature.

6. *They are in variety.* There was a necessity for a great variety of types to give anything like a correct idea of the Messiah. Just as a single letter, or a very few letters from the alphabet could not express the full ideas of authors, so no type could

fully exhibit the promised Savior in the dignity of his person, the mystery of his incarnation, excellency of character, union of offices, depth of humiliation, etc. Moses was an eminent type as a prophet, but he was no priest; Aaron was a chosen priest, but no prophet; David was a king and prophet, but no priest. While one goat *slain* was a type of the death of Christ, another must be sent away *alive* to typify his resurrection.

Importance of Studying Types:

1. Absolutely necessary if we are rightly to understand the revelation of God.

   Types and their antitypes are like a book with a large number of *pictures* of things, institutions, events followed by words of descriptions and explanations. It is difficult to conceive of any one trying to understand the descriptions and explanations without referring to the *pictures* themselves. Yet this is how the Bible is often treated. Many people are satisfied to read the N.T. without any reference to the types of the O.T.

   The typology of the O.T. is the very *alphabet* of the language in which the doctrine of the N.T. is written.

2. It is very clear that God himself sets great value upon types. In Hebrews we learn that in the construction of the Tabernacle every detail was planned by Him. And He warned Moses to *follow* those details! For example: The veil in the Tabernacle was not merely a curtain to divide rooms . . .there was great meaning . . . a great lesson conveyed in that vail.

   God Himself rent that veil from top to bottom. He added the finishing touches to that picture! Doesn't this show the great importance God puts upon the types!?

3. Jesus set great value upon types. Again and again He referred to them and showed how they pointed to Himself (Manna from heaven; Jonah's death and resurrection from the whale; Light of World; etc.)

4. The very high place that is accorded types by the writers of

the N.T. show their importance (Hebrews, Romans, Gospel of John, Revelation). The Epistle to the Hebrews is almost entirely made up of references to the O.T. The O.T. is the shadows—Christ is the substance.

We sometimes forget that the writers of the N.T. were students of the O.T.; that it was their Bible, and that they would naturally allude again and again to the types and shadows, expecting their readers also to be familiar with them. If we fail to see these allusions, we lose much of the beauty of the passage, and cannot rightly understand it.

5. We fit the type to the antitype as a glove to the hand . . . as we prove a criminal's steps by fitting his boot into the tracks, so are we enabled, by a comparison of these types, to declare to the world that we have not followed any cunningly devised fables when we made known the power and coming of our Lord Jesus. He alone answers to the typical photographs . . . Such is the unity of the Divine purpose, that, look at what portion of it we will, there meets us some allusion to or emblem of our common salvation. The Scheme of Redemption is one gorgeous array of picture-lessons. The nation who typified it was a rotating black-board, going to and fro, and unfolding in their career the Will of the Eternal. Let us not despise the day of small things.

Some Rules for Interpreting Types:

1. The literal meaning of the word (strike) is not that which is generally found in the Scriptures.
2. We must never expect the type and the antitype to be the same. It is therefore utterly impossible to find something in the antitype that is analogous to every feature of the type —or that the type has perfectly prefigured the antitype.
3. For one purpose, generally, the type has been selected. Always remember—one point, or, at most, for but a very few features of similarity only.
4. It must predict something.

5. It must have been *intended* to represent something. Types are not coincidental.

6. The Scriptures should be allowed to interpret them, as far as possible.

7. We are always safe in calling anything a type that is so named in the word of God. But it is not necessary to suppose that we are limited to these named ones only.

8. Just like in the interpretation of symbols, the *similarity* between type and antitype will lead, in most cases, to the true meaning. (Lamb, Laver, Priest, etc.).

9. Anything, to be a type, must have been a real person, thing, event, or office.

10. The antitype is always superior to the type. The type is always visible at the time it is given, because it is material; but the antitype contains divine or spiritual thought.

11. Sometimes figurative language is employed in giving a typical event.

12. The rules for the interpretation of symbols apply as well as to types.

    a. Many of the symbols have been interpreted in whole or in part by their authors. Let them interpret, first.
    b. Other symbols have been interpreted by other inspired authors. Second choice of interpretation.
    c. Other scripture illustrations help where authors have not interpreted. Third choice of interpretation.
    d. Names of symbols are to be understood literally.
    e. There must be found a resemblance, more or less clear, between the symbol and the thing signified.
    f. The condition of those to whom the symbol was given must be known, if possible . . . to get the meaning the author intended for his primary audience.

Why types:

I. There was something *ultimately* greater and more perfect than the OT.

A. The Gospel age is the "end of the ages" (I Cor. 10:11; Heb. 11:40; etc.)
B. The Gospel age is called "the dispensation of the fulness of time" (Eph. 1:10).
C. In the Gospel dispensation only is the great mystery of God in connection with man's salvation disclosed (Lk. 1:78; I Jn. 2:8; Rom. 16:25-26; Col. 1:27; I Cor. 2:7-10).
D. In the NT are the realities which were before in the OT mere shadow and partial revelations (Col. 2:17; Heb. 8:5).
E. Even the most eminent of people in the OT (John the Baptist) were said to be inferior to the least in the Messiah's kingdom (Mt. 11:11).
F. The OT predicts its own fulfillment by something ultimate (Jer. 3:15-18; 31:31-34, etc.).

II. To prepare the way for the introduction of these *ultimate* objects, He placed His chosen people under a course of training which included instruction by types (designed resemblances) of what was to come.

A. There must have been in the Old the same great elements of truth as in the antitypes of the New.
   1. Spiritual necessities of men have been the same in every age. So the truth revealed to meet these necessities, however basic or progressive, must have been fundamentally the same or essentially one in every age.
   2. Primary elements of truth embodied in Gospel (atonement, sacrifice, purification, etc.) had their origin as primary elements of truth even in the types.
B. Presented more simply and palpably in the OT types.
   1. In a shape or form the human mind could easily grasp.

2. From type to antitype involves a stretch of the mental faculties.

THIS IS REALLY THE FOUNDATION OF THE WHOLE IDEA OF TYPOLOGY: One truth in both type and antitype, but that truth existing first in a lower, then in a higher stage of development.

III. Something more was needed than mere prophecy.

A. Training (experiential) of a very peculiar kind was needed.
B. Touching, seeing, tasting the spiritual realities which could *not* be seen and touched was needed.
C. The Jew had constantly presented to his sight and touch, in the outward and earthly things, the fundamental truths and principles of eternal-spiritual relationships which cannot be seen and touched.

Several kinds of types: (not exhaustive)

1. *Typical persons*
   a. Adam (type of Christ in that he was opposite from Him, Rom. 5:12-19; I Cor. 15:22, 45).
   b. Moses (type of Christ as leader, prophet and mediator, Dt. 18:15-18; Acts 3:22-24)
   c. Joshua (leader)
   d. Melchizadek (priest and king together—not from Levitical genealology, Gen. 14:18-20; Ps. 110:4; Heb. 5:5-10; 6:20; 7:1-17).
   e. David (king after God's heart, Acts 13:33-35; Isa. 9:6-7).
   f. Solomon (II Sam. 7:13-15; I Ki. 8:18-20; Rom. 1:1-4)
   g. Zerubbabel (Hag. 1:1-12; Zech. 4:1-10; 6:12-14).
   h. Cyrus (a type of Christ as deliverer and anointed of God, Isa. 44:27-29; 45:1-4); as Servant of God also.
   i. Ahithophel (type of Judas, II Sam. 15:30-35; Psa.

41:9; 55:12-20; Acts 1:16-20).

j. Elijah (type of John the Baptist, Mal. 3:1; 4:5-6; Isa. 40:3-4; Mt. 3:1-3; Lk. 1:17; Mt. 11:7-15; 17:9-13).

2. *Typical things*
   a. Tabernacle (Heb. 9:9-10)
   b. Temple (Jn. 2:13-22; Eph. 2:19-22; I Cor. 3:16-17)
   c. Serpent in the wilderness (Jn. 3:14; Num. 21:9)
   d. Lambs slain by priests (Jn. 1:35; Rev. 5:6, 12).
   e. Laver before the tabernacle (Titus 3:5-7; Heb. 10:22).
3. *Typical institutions*
   a. Sacrifices and offerings of patriarchs and Law (Heb. 10:1f)
   b. Day of Atonement; Jubilee (Heb. 9:25; Lk. 4:18-21).
   c. Sabbath (Heb. 4:1-10; Mt. 11:28-30)
   d. Cities of refuge (Num. 35:9-34; Heb. 6:18-20).
   e. Passover, Pentecost, Tabernacles (I Cor. 5:7; 15:20; Jn. 7:37-39; 8:12)
   f. Ablutions, laying on hands, etc. (Heb. 6:1-8)
4. *Typical offices*
   a. Prophet
   b. Priest
   c. King
5. *Typical conduct*
   a. Abraham's faith, type of Christian response (Rom. 4:1-25; Jas. 2:18-26; Heb. 11:8-12).
   b. Many of the prophets performed deeds that were typical (Jeremiah, Hosea, etc.)
6. *Typical events*
   a. Passage through the Red Sea (I Cor. 10:1-10).
   b. The Flood (I Pet. 3)
   c. The Manna in the Wilderness (Jn. 6)
   d. The deliverance from Egypt (Hos. 11:1)
   e. Wilderness Journey (Heb. 3)
7. *Typical places*

a. Egypt (Bondage and sin)
b. Jordan (death)
c. Canaan (heaven)
d. Babylon (proud paganism opposing God's people)

THE TABERNACLE

I. The earthly tabernacle was a *parabole* of the Christian age (Heb. 9:9)

A. It is said to be a "shadow" of the heavenly, Heb. 8:5
   1. All the law of Moses was a shadow of the good things to come, Heb. 10:1
   2. Thousands of years before the N.T. church was instituted it was typified, and prefigured in the Tabernacle, built "according to the pattern."
      (The pattern was for the tabernacle, not the N.T. church)

B. The Altar of Burnt Offering
   1. Sacrifices twice daily, besides all the feasts
   2. For atonement of sins; offerer must lay hands on head of sacrifice (doctrine of laying on hands, Heb. 6), to signify substitutionary nature, Lev. 1:3-4
   3. Christ is our Lamb; He was a willing sacrifice (Heb. 10), not the blood of dumb animals
   4. We lay hold of our sacrifice by faith and obedience to the initiatory commands of the Gospel, demonstrating that He died for us and we accept His death in our place.

C. The Laver
   1. Priests must wash hands and feet (complete cleanness and sanctification) before entering Holy Place; on penalty of death, Ex. 30:17-21
   2. Laver is certainly figure of our cleansing and separation from world unto God; would then be typical of baptism
      a. I Pet. 1:22

b. Eph. 5:26
c. Titus 3:5

3. We have two things to do before entering God's new Holy Place (the church); accepting in faith the substitutionary death of Jesus; cleansing in the laver of regeneration, I Pet. 3:21

D. The Lampstand

1. It was for a light in the Holy Place, Ex. 25:37
2. It was to be made of pure gold and burn pure oil
3. It was to burn continually, night and day; no other light was to shine in the Holy Place
4. It typifies the Word of God in the church
   a. Thy word is a lamp unto my feet and a light unto my pathway
   b. We have been delivered from the power of darkness into the light of his kingdom by the word of God
   c. The church is to continue stedfastly in the apostles doctrine
   d. The word is sufficient light (II Tim. 3:16-17; II Pet. 1:2-4)
   e. The church is the pillar of truth, I Tim. 3:15
   Christ symbolized the church with seven lampstands in Rev. 2 and 3 as pillars of truth in Asia Minor

E. The Table of Shewbread (Presence)

1. Twelve loaves renewed each week (Lev. 24:5-7)
2. Eaten as memorial each week to deliverance from Egypt and as a memorial to their being set apart to good works
3. Priests had to partake each week
4. Apparently typifies the Lord's Supper, a memorial of our deliverance, Christ's presence, our sanctification to good works.

F. Altar of Incense

1. Just before the veil and smoke and scent of incense permeated the whole tent (drifting even into the Holy

of Holies)

2. Was to be made according to the will of God and to be pure (Nadab and Abihu were slain for offering incense contrary to God's will)
3. Burned at times of prayer
4. A figure of prayer in the N.T. church
   a. Psa. 141:2 "Let my prayer be set forth as incense before thee."
   b. Rev. 5:8; 8:3-4, prayers of saints going up as incense before throne
   c. Our prayers must be according to God's will (I Jn. 5:14-15)

G. Ark of the Covenant

1. God's presence was there in the Shekinah glory (Spirit)
2. It was the place of mercy
3. The people were separated from it by a veil, signifying that an open and free access to mercy and glory had not yet been made
4. The High Priest entered once a year to atone for sins
5. The veil in the temple was rent from top to bottom when Christ was crucified, signifying that the way into mercy and glory had been made and we may now enjoy (every one, not just High Priest) the presence of God in the Spirit—the church is the habitation of God in the Spirit (Eph. 2)

BIBLIOGRAPHY

1. *The Typology of Scripture,* Fairbairn, Baker
2. *Hermeneutics,* D. R. Dungan, Standard Publishing Co.
3. *Baker's Dictionary of Theology,* Baker, pg. 533-534
4. *Principles of Interpretation,* Clinton Lockhart, Central Seminary Press
5. *Types and Metaphors of The Bible,* J. W. Monser, John

Burns Book Co.
6. *Shadow and Substance,* Victor E. Hoven, Northwest Christian College Press
7. *The Study of The Types,* A. R. Habershon, Kregel
8. *Christ: The Fulfillment of the Law and the Prophets,* James D. Bales, Lambert Book House
9. *Things Old and New In Religion,* Hoyt Bailey, C.E.I. Pub. Co.
10. *Survey Course In Christian Doctrine, Vol. II and IV,* C. C. Crawford, College Press, Pg. 256f
11. *International Standard Bible Encyclopedia,* Vol. V, art. "Types" Eerdmans
12. *The Theology of the Older Testament,* Payne, Zondervan
13. Class notes from Hebrew Epistle, Butler, unpublished.
14. *Bible Types and Shadows,* John W. Wade, Standard Pub. Co.

3. SOVEREIGN OVER NATIONS, CHAPTERS 46 - 47

a. CONDEMNING THEIR GODS

TEXT: 46:1-13

1 Bel boweth down, Nebo stoopeth; their idols are upon the beasts, and upon the cattle: the things that ye carried about are made a load, a burden to the weary beast.
2 They stoop, they bow down together; they could not deliver the burden, but themselves are gone into captivity.
3 Hearken unto me, O house of Jacob, and all the remnant of the house of Israel, that have been borne by me from their birth, that have been carried from the womb;
4 and even to old age I am he, and even to hoar hairs will I carry you: I have made, and I will bear; yea, I will carry, and will deliver.
5 To whom will ye liken me, and make me equal, and compare me, that we may be like?

6 Such as lavish gold out of the bag, and weigh silver in the balance, they hire a goldsmith, and he maketh it a god; they fall down, yea, they worship.
7 They bear it upon the shoulder, they carry it, and set it in its place, and it standeth; from its place shall it not remove: yea, one may cry unto it, yet can it not answer, nor save him out of his trouble.
8 Remember this, and show yourselves men; bring it again to mind, O ye transgressors.
9 Remember the former things of old: for I am God, and there is none like me;
10 declaring the end from the beginning, and from ancient times things that are not yet done; saying, My counsel shall stand, and I will do all my pleasure;
11 calling a ravenous bird from the east, the man of my counsel from a far country; yea, I have spoken, I will also bring it to pass; I have purposed, I will also do it.
12 Hearken unto me, ye stouthearted, that are far from righteousness:
13 I bring near my righteousness, it shall not be far off, and my salvation shall not tarry; and I will place salvation in Zion for Israel my glory.

QUERIES

a. Whose gods were named Bel and Nebo?
b. Who is the "ravenous bird from the east"?
c. When is salvation placed in "Zion"?

PARAPHRASE

Bel and Nebo, the images of Babylonian gods, are as good as gone! They are about to be loaded on camels and horses and taken captive along with their worshipers. Those pagan gods you carried about with such fondness and care are to be unceremoniously loaded on animals like so much burdensome baggage. Where are the gods these images represent? Why do they not save the images from such humiliation? Because the gods consist of nothing more than the wood and metal of which their images are composed! Therefore the Babylonian gods disappear into captivity. Listen to Me, descendants of Jacob and all you who remain of My covenant people, Israel; take heed to the One who gave you birth as a people and who has given you paternal care ever since. I am your Father through all your lifetime; even when your hair is white with age I will continue to take care of you. I created you and I will sustain you. I am not like the pagan gods—I will deliver you. Is there any pagan god with whom I may be compared? None! All other gods are made of metal and stone by human hands. That is what the Gentiles worship—a creation of their own hands. They take metal or wood, make themselves a god, carry it around wherever they wish and when they set it down any place it stays there, for it is unable to move! And when those who made it cry out to it in prayer and supplication it does not answer, nor does it deliver those who are in trouble. It is not really a god at all—just a piece of wood or metal!

Do not forget what I have just told you, My people, and fix it firmly as a part of you; take it to heart you sinners! Do not forget all the former demonstrations of My sovereignty, both to you and your forefathers. Remember that I, Jehovah, am God and there is not another like me. I predict the events of history and the affairs of men's lives many centuries before they happen. Now, what I have predicted shall just as surely come to pass! My sovereign decree that a "bird of prey" (Cyrus) shall come from the east, a man from a far away country to carry out My counsel, will be brought to fulfillment. I, Jehovah, have planned it and I will surely do it! Listen to Me, you stubborn-hearted who are resisting the idea that I will certainly fulfill My predictions of righteous judgments; I am very near to showing My righteousness—it is not far away. And all I have predicted concerning My salvation will soon come to pass. "Zion" will be the location of My salvation and the true Israel will be the recipient of My glory.

COMMENTS

v. 1-7 DEMISE OF IDOLS: Bel (otherwise known as Merodach or Marduk) was the principal god of the Babylonians. Nebo (or Nabu) was the son of Bel and in later times was identified with the Greek god Mercury because Nabu means "speaker." The Babylonian gods were (as the name Bel indicates) "descendants" of Baal, the Canaanite god (see *Minor Prophets,* by Clinton Gill, pub. College Press, for a special study on Baalism). Bel's major temple was in Borsippa, twelve miles to the south of Babylon. According to the historian Herodotus, the image of Bel was gold and 18 feet tall. These great, impressive, expensive images with the authority of centuries of pagan heritage added, which seem invincible, will be dismantled and carried away from their place to a foreign pantheon. When will this happen? When Cyrus conquers Babylon, October 29, 539 B.C.! (for details of Cyrus' conquest of Babylon see, *Daniel,* by Butler, ch. 5, 7, 8, pub. College Press). The thrust of Isaiah's message here is: these pagan images, impressive as they may be, powerful as their people claim they are, will suffer humiliation and defeat. They will be carried away on the backs of *khayyah* (wild animals, probably asses) and *behemah* (large animals, probably oxen). Those objects of metal (precious gold they may be) of which the Hebrew people were so enamored will ignominiously disappear, loaded unceremoniously onto the backs of dumb brutes and transported at the whim of a conquering emperor. Where are the gods these images represent? If they are images of a real god surely this god would not allow his image to be thus humiliated and obliterated! The answer is: there are no gods. Otherwise they would deliver their images. The gods are figments of human imagination—mere fantasies—less than the wood and metal of which their images are composed. This was fulfilled in a way which would not be admitted by Cyrus. He had claimed that it was under the auspices of the gods that he had marched into Babylon. But the idols were powerless (v. 7); it was the Lord, Jehovah, who was bringing his conquest of Babylon and its gods to fulfillment.

After exposing the nothingness of Babylon's gods, Jehovah calls the remnant of the Jews to attention. Why should they put their trust in the gods of foreign nations when it was Jehovah who gave birth to them as a people and a nation (cf. Isa. 44:2; 44:24; 49:5). He "bore" them (sustained) them through centuries of deliverance from enemies all around them many times more powerful than they (cf. Deut. 1:31) 33:27; Isa. 40:11). Jehovah nurtured them, chastened them, enriched them and kept them free (cf. Ezek. 16:1f), but they turned to other gods. He wants to care for them when they become aged and silver-haired, even for all their lives. But He cannot care for them if they refuse His covenant of care. They should know by now the difference between pagan gods and Jehovah. There are no pagan gods in all the history of mankind which can compare at all to Jehovah. He delivers! He keeps His word! He is invincible! He cannot be moved by men. The gods of the Gentiles are made by craftsmen (cf. Isa. 44)—works of human hands—and then human beings fall down and worship the works of their own hands. Utterly absurd! Furthermore, these man-made gods are carried about from place to place. They can be manipulated, misplaced, displaced, burned up, melted down, and carried off to foreign temples. They cannot move once they are set in one place by human hands. It takes human hands for them to move again. Men cry to them, offer sacrifices to them, disfigure themselves in fear of them and all to no avail—the images of wood and metal say not a word. They cannot answer; they cannot deliver anyone from trouble nor can they bless anyone. They are dead! They were never alive!

v. 8-13 DIRECTION FOR ISRAEL: The stance Israel is to take in light of the soon demise of Babylon's gods is to *remember.* They are reminded of two things: (a) it is sinful to worship gods other than Jehovah; (b) there is no One but Jehovah whose word is sovereign. The Hebrew word *hitheaoshashu* ("show yourselves men" v. 8) means literally, "firmly founded." God's direction for Israel is that she remember *who* He is and *fix it firmly* in her heart. This is the only solution for Israel's idolatrous rebellion. She is a nation of *phosheiym* (from *pasha'*) "rebels." The word means "refuse subjection to rightful authority." The only solution to rebellion and sin is to remember *who* God is! Remember how He has dealt with man and sin in the past; punishment for the incorrigible rebel and forgiveness for the penitent believer. God is omnipotent and omniscient. He not only knows and predicts the future, He controls it and uses it for His redemptive purposes. What He has said about Cyrus will surely come to pass. God will certainly call an *'Ayit* ("ravenous bird") from the east. The Hebrew word means, "to be angry with; to rush or fall upon with fury." Cyrus will come from a "far country" to carry out the counsels of God. This is the "servant" of Jehovah—this bird of prey. He hasn't even been born yet, but his birth, crowning and service to God is as certain as if it had already been done because it is the will of the sovereign Jehovah! Cyrus is not merely another conqueror—he is the divinely commissioned executioner of Babylon and her gods. More sovereign control of the events of history and the destinies of men could not be visualized than is described in these chapters by the prophet Isaiah! When God speaks His word never fails of completion! When God purposes, it is as good as done!

The word *abbiyrey* ("stout-hearted") literally means, "strong" but is probably synonymous with "strong-minded" or "stubborn-hearted." The context would indicate this usage. They are stubborn-hearted and "far from righteousness." "Righteousness" in this instance must mean the righteous purposes of Jehovah in what He has been announcing concerning Israel's captivity, release by Cyrus and Cyrus' destruction of the Babylonian gods Israel had grown so enamored of. Israel was stubbornly staying away from those conclusions. She refused to accept these decrees of the sovereign Jehovah. But Jehovah is about to bring "near" His righteous goal. Its beginning is not far off. In a little over a century it will all begin just as the prophet is predicting it. Jehovah's salvation for all mankind (including the *goiyim*) will come without fail. "Zion" will be the location of God's salvation (see comments in *Minor Prophets,* Butler, pub. College Press, Obadiah 17; Joel 2:28—3:21). "Zion" is the N.T. church (cf. Heb. 12:22). Of course, the climax of this salvation will not come for some 600 years after Cyrus—but what is 600 years viewed from Jehovah's perspective? Less than a day! For the believer who by faith sees all things from God's perspective "redemption draweth nigh." Not only salvation, but glory!

QUIZ

1. Where did the gods Bel and Nebo have their origin?
2. Who carried these gods off on the backs of animals?
3. Give four reasons men should be able to know that idols are not gods.
4. To what extent are the people of Israel rebelling against God's purposes?
5. How emphatic is this text on the sovereignty of God?
6. Where is "Zion"?

b. CONQUERING THEIR GOVERNMENTS

TEXT: 47:1-15

1 Come down, and sit in the dust, O virgin daughter of Babylon; sit on the ground without a throne, O daughter of the Chaldeans: for thou shalt no more be called tender and delicate.

2 Take the millstones, and grind meal; remove thy veil, strip off the train, uncover the leg, pass through the rivers.

3 Thy nakedness shall be uncovered, yea, thy shame shall be seen: I will take vengeance, and will spare no man.

4 Our Redeemer, Jehovah of hosts is his name, the Holy One of Israel.

5 Sit thou silent, and get thee into darkness, O daughter of

the Chaldeans; for thou shalt no more be called The mistress
of kingdoms.
6 I was wroth with my people, I profaned mine inheritance,
and gave them into thy hand: thou didst show them no
mercy; upon the aged hast thou very heavily laid thy yoke.
7 And thou saidst, I shall be mistress for ever; so that thou
didst not lay these things to thy heart, neither didst remember the latter and thereof.
8 Now therefore hear this, thou that art given to pleasures,
that sittest securely, that sayest in thy heart, I am, and
there is none else besides me; I shall not sit as a widow,
neither shall I know the loss of children:
9 but these two things shall come to thee in a moment in one
day, the loss of children, and widowhood; in their full
measure shall they come upon thee, in the multitude of thy
sorceries, and the great abundance of thine enchantments.
10 For thou hast trusted in thy wickedness; thou hast said,
None seeth me; thy wisdom and thy knowledge, it hath
perverted thee; and thou hast said in thy heart, I am and
there is none else besides me.
11 Therefore shall evil come upon thee; thou shalt not know
the dawning thereof; and mischief shall fall upon thee; and
thou shalt not be able to put it away: and desolation shall
come upon thee suddenly, which thou knowest not.
12 Stand now with thine enchantments, and with the multitudes
of thy sorceries, wherein thou hast labored from thy youth; if
so be thou shalt be able to profit, if so be thou mayest prevail.
13 Thou art wearied in the multitude of thy counsels: let now
the astrologers, the star-gazers, the monthly prognosticators,
stand up, and save thee from the things that shall come
upon thee.
14 Behold, they shall be as stubble; the fire shall burn them;
they shall not deliver themselves from the power of the
flame: it shall not be a coal to warm at, nor a fire to sit
before.
15 Thus shall the things be unto thee wherein thou hast labored:
they that have trafficked with thee from thy youth shall

wander every one to his quarter; there shall be none to save thee.

QUERIES

a. How did God "profane" His inheritance? (v. 6)
b. Why did Babylon say, "I will not sit as a widow . . ."?
c. Who are the "monthly prognosticators"?

PARAPHRASE

Babylon, you may be a virgin in respect to foreign invasion, but you will come down from your delicate luxury and your face will be rubbed in the dirt. From haughtiness to humiliation you will come because Jehovah has commanded it. No longer will you sit upon the throne of the world like a queen. You, O Chaldea, will be forced into a humiliation like the lowliest slave-girl. You will be subjected to the worst degradation, shame and toil. You are going to be exposed for what you really are, Babylon, a shameful, wicked nation. I, Jehovah, will see that vengeance is done upon you and no man will stop Me. Yes, Babylon, our Redeemer is Jehovah of hosts, the Holy One of Israel and He is sovereign. Jehovah says to Babylon, You will be dumbfounded with grief and anguish when I judge you. No more will you be the center of world attention—the darling of the nations. I was angry with My people, says the Lord, so I allowed My possession to be captured by this pagan, wicked Babylon. But you, Babylon, did not show them any mercy or kindness; even the elderly you despised and persecuted.

In addition, O Babylon, you have said, I shall be the darling of the world forever. You have not given heed to the warnings of history or conscience and therefore you do not recognize that you are headed for destruction. So now pay attention to this you sensuous city, secure in your wicked wealth and power. You may say to yourself that you are sovereign of the universe and there is no other people or nation that will ever bring you down; you may think you will never know the bereavement of a widow or of a mother having lost her children. However, this is exactly the kind of fate you will suffer. In spite of all the hocus pocus of your magicians and soothsayers you will become as destitute and bereaved as a widow and a mother who has lost all her children. This will come upon you because you have trusted in your apparent ability to do as evilly as you please and get away with it. You have said, There is no power higher than I, to whom I must give account. You have become too sophisticated and wise for your own good. Your wisdom has led you to an arrogant self-delusion and to believe you are sovereign ruler of all creation. Because of this attempted usurpation of Jehovah's sovereignty, judgment shall come upon you which you will not, with all your magicians, be able to "charm" away. Destruction is going to come upon you and you cannot pay the price to take it away. You are going to be a wasted, desolate place with such suddenness it will be beyond human understanding or explanation.

Go on using your hocus pocus magic charms by the thousands, like you have since your nation's beginning, if it is the only thing you have to ward off the destruction that is sure to come. You have had so many magicians and such a complex system of magic that most of your people have grown tired of it all. But go ahead, let the astrologers, (those who study the stars) and horoscope-casters arise and save you from the judgments predicted upon you if they are able to do so! Soon it will be apparent to all that they are powerless as stubble which is so easily and quickly consumed by fire. They will, like straw in a fire, be gone almost instantly. They will not even be around long enough to provide an afterglow like the coals of a wood fire. How quickly shall all that disappear for which your generations have expended their energy and wages. In the end all those upon whom you relied for military and financial assistance since your beginning shall desert you. Your allies will not help you; they will not want to have anything to do with you lest they suffer the same destruction. There is not anyone who can save you!

COMMENTS

v. 1-6 ABASED: Babylon is going to come down from its pinnacle of world rulership. In fact, she is going to lose her identity as a nation altogether. The Hebew word *bethulath* is translated virgin. It probably refers to the idea that Babylon (from her conquest of Nineveh about 612 B.C. until being conquered by Cyrus 539 B.C.) never suffered foreign invasion. She was untouched until Cyrus spoiled her.

The words *raccah* and *'anuggah,* translated *tender* and *delicate* probably emphasize the luxuriousness of Babylonian life; *raccah* literally means *effeminancy* and *'anuggah* means *pleasure, luxury, sport.* They are descriptive of the indulgent, immoral wickedness of Babylon. From her position as pampered, indulged, haughty queen of the world she would be dethroned and abased. She would become like the lowliest servant-girl doing the most humiliating tasks. Grinding meal is the hardest, most menial task for women slaves. Removal of the veil and stripping off the train means to take off the clothing of a lady of leisure and put on the clothing of a common slave. Uncovering the leg and passing through the rivers probably pictures a slave-girl rolling up her garments to walk across streams and rivers bearing burdens for her master. Slaves were simply the property of their owners and could be treated anyway the owner desired. Most of them, especially women, were treated shamefully. When sold in the slave market they were undressed and their bodies exposed, more to humiliate them than anything else. Jehovah is going to expose Babylon for what it really is. The whole world will see Babylon naked, without all the false luxury and haughtiness she arrogated to herself. God will spare no man—no human being on the face of the earth will deter Jehovah from His humiliation of Babylon.

Verse four is a pause of praise on the part of the prophet. It is like those digressions of the apostle Paul in Ephesians and Romans. The sovereign program of God's redemption for Israel elicits spontaneous testimony from Isaiah to Babylon that the Redeemer of Israel is Jehovah (Covenant-God) of hosts, the Holy One of Israel. The testimony also serves to show the contrast between Israel's God and the gods of Babylon. Israel's God would raise her out of humiliation to glory (through the Servant-Messiah to come), while Babylon's gods would be impotent to save them from going from glory to humiliation.

When Babylon's degradation comes at the hand of Jehovah she will sit silently dumbfounded. Her shameful humiliation by the conquering Medes and Persians was totally unexpected and incomprehensible from a human point of view. She was the one upon whom the spotlight of the world was focused; but her prominence will soon be gone—all will be darkness for her. She shall no longer be the queen of the world. The Hebrew word *gevereth* is translated *mistress* but it does not mean *mistress* in the sense of a "kept woman" or a fornicator. *Gevereth* means *mistress* in the sense of *royalty,* hence, a *queen.* The proper name *Gabriel* comes from the same root. The wealth and luxury and power of Babylon was almost unbelievable. No other empire before had exerted such influence on the world. But it would all disappear suddenly because she opposed and humiliated the covenant people of Jehovah.

God has been talking of mighty Babylon, but suddenly the little nation of Judah moves into the center of the picture. The center of history is God's covenant people not the mighty empires which seem to dominate the world. God's people strayed from their messianic destiny and incurred the holy wrath of God. He allowed profane Babylon to swallow up Judah for a proper period of chastening. But even profane and pagan people are subject to certain moral standards before the Absolute God (cf. our comments in *Minor Prophets,* Amos ch. 1-2, pub. College Press). The obvious standards of humane treatment were not observed toward the Jews, especially toward older people. Babylon apparently ignored the commonest laws of reasonableness and mercifulness (cf. Rom. 1:18f) written on the consciences of most human beings (cf. comments on verse ten below). Therefore Jehovah will judge her. One should read Isaiah ch. 13-14; Jeremiah 50-51; Daniel 1-5 in connection with these verses.

v. 7-11 ABUSED: Babylon boasted that she would be *gevereth* (mistress) or queen forever. She never gave a thought to the warnings of conscience or the lessons of history. Those who will not learn from history are doomed to repeat it! She seemed unaware of the natural law all around that whatever is sown is eventually reaped. She did not seem to consider where such haughty disregard for humaneness and mercy might lead. The failure of tyrants and dictators to learn where cruelty and immorality ends is almost incredible! It was difficult for most of the world of the 1940's to believe Adolph Hitler was ignorant that the atrocities of the Third Reich would lead to self-destruction. But Hitler "did not remember the latter end thereof" and slaughtered over six million people in his concentration camps which eventuated in degradation and partitioning of Germany which it had never known before.
'Aediynah is from the Hebrew root *'adan* and means *voluptuousness, pleasurable, luxurious, sensuous.* It is the same root from which we get *Eden* (Gen. 2:8, etc.). One only has to read Daniel ch. 5 to understand that Babylon was characterized by its bent to pleasure. The kings of Babylon apparently had as their goal the satisfaction of their every pleasure. Wealth, wine and women gave them security. They used their wealth to build gold-plated gods and temples; a massive city with huge, thick walls; hanging gardens and banquet halls; then retired to admire the work of their hands and revel in the sensuous luxury of it all. They told themselves "this is great Babylon. . ." (cf. Dan. 4:28-30). All the world, even the majority of the Jewish people, stood in awe of mighty Babylon. The world expected Babylon to exist forever. Certainly Babylon herself never expected to mourn like a widow or a mother who has lost her children. She anticipated eternal reveling and gaiety and luxury. Apparently the emperors of Babylon decreed themselves to be gods (cf. Isa. 14:12-14), and believed themselves to be invincible (much like Adolph Hitler, centuries later). But the real Sovereign of the world, Jehovah, predicts that exactly what Babylon said could never happen would happen suddenly and fully. The haughty and satiated Babylonians

would one day mourn and grieve like a woman who has lost her husband and a young mother whose children have died tragic deaths. Their affliction would be without warning and in full measure. One day on top of the world; the next day devastated and conquered by the Persians. Babylon fell in one night! (cf. Dan. ch. 5). Babylon was noted for its multitude of astrologers and sorcerers. She was famous for her magic. No other nation since has been as prolific or elaborate in its cultivation of such sorcery. Babylon's whole culture, political, economic and religious was built around its astrologers and enchanters and wise-men. In spite of this elaborate and long established system of pseudo-science and religion, Babylon would fall. Her "star-gazers" would not be able to work magic or charm away the judgment of Jehovah.

Babylon trusted in its wickedness. There is a false sense of autonomy and sovereignty that comes as a result of deliberately practiced wickedness. That is what the devil promised Eve in the Garden of Eden (". . . in the day you eat from it your eyes will be opened, and you will be like God, knowing good and evil . . ."). Professing to be wise, they became fools. They exchanged the truth of God for a lie. They refused to have God in their knowledge (cf. Rom. 1:22-32). Babylon trusted in her cruelty and cunning and decided she could do as she pleased and no one could stop her. She believed she was sovereign. There was no One to whom she could be held accountable ("None seeth me . . ."). This wicked exercise of power seared Babylon's conscience—it perverted her reason. She went against the most fundamental revelation of nature itself (that there is a divine power higher than man to whom man is morally responsible—cf. Rom. 1:18-21) and denied the existence of God.

But judgment (evil) will surely come upon haughty Babylon. She will now know the *shakherah* (dawning) of it. This probably means (in keeping with the context) she will not "be able to conjure away" or able to keep it from coming by all her incantations and sorceries. There are three different Hebrew words used to describe the judgment: *ra'ah* (break in pieces, calamity, evil); *hovah* (mischief, or, literally, yawning—utter destruction); *sho'ah* (deserted, wasted, desolation). These words give a graphic description of the process of Babylon's judgment. It will come *suddenly.* Daniel, ch. 5, records that Babylon's overthrow came in *one night!* It was completely unexpected! First she was broken, then came the destruction and to this day there is only a deserted waste place where once mighty Babylon stood. The fall of Babylon is inexplicable except as one understands the prophecy of God by Isaiah!

v. 12-15 ANNIHILATED: Jehovah now challenges Babylon to call upon the full force of its massive and complex system of sorcery, astrology and magic to save it. The ancient peoples not only worshiped the stars, but many of them built their political and economic structures on a "science" of star-gazing and horoscope casting. These pseudo-sciences were elaborately constructed and Babylon was more prolific than all the ancients. Determining things from the motions of the stars was not something Babylon merely toyed with. She had built her whole national identity on this from her very beginning. She went to war or sued for peace on the basis of what the stars "said." She crowned emperors or deposed them only after casting a horoscope. She conducted business and built buildings and practiced the healing arts by interpreting dreams, saying incantations and practicing sorcery. So, if Babylon had any resource greater than any other empire of the past (Egypt, Assyria, etc.) it would be her star-gazing. If she was to prevail against the God of Israel her elaborate system of astrology would have to stand up. The many hours of study devoted to astrology, the voluminous writings of the wisemen and the staggering (and sometimes repulsive) amount of time consumed to practice all the hocus pocus involved wearied the general populace. There is evidence that even emperors became exasperated at the sham of it all (cf. Dan. 2:1-12). The Hebrew word *modiy'iym* (prognosticators) is from *yada'* (to know, perceive, discern) and the word *khadashim* means, new moons or months. The position of the moon was a determining factor in the Babylonian system of astrology.

But none of this shall save Babylon! Even this great, elaborate pervasive system of astrology shall be as vulnerable as dry wheat stubble thrown on a fire. It will go up in smoke, suddenly. Nothing will be left of it. Wood thrown on a fire leaves coals and lasts long enough to provide warmth. But poof, like stubble, Babylon and all her star-gazers will be gone! So much for all the years of toil and energy invested in Babylon's elaborate system of astrology! All those *sokherayik* (traveling merchants) who "trafficked" with Babylon were interested only in financial gain. As long as they were making profit from trading with Babylon they were her friends. But when she needed assistance against her enemies they "wandered to their own quarters," not wishing to suffer the judgments coming upon her. They have merely taken advantage of Babylon and have no genuine concern for her no matter how glibly they may have dealt with her when she was alive and prosperous. It was predicted that the magnificent Roman empire of the apostle John's day would come to the same despicable ruin (cf. Rev. 17 and 18). Rome would say in her heart she was a "queen" and not a "widow." Rome would be burned with fire. The merchants of the earth would mourn Rome's demise because it would mean financial loss for them (not that anyone was genuinely concerned for Rome's fall). Thus "Babylon" is used as a symbol, a type, of the Roman empire (Rev. 14:8; 17:5; 18:2, 10, 21, etc.).

Babylon fell! Great and sudden was her fall! It was totally unexpected! During a night of drunken revelry and carousing by the emperor (Belshazzar), his noblemen and concubines, Cyrus the Persian marched in on a dry river bed (whose waters had been diverted by Cyrus) and Belshazzar was slain. For further details see *Daniel,* by Butler, pub. College Press, pg. 200-208. Rome's fall was not quite so sudden, but it fulfilled the predictions of John just as certainly as Babylon's fall fulfilled the predictions of Isaiah and Jeremiah. And just as certainly, all human governments must ultimately fall and give way to the kingdom of God for whom the new heavens and the new earth are to be created.

QUIZ

1. Why is Babylon called a "virgin"?
2. What is meant by calling Babylon the "mistress" of kingdoms?
3. Why may Babylon be judged accountable for knowing that she was headed for judgment by her actions?
4. In what did Babylon place her trust?
5. Describe the fall of Babylon?
6. How did those who had traded with Babylon react to her downfall?

4. SOVEREIGN IN WISDOM, CHAPTER 48

a. PROOF

TEXT: 48:1-8

1 Hear ye this, O house of Jacob, who are called by the name of Israel, and are come forth out of the waters of Judah; who swear by the name of Jehovah, and make mention of the God of Israel, but not in truth nor in righteousness.
2 For they call themselves of the holy city, and stay themselves upon the God of Israel; Jehovah of hosts is his name.
3 I have declared the former things from of old; yea, they went forth out of my mouth, and I showed them: suddenly I did them, and they came to pass.
4 Because I knew that thou art obstinate, and thy neck is an iron sinew, and thy brow brass;
5 therefore I have declared it to thee from of old; before it came to pass I showed it thee; lest thou shouldest say, Mine idol hath done them, and my graven image, and my molten image, hath commanded them.
6 Thou hast heard it; behold all this; and ye, will ye not declare it? I have showed thee new things from this time, even hidden things, which thou hast not known.

7 They are created now, and not from of old; and before this day thou heardest them not; lest thou shouldest say, Behold, I knew them.
8 Yea, thou heardest not; yea, thou knewest not; yea, from of old thine ear was not opened: for I knew that thou didst deal very treacherously, and wast called a transgressor from the womb.

QUERIES

a. What are the "waters of Judah"?
b. What are the "former things" Jehovah showed?
c. What are the "new things" being shown?

PARAPHRASE

Listen to this, you descendants of Jacob whom I have called Israel, you who are from the royal tribe of Judah and who take their oaths in the name of Jehovah boasting of your relationship to Him; I know that your relationship is not in truth or righteousness! You boast of your citizenship in the holy city of Jehovah and of your dependence upon Him; but do you not realize He is the Lord God Almighty?!

The Lord says to Israel, For centuries I have been proving to you My sovereignty in wisdom by predicting what would take place; then suddenly I brought it to pass. I knew beforehand that you would be stubborn and unbending and hard-headed. And so I predicted your future long ago, telling you through prophets what was going to happen to you before it happened. I had my prophets predict your future centuries in advance so you would realize I am sovereign in wisdom and not the idols of wood and stone you worship. You have seen all My prophecies come true thus far, but you have refused to confess the truth of it, haven't you? Now I am predicting, through My prophets, new revelations—things impossible for you to know unless I tell you. These are completely new things; nothing like this has taken place in the past. You cannot say of these things, This is no proof of Jehovah's sovereignty—we knew this all along! The reason you never got the message from all My revelations, both present and past, is you deliberately chose to close your ears to My word. I know you, Israel, you have been treacherous and rebellious from the days you became a nation!

COMMENTS

v. 1-5 PERSEVERANCE OF JEHOVAH: God addresses the people of Isaiah's day sternly. *Shama* ("hear") means to heed and obey. It appears they call themselves "Israel" but God addresses them as "house of Jacob." Whether there is an intended sarcasm on the part of Jehovah or not is not easy to determine. Certainly God permitted writers of the Bible to employ sarcasm in their attempts to call men to repentance. We have discussed the difference between the terms Jacob and Israel earlier. "Coming forth out of the waters of Judah" simply means the audience of Isaiah's writing are the people of the southern kingdom whose main source is Judah (see Deut. 33:28; Psa. 68:26 for similar phraseology). The main point in citing the three names (Jacob, Israel and Judah) is to emphasize their culpability for not trusting the message Isaiah is giving them about captivity, Cyrus' future return of the exiles and the messianic destiny in their future. These are people of Jehovah—they are His specially graced people, but they do not "hear." They "make mention" of Jehovah but not in truth or righteousness. To acknowledge the name of God in truth means to hear and obey what God has revealed for man to obey. Whoever says "I know Him" but does not keep His commandments is a liar and the truth is not in him (cf. I Jn. 2:3-6). They worshipped Jehovah with lip-service but their hearts were far from Him (cf. Isa. 29:13-14). They boasted of their citizenship in the "holy" city (where the temple of Jehovah was located) and they glibly declared their allegiance to Jehovah but it did not seem to register on their minds that He Is Jehovah-Zev'oth (*zev'oth* is Hebrew for "armies, hosts, myriads" and is also used for "war, battle, etc."). In other words, Jehovah is Lord of all! He is Lord of earth and heaven. He is Lord of the inward man as well as the outward man. He knows everything created everything and commands everything.

Judah should have acknowledged His lordship with their hearts as well as their lips for Jehovah had proven His sovereignty in centuries past by predicting (through the mouths of His messengers) the events of Judah's history long before they came to pass. Jehovah also demonstrated through His prophets that He knew the hidden, secret thoughts of men (e.g., Nathan and David). The nation and individuals often knew years and centuries in advance of the coming of minutely-detailed events. Many of these events came to pass *suddenly* without any gradual development or advanced signals. Two needs of the Hebrew people are the motivation prompting Jehovah to predict their future; (a) their obstinacy and hard-headedness toward His sovereignty must be broken; (b) they must acknowledge once and for all that idols are not gods—there is only One God, Jehovah. This indicates that God's primary purpose in predicting the future is not simply to satisfy the curiosity of man about tomorrow. No theology should be built on eschatology! Our theology should be built on the character of the One who knows about tomorrow, not on when and what tomorrow will bring. The only reason God foretells the future is to demonstrate His sovereignty! That is the point! Once man surrenders to His omnipotence and omniscience he does not need to know the future (cf. Mt. 6:25-34; Acts 1:7). Prophecy fulfilled is a means to an end, not an end in itself. The end is to believe God's revelation of Himself and to accept His written word from the hands of the writers as being validated (cf. II Pet. 1:16-21, etc.).

v. 6-8 PERVERSITY OF JUDAH: The onus is put squarely upon the perverse people of Judah. "You have had opportunities to know all these past predictions and their fulfillments;

I remind you to study them again," would be Jehovah's challenge to Judah. The question of verse six is undoubtedly rhetorical: "And you, you will not declare it, will you?" or, "And you, how can you not declare it?" The meaning is that what the Lord predicted came to pass and they must acknowledge the factuality of it even if they do not obey the moral implications of it! This shows that unbelief is a moral problem, not an evidential one!

But now, the Lord is predicting *new* things (things that will have their fulfillment yet in the future). Among these things (so incredible for Judah to accept) were the captivities, release from captivity by a pagan ruler and a coming Messiah who is bringing a way of salvation which is absolutely foreign to their present dispensation. Salvation by grace, through faith in the substitutionary atonement of the Messiah (Isa. 53, et al.) had to be by *revelation*—it had to be a "new" prediction because it could never have been "thought-up" by the human mind (cf. I Cor. 1:18—2:16). This plan of salvation was "created" by God and worked out in His sovereign plans (cf. Rom. 9, 10, 11) as a "mystery to be revealed" (cf. Eph. 1:3-10, etc.). God predicted it all and typified it all in the Old Testament dispensation, to be sure (cf. Rom. 3:21-22; see special study, "The Righteousness of God As Revealed by The Prophets," page 282), but it was dim and abstruse (cf. Heb. 1:1). The Lord predicts and rules in history toward His goal of redemption. He *reveals* His will and plan for man; He reveals Himself (His own person, nature, character—even in the flesh!). Man cannot know God's plan or God's nature until God *reveals* it. Man may not even be able to understand it all when it is *revealed.* But God revealed enough of it in *human language* (which is human experience) (cf. I Cor. 2:13) and in *human flesh* (Jesus Christ; cf. Jn. 1:1-18; I Jn. 1:1-4, etc.) that man can *know* His will for salvation and *obey* His will for salvation.

In verse eight we have the reason God chose to hide these "new" things from Judah until He was ready to *reveal* them. The Hebrew syntax would indicate the latter half of the verse should read literally: "dealing treacherously you would deal treacherously. . . ." God did not let them know—He did not "open their ear" to these new things because of their perversity. They were spiritually unprepared to hear them. He had yet to put them through a long period of "indignation" (the captivities, the return from exile, the centuries of the Greek-Seleucid oppression and the Roman oppression) before the "new" dispensation could come and be accepted. This verse definitely teaches the sovereign wisdom of God in a *gradual* revelation from Old Testament times to the New. There were things Jesus could not reveal to the twelve until after He had "gone away" because they were unable to "bear" them while He was with them in the flesh (cf. Jn. 16:1-15). Fleshly-mindedness prohibits man from listening to God's word even when it is being spoken and revealed (cf. I Cor. 2:6; 3:1-4; Heb. 5:11-14, etc.). It was difficult for the apostle Peter to accept the revelation of Christ about His atoning death (cf. Mt. 16:21-23) because Peter simply *refused* to accept the concept of a dying Messiah! So, Isaiah says, until Judah stops its rebellion against Jehovah's sovereignty, she is not going to "hear" the "new" things Jehovah wants to reveal.

QUIZ

1. What is Isaiah's point in mentioning the three names of the covenant people?
2. Why must one obey the commandments of God to say "I know Him"?
3. What two needs of the people prompted the Lord to reveal their future?
4. Why should a theology not be built on an eschatological system?
5. Has God revealed enough of His will to man?
6. Why do most men not know God?

b. PERSPECTIVE

TEXT: 48:9-16

9 For my name's sake will I defer mine anger, and for my praise will I refrain for thee, that I cut thee not off.
10 Behold, I have refined thee, but not as silver; I have chosen thee in the furnace of affliction.
11 For mine own sake, for mine own sake, will I do it; for how should my name be profaned? and my glory will I not give to another.
12 Hearken unto me, O Jacob, and Israel my called: I am he; I am the first, I also am the last.
13 Yea, my hand hath laid the foundation of the earth, and my right hand hath spread out the heavens: when I call unto them, they stand up together.
14 Assemble yourselves, all ye, and hear; who among them hath declared these things? He whom Jehovah loveth shall perform his pleasure on Babylon, and his arm shall be on the Chaldeans.
15 I, even I, have spoken; yea, I have called him; I have brought him, and he shall make his way prosperous.
16 Come ye near unto me, hear ye this; from the beginning I have not spoken in secret; from the time that it was, there am I: and now the Lord Jehovah hath sent me, and his Spirit.

QUERIES

a. Why would God stop His anger for His own sake?
b. Does God love Cyrus (the one who shall perform God's pleasure on Babylon)?
c. Who is the "me" whom the Lord Jehovah has "sent"? (v. 16)

PARAPHRASE

In order that the faithfulness and mercifulness of My nature may be manifested and praised I am putting a muzzle on My anger and I will not utterly destroy you, Judah. I have put you to the test in the furnace of affliction, like silver is refined, but I have found no silver in you. Therefore, I want you to know that what I am going to do in redeeming you, this "new thing" I am predicting, is not because you deserve it but because I do not intend for My name to be dishonored. The inviolability of My name is of supreme importance to all men lest they think My absolute sovereignty and glory can belong to another. Listen to Me My chosen people, Israel. I am the Absolute God; I am the only God there is—first, last, and always. I created the earth and the heavens; they are at My command and when I command, they obey! Get yourselves together, Israel, and decide this; which of the heathen gods has predicted or is able to command the future like I am commanding Cyrus now before he is even born!? Jehovah has chosen Cyrus as the object of His pleasure to execute Jehovah's will upon Babylon; yes, it shall be the arm of Cyrus descending upon the Chaldeans on My behalf. I, the Absolute Sovereign of all creation, have spoken; I have determined that it shall be Cyrus; I will support him in My work, and nothing shall keep him from doing My purpose. Draw near to Me and pay close attention to what I am telling you: From the time I began speaking to man My will has always been clearly made known and not secret like the heathen oracles; My sovereign will has been present in everything that has happened to you and it will continue to be present in what is going to happen through Cyrus—even to the coming of the "new" things of the messianic age. Now, I the Suffering Servant, tell you, Israel, the Lord Jehovah sends Me along with His Holy Spirit.

COMMENTS

v. 9-11 JEHOVAH'S GOODNESS: What Jehovah is doing with Judah (Israel), He is doing because of His goodness not theirs. To keep His own absolute goodness and faithfulness and mercifulness inviolate He will act to redeem them from captivity. That which motivates Jehovah is His own graciousness—Judah does not merit redemption. The Hebrew word *'ekhetam* is translated *refrain* but literally means *muzzle;* it is the same Hebrew word used in Deut. 25:4 concerning the muzzling of an ox when treading out the grain. Jehovah decides by His own sovereign grace to muzzle Himself and not utterly destroy His covenant people. The Lord chose His people "in the furnace of affliction." Israel was in the Egyptian "furnace" when first chosen. Then the Lord submitted them to a "refining" process through the wilderness, the period of the judges, the period of the monarchy and the divided kingdoms, to see if there was any "silver" in them. He found none! As good as some of the faithful (like Isaiah, Hezekiah, and some others) remnant may have been, put to the refinement of Jehovah none deserved the approbation, "silver." Jeremiah was instructed to find *one* righteous man in Jerusalem, if he could (Jer. 5:1f). If God refined your community in His crucible today He would not find *one* righteous man who deserved redemption—no man (except the Man, Very Man, Jesus Christ) deserves redemption. All have sinned and come short of the demand of God. But the Good News is that Jesus Christ did come in the flesh, earned absolute righteousness in the flesh, died as the substitute-sinner for all mankind and arose from the dead victorious over that penalty and offers the grace of God to every man conditioned upon that man's faith and covenant relationship. The whole point of this passage is that the inviolability of the name of Jehovah is absolutely necessary to the redemption of Judah because there is no other basis upon which Judah may be redeemed! If Jehovah's absolute goodness and mercifulness and faithfulness cannot be trusted, then all is lost! If Jehovah cannot and does not keep His word

He is no better than the impotent gods of the heathen. The redemption of man rests not in the failing, falling inconsistencies of humanness, but in the *never* failing consistency and absolute changelessness of God and His Son, Jesus Christ. If Jehovah's name can be profaned and His glory given to any other then there is no Absolute Being and man must have an Absolute Being. If this be the case, the focus of all prophecy and preaching should be the character of God and His Son. The Good News is Who God Is and what He has done—not who man is and what he must do! The Gospel is preaching the *person* of Christ, not a religious system. Of course, the good news also reveals how man may enter into a covenant with that *Person.* It is by obedient faith, but not of meritorious works lest any man should boast.

v. 12-16 JEHOVAH'S GREATNESS: This chapter is a summation of the section discussing the *Power of the Lord's Servant* (ch. 44-48). The power of Jehovah is going to be demonstrated through His servant Cyrus (and ultimately through His Servant the Messiah) in order that His name may be vindicated as Absolute Sovereign. This is necessary that once and for all men may realize there are no other gods. Man must trust his eternal life to Jehovah and His sovereign plans and servants. Jehovah is Creator. He made the earth and heavens. Even inanimate creation is His servant. There is nothing made that is useless—Jehovah created everything and made it to be His servant and do His bidding. All of creation "stands at attention" to serve His purpose (cf. Psa. 119:90-91; I Cor. 3:21-23; Heb. 1:7, 14, etc.).

So all Israel (Judah) is commanded to assemble itself and hear the sovereign challenge of Jehovah about His servant's work. Which of the heathen gods or false prophets has ever told Israel all that Jehovah is now telling her about His redemptive plan, the use of Cyrus, and the coming of the Messiah-Servant? None! They do not because they cannot! They are not gods but pieces of wood and stone. He "whom Jehovah loveth" is undoubtedly referring (in context) to Cyrus. Of course, Jehovah loves Cyrus, but not in the same way He loves a believer simply because Cyrus (being an unbeliever) will not *allow* God to love him in a covenant relationship. The word *love* (Heb. *aehevo* from *ahav*) here probably means simply that Jehovah has chosen Cyrus to be the object of His care and providence to serve Him in conquering Babylon and freeing the Jewish exiles. At one time Nebuchadnezzar was chosen to be the recipient of the special favor of Jehovah (cf. Jer. 27:5f); at another time Alexander the Great was given dominion (Dan. 7:6f). The emphasis here is not on Cyrus but on the sovereignty of Jehovah. Jehovah has spoken! Jehovah has called Cyrus! Jehovah will bring (sustain) Cyrus and Jehovah shall make Cyrus prosper in what Jehovah wants, but Cyrus will not prosper when Jehovah does not want him to prosper!

The intent of it all is that Judah might see things from *Jehovah's perspective!* This is the whole point of *revelation;* man must see (or understand) what "is" from the perspective of "Who" Made What "Is!" Man must see that all of creation stands at attention and serves the *eternal* purpose of God which is the redemption of creation. The coming captivity of Judah, the coming conquest of Babylon by a Persian emperor yet unborn (Cyrus), the far distant coming of a Messiah-Servant—all must be seen by man, not through human perspective (carnal, limited, temporal), but through divine perspective which is eternal, righteous, true, pure and glorious. God calls Judah, "Come near unto me, and pay close attention" to what I am about to say. However much of His will God has deemed necessary for man to know and obey at any time, God has not been secretive about it. It was never God's business to keep His will as secret as He possibly could. He has always desired to reveal as much of His will as He possibly could. The only hindrance to revelation has been man's spiritual rebellion. God's revelation of Himself in Jesus Christ is hindered by man's unwillingness to want that revelation. We would *know* His will more fully if we were more willing to *do* His will (Jn. 7:17; 13:17). God spoke plainly and openly through His messengers from the very beginning. Often times He spoke more plainly than the people wanted Him to speak (cf. Isa. 30:9-11; Amos 9:10-17; Micah 2:6-11, etc.). Jehovah's presence was apparent in every prophecy made by any prophet of His. Now it should be apparent to Judah that Jehovah's presence and will is being expressed in the prophecy concerning Cyrus.

The last half of verse 16 presents a problem for commentators. Keil and Delitzsch say the "me" who is sent by the Lord Jehovah is "the One unequalled servant of Jehovah" (the Messiah); Edward J. Young calls Him "the Servant *par excellance*" (the Messiah); Leupold believes the "me" is the prophet Isaiah. Of course, it is unusual to have such a sudden transition from the speaking of Jehovah directly to the speaking of the Messiah. But it is not altogether unparalleled. Certainly Isaiah 61:1f are the words of the Messiah. It appears that Isaiah ch. 49 is also a dissertation by the Messiah Himself. Keil and Delitzsch cite Zech. 4:9 as another example of such transition. It would appear that the context supports the messianic view. Jehovah has been emphasizing the "new" thing He is going to do as a consequence of Cyrus' return of the exiles. That "new" thing can only be the messianic age. It is therefore altogether appropriate that the "Unequaled" Servant speak here of His commission or sending. In this text is emphasized also the unique companionship of the Spirit the Messiah will have in His mission (cf. Isa. 42:1f; 61:1f). The Suffering Servant (Messiah) did not come alone. The Holy Spirit was with Him; in fact, He was the Holy Spirit in the flesh (cf. Jn. 14:15-17). From this point on (and of chapter 48) more and more emphasis is put on the program of the coming "unequalled" Servant. The work of Cyrus and the restoration of Israel to Palestine was simply a preparatory step for His coming. There is going to have to be centuries of repentance and sanctification in a remnant of Israel in preparation for His coming. Cyrus and the restoration was just the beginning of it all. From verse 16a to 16b the reader has been transported over a span of more than 600 years. But such "telescoping" of history is not unusual in the writings of the prophets (see Shortened Perspective, in *Minor Prophets,* by Butler, pub. College Press, pg. 32;

comments on Joel 2:27-28, pg. 184-188).

Jehovah wants Israel to see her destiny from *His perspective,* not from the limited human perspective. Jehovah knows everything from beginning to end. He created everything. He is absolute Sovereign. When He says His people will be taken captive, released by a pagan emperor (yet unborn), and that His Servant will come to bring them everlasting victory and peace, Israel should "see His day" (cf. Jn. 8:56-59; 12:41; I Pet. 1:10-12) by faith.

QUIZ

1. What was the basis upon which Jehovah acted to redeem Judah?
2. Why must Jehovah do things for the sake of His name?
3. Why emphasize here that Jehovah is Creator?
4. What hinders man from knowing God's revelation of Himself?
5. Why should man need to see everything from the perspective of divine revelation?
6. Why the transition from Jehovah's speaking to the Servant's speaking in verse 16?

c. PRACTICE

TEXT: 48:17-22

17 Thus saith Jehovah, thy Redeemer, the Holy One of Israel: I am Jehovah thy God, who teacheth thee to profit, who leadeth thee by the way that thou shouldest go.
18 Oh that thou hadst hearkened to my commandments! then had thy peace been as a river, and thy righteousness as the waves of the sea:
19 thy seed also had been as the sand, and the offering of thy bowels like the grains thereof: his name would not be cut

off nor destroyed from before me.
20 Go ye forth from Babylon, flee ye from the Chaldeans; with
a voice of singing declare ye, tell this, utter it even to the
end of the earth: say ye, Jehovah hath redeemed his servant
Jacob.
21 And they thirsted not when he led them through the deserts;
he caused the waters to flow out of the rock for them; he
clave the rock also, and the waters gushed out.
22 There is no peace, saith Jehovah, to the wicked.

QUERIES

a. How may peace be like a "river"?
b. When were they to "go forth from Babylon"?
c. Why do the wicked not have peace?

PARAPHRASE

This is what Jehovah, your Redeemer, the Holy One of Israel says: I am your covenant-God, Jehovah, who wishes to teach you to help you and who wishes to direct you in the way you should go. If only you had obeyed My commandments. Then you would have had peace in your soul deep, steady, living and ever-flowing just like a river and you would have had a rightness in your soul that was powerful and never exhausted itself, just like an ocean. Your descendants would have been as numerous as the grains of the sand on the seashore and I would not have had to take away your nationhood. Now when the time comes for your release from exile, leave Babylon and everything she stands for; you are going to be freed from that pagan oppressor so leave all her paganism behind and flee! Go, singing about your deliverance so the whole world can hear about it; make sure everyone knows it is Jehovah who has delivered His covenant people. The Lord God will sustain you in your deliverance, you will not need to cling to Babylon as if you need her. When Jehovah led His people through the deserts in the days of Moses He sustained them. They did not need Egypt to give them water and food. The Lord made water come from a rock for them; He split the rock open and water flowed out. If you will be firm in your commitment to My commandments you will have deliverance, peace and righteousness, but there is no peace for those who are wicked and who are lax about My commandments, says Jehovah.

COMMENTS

v. 17-19 THE WAY: The Lord God of Israel has made every effort, from Abraham to Isaiah, to lead this people in the only way profitable for them. The Hebrew word *ya'al,* translated *profit,* means literally, *helpful, good, useful.* It is also used as a proper name, *Jael* (see Judges 4:18; 5:6, etc.). Jehovah *teaches* His people in order to *help* them to peace and righteousness. Joel 2:23 speaks of the "teacher unto righteousness" (see our comments, *Minor Prophets,* by Butler, pub. College Press, pg. 180-183). This is the *way* Israel should have gone—the way of peace and righteousness. It is the "ancient" way wherein is goodness and rest (cf. Jer. 6:16). But Israel, of her own free choice, refused to walk in that way. She chose "bypaths" and "stumbled" (cf. Jer. 18:15-17). The *way* of the Lord is in His *commandments.* They called Jehovah "Lord" but did not do what He commanded (cf. Isa. 29:13; Mt. 15:8-9; Lk. 6:46; I Jn. 2:3-6, etc.). If Israel had only obeyed God's commandments (the law of Moses and the revelations of the prophets) she would have had peace and righteousness in abundance (cf. Amos 5:24; Isa. 11:9; 44:4), like a deep, steadily flowing, life-giving *river.* The figure of the river and the sea stands in emphatic contrast to Palestine's hundreds of shallow, wadis which were dry most of the year and ran with water only occasionally, during downpours, and then soon ran dry again. The peace and righteousness Jehovah gives through His *way* (His commandments) is deep, not shallow; it is steady, not vacillating. It is this because it is imputed, not earned. Man cannot earn peace with God; he may have it as a gift from God by entering into discipleship with Christ (cf. Mt. 11:25-30). This is the peace available to the new, true Israel of God (cf. Gal. 6:11-16) and comes not by legal attainment but by new birth. Discipleship and new birth comes through a willingness to be taught, to be baptized, and to be taught the way of Christ for the rest of one's life (cf. Mt. 28:18-20; Jn. 3:3-5; Gal. 3:26-27; Col. 2:12-13; Rom. 6:1-19). If Israel had only listened to Jehovah, He would have made of her a great nation. Of course, of the "seed" (singular) of Abraham, God has made a "great" people (the church) (cf. Gal. 3:6-18). But what great things Israel could have done as a testimony to Jehovah unto the Gentiles long before Christ ever came if she had only walked in His way! God brought His redemption to the world *in spite of* Israel's stubborn disobedience; what could He have done had Israel been a willing, humble, obedient servant!? (cf. Rom. 11:15). Had Israel obeyed, God could have had a holy nation as numerous as the grains of sand on a seashore. But she disobeyed. God had to give her up to wars, pestilence, famine and finally complete national oblivion in captivity in order to sanctify for Himself a small remnant for His messianic use. What great good could be done for mankind today if all Israel according to the flesh would obey and become part of Israel according to faith in Christ, the Messiah! Fleshly Israel's disobedience has been a great hindrance to the gospel. The disbelief and disobedience of the majority of the Jews was a constant source of heart-rending pathos to Jesus!

v. 20-22 THE WAYFARER: The *way* of Jehovah is in His commandments. The wayfarer is not forced to take that way; he is exhorted to choose Jehovah's way by a deliberate exercise of his will which is expressed by both a negative and positive action. First he is to "flee Babylon" and second, he is to "declare" Jehovah's redemption. These verses are prophetic commands anticipating Judah's captivity by Babylon and release by Cyrus. There were strong temptations for many of the Jews to remain in Mesopotamia after the Persian edict restoring them to their homeland. Many of them did, in fact, remain (cf. Ezra, Nehemiah and Esther). Although most of the Jews retained much of their cultural identity, many of them, influenced by the paganism around them, lost their firm faith in the Scriptures and they produced succeeding generations whose faith was in their past, not in their supernatural messianic future.

The Lord's command, "Go ye forth from Babylon, flee ye from the Chaldeans . . ." anticipated more than physical escape from captivity. It is also a command to holiness; it is an exhortation to Israel to separate herself from the wickedness of Babylon and from dependence upon Babylon for sustenance. The true meaning of this finds its fulfillment in the exhortation to the true Israel (the church) to flee the paganism of Rome ("Babylon") (cf. Rev. 18:4-5), and not "partake of her sins." Singing of the Lord's redemption is a favorite figure of Isaiah (cf. Isa. 14:7; 24:14; 26:19; 27:2; 35:6, 10; 38:20; 42:11; 44:23; 49:13; 51:11; 52:8-9; 54:1; 55:12; 65:14). It is a song of praise and testimony the wayfarer is to sing. It is a song about what Jehovah has done—not how the wayfarer feels! Modern "gospel" music focuses too much on subjective experiences and feelings. All the exhortations of God are to sing about what God has done objectively and who God is revelationally! It is interesting that the Psalms, written to be sung, are focused on what God has done and who He is. See Psalm 81:13-16 which especially sounds like this passage in Isaiah.

Israel does not need to be afraid to break all ties with Babylon and separate itself unto its messianic destiny. Babylon's material riches and carnality cannot be the source of Israel's security and sustenance. God will keep His promises to sustain them. He kept His covenant with Israel when she separated herself from Egypt. Even when some of the wilderness wayfarers wanted to return to Egypt for security, Jehovah provided them water in the desert. He clave the rock and water gushed out (Ex. 17:1-7; Deut. 8:15). The fundamental essence of Christ's church, according to the New Testament, is its separation from worldliness. Much of the modern-day church, however, has not "come out of Babylon" but still clings to worldly-attitudes (bigness for bigness sake, spectacularism, subjectivism, manipulation, exploitation) and worldly behavior (wastefulness, sensualness, legalism, show-offishness, shallowness). The church must learn to depend totally on God, not on human programs.

For there is no peace to the wicked. The Hebrew word *resha'iym* is from the root word *rasha'* and refers mainly to the activity of *wickedness* which is *disquietude, confusion, tossing, restlessness, disturbing.* Keil and Delitzsch say the primary meaning of the root word is, *laxity* and *looseness.* It is to describe those whose inward moral nature is without firmness and therefore in a state of moral confusion and tossing to and fro; moral upheaval (cf. Isa. 57:20-21). Cunning and deceitful men, Paul warns the Ephesian church, would like to bring wickedness into the body of Christ and cause it to be "tossed to and fro with every wind of doctrine" (cf. Eph. 4:11-16). Many people do not understand that doctrinal vacillation leads to moral confusion. Paul wrote to the Corinthian church (I Cor. 15:33-34) that "evil *homilia* (teaching, sermonizing) corrupts good morals." And this is the precise point of this passage in Isaiah. Israel must walk in the commandments of Jehovah if she is to have peace. True peace is a result of preaching and doing true doctrine.

QUIZ

1. What "profit" would God's teachings be to Israel?
2. What is God's way?
3. What might have been the result if Israel had been obedient to the commandments of God?
4. Does the exhortation to "Go forth from Babylon" have any application for believers today?
5. Why would the Jews be inclined not to leave Babylon?
6. What is necessary to true peace? Why do the wicked not have it?

EXAMINATION

CHAPTERS FORTY-FOUR THROUGH FORTY-EIGHT

DEFINITION

(Define the following words or phrases as they were discussed in the comments.)

1. *Jeshurun*
2. graven *image*
3. *delight*
4. *shut* their eyes
5. *seen* the fire
6. *liars*
7. *anointed*
8. *hidest* thyself
9. *Nebo*
10. *show* yourselves men
11. *virgin*
12. *mistress*
13. *tender, delicate*
14. *profit*

MEMORIZATION

I am Jehovah, and there is ______ else; besides me there is no ______. I will gird thee, though thou hast not known me; that they may know from the ______ of the sun, and from the west, that there is ______ besides me; I am Jehovah, and there is none else. I ______ light, and ______ darkness; I make ______, and create ______; I am Jehovah that ______ all these things. (45:5-7)

For my ______ sake I will defer mine anger, and for my ______ will I refrain for thee, that I cut thee not ______. Behold, I have ______ thee, but not as silver; I have chosen thee in the furnace of ______. For mine ______ sake, for ______ own ______, will I do it; for how should my ______ be profaned? and my ______ I will not give to another. (48:9-11)

EXPLANATION

1. Explain the stupidity of idol making.
2. Explain how God shuts the eyes of idolaters.
3. Explain how Cyrus could be used of God in redemption.
4. Explain how God proves that idols are not gods.
5. Explain what was "new" about some of Jehovah's predictions.
6. Explain why Jehovah always acts primarily for His own name's sake.

APPLICATION

(In its context every scripture has one meaning—the author's intended meaning. How may the following be applied in the believer's life?)

1. Would man in our enlightened age be stupid enough to call a "thing" God?
2. Does God's statement that He creates both goodness and calamities apply to modern history?
3. What application may we make of God taking an oath on His own name?
4. Of what value is biblical typology today?
5. Why is the teaching about idolatry so continually relevant to every age of civilization?
6. Is the teaching about listening to false prophets relevant for today?
7. Is there an application concerning the practice of astrology today from the teachings of Isaiah concerning Babylon's astrology?

C. PROGRAM OF THE LORD'S SERVANT, CHAPTERS 49 - 53

1. RESCUE, CHAPTER 49

a. DESPISED SERVANT

TEXT: 49:1-6

1 Listen, O isles, unto me; and hearken, ye peoples, from far:
Jehovah hath called me from the womb; from the bowels of
my mother hath he made mention of my name:
2 and he hath made my mouth like a sharp sword; in the
shadow of his hand hath he hid me: and he hath made me a
polished shaft; in his quiver hath he kept me close:
3 and he said unto me, Thou art my servant; Israel, in whom
I will be glorified.
4 But I said, I have labored in vain, I have spent my strength
for nought and vanity; yet surely the justice due to me is with
Jehovah, and my recompense with my God.
5 And now saith Jehovah that formed me from the womb to be
his servant, to bring Jacob again to him, and that Israel be
gathered unto him; (for I am honorable in the eyes of Jehovah:
and my God is become my strength;)
6 yea, he saith, It is too light a thing that thou shouldest be
my servant to raise up the tribes of Jacob, and to restore the
preserved of Israel: I will also give thee for a light to the
Gentiles, that thou mayest be my salvation unto the end of
the earth.

QUERIES

a. Who is this Jehovah "hath called from the womb"?
b. Why is he disappointed that he has labored in "vain"?
c. Why increase his burden to "the end of the earth"?

PARAPHRASE

Listen to Me, all you peoples in far distant parts of the earth, Jehovah called Me to be His servant long before I was ever born. From within the womb of My mother I was given My name by Jehovah. Jehovah is going to make My words His weapon, like a sharp sword. I will be the greatest weapon in His hand. He will make Me like a finely polished and sharpened arrow, ready in His quiver for His warfare. Jehovah said to Me, You are My Servant, My Prince, and people will praise Me because of You. But I replied, My work as Your instrument seems fruitless. I have spent My strength and it appears I have accomplished nothing! Nevertheless, I will commit it all to Jehovah—I know He will do what is just and give Me the reward I should have. And now, says Jehovah—the One who is is going to incarnate Me in a woman's womb to be His Servant, to gather Israel unto Him, the One who has honored Me with this task and gives Me strength to do it, He says to Me, I have a greater task for You than gathering just a remnant of the Jews to Me; I will also make You a revelation of My truth to the Gentiles and You will be My salvation to the whole world.

COMMENTS

v. 1-3 Call: Who, other than the Messiah-Servant, could be speaking in these verses? Note the following:

1. Called from the "womb" (he is to be born of a woman) (cf. Isa. 7:14; 9:6; Micah 5:2, etc.).
2. Named while still in the womb (Mt. 2:18-25; Lk. 1:30-35; Isa. 7:14; 9:6).
3. His mouth a "sharp sword" (Rev. 1:16; 2:12, 16; 19:15; Heb. 4:12)
4. He is hid in shadow of Jehovah's hand (Col. 3:3)
5. He is called "Israel" (Prince of God) (Isa. 9:6; Dan. 9:24-27; Lk. 1:30-35, etc.).

6. Jehovah is to be glorified in Him (cf. Jn. 12:27-36; 17:1-5)
7. He is to bring Jacob back to Jehovah (Lk. 1:33)
8. He is honorable in the eyes of Jehovah (Jn. 12:27-36; Lk. 3:21-22; Mt. 17:5-8; Acts 2:22-36; Acts 3:17-26, etc.).
9. He is to be a light to the Gentiles (Isa. 9:1-2; Mt. 4:12-17; Lk. 2:29-32, etc.)
10. He is Jehovah's salvation to the end of the earth

A new emphasis is begun by the prophet Isaiah. From this point on Babylon and Cyrus are not directly mentioned. The Messiah-Servant and the glory of His future kingdom will be pre-eminent. Everything the prophet has to say to his contemporaries will, from this point on, be in relationship to the future messianic glory.

Note the absolute authority with which the Servant addresses the world, commanding the isles and all afar off to listen to Him. Jehovah has made the Servant His instrument of conquering warfare. The Servant is a "polished arrow" and His words are a sharp sword. The Servant is kept in Jehovah's "quiver" until the proper time for battle. The word of Christ is more powerful than any sword or arrow or any other carnal weapon. The word of Christ converts the mind and soul—carnal weapons only subdue bodies (cf. II Cor. 10:3-5; Eph. 6:10-20; Heb. 4:12). It is imperative that the people of God today remind themselves they are engaged in the *warfare* of God. God sent His Son as a sword and an arrow! God so loved the world that He sent His Son, but He was sent to engage in a "life and death" struggle, a war, with the devil and his henchmen. The devil has been defeated and bound, but he still struggles against his "chain" and will devour all who willingly put themselves within his sphere of influence. God does not see the world, the flesh and the devil as a "good place, every day and every way getting better and better." The world, the flesh and the devil are condemned, doomed, judged. Only those who bring every thought into captivity to obedience of

Christ will survive the final judgment of the world.

The Messiah-Servant is also called to be anointed "Israel" (Prince of God). The Hebrew word *yiserael* means "Prince of God." Jesus was descended from David according to the flesh (Rom. 1:1-6), and promised the throne of His earthly father and His Heavenly Father—therefore, Prince (cf. Isa. 9:6; Dan. 9:24-27; Lk. 1:30-35, etc.). To glorify is to honor. The highest form of praise or compliment is imitation and impersonation. Jesus reflected the very image of God (Heb. 1:3); to see Jesus was to see God (Jn. 14:8-10); in Him dwelt all the Godhead bodily (Col. 1:15-20; 2:9); Jesus was the Word become flesh (Jn. 1:1-18); He glorified the Father on earth (Jn. 12:27-36; 17:1-5).

v. 4 COMMITMENT: This verse is one of the most unique verses of all the Bible! It predicts, in the words of the Servant-Messiah Himself, a point in the Servant's ministry when He will cry out in frustration and disappointment. Edward J. Young comments, "The expression of discouragement is no thought of unbelief, but simply of a genuine modesty borne from a consciousness of one's own weakness." Jesus, the Eternal Son, pre-existent with the Father, humbled Himself, emptied Himself and took upon Himself the form of flesh (cf. Phil. 2:5-11). He partook of the same nature as man (Heb. 2:10-18) and was tempted in all points like we are tempted (Heb. 4:14-16) yet without sinning. It was in this incarnation that He partook of human weaknesses. Part of that weakness was the frustration and disappointment men know when they love other men and want to lead them to God's redeeming grace and when sinful, rebellious men refuse to be led (cf. Mt. 19:16-22; Mt. 23:37-39; Mk. 3:1-6; Lk. 19:41-44; Jn. 12:27-36; Mt. 26:36-46). Did Jesus agonize? Did He have to cry out to God in prayer? Yes! (cf. Heb. 5:7-9). Jesus was "astonished" at the unbelief of His countrymen (Mk. 6:6); He wept at the grief of Mary and Martha (Jn. 11:35); He even despaired of finding faith on the earth at His second coming (Lk. 18:8). The earthly ministry of Jesus was not spectacular in its personal results—judged by human standards. He made more enemies, per capita, than friends. He convinced only 12 men to follow Him, one of them was a traitor, and the others disavowed Him at His death. He came unto His own and His own received Him not (Jn. 1:9-11). This was predicted (Isa. 52:13—53;12)!

In spite of the fact that the Messiah experienced discouragement and disappointment and was "a man of sorrows and acquainted with grief," He realistically committed His cause to Jehovah for vindication, justification and reward. The Christian must be a realist also! If they persecuted the Master they will persecute the disciple (cf. Jn. 15:18-27; I Pet. 4:12-19, etc.). There will be emotional lows as well as emotional highs for the Christian. The implication that believers should have a constant, happy glow about life is a form of Christian schizophrenia. Christian emotional dishonesty often can lead to deep despair and other psychological problems. A Christian psychologist says: "God allows us to experience the low points of life in order to teach us lessons we could not learn in any other way. The way we learn those lessons is not to deny the feelings but to find the meanings underlying them. . . . Emotional dishonesty may be creating problems for others . . . Emotional honesty is necessary for one's own spiritual growth and it also helps others to get the right perspective on their own experience." Commitment to God is not built on human feelings as a basis—they are too subjective, biased and vacillating. Christ did not "feel" like going to the cross (". . . let this cup pass from me . . ."). Commitment to God is built on faith in the facts about who God is as they are objectively revealed in the Scriptures and in the Person of Jesus (". . . nevertheless, not my will but thine be done . . ."). Even the Messiah, in His incarnate humiliation, knew emotional depression and could overcome it only by commitment and faith in the knowledge of who the Father is. The Messiah knew He could depend upon the faithfulness of Jehovah to see that justice was ultimately done and that His ministry would receive its eventual reward. Eventually the work of the Messiah would produce a "great multitude" of believers "which no man could number" (Rev. 7:9f), but not in the earthly lifetime of the Messiah. Christians need to learn the lesson of the parable . . . "first the blade, then the ear, then the full grain in the ear" (Mk. 4:26-29).

v. 5-6 COMMISSION: The Servant is born incarnate to accomplish a specific mission. He is to bring back Jacob and gather Israel to Jehovah. *Ye'seph* is the Hebrew word translated *gathered* and means, "to be brought in; placed in safety." His commission was to go to the "lost sheep of the house of Israel." This He did. And He brought to safety all of the true Israel (cf. Gal. 6:16; Rom. 11:25-32). The parenthetical statement is the Messiah-Servant's reiteration that He has committed His cause to Jehovah and He is sure Jehovah will vindicate His ministry with honor and strength.

The Messiah-Servant's commission is much broader than physical Israel, although in the sovereign plan of God that is where redemption began (Acts 1:8). The Messiah was for the whole world. He was to gather sheep not of Israel into the flock of God to become part of the true Israel (cf. Jn. 10:16). Paul the apostle quotes Isaiah 49:6 in Acts 13:47 to give us the inspired interpretation of this prophecy. Jesus Christ is no provincial Messiah; He is not just a prophet of the Jews—He is Savior of the whole world. He is the Light of the world (Jn. 8:12f). One religion is not as good as another—not even to Isaiah. There is salvation in no other name (Acts 4:12). Isaiah is the prophet of world missions. Strangely enough, Isaiah says more about the salvation of the Gentiles than any O.T. book, and yet he is the one most read in the Jewish synagogues! Of course, most of the Jews have a different view of what God has in store for the Gentiles than Isaiah predicted (cf. Lk. 4:16-30).

QUIZ

1. How may we be certain this passage is a prediction of the Messiah?

2. How was the Messiah to be used as God's instrument?
3. Does the N.T. support the idea that the Messiah may have been disappointed in His earthly ministry?
4. Why can't we base our relataionship to God on our feelings?
5. What N.T. scriptures indicate that the Gentiles were to be given an opportunity to become part of "true Israel."?

b. DESIRABLE SAVIOUR

TEXT: 49:7-13

7 Thus saith Jehovah, the Redeemer of Israel, and his Holy One, to him whom man despiseth, to him whom the nation abhorreth, to a servant of rulers: Kings shall see and arise; princes, and they shall worship; because of Jehovah that is faithful, even the Holy One of Israel, who hath chosen thee.
8 Thus saith Jehovah, In an acceptable time have I answered thee, and in a day of salvation have I helped thee; and I will preserve thee, and give thee for a covenant of the people, to raise up the land, to make them inherit the desolate heritages;
9 saying to them that are bound, Go forth; to them that are in darkness, Show yourselves. They shall feed in the ways, and on all bare heights shall be their pasture.
10 They shall not hunger nor thirst; neither shall the heat nor sun smite them; for he that hath mercy on them will lead them, even by springs of water will he guide them.
11 And I will make all my mountains a way, and my highways shall be exalted.
12 Lo, these shall come from far; and, lo, these from the north and from the west; and these from the land of Sinim.
13 Sing, O heavens; and be joyful, O earth; and break forth into singing, O mountains: for Jehovah hath comforted his people, and will have compassion upon his afflicted.

QUERIES

a. Why the change from abhorrence to worship (v. 7)?
b. How is a person given for a covenant (v. 8)?
c. When did Jehovah "comfort" His people (v. 13)?

PARAPHRASE

Jehovah, Redeemer, and Holy One of Israel speaks to the One whom men will at first despise, for whom His own nation will feel revulsion, and whom men in high places will esteem lower than a slave, His Servant, and says: Do not be discouraged, kings and princes will one day recognize Your deity and will respectfully worship You. This will happen because Jehovah is absolutely faithful to fulfill His divine purpose of redemption in You. Jehovah also says, At the time acceptable to Me, at the time when, according to My sovereign will, I decide to accomplish My salvation of the world, I will deliver You from those who would try to thwart Your mission and I will make You, personally, My covenant. Through You My people shall receive the inheritance I promised to their forefathers; through You I will say to those in bondage—you are freed; to those in blindness—you may now see. My people, like sheep, shall be fed in green pastures and on grassy hill-sides. They shall not be hungry or thirsty for righteousness; nothing will be allowed to hurt them any more for they will be led by One who loves them to an everlasting source of living water. I will remove all obstacles in their way and smooth out all the rough places. Behold, these people of Mine will be coming from the fartherest reaches of the world—even from the far east. All of creation is invited to sing praises unto Jehovah because, when He has done what He here predicts through His Servant, He will have comforted His afflicted people as He promised to do.

COMMENTS

v. 7-8 VINDICATION: Jehovah calls Himself "Redeemer of Israel." Redeemer is from the Hebrew word, *go'el,* which means, *avenger, vindicator, ransomer, retributor, recoverer* (often translated, *kinsman,* esp. in Ruth). Jehovah is going to redeem mankind through His Servant, and when He does His Servant will be vindicated. During His earthly tenure, the Servant, because of His humble station and His sinless purity, will be despised by rebellious, sinful men. In order to destroy the wisdom of the wise and thwart the cleverness of the clever, God chose what is weak, low, despised and foolish to the world in order to save the world. Man must learn to trust *completely* in God. If man is given any margin for egotism or boasting in self, he cannot trust God completely (cf. I Cor. 1:18-31). So God chose to send the Messiah, born in a Bethlehem barn, of poor parents, not tutored in the rabbinical schools, reared in Galilee (circuit of the Gentiles), a friend of fishermen, tax-collectors and harlots. He was abhorred by His own people. They called Him, "Samaritan," "demon-possessed," "friend of sinners." He had no "form or comeliness . . . that they should desire Him," (cf. Isa. 53:1f). They were sure no good thing could come out of Nazareth (Jn. 1:46). Finally, they murdered Him (cf. Acts 2:22-24; 3:13-16; 13:26-32, etc.). But Jehovah raised Him from the dead and exalted His name above every name (cf. scriptures just cited plus Phil. 2:9-10; Rev. 1:5; 5:5; 15:3-4; 19:11-16). After the exaltation of the Servant, kings and princes and men in high places became His followers and worshipped Him (cf. Acts 13:7; 17:32-34; 18:8; Rom. 16:23; Phil. 1:13). In succeeding centuries many kings and national leaders have become Christians. The Son was, for a little while, made lower than the angels (cf. Heb. 2:9). After He suffered the necessary humiliation and accomplished atonement for sin, He was enthroned at the right hand of the Majesty on high (Heb. 1:3f) and was restored to the glory He had with the Father from the beginning (Jn. 17:5). All this was according to the definite plan and foreknowledge of God (Acts 2:23f) and God kept His word (Acts 3:12-26).

The "acceptable time" (Heb. *be'eth ratzon*) means literally, "delightful, pleasing, gracious, satisfying time." It is the "time" pre-figured in the Year of Jubilee (Lev. 25:8ff), when tribal inheritances were restored and bond-slaves were set free—a time for great rejoicing. Jubilee was a type of the time of delight and grace that would come when the Messiah appeared (cf. Isa. 61:2) to release captives, etc. "Day of salvation" (Heb. *yom yeshu'ah*) is, interestingly, "day of Jesus" or "day of Joshua." The apostle Paul apparently quotes this verse in II Cor. 6:2 and applies it to the N.T. dispensation. In the fulness of time, God sent His Servant (Gal. 4:4) to bring salvation and, in person, be a "covenant" of the people. Isaiah has already revealed that the Servant will Himself be given as a *covenant* to the whole world (cf. Isa. 42:6). How does the Servant *become* a covenant? Girdlestone says in his, *Synonyms of The Old Testament,* "The Lord Jesus is called the mediator of the New Covenant, because He is the medium wherein the Disposition of God is carried into effect, whether as regards the individual or the race as a whole (Heb. 8:6; 9:15; 12:24). The inheritance which was given by *promise* to Christ (Gal. 3:16) was conveyed by *covenant* (through His blood-shedding) to all believers (Gal. 3:17, 29), who are made *one* with Him by faith; and it is this union of God with man, and of man with God, in Christ, which is summed up in the N.T. sense of the word *berith.*" Jesus, in the offering of Himself to die the "second death" for all sin, became personally a covenant. Covenant relationship is relationship to Christ, the Person, not to a legal system. He said His blood (death) was the covenant (Mt. 26:26-29). All the promises of God find their Yes in Him (II Cor. 1:20). Christ became a servant . . . to show God's truthfulness, in order to confirm the promises given . . . (Rom. 15:8). When God could find nothing higher to swear by in order to show the unchangeable character of His purpose, He interposed (Himself) with an oath (Heb. 6:17). Malachi calls Him the "messenger of the covenant" (Mal. 3:1-2). Daniel says the "prince, the anointed one" who is to be cut off will make a strong covenant with many (Dan. 9:24-27). The renovated "land" of verse eight is all part of the imagery of the fulfillment of Jehovah's covenant with Abraham and his spiritual descendants, and is not to be understood literally. We come into covenant relationship with God by being "joined" in discipleship to Jesus. Disciples of Jesus are those who have been baptized into Him and keep His word (Mt. 28:18f; Jn. 8:31f).

v. 9-11 VIVIFICATION: The Servant will give Jehovah's people back their life. Men will be released from their bondage to sin and delivered from their blindness (darkness) (cf. Isa. 61:1-3; Lk. 4:16-30; Jn. 8:12; 9:39; I Jn. 1:7; 2:10; etc.). Furthermore the Servant will shepherd Jehovah's people (see comments on Isa. 40:11). God's people will not have to wander in the deserts of unbelief and sin aimlessly. They will be led by the Incarnate Messiah-Son who has partaken of their nature in order to become The Good Shepherd (cf. Jn. 10:1f). They will pasture in ways that formerly would not provide or were inaccessible. The Servant will change everything! The Servant's people will not want (Psa. 23); when they hunger or thirst after righteousness, they will be filled (Mt. 5:6). The Hebrew word *sharav* may be translated *heat, drought,* or *mirage.* It is the same word used in Isa. 35:7 and there translated "glowing sand" which would seem to mean *mirage.* The mirage was a common experience of the thirsty Palestinian traveler, who often thought he saw water where there was none. The Servant will not delude the many dying of spiritual thirst—He will provide living water and that in abundance. The Hebrew word *mabbu'ey* is translated *springs* and means, *to gush out, effervescent, bubbling out, abundant.* It is also found in Isa. 35:7, translated *springs.* The final thing the Servant will do will be to make mountains into highways and raise the roads through deep valleys up to where they are safe and easily accessible. Apparently the mountains and valleys here stand for obstacles that are to be overcome by the Servant on behalf of His people (cf. 40:4). Faith in Christ makes mountains into mole-hills (cf. Mt. 17:20; 21:21; Mk. 11:23). Every obstacle to the knowledge of God may be destroyed with the weapons of the Servant (II Cor. 10:3-5).

v. 12-13 VERIFICATION: The Servant will also verify that God has kept His promise (Isa. 40:1-2) to "comfort" His people and bring their "warfare" to an end (see comments on Isa. 40:1-2). The Servant's people are to come from the far reaches of the world. We have again the universal nature of the messianic salvation. The return from exile in Babylon is no longer the focus. The prophet's revelation is now expanded to the whole world. The word *Siyniym* (Sinim) means, some commentators say, people of the wilderness of Sin, or the Sinites, a people of Canaan (Gen. 10:17; I Chron. 1:15). Gesenius says it means *Chinese.* Kyle and Delitzsch also believe it refers to people of the ancient land of China. The word *Tsin* can be traced back to about 1122-1115 B.C. as a name (in many different forms) of small states into which the empire of China was divided after the reign of Wu-wang. *Tsin,* according to the Sinologist Neumann, was the name of a feudal kingdom of some importance in Shen-si, one of the western most provinces of the land of China, and *Fei-tse,* the first feudal king of *Tsin,* began to reign as early as 897 B.C. It would be quite possible then for Isaiah to have heard of the land of the *Sinese.* Of course, there were no exiles in China from the Babylonian dispersion. However, there is documentation that there were Jews who immigrated from Persia to China during the Han dynasty (205 B.C.—220 A.D.). If Isaiah is speaking of the messianic era, as we think he is, then there is no problem with some people from China (Sinim) becoming followers of the Messiah. Since the emphasis is on distance from Palestine, China is more acceptable than the first two suggestions. Whatever the case, the whole universe is commanded to acknowledge in a hymn of praise that Jehovah has comforted His people and shown compassion to the afflicted. He has done it in the Person of the Servant who, despised and abhorred, tested in the crucible of incarnate weakness and disappointment, is now the exalted and desirable Savior.

QUIZ

1. What does the word Redeemer encompass?
2. Why was the Servant abhorred?
3. Can you name some of the kings and princes who worshiped Him?
4. What is the "acceptable" time?
5. What do you know about the Servant becoming a covenant?
6. Where do all the people come from to be comforted through the Servant?

c. DEJECTED ZION

TEXT: 49:14-21

14 But Zion said, Jehovah hath forsaken me, and the Lord hath forgotten me.
15 Can a woman forget her sucking child, that she should not have compassion on the son of her womb? yea, these may forget, yet will not I forget thee.
16 Behold, I have graven thee upon the palms of my hands; thy walls are continually before me.
17 Thy children make haste; thy destroyers and they that made thee waste shall go forth from thee.
18 Lift up thine eyes round about, and behold: all these gather themselves together, and come to thee. As I live, saith Jehovah, thou shalt surely clothe thee with them all as with an ornament, and gird thy self with them like a bride.
19 For, as for thy waste and thy desolate places, and thy land that hath been destroyed, surely now shalt thou be too strait for the inhabitants, and they that swallowed thee up shall be far away.
20 The children of thy bereavement shall yet say in thine ears, The place is too strait for me; give place to me that I may dwell.
21 Then shalt thou say in thy heart, Who hath begotten me

these, seeing I have been bereaved of my children, and am solitary, an exile, and wandering to and fro? and who hath brought up these? Behold, I was left alone; these, where were they?

QUERIES

a. Why would Zion think Jehovah had forsaken her?
b. How would Zion "clothe" herself with those coming to her?
c. Why does she ask, "Who hath begotten me these"?

PARAPHRASE

But those in Zion who have been listening to these predictions of their glorious future say, How can all this come to pass if we are to go into captivity? Surely Jehovah is showing that He has forsaken us and forgotten us if we must go away to Babylonian exile! So Jehovah answers, As incredible as it may seem, occasionally a mother may disown her own baby, but I will never disown My true Zion. Look! I have cut your name deeply into the flesh of the palms of My hands. Your walls may be broken down from time to time but I see them ultimately and eternally built up. When the time of the Servant comes I want you to observe that many of those who have previously been your destroyers will cease opposing you and will come to you and become a part of Zion. Your beauty will be enhanced by their joining you. You will look as lovely as a bride dressed for her wedding. You think your population will be decimated by the captivity, and your nationhood destroyed. I tell you you will become so populous you will think there is no room for all the people joining themselves to you and your destroyers will be made powerless. The descendants of those who shall go into exile will one day shout to you, Zion is not large enough for all these people; it must be enlarged. Then you will say in amazement, Where did all these children of Zion come from, seeing I have suffered so much destruction and death of my own children? I have spent most of my existence wandering to and fro, so how could I have produced all these children? Look, I was left all alone in captivity and no one seemed to come forth to help me, so where have all these children been hidden all this time?

COMMENTS

v. 14-18 MELANCHOLIA: The people of Zion are represented as being in a state of deep despondency. This is anticipating the nation of Judah in exile in Babylon. The Psalmist of the exile wrote: "By the rivers of Babylon, there we sat down, yea, we wept, when we remembered Zion . . ." (see Psa. 137:1f). The promises of the prophets were glorious but only the most thoroughly committed believer put much hope in them. All recent history taught the Jews was that nations taken captive into Mesopotamia disappeared or lost their national identity. The great empires had never allowed a conquered nation to return to its own homeland. Judah was certain Jehovah had forsaken her (cf. Lam. 5:1f).

The Lord left His people in Babylon for 70 years (two generations would have been born and reared in a foreign land). Some of those who were taken down to Babylon as captives of war undoubtedly died there without ever seeing their homeland again (perhaps Daniel and his three friends). It was a great temptation for many Jews to despair and to spread their discouragement among others. The Lord works slowly, as men are prone to count time, but He is absolutely faithful to keep His promises. One of the most beautiful promises of the Old Testament is pictorialized in verses 15-16. The Hebrew word *'ulah* is translated "sucking child" but means more literally an *infant* (newly born). On rare occasions one learns of a mother deserting her new-born child, but it is very unusual. The Lord's love for Zion is indestructible! He *cannot* forget her—it is not in His nature at all to forget His promises. He is preparing to sacrifice His only Son for her. True Zion is precious to Him. He has *khakak,* graven, them on the palms of His hands (not tattooed, but carved, etched deeply). He is constantly reminded of Zion! Her walls may be torn down by her enemies but in God's sovereign vision, they are constantly before Him as built up forever. Whatever God dreams or envisions comes to pass. God's dreams are not sand-castles. He has proven this through dreams and visions He manifested to the world by the instrumentality of His prophets. They all came to pass! So when God envisions the wells of Zion built forever, they shall be built forever! Maybe not in the lifetime of Isaiah, or the returned exiles, but when the Messiah arrives, He shall build the eternal walls of Zion (cf. Heb. 12:25-28, "a kingdom that cannot be shaken" is already being received by the recipients of the Hebrew epistle)!

Those contemporaries of Isaiah who read his prophecy should look and see that what God has promised about Zion is already beginning to happen, and believe. Already the *true* Zion is beginning to take shape. Already the sifting process is taking place. True believers in the long-range program of God are starting to separate themselves from those who are "destroyers" of Zion (unbelievers). Already Isaiah's teaching had begun to form a small band of "disciples" (Isa. 8:16-18), a "remnant," which would eventually include all "those who walked in darkness" even the Gentiles (Isa. 9:1-7). Jehovah swears by His own life (which is, of course, never ending and absolute) that Zion shall one day wear these few, faithful believers (of Isaiah's day) as a bride would her wedding finery (cf. Eph. 5:26-27; Rev. 12:1; 19:7-8; 21:2).

v. 19-21 MARVEL: Zion's melancholia would eventually turn to *marvel.* These verses indicate Isaiah is predicting a "spiritual" land of Zion. Zion's literal land has never been too small for her. She has never thought she had too many literal, physical "children." There were times, however, after the establishment of the New Testament church that some of the Jewish Christians (even Peter) wondered about the amazing and rapid growth of the new Zion (the church). Many were wondering how God could make room in "Zion" for Gentiles from all over the world! There has never been a time (especially after the return from exile) that the enemies ("those who swallowed up") of the Jews were literally far away. Enemies of the Jews have always been near and have continually oppressed them and "swallowed them up" (e.g., Sanballat, Alexander the Great, Antiochus IV, Pompey, the Mohammedans; in our lifetime, the Germans, Russians and Arabs). But spiritually, the Messiah defeated the arch-enemy of Zion, the devil, and bound him for a thousand years so that Zion's enemy is "far away." It is a constant source of wonder and amazement that Jehovah could take the small minority of believers exiled in Babylon and preserve them through centuries of "indignation" and eventually make of them a world-wide Zion (cf. Acts 11:1-8; 15:1-21, etc.).

We quote from Edward J. Young, "Even during the exile the tide was turning. God was raising up Cyrus, who would make it possible for the exiles to return to their home. In this return there is seen the first fulfillment of this promise, but in the deeper sense the fulfillment takes place in the distant future when the Gentiles are brought into the Church of Christ. Zion is bereaved, but she has children, so many that there is no room for them."

The remainder of this chapter confirms the messianic intent of the prophet.

QUIZ

1. What are other scriptures to indicate the despondency of the exiles?
2. Why is God unable to forget Zion?
3. When did they "remember" Zion?
4. How could the land be "too strait" for Zion?
5. Why can't this be literal Zion?

d. DELIVERED SOCIETY

TEXT: 49:22-26

22 Thus saith the Lord Jehovah, Behold, I will lift up my hand
to the nations, and set up my ensign to the peoples; and
they shall bring thy sons in their bosom, and thy daughters
shall be carried upon their shoulders.
23 And kings shall be thy nursing fathers, and their queens
thy nursing mothers: they shall bow down to thee with their
faces to the earth, and lick the dust of thy feet; and thou
shalt know that I am Jehovah; and they that wait for me
shall not be put to shame.
24 Shall the prey be taken from the mighty, or the lawful
captives be delivered?
25 But thus saith Jehovah, Even the captives of the mighty
shall be taken away, and the prey of the terrible shall be
delivered; for I will contend with him that contendeth with
thee, and I will save thy children.
26 And I will feed them that oppress thee with their own flesh;
and they shall be drunken with their own blood, as with
sweet wine: and all flesh shall know that I Jehovah, am thy
Saviour, and thy Redeemer, the Mighty One of Jacob.

QUERIES

a. Why put up a signal for the "nations"?
b. How does God contend with those who contend with Zion?
c. When did Jehovah take the "prey" away from the mighty?

PARAPHRASE

Now this is what the Lord Jehovah says, Look! I will give directions to the Gentiles and point out to them the sign I have set among the covenant people of My presence among men and they shall bring Zion's sons and daughters to her in gentle safety. Gentile kings and queens will be like foster-fathers and foster-mothers to you. They will humiliate themselves to Zion and serve her like slaves. Then you will acknowledge that I am Jehovah and realize that trusting in Me with faith and patience will result in victory. Now you are despondent, saying, It is utterly impossible for us to be rescued from mighty Babylon—the righteous usually do not escape from the unrighteous. But Jehovah replies, Quite to the contrary, and as incredible as it may seem, I will do as I have promised and rescue my people from the giant. They shall be the prey of the tyrant no longer. I, Jehovah, will make war against those who make war upon you. I will make your enemies feed upon one another—they will make war upon one another, until they stagger and reel with defeat like drunken men. When all this comes to pass then all mankind will have evidence to know that I am the One Sovereign Lord who saved His people and sets them free. This will be the revelation to all the world that I am the Mighty One of Jacob.

COMMENTS

v. 22-23 SIGNAL: Two different Hebrew words are used to denominate the recipients of Jehovah's "ensign"—*goim* (Gentiles, or nations) and *'ammim* (peoples). Girdlestone says, ". . . the word *goim* primarily signifies those nations which lived in the immediate neighborhood of the Jewish people; they were regarded as enemies, as ignorant of the truth, and sometimes as tyrants . . . If *goi* denotes a nation regarded from without, *'am* signified a people as viewed by one of themselves. Sometimes it (*'am*) is used in the familiar and domestic way in which we speak of 'folk' . . . It is often brought into direct . . . contrast with *goi.* Thus Moses, speaking to God concerning Israel, says, 'This nation (*goi*) is thy people (*'am*),' Exodus 33:13. *'Am* is used by Isaiah (and other prophets) to distinguish Israel as God's people, and to mark them off from the heathen *goim.*" Often Isaiah predicts that the *goim* who had not been *'ammim* should become the people of God through the messianic redemption. Psalms 18:43; for example, reads, "Thou hast made me the head of the heathen (*goim*); a people (*'am*) whom I have not known shall serve me." This will come to pass when Jehovah shall be acknowledged as holding rule as "King of the *goim*" (Jer. 10:7; Hos. 1:9-10; 2:23).

This by-play upon the words *goim* and *'ammim* in verse 22 seems to indicate the delivered society referred to, although it may begin with deliverance from exile by Cyrus, has its ultimate goal as the messianic society (the church). The setting up of an "ensign" (a battle standard upon a pole; a rallying flag) is one of Isaiah's favorite pictures of the coming Messiah (11:12; 18:3; 62:10). When God sends His Messiah to the world, the pagan nations are going to deliver up (by the preaching of the gospel) all whom God in His omniscience knows are His (both Jew and Gentile). The Lord once told Paul "I have many people in this city . . ." That city was Corinth (Acts 18:9-11). "Nursing fathers" is from the Hebrew word *'omenayik* (root word is *'man*) which means "foster-father" and its root meaning is "to stay, to support." The Hebrew word *yanak* ("nursing mothers") means literally "to suckle" and therefore may be translated "foster-mother." The whole idea is that kings and queens of the *goim* (heads of state of heathen nations) will one day become, as it were, parents or supporters of Zion! And the once haughty, domineering *goim* will come to Zion in all humility to serve as slaves of Zion and her King. This is the only way anyone can join Zion—humility and service. When Jehovah begins the great work He is predicting here then many will begin to acknowledge Him as Sovereign and look forward in faith to the completion of it all in the messianic kingdom (just when the completion is to come they will not know, cf. I Pet. 1:10-12). Those who thus "wait" in patient faith upon Jehovah's promises, even though they do not live to see them accomplished, (Heb. 11:13-16), will not be put to "shame" but will "stand at their allotted place at the end of the days . . ." (Dan. 12:13).

v. 24-26 SPECTACLE: Zion is not yet convinced. If Zion is taken captive by the mighty (*gibbor*) one (Babylon) how is it possible that she shall ever see kings and queens coming to her in humble service? The *lawful* captives are, in Hebrew, the *tsadiyk* or *righteous* captives. They are righteous compared to Babylon. The "righteous" are Jews essentially non-warlike as compared to "unrighteous" Babylon. It was historically unheard of that a nation taken from its homeland into exile by such self-serving empires as Babylon should ever reappear again in its own homeland. Jehovah predicts that Zion shall not only be returned to her homeland but her enemies shall serve her. Incredible as it may seem, Zion is going to be delivered from her mighty and terrible enemy. These verses apply to the return of the Jews from Babylonian exile at the decree of Cyrus the Persian. This is a prelude to the signal to the *goim* of verses 22-23 and their becoming foster-parents to Zion (the church). Zion needs first to believe that Jehovah will deliver her from Babylonian captivity. This is the first obstacle in the way to the formation of a remnant which will in turn perpetuate the true Zion through the centuries until the King of Zion appears. So God says, I will make war upon those who contend with Zion. This is one of the fundamental warnings of the Bible; "Leave God's people alone—do not harm them—for He is jealous for them." Whoever would attack the people of God attacks God! God even holds the world responsible for "standing aloof" when His people are being set upon (cf. our comments, Obadiah, v. 10-14, *Minor Prophets*, Butler, College Press). All God has to do is give pagan empires up to their own paganism and they turn on one another and bite and devour one another (cf. Rom. 1:24-32). The history of the unbelieving world of human governments is one long tale of war, tyranny, destruction and politico-socio cannibalism. Man, in his perverse rebellion against God, goes on devouring himself! It is a matter of history that when Cyrus took up the conquest of Babylon some of the satrapies of the Babylonian empire revolted and fought with the Persians against their former rulers. Isaiah's prediction came to pass specifically and generally.

QUIZ

1. Who are the "nations" and "peoples"?
2. Who is the "ensign"?
3. How will kings and queens become "nurses"?
4. How will those who wait upon Jehovah not be put to shame?
5. Why does Zion still think they may not be delivered from captivity?
6. How does Jehovah "feed" oppressors with their own flesh?

SPECIAL STUDY

PEOPLE OF THE PROPHETIC PROMISES

by Fred Long

I. Pre-Assyrian Prophets
   A. Obadiah
      1. v. 15-21 "The Kingdom shall be Jehovah's"
         a. Who: House of Jacob means God's covenant people (Acts 15:13-18, 13:29-37).
         b. When: Christian age, when Gentiles were added to kingdom (Acts 15:13-18).
         c. Where: Mt. Zion is the Church (Heb. 12:18-29).
   B. Joel
      1. 2:28-32 Promise of Holy Spirit
         a. Who: Twelve Apostles (Acts 2:14-21)
         b. When: Day of Pentecost—Christian age (Luke 1:68-75)
         c. Where: In Jerusalem (Heb. 12:22)
      2. 2:30—3:3 "Great and Terrible Day of the Lord"
         a. Who: Children of promise (Rom. 9:6)
         b. When: Second coming of Christ (Matthew 24:29)
         c. Where: Valley of Jehoshaphat—symbolic of Last Judgment

3. 3:17-21 Jerusalem shall be holy
    a. Who: Jerusalem—symbol of Church, Christians
    b. When: Messianic age (Hebrews 6:17-20)
    c. Where: Zion, Jerusalem is the Church (covenant people)

C. Jonah
1. 1:17 Jonah—symbol of Christ's death (Luke 11:30)
    a. Who: Christ (Matthew 12:40, 41—Matthew 16:4)
    b. When: Messianic age
    c. Where: Jerusalem (literal), Nineveh is type of Gentiles

D. Amos
1. 9:11-15 Raise up the Booth of David
    a. Who: Gentiles (Acts 15:14-18)
    b. When: Messianic age
    c. Where: Church

E. Hosea
1. 1:10-11 Great shall be Day of Jezreel
    a. Who: Gentiles (Romans 9:24-26; I Peter 2:9, 10)
    b. When: Messianic age (John 10)
2. 2:21-23 Pity on Not Pitied
    a. Who: Gentiles (Romans 9:25, 26)
    b. When: Messianic age
3. 3:4, 5 Israel shall return and seek Lord
    a. Who: Israel—Church (Hebrews 12:22)
    b. When: In latter days (Messianic)

II. Assyrian Prophets

A. Isaiah
1. 2:1-4 Mt. of the house of the Lord established as highest
    a. Who: Covenant people (Luke 24:47)
    b. When: Messianic age (Hebrews 12:22, 23; Col. 1:23)
    c. Where: Jerusalem (Church) (Romans 10:18)
2. 6:9, 10 Jews reject the Gospel
    a. Who: Jews (Matthew 13:14, 15; Mark 4:12)

   b. When: Jesus' ministry (parables) (Luke 8:10; John 12:40) (Romans 11:8)
3. 9:1, 2 Gentiles of Zebulun and Naphtali see Great Light
   a. Who: Gentiles (Matthew 4:13-17)
   b. When: Jesus traveled to Zebulun and Naphtali (Luke 1:32)
4. 10:21-23 Only remnant of Jacob will return
   a. Who: Gentiles (Romans 9:27, 28)
   b. When: Christian age
   c. Where: Church
5. 11:1-6 Shoot from the Stump of Jesse
   a. Who: Christ (Acts 13:23)
   b. When: Messianic age (Romans 15:12; Romans 12:12)
6. 29:13, 18, 19 Deaf shall hear, Blind shall see
   a. Who: Hypocracy of Jews (Matthew 11:5; 15:8-9)
   b. When: Jesus' ministry (Mark 7:22)
7. 35:8-10 Highway called the Holy Way
   a. Who: Covenant people (Matthew 13:14)
   b. When: Christian age
   c. Where: Zion—symbol of Church
8. 42:1-4 My Servant Brings Justice to the Nations
   a. Who: Gentiles (Matthew 11:4-5; 12:18-20; 3:16, 17)
   b. When: Jesus' ministry (Matthew 17:5)
9. 49:6 Light to the Nations
   a. Who: Gentiles (Luke 2:32)
   b. When: Christian age (Acts 13:47; 26:23)
   c. Where: Ends of the earth
10. 54:1, 13 Children of the desolate
   a. Who: Gentiles (Gal. 4:27)
   b. When: Christian age (John 6:45)
11. 55:3 Everlasting Covenant
   a. Who: Covenant People (Christians) (Romans 10:5; Acts 13:34)
   b. When: Christian age (Luke 22:37)

12. 56:8 I will gather others
    a. Who: Gentiles (John 10:16)
    b. When: Jesus' ministry
13. 61:1, 2 Day of Vengeance
    a. Who: Jesus (Luke 4:18; Matthew 5:4)
    b. When: Jesus' ministry (read in synagogue) (Mark 4:17-21; Luke 21:21-28)
    c. Where: Nazareth
14. 65:1, 2 Jews rebellious
    a. Who: Jews (Romans 10:20, 21)
    b. When: Messianic age

B. Micah
   1. 4:1-7 Mountain of the House of the Lord (Isa. 2:2-4)
      a. Who: Covenant people (Luke 24:47)
      b. When: Messianic age (Heb. 12:22; Col. 1:23)
      c. Where: Jerusalem (Church) (Romans 10:18; Luke 1:33; Rev. 11:15)

C. Nahum

III. Chaldean Prophets

A. Zephaniah
   1. 2:7 Seacoast shall become possession of remnant of the house of Judah (Luke 1:68)
      a. Who: Covenant people (remnant of Judah)
      b. When: Birth of Christ
      c. Where: Bethlehem

B. Habakkuk
   1. 1:5 Unbelief of Jews
      a. Who: Jews (Acts 13:41)
      b. When: Christian Age
   2. 2:4 Righteous shall live by Faith
      a. Who: Gentiles (Hebrews 10:38, 39)
      b. When: Christian age (Romans 1:17; Gal. 3:11)

C. Jeremiah (and Lamentations)
   1. 3:14-18 Jerusalem called Throne of the Lord
      a. Who: All nations

b. When: Christian age (Acts 20:28)
c. Where: Jerusalem and Zion—symbol of Church

2. 6:10 Jews reject the Gospel
   a. Who: Jews (Acts 7:51)
   b. When: Christian age
   c. Where: Jerusalem
3. 9:25 Punishment of "uncircumcised" in heart
   a. Who: Jews (outwardly) (Romans 2:8, 9, 28)
   b. When: Christian age
4. 17:25 Jerusalem inhabited forever
   a. Who: Covenant people (Christians) (Luke 1:32)
   b. When: Christian age (Hebrews 12:22)
   c. Where: The heavenly Jerusalem (Church)
5. 31:1 All Israel will be saved
   a. Who: Gentiles (Romans 11:26-28)
   b. When: Christian age
6. 31:31-34 Promise of a New Covenant
   a. Who: Covenant people (Gentiles) (John 6:45)
   b. When: Christian age (Hebrews 8:8-12; Romans 11:27; I Thes. 4:9)
7. 33:16-18 Judah will be saved
   a. Who: Covenant people (Hebrews 13:15; Phil. 3:9)
   b. When: Christian age (Luke 1:32, 33)

IV. Exilic Prophets

A. Ezekiel

1. 39:29 Promise of Holy Spirit
   a. When: Pentecost (Acts 2:17)
2. 47:21-23 Aliens shall be allotted an inheritance
   a. Who: Gentiles (Romans 10:12)
   b. When: Christian age (Eph. 2:12-14; 3:6)
   c. Where: In the Church (Col. 3:11)

B. Daniel

1. 2:44-45 God's Kingdom set up—never be destroyed
   a. Who: Christians (I Cor. 15:24)
   b. When: During Roman Empire (Iron Kingdom)
   c. Where: Heavenly Kingdom

2. 9:24-27 Promise of Coming Kingdom
   a. Who: Covenant people (Christians) (Matthew 9:12; Luke 19:43)
   b. When: After seventy weeks of years—Christian age
   c. Where: Jerusalem (heavenly)—Church (Matthew 24:15; Luke 21:20)

V. Post-Exilic Prophets

A. Haggai
   1. 2:6, 7 I will shake the heavens and the earth
      a. Who: New Covenant people (Hebrews 12:26)
      b. When: Christian age
      c. Where: Heavenly Kingdom—Church
B. Zechariah
   1. 13:1 Fountain opened for the House of David
      a. Who: Covenant people (Hebrews 9:14)
      b. When: Christian age
      c. Where: Jerusalem (heavenly)—Church
C. Malachi
   1. 4:5, 6 Return of Elijah the Prophet
      a. Who: John the Baptist (Matthew 11:14)
      b. When: Before Jesus' ministry (Mark 9:11)
      c. Where: Israel (literal) (Luke 1:17)

VI. New Testament scriptures that show the Gentiles taking part in prophetic promises:

Acts 26:17-23
Acts 28:25-29
Romans 2:28, 29
Romans 9:6-8
Romans 9:24-31
Romans 10:13
Romans 11:11, 25
Romans 15:12
Ephesians 2:11-16
Galatians 4:24-31
Hebrews 12:18-24

2. TEACH, CHAPTER 50

a. OBJECTIONS CANCELLED

TEXT: 50:1-3

1 Thus saith Jehovah, Where is the bill of your mother's divorcement, wherewith I have put her away? or which of my creditors is it to whom I have sold you? Behold for your iniquities were ye sold, and for your transgressions was your mother put away.
2 Wherefore, when I came, was there no man? when I called, was there none to answer? Is my hand shortened at all, that it cannot redeem? or have I no power to deliver? Behold, at my rebuke I dry up the sea, I make the rivers a wilderness: their fish stink, because there is no water, and die for thirst.
3 I clothe the heavens with blackness, and I make sackcloth their covering.

QUERIES

a. Why bring up the subject of divorce?
b. What is meant by the question, ". . . was there no man"?
c. What do "stinking fish" have to do with the subject?

PARAPHRASE

This is what Jehovah says to your objections: I am the husband, you are my wife. You know My law says when a husband divorces his wife he must give her a written certificate of divorce. You say I have divorced you, Israel, and I am putting you away—where is the certificate? No, I have not divorced you, you have left me. Look at it another way: Do you think you have gone into slavery because I sold you to pay somebody a debt I owed them? I owe no one! You are going into slavery because you wanted to be as much like the Babylonians as possible.

It is your rebellion against Me and your infatuation with and dependence upon ungodly men that will bring about your enslavement to them. Why did everyone try to hide and keep away from Me when I came to save you? Why did no one answer Me when I called through My prophets? Have I ever given anyone reason to think that I could not save you from every enemy? No, you and all your ancestors have seen with your own eyes that I have saved you from greater powers than men. I have dried up seas and rivers and some of you have seen the heaps of rotting, stinking fish when this has happened. I have also worked great miracles in the heavens which some of your ancestors saw and have written in your scriptures. No, you are not going to be enslaved because I am powerless to help you or because I wanted it that way, says Jehovah.

COMMENTS

v. 1 ACCUSATIONS: Judah is trying to justify herself against Jehovah's accusations (through His prophets) and against His promise of her impending captivity, with some accusations of her own! Judah is trying to blame Jehovah for her troubles with Babylon. She is accusing Jehovah of casting her off "illegally," or without justification. That is the impenitent sinner's usual ruse. Jehovah answers by referring them to His Law. The Law of Jehovah is, of course, His will—a revelation in human terms of His very nature. It is not Jehovah's nature to do anything without justification. In the matter of divorce, for example, if there is legal cause for a man to put away his wife, he must certify the legality of it by a written bill of divorcement (Dt. 24:1f). There is no written "bill of divorcement" from Jehovah. Israel is separated from Jehovah by her own doing—not His! She has gone after other lovers (cf. Hosea 1-3). The Lord did not want the separation, nor is He responsible for it. Another objection Israel might propose is that the Lord will give her up to slavery because Babylon has some claim upon Him. The thought is preposterous. Jehovah owes no one! Jehovah is not man that He has creditors. No one has any claims upon Him! Israel will go away into slavery because of her own weaknesses, not God's. Judah had flirted with the Babylonians off and on for a number of years (cf. comments on Isaiah, ch. 36-39). The separation was her doing, not the Lord's. Jehovah's attitude toward Israel is graphically portrayed in the experience of Hosea with his wife.

v. 2-3 ACTUALITIES: Israel has accused Jehovah of insensitively casting her off. The actual facts are quite different. Many times Jehovah came to Israel (through prophets and providential judgments and redemptions) to rescue her from her headlong plunge into pagan slavery, but she would not listen. This is the historical record! Furthermore, the actual facts are that God demonstrated that He not only wanted to save Israel from enslavement but He had the power to save her. Time and time again He came, but none responded. In fact, He was rejected (cf. Isa. 30:8-11), until in the fulness of time He came incarnate to His own and they crucified Him! Delitzsch interprets these as the words of The Servant. Certainly 50:4f would seem to be The Servant's, and these may very well be His also. The apparent reference to the Red Sea exodus (". . . at my rebuke I dry up the sea . . .") would indicate these to be the words of Jehovah. Since Jehovah and the Servant are essentially One (Jn. 1:1-18; 14:8-11; Col. 1:19; 2:9), Isaiah constantly shifts from One to the other in these latter chapters. This is not unusual. It is the "shortened perspective" aspect of O.T. prophecy. It may be nearer the correct interpretation to understand Jehovah as the speaker in 50:1-3 and the Servant in 50:4-11. Whatever the case, the point of this passage is to emphasize the righteousness and justness of God in Israel's imminent enslavement and to implore Israel again that He is not only willing but able to save her if she will hearken to His leading. The final and full revelation of Jehovah's redemptive purpose will be in the Person of The Servant, and that is who addresses Israel next.

QUIZ

1. What kind of accusation is Jehovah countering by the reference to a bill of divorcement?
2. What accusation would be answered by speaking of "creditors"?
3. Why did Israel go away into captivity?
4. Who is speaking in verses one-three?
5. How has Jehovah demonstrated His power to save?

b. OBEDIENT CHRIST

TEXT: 50:4-9

4 The Lord Jehovah hath given me the tongue of them that are taught, that I may know how to sustain with words him that is weary: he wakeneth morning by morning, he wakeneth mine ear to hear as they that are taught.

5 The Lord Jehovah hath opened mine ear, and I was not rebellious, neither turned away backward.

6 I gave my back to the smiters, and my cheeks to them that plucked off the hair; I hid not my face from shame and spitting.

7 For the Lord Jehovah will help me; therefore have I not been confounded: therefore have I set my face like a flint, and I know that I shall not be put to shame.

8 He is near that justifieth me; who will contend with me? let us stand up together: who is mine adversary? let him come near to me.

9 Behold, the Lord Jehovah will help me; who is he that shall condemn me? behold, they all shall wax old as a garment; the moth shall eat them up.

QUERIES

a. What is the "tongue of them that are taught"?
b. What is significant about "plucking" hair from the cheek?
c. How did he "set his face like a flint"?

PARAPHRASE

The Servant of Israel who comes to redeem Zion speaks. The Lord Jehovah gives Me words of divine wisdom so that I may sustain the weary and despairing. I am in constant communion with the will of Jehovah just like an obedient disciple to His Master. The Lord Jehovah speaks His commandments to Me and I keep them—I do not rebel and turn away from them. I willingly conform to Jehovah's plan and will offer my back to those who will smite me. I will suffer the humiliation of having thc hairs of my beard plucked out by my tormentors. I will not be resentful or rebel when my enemies try to shame me by spitting in my face. I will trust completely in the Lord Jehovah for He will come to My aid. My intention to do His will cannot be thwarted by such actions and I will not be distracted from His will by them. I have set my will as hard as diamond to do His will and I know that ultimately I will be glorified in doing so. He is always present and He will vindicate My trust in Him. He will show to the world once and for all that I am sinless and righteous. If there is someone in all creation who can prove any unrighteousness against Me, let him stand up and present his case! There is no one! The enemies of the Servant may falsely accuse Him, but they will all be put to shame as easily as a moth devours old, worn-out clothes.

COMMENTS

v. 4-7 DISCIPLINED: The Hebrew word *limmudiym* (them that are taught; could be translated *disciples* for it is the same word as is used in Isaiah 8:16. It is the root word from which the later Hebrew word *Talmud* (instruction) was derived. Jehovah will equip the Servant with divine wisdom and instruction. The obedient character of the Servant is being emphasized. He will hear the commandment of Jehovah and do it (cf. Mt. 3:17; 17:5; Jn. 8:29; 14:31; 15:10; Rom. 5:19; Phil. 2:5-8; Heb. 5:8; 10:9), as compared with Israel who had the commandment of God taught to them by the prophets and did *not* hear and obey. The Servant, experiencing obedience, will become the "pathfinder" (Gr. *archegon,* in Heb. 2:10) of our salvation. He will be able to "succor" those who must also experience obedience (Heb. 2:18). Why did the Servant (Jesus) need to "learn obedience through the things He suffered" (Heb. 5:8-9)? Was He disobedient? Was He less than perfect? Were there things He did not know and could only know by chastening and instruction? Perhaps we shall never know fully the profound, divine mystery of the *kenosis* (humiliation) of the Son of God. Perhaps, in His willing choice to suffer the humiliation of incarnation (becoming flesh), He must, in some way *experience* discipline in order to fulfill the whole experience of incarnation. He was subject to His earthly parents as well as to His Heavenly Father. He did grow in wisdom and stature and in favor with God and man (cf. Lk. 2:40, 51, 52). Perhaps He did not need to experience obedience for His own sake but for ours. If we are to really believe He knows and cares about our chastenings—if we are to have realistic (not superficial) commitment and discipleship to Him—then the Servant must experience suffering and obedience. He must obey the Father's commandments at the cost of self—not for Himself but for us. So the Servant, God-incarnate, is given the tongue of them that are taught, that He may know how to sustain with words him that is weary.

The phrase "he wakeneth morning by morning" emphasizes the continuous, unreserved obedience of the Servant. He always obeys. He never takes a day off from obeying the Father. It was His *mission to obey* the Father! (Jn. 12:27; Heb. 10:5f). It was His mission to teach mankind what obedience to the Father involved and produced. There was not the slightest rebellion in the Servant. He was tempted; He was tested—supremely—but He did not yield. Moses, Jeremiah, Jonah, and a host of other servants objected and some even tried to resist the Lord's call (cf. Ex. 4:10ff; Jer. 20:7ff; 17:16; Jonah 1:3). The Servant did not turn back from serving Jehovah for one moment (cf. Mt. 4:1-11; Jn. 4:34; 9:4; Heb. 10:5-10, etc.).

The Servant's experience of obedience involved "giving His back to the smiters." He was to be delivered up for such humiliation and suffering according to the definite plan and foreknowledge of God (cf. Acts 2:23). Yet it was not without His willing surrender to God's plan for He had the power to lay down His life and the power to take it up. No one took His life from Him (cf. Jn. 10:17-18). Whatever He did or whatever was done to Him, He allowed it to be (cf. Jn. 19:10-11) in obedience to the plan of His Father. He allowed His tormentors to "pluck off the hair" which refers no doubt to His beard. Many passages in the Bible seem to show that the Jews let their beards grow. Psalm 132 directly states that Aaron, Moses' brother, had a beard; and balm flowed down it to the very skirts of his robe. The Oriental regarded the beard as a sign of freedom and respect, and to pluck out the hair of the beard is to show utter contempt. The most heinous and degrading insult is to spit in the face of another. It is nothing short of impossible to willingly subject oneself to such humiliation without resentment, rebellion and perhaps revenge. But the Servant did it! (cf. Mt. 26:67; 27:26; Jn. 19:1ff). And He did it for us!

v. 7-9 DEFENDED: The power of the Servant to render such unreserved obedience is in His unreserved trust in Jehovah to vindicate Him. Whatever the Servant has to suffer, Jehovah will ultimately make right. Furthermore, Jehovah will give the Servant divine assistance. The Servant's secret is godly faith and dependence (cf. Heb. 5:7) that Jehovah will, in His own good time, turn the Servant's humiliation into everlasting exaltation. So the Servant sets His face "like a flint" to do Jehovah's will (cf. Lk. 9:51-53). The Hebrew word *hallamiys* is translated "flint" but Young says it is comparable to the

Akkaddian word *elmesu* which means *diamond.* The point to be illustrated is that the Servant will not be detered by anything from doing the will of Jehovah because the servant has complete confidence in Jehovah's justification. The reason the Servant has such confidence is His constant companionship and communion with Jehovah (cf. Jn. 14:10-11; 15:9-10; 16:25-28; 17:1-26, etc.). Jesus knew, mentally, emotionally and experientially the constant presence of Jehovah and He *lived,* not by bread alone, but by God's abiding presence (Mt. 4:4; Jn. 4:34)—that is how *near* God was to Jesus. When God justifies, who is there to condemn (cf. Rom. 8:31-39)?! The enemies of the Servant abused Him, slandered Him, perjured themselves bearing false witness against Him, tormented Him, accused Him and crucified Him as a criminal, but God raised Him from the dead showing the Servant was right and not His accusers! The cause of the Servant's enemies was "as full of holes as a garment eaten by moths." They went the way of all flesh, but the Servant lives forever! The same exaltation given the Servant is offered to all who faithfully serve the Servant. If we belong to the Servant, God is for us. If God is for us, who can be against us! We are justified because our faith is in the justified Servant.

QUIZ

1. What characteristic of the Servant is being stressed in this text?
2. Why did the Servant need to experience obedience?
3. What is the meaning of "morning by morning"?
4. Why say the Servant "gave" his back to the smiters?
5. How did the Servant have the ability to render such unreserved obedience?
6. How did Jehovah justify the Servant?

c. OUTCOME CONFIRMED

TEXT: 50:10-11

10 Who is among you that feareth Jehovah, that obeyeth the voice of his servant? he that walketh in darkness, and hath no light, let him trust in the name of Jehovah, and rely upon his God.
11 Behold, all ye that kindle a fire, that gird yourselves about with firebrands; walk ye in the flame of your fire, and among the brands that ye have kindled. This shall ye have of my hand; ye shall lie down in sorrow.

QUERIES

a. How could people of Isaiah's day obey the "servant"?
b. What is the "fire" that is kindled?

PARAPHRASE

Whoever among Israel says he fears Jehovah must give obedient belief to all I have said about the coming Servant. There will be times when you will have to struggle through dark hours of tribulation because you belong to Jehovah and you may not be able to understand it all. Remember what I say about My Servant. He too shall suffer dark tribulation. But you, Israel, follow the Servants obedient life and trust in the name of Jehovah. Put yourself totally dependent upon your God. On the other hand, you among Israel who ignite the hellish fire of rebellion against Me and My Servant and arm yourselves with the fiery darts of Satan, you go ahead and build your fires as big as you want and gather as many of Satan's firebrands as you desire. Those who play with that fire are sure to be burned up with it. I will take this fire you have ignited and turn it upon you and you will be struck down to suffer torments.

COMMENTS

v. 10 STRENGTH: Israel is offered two options in relation to Jehovah's prediction of the coming Servant. The outcome depends on one's attitude toward Jehovah's coming Servant. Parenthetically, it may be well to point out here that the "Servant" cannot possibly be the nation Israel since fearing the Lord and hearkening to the voice of the Servant are synonymous. Hearkening to human Israel (even the best of Israel) cannot be seriously equated with fearing Jehovah. By "obeying" the voice of the Servant is meant believing, accepting and obeying the predictions of the coming Servant insofar as their limited revelation of God's will at that time would direct them in such obedience. Israel must believe that God's redemptive purposes were to be fulfilled in a coming "suffering Christ" (I Pet. 1:10-12) and prepare themselves to be used by Jehovah as the instrument of that coming by obeying God's instructions for them. Israel may have to walk in centuries of "darkness" (tribulation and indignation) but she must trust in the name of Jehovah and *yisshae'n* (Hebrew for "lean upon for support") *rely* upon God. Israel is to follow the example of the mysterious Servant who will come and be willingly obedient even in the face of extreme humiliation. Then Israel may expect to be vindicated and exalted as is predicted of the Servant. That is Israel's first option—the one Jehovah desires she choose.

v. 11 SORROW: The other option is rebellion. Those who opt for rebellion are those who play with fire. Fire is used chiefly as a figure of destruction, doom, torment, wrath, anger. Those who rebel against God are toying with forces that destroy those who continue to kindle them. Rebellion against the Creator is self-destructive for the creature (Rom. 1:18ff). Jehovah speaks ironically, "walk ye in the flame of your fire . . ." or, "Go ahead and rebel if you insist. . . ." (cf. Isa. 1:2, 20; Ezek. 2:3; 20:8, 13, 21; Dan. 9:5, 9; Isa. 30:1, 9; 65:2, etc.). The Lord will take this rebellion in His hand and turn it against the rebels until they are struck down in sorrow. Rebellion can never lead to happiness. It always leads to sorrow. When the

Jewish people rejected their Servant-Messiah their rebellion eventuated in the Roman holocaust. The sorrow of the Jew has been unceasing. He can never find happiness until he "obeys the voice of the Servant."

QUIZ

1. Why does this verse preclude the possibility of national Israel being the "Servant"?
2. How may Israel of Isaiah's day obey the voice of the Servant?
3. Why is rebellion self-destructive?
4. How did the rebellion of the Jews against the Servant lead to their sorrow?

3. RULE, CHAPTER 51

a. TURN TO JUSTICE

TEXT: 51:1-8

1 Hearken to me, ye that follow after righteousness, ye that seek Jehovah: look unto the rock whence ye were hewn, and to the hole of the pit whence ye were digged.

2 Look unto Abraham your father, and unto Sarah that bare you; for when he was but one I called him, and I blessed him, and made him many.

3 For Jehovah hath comforted Zion; he hath comforted all her waste places, and hath made her wilderness like Eden, and her desert like the garden of Jehovah; joy and gladness shall be found therein, thanksgiving, and the voice of melody.

4 Attend unto me, O my people; and give ear unto me, O my nation: for a law shall go forth from me, and I will establish my justice for a light of the peoples.

5 My righteousness is near, my salvation is gone forth, and mine arms shall judge the peoples; the isles shall wait for me, and on mine arm shall they trust.

6 Lift up your eyes to the heavens, and look upon the earth beneath; for the heavens shall vanish away like smoke, and the earth shall wax old like a garment; and they that dwell therein shall die in like manner: but my salvation shall be for ever, and my righteousness shall not be abolished.
7 Hearken unto me, ye that know righteousness, the people in whose heart is my law; fear ye not the reproach of men, neither be ye dismayed at their revilings.
8 For the moth shall eat them up like a garment, and the worm shall eat them like wool; but my righteousness shall be for ever, and my salvation unto all generations.

QUERIES

a. Why look unto Abraham and Sarah?
b. Is the garden of Eden to be reestablished on earth?
c. How could anyone have the law of God in their heart before Christ?

PARAPHRASE

Listen to Me, you small and fearful remnant: If you are truly seeking to know Jehovah and wanting His way of life, look unto the character of your ancestors Abraham and Sarah—that is where you will find an example of what you seek. I called this one man, Abraham, and he responded in faith and obedience. I delivered him from all that opposed him and made of him a great nation. Now Jehovah has promised to deliver and strengthen true Zion, a small remnant though she may be. He has promised to change Zion's despair and destitution into a salvation that will restore the fellowship between Him and man which was present in Eden. True joy and thanksgiving will abound when this has come to pass. Listen to Me, O My people: I am going to send into the world the final and full expression of My will and it will be a revelation to the Gentiles as well, to bring them to salvation. This is near—it is as good as done. When it comes to fulfillment (and it is beginning now), it will be both salvation and judgment; salvation for all (even Gentiles) who trust in Me, and judgment upon those who reject My will. Study the universe: both the heavens and the earth are doomed to disintegration and dissolution. All humanity likewise is dying. But what I will and what I work shall endure forever. Listen to Me, you who have allowed My will to rule your mind and heart so that you are doing right: Do not fear the threats of human beings, no matter how powerful they may appear to be. They will all be consumed and disappear like a garment eaten by moths, but My righteousness and salvation will endure forever.

COMMENTS

v. 1-5 ESTABLISHED: This chapter predicts the coming of Jehovah's rule of justice through His law. It is, of course, an integral part of the whole section discussing *Salvation Through God's Servant* (*ch. 40-53*). Thus we are to understand Jehovah's predicted rule of justice will be through the coming Servant. This chapter is a special message to that small remnant of true believers contemporary with Isaiah. They are designated "ye that follow after righteousness, ye that seek Jehovah." The majority of people in Isaiah's day did not follow after righteousness. And even the remnant which did was sorely tempted to give up all hope. In view of the depraved morality and hypocritical religiosity of most of Israel and in view of the dreadful predictions of the true prophets of God that Babylonian captivity was near, the remnant must be encouraged. This remmant was sincere in its search for righteousness. The Hebrew word *rodephey* is translated *follow after* in the ASV, but is stronger and more properly translated *pursue* as in the RSV. There was not much righteousness to be found among this nation. They were a people "laden with iniquity" (Isa. 1:4, etc.). Only a few "disciples" of Isaiah (Isa. 8:16) desired real justice and the rule of Jehovah. The Lord encourages them to believe that He will establish His rule of justice by directing them to look backward to what He did through Abraham and to look forward to what He promises to do in the future. To the tiny remnant of Isaiah's disciples it may appear impossible that Jehovah's rule of justice will ever be established. However, Jehovah is able to do the impossible! Let the remnant look back to the "rock from which" the nation was hewn—Abraham—and the "hole of the pit" from which it was digged—Sarah. That Jehovah could produce a nation of many people from one man and woman who were past the age of child-bearing was thought impossible. Nevertheless, from one lone sojourner who had a wife whose womb was barren and who was beyond the age of bearing children and who bore only one child, God produced a nation. Of course, Jehovah could not have done it without the faith of Abraham and Sarah (cf. Rom. 4:1-25; Gal. 3:6-9; 4:21-27; Heb. 11:8-12; Heb. 11:17-22; James 2:18-26). This is the point. God is able to save this remnant and through them establish His rule of justice, but they must be people of stedfast faith like their forefather Abraham. Through one man, Abraham, and through the one son of Abraham, Isaac, God formed a people for Himself. But this people rejected His rule. Through the one "Seed" (Christ) of Abraham, Jehovah will produce a new Israel who will submit to His rule (cf. Gal. 3:15-29; 6:13-16). Isaiah's "remnant" must believe even though they may not receive what is promised; they must see it and greet it from afar (cf. Heb. 11:13-16). A remnant must be preserved through which the Messiah-Servant may come and establish the rule of Jehovah's justice (cf. Isa. 9:7; 11:1-9, etc.).

Jehovah's *comforting* of Zion will reach its culmination in the coming Servant (cf. comments Isa. 40:1-11; 49:13). Verse three is in the "predictive present." What Jehovah will do through the Servant is so certain it may be spoken of by Him as having already been accomplished! When the Servant finishes comforting Zion, all Zion's spiritual desolation and moral destitution will be turned into a righteousness that will be like Eden restored. The prophet is not here intending that the land of Palestine shall be physically restored to the flora and fauna of pre-fallen Eden. This world is destined (including Palestine) for destruction (cf. II Pet. 3:1-13). The prophet is speaking of a restoration of spiritual paradise; a restored Zion over which Jehovah rules in righteousness and justice, in which there shall be joy and gladness (see comments Isa. 35:8-10).

Jehovah will comfort Zion through a rule of *torah* (law). This is not the law of Moses in commandments and ordinances which "stood against us" (Col. 2:13-15). No man could be justified by that law (cf. Gal. 3:10-14; 5:1-6). This is the "law of the Spirit of life in Christ Jesus" (cf. Rom. 8:1-17). Young calls it, "in particular . . . the law of faith, given 'by the commandment of the everlasting God, made known to all nations for the obedience of faith' (Rom. 16:26)." It is that final and full revelation of the will of God for man's salvation which also sets before man what God requires of him. It is the same going forth of His law as predicted in Isaiah 2:1-4. This rule of Jehovah through the law of the Servant will provide light for all people (cf. comments on Isa. 9:1ff).

The Lord's righteousness is *near.* Near is relative to God's perspective! All time is as one day with Jehovah. When He declares a thing, it is as good as done. He will begin His great work toward this coming of the Servant with the Babylonian captivity and release from it through Cyrus. Israel may know Jehovah's salvation is on its way when they see Him "judge" the peoples by His arm. When these great empires fall and Israel continues to survive she may know that His salvation is so certain it may be said to be *near* (Heb. 11:13-16). For a discussion of the meaning of "isles" see comments on 41:1ff.

v. 6-8 ENDURING: What seems as if it will go on and on, unalterably fixed and sure (the heavens and the earth) will one day vanish. Even the perpetuity of the human race *seems* assured. But it too will expire. Only that which is saved by Jehovah will endure forever. What is declared *right* (His righteousness) by Jehovah is eternal because that is truth. Anything declared *not right* by Jehovah will perish. And how does man know what God declares right?—by hearkening unto God's law! And what is this law which is in the heart?—it is the law of Christ, the law of faith which was in the heart of Abraham and by which he was justified (cf. Rom. 4:1-25). It is the will of God concerning redemption through the Servant (cf. Isa. 42:1-4)—the Servants law. That this law (or will) of God concerning future salvation through an atoning Servant was written on the hearts of some before Christ was born is evidenced by Abraham rejoicing to see Christ's day (Jn. 8:56), Isaiah seeing the glory of the Christ (Jn. 12:41), the prophets inquiring about Him (I Pet. 1:10-12) and from all the faithful in Hebrews, chapter 11. The prophecy in Jeremiah 31:31-34 does not exclude every Jew of the Old Testament dispensation from the capacity to have God's law written on their heart through faith. If that should be the case, it would contradict Romans 4, et al. The Jeremiah 31 passage, taken in harmony with this passage in Isaiah, seems to say that out of a *small* remnant of O.T. saints who believe God's promises about an atoning Servant (the law of Jehovah about the Servant "written on their hearts"), Jehovah is going to form a new covenant people who will be covenant people *only* because they have His law written on their hearts and not because they were physically born to a particular nationality. In other words, there was a nucleus of people in the O.T. with Jehovah's will (law) written on their hearts and they were justified, in prospect, by their faith. When the Servant came and fulfilled the predicted atonement, these O.T. believers were justified in fact (cf. Heb. 9:15-16). The message of God expressed in all the sacrifices and offerings and in all the prophecies of the suffering Servant was that man could not atone for his sins by any works—God alone could provide atonement. Now when the O.T. believer *took that to heart*, with the moral and doctrinal implications it had for his life, then he had the law of God written on his heart! The goal of all this is, of course, the New Testament dispensation. Without that goal the faith of the O.T. believer could not have justified him. If the Servant had not come and accomplished the atonement which was typified and prophesied there could have been no law of God written on any heart either before the fact or after. The N.T. covenant is enacted upon better promises because it is after the fact of the Servant's work.

Those who have the law of faith written on their hearts do not need to fear the threats of those who stand in opposition to the rule of Jehovah's Servant. Those who stand for the rule of the Servant will always be in the minority. Those who stand against the rule of the Servant will always be in the majority and will control all the resources of human power. But Jehovah has revealed historically that He is more powerful than all human power put together. His righteousness (what He declares right) will endure every opposition. There may be those of ethnic Israel who do not want to know that what God says is right (cf. Isa. 30:9-11), but those who are true Israel do not need to fear for what God says is right and will last forever.

QUIZ

1. What is "following" after righteousness?
2. What relationship does Abraham have to the needs of Isaiah's audience?
3. How will Jehovah comfort Zion?
4. What is the law that goes forth from Jehovah?
5. How is the Lord's salvation near?
6. How may we say some of the people of Isaiah's day had the the law of God written on their hearts?
7. How are they to know the righteousness of God can withstand all opposition and endure forever?

b. TRUST IN JEHOVAH

TEXT: 51:9-16

9 Awake, awake, put on strength, O arm of Jehovah; awake,
as in the days of old, the generations of ancient times. Is

it not thou that didst cut Rahab in pieces, that didst pierce
the monster?
10 Is it not thou that driedst up the sea, the waters of the great
deep; that madest the depths of the sea a way for the redeemed to pass over?
11 And the ransomed of Jehovah shall return, and come with
singing unto Zion; and everlasting joy shall be upon their
heads: they shall obtain gladness and joy; and sorrow and
sighing shall flee away.
12 I, even I, am he that comforteth you: who art thou, that
thou art afraid of man that shall die, and of the son of man
that shall be made as grass;
13 and hast forgotten Jehovah thy Maker, that stretched forth
the heavens, and laid the foundations of the earth; and
feareth continually all the day because of the fury of the
oppressor, when he maketh ready to destroy? and where is
the fury of the oppressor?
14 The captive exile shall speedily be loosed; and he shall not
die and go down into the pit, neither shall his bread fail.
15 For I am Jehovah thy God, who stirreth up the sea, so that
the waves thereof roar: Jehovah of hosts is his name.
16 And I have put my words in thy mouth, and have covered
thee in the shadow of my hand, that I may plant the heavens,
and lay the foundations of the earth, and say unto Zion,
Thou art my people.

QUERIES

a. Does Jehovah have to be awakened?
b. Who is the captive exile?
c. Into whose mouth has Jehovah put his words?

PARAPHRASE

Help! Help! Come forth to help us girded with power as You did for our ancestors in olden times, O Lord. Did You not slay the "Big Mouth" dragon, Egypt? Did You not dry up a path through the great Red Sea for Your people to walk across and escape from Egyptian slavery? You have promised: Those whom the Lord purchases with a ransom-price will return to Him and to Zion rejoicing with songs about their redemption. Everlasting joy will crown their whole lives. They shall finally find the refreshment of their souls for which they have longed. All that would frustrate or hinder their travel will be made to disappear. Jehovah answers: Yes, I, the same God who delivered your ancestors, Am the God who is coming forth to deliver you. What kind of people are you that are so afraid of human beings? Mortal man is no more enduring than the grass of the field! Have you forgotten Jehovah, your Maker, who spread the stars through the skies and brought the earth into existence? Are you in constant dread of the oppressions of men? Are you paralyzed with terror at the anger of your enemies. Soon Zion shall be set free; dungeon, starvation and death are not going to put an end to Zion. Remember, I am Jehovah, your God, Lord of all creation. I control the sea and everything else. Zion's deliverance will be revealed and accomplished through My Servant, for I have put my words in His mouth and I protect Him with My mighty hand. Through Him I will make a whole new creation, a new Zion, who shall truly be My people.

COMMENTS

v. 9-11 PLEA: The Hebrew words *'uriy 'uriy* (Awake, awake) do not mean to convey that Isaiah thought God had fallen asleep. The word is also used in Dan. 4:10, 14, 20 and translated, *watcher.* The idea of the word is *watchfulness, alertness* or *awareness,* that motivates action. In view of the impending Babylonian captivity, the prophet is calling upon the Lord to act on behalf of the small minority of believers and save Zion. God has promised protection from Babylon, but God has not acted. Men, even prophets, often run ahead of the Lord. Isaiah is representing the remnant, of course, and they are expressing their terror at the threats of Babylon. It appears from their fearful perspective as if God is either unaware of their plight or is aware but is not intending to do anything about it. Their appeal for action is based on what they know of His previous deliverance of Israel from Egypt. Their ancient writings tell of Moses' and Israel's passage from slavery in Egypt through the Red Sea. Egypt is called "Rahab" (which means "loud mouth" in Hebrew; see 30:7) and *thanniyn* "the monster"; *thanniyn* is translated *serpent* in most uses (cf. 27:1). Jehovah delivered from the dragon Egypt, will He now allow Zion to be destroyed by the lion Babylon? The sea which was dried up must refer to the Red Sea crossing (Ex. 14:1ff).

Verse 11 forms an excellent conclusion to Isaiah's plea. It is a quotation, almost letter for letter, from 35:10 which likewise forms a conclusion to a messianic section. Isaiah quotes himself (and why not, since it was such a beautiful and emphatic promise of God the first time it was spoken) as part of his pleas as if to remind Jehovah of His recently promised redemption; see comments 35:8-10.

v. 12-16 PROMISE: Jehovah answers the plea of Isaiah and the remnant by affirming that He is indeed that same Jehovah who kept His covenant with Israel and delivered them from Egypt. The "I, even I . . ." appears to be a retort in irony to "awake, awake." Jehovah is who He is and will always be the same. What the remnant needs is to find its own identity. And that is the interesting thing here; the remnant's identity is to be found in who Jehovah is! In other words, if Jehovah is always the same, then who are those who believe and trust in Him? They are those who need not fear mortal men. The same truth is relevant for today. Men and women can only find their true identity in relationship to their commitment to God. If they trust Him and follow Him, they are invincible; He will save them from all that threatens. If they do not trust Him and do not follow Him they will be lost. The fundamental identification of man is his savedness or his lostness! That is who he is! When man forgets his Maker—when man forgets that he is creature and Jehovah is Creator—he is a slave to fear and falsehood. When man forgets his Creator his whole perspective is warped. Anyone who searches for self-identity without first knowing who God is (and all that such knowledge of Him implies) searches in vain! If the remnant of Isaiah's day remembers its Maker, it will be freed from fear of its enemies.

The Hebrew word *tzo'eh* means "to bend down; to stoop" as though burdened down and is translated "he who is bowed down" in the RSV. It is predicting the circumstances of the Babylonian exiles being "bowed down" in chains or in prisons. Zion (the remnant of believers; disciples of Isaiah) may have to go into captivity but she shall "speedily" be released (70 years). Most assuredly, Jehovah does not intend Zion's ultimate destiny to be imprisonment, starvation and death! She will suffer chastening but Jehovah will work through her to create a new Zion.

The final word of Jehovah (v. 16) is manifestly addressed to the Servant because it shall be particularly through the Servant that Jehovah creates the new, ultimate Zion (cf. Heb. 12:22). Jehovah reaffirms His promise (cf. 50:4-11) that the Servant will be sent with the incarnate word of the Lord ("my words in thy mouth"). The special, intimate, divine companionship to the Servant is also reiterated ("covered thee in the shadow of my hand"). Jehovah will "plant" and "lay the foundations" and "say unto Zion. Thou art my people." Some commentators think this refers to the creation of a new heavens and earth, or a new cosmos, after the present one is destroyed by fire (as per II Pet. 3, etc.). That may be the ultimate outcome of the "new creation" ushered in by the Messiah at His first coming, but we believe Isaiah is not really focusing on the end of the messianic age but on the beginning of it. The messianic age is often pictured as a "new creation" of Zion (cf. Isa. 66:22-24; II Cor. 5:16-21, etc.). The Zion of the N.T. was created after the "removal of what is shaken" (Heb. 12:25-29). The old "creation" (Judaism) was shaken down and the new "creation" (Christianity) remains and cannot be shaken. The abrogation of the old dispensation and the creation of a new dispensation (especially a dispensation which would include Gentiles in God's covenant) would not be possible in Jewish thinking without a whole new creation (new heavens and earth)! The prophet figuratively accommodates his language to the Jewish thought-pattern. Of course, God did not intend to create a new physical heaven and earth when He sent the Servant on His first advent. And this is one of the major causes of Jewish rejection of the Messiah! They could not adjust their thought-patterns to the reality of the revelation that Jesus was the Christ and that He came to form a spiritual kingdom in this present earth and not to form a political kingdom in a rejuvenated physical earth! Certainly, God will one day destroy this present cosmos and create a new one. But mankind must be reborn and accept citizenship in a newly created Zion before he is ready for the new cosmos. The Jew, as well as the Gentile, must become a new creature first. Toward this first goal the prophets primarily pointed! "Thou art my people" is definitely a messianic term (cf. Hosea 1:10-11; 2:16-23; Rom. 9:23-33; I Pet. 2:9-10).

In the light of so much contemporary emphasis on personal subjectivism and feeling as criteria for proper relationship to God, it is important to notice in this chapter thus far the criterion for proper relationship to God is the objective revelation of His nature. Man's relationship to God is properly built on who God is—not on how man feels. And God has objectively demonstrated—in historical deeds—that He is absolutely powerful and absolutely faithful. Isaiah's contemporaries are exhorted to look back at what Jehovah has done; look now at what He is doing; and look forward to what He promises to do. They are never asked, what do you think He ought to do, or, What is He doing to your feelings!

QUIZ

1. What does Isaiah mean when he cries to Jehovah, "awake, awake"?

2. What event in Israel's history is appealed to in reference to the "sea"?
3. Why can man only find out who he is when he finds out who God is?
4. Why will God not leave the exiles to starve and die?
5. Why do we think God is addressing the Servant in verse 16?
6. What are the "heavens and . . . earth" God is going to plant?
7. Why did the Jews think the "heavens and . . . earth" would have to be physical?
8. What criterion of man-to-God relationship is appealed to in this chapter?

c. TORMENTORS JUDGED

TEXT: 51:17-23

17 Awake, awake, stand up, O Jerusalem, that hast drunk at
the hand of Jehovah the cup of his wrath; thou hast drunken
the bowl of the cup of staggering, and drained it.
18 There is none to guide her among all the sons whom she
hath brought forth; neither is there any that taketh her by
the hand among all the sons that she hath brought up.
19 These two things are befallen thee; who shall bemoan thee?
desolation and destruction, and the famine and the sword;
how shall I comfort thee?
20 Thy sons have fainted, they lie at the head of all the streets,
as an antelope in a net; they are full of the wrath of Jehovah,
the rebuke of thy God.
21 Therefore hear now this, thou afflicted, and drunken, but
not with wine:
22 thus saith thy Lord Jehovah, and thy God that pleadeth the
cause of his people, Behold, I have taken out of thy hand
the cup of staggering, even the bowl of the cup of my wrath;
thou shalt no more drink it again:
23 and I will put it into the hand of them that afflict thee,

that have said to thy soul, Bow down, that we may go over; and thou hast laid thy back as the ground, and as the street, to them that go over.

QUERIES

a. When did Jerusalem drink the cup of Jehovah's wrath?
b. Why was there none to guide her among her sons?
c. Who made her "bown down" and where did they "go over"?

PARAPHRASE

Attention! Be alert, Zion! You will soon drink of the cup of Jehovah's punishment. You will have drained every drop; you will have been made to reel under your punishment. You must now decide what course you shall take. You cannot depend on any of this generation of Israelites to take spiritual leadership of Zion. None of them are capable of stopping the desolation and destruction that is coming upon you. Starvation and war and captivity is coming and how will I, Jehovah, save you? Your young men, in whom you hope for leadership, have collapsed everywhere from spiritual and moral weakness. They are as helpless as deer caught in a hunter's net. They shall feel the full force of the Lord's wrath. On account of this, you suffering people of Zion, you shall reel under the Lord's punishment but the Lord your God will defend you. You can believe this: I will take the cup of staggering punishment out of your hand. You will not drink from My wrath-filled cup again when I comfort you through My Servant. I will put that cup of judgment in the hand of your tormentors. Those who have forced Zion to surrender to the chains of captivity and those who have oppressed and trampled her, body and soul, into the dust—they shall stagger under My judgment.

COMMENTS

v. 17-20 STAGGERED: Again, this is Servant-centered. And again, we have the prophet predicting the captivity of Zion, her release, and out of that the ultimate comforting of Jehovah in the coming Servant. Jerusalem (Zion) is roused to wakefulness to prepare herself for the coming "cup" of God's wrath (cf. Jer. 25:15-29; Ezek. 23:31-35); Zion will drink the whole cup Jehovah has for her—exile into a pagan land. Her walls and her temple will be leveled to the ground by a pagan people. The sacred vessels will be desecrated and carried away. Her people will be marched away in chains like slaves. They will be utterly cut off from Jehovah without a temple or a priesthood, unable to offer sacrifices or be ritually cleansed. This would be "staggering" to a Jew. The religious-psychological-moral shock would be more staggering than the physical suffering. People can endure great physical privation when they know they are not suffering the disfavor of God.

Zion is to learn something from this "cup of staggering." She is to alert herself to the fact that only Jehovah can deliver her from the fix she has gotten herself into. None of Jerusalem's wise old men could rescue her from the consequences of her sins. None of Jerusalem's bright young men had the capability to step forward and deliver her from the coming ruin. In fact, those who were capable of leadership had become so self-centered and cynical they did not even *want* to become involved with civic mindedness (cf. Isa. 3:6-12; 4:1, etc.). Jerusalem is headed for desolation, destruction, starvation and slaughter; who will rescue the remnant of Zion? Jehovah asks the rhetorical question, "How shall I comfort thee?" If there are no "sons" of Jerusalem through whom Jehovah may work, what shall be the instrument of His salvation? All the "sons" of Jerusalem are as helpless as the antelope caught in the hunter's net. The Hebrew word *toa* is translated *oryx* (Gr.) in the LXX and *wild bull* in the KJV. It is probably the *dorcas gazelle,* common to Syria, Palestine and Arabia, or the *oryx beatrix* (Arabian oryx). The Hebrew root word, *tha'ah,* means literally, "to outrun," thus signifying the antelope-gazelle animal which is extremely fast but physically weak. The men Jerusalem expected to be leaders and deliverers will become victims like everyone else. They too have drunk the cup of the Lord's wrath dry. They have imbibed of the same heady wine of rebellion and moral corruption in which the populace has indulged. Now they will all stagger and reel. How shall Zion be delivered?

v. 21-23 SAVED: The word "therefore" is meant to be understood, "on account of this . . ." On account of Zion's inability to save herself, Jehovah will "plead her case." (the Hebrew word *riyv* is a term of the court; cf. 45:9; 49:25; 50:8). When the proper time comes, Jehovah the judge will discontinue Zion's punishment and give the cup she was drinking into the hand of her enemies. Undoubtedly this refers initially to the deliverance from Babylonian exile. This great event is predicted over and over by Isaiah (and other prophets). It will begin in the days of Cyrus, ruler of the Persian empire. But almost always, wherever the return from the captivity is predicted, it is pointed to as the initial step in a glorious program of redemption which shall culminate in the messianic age. Jehovah certainly did not *literally* take away Jerusalem's "cup of staggering" with the return from exile. Jerusalem suffered severe physical warfare under the Seleucids and the Romans (predicted in Daniel). There are two possible interpretations of the phrase "thou shalt no more drink it again": (a) The removal of the cup was to be conditional. Jerusalem would never stagger again after the captivity as long as she remained true to Jehovah. She did not remain true as evidenced by Haggai, Zechariah and Malachi, and as evidenced by her murdering of the Messiah, so Jerusalem was given the cup of staggering again; or (b) the promise is to Zion, the true Jerusalem, the Jerusalem that is above (pre-eminent, cf. Gal. 4:26), the messianic kingdom, the church. The true people of God, the born-again kingdom, shall never suffer being cut off from the presence of God as were the Jews of the exile. The N.T. church will always have its one and only sacrifice (the Lamb of God).

It shall always have its sanctuary in the heavens and its Eternal High Priest. Of course it may suffer trial and tribulation in the physical sense here on earth, but it shall always enjoy the favor of God. The cup of staggering is taken from the hand of God's true Israel by the atoning death of the Servant. He became a "curse for us" (cf. Gal. 3:10-14), and delivered all who submitted to the rule of God in Christ from the wrath of God that is to come upon the sons of disobedience (Eph. 2:1-22). The cup of staggering is put into the hand of "Babylon" (humanity opposed to God) and it shall reel and fall under the wrath of God (Rev. 16:19; 17:6; 18:4-8). God will accomplish all this through the Suffering Servant and for the new Zion (the N.T. church and the O.T. saints who believed which form the one great Mt. Zion pictured in Heb. 11:22-29). And thus we approach the climactic chapter of Isaiah's entire work—chapter 53—the Suffering Servant. But first the transition-chapter, chapter 52. Actually, 52:1-12 serves as the transition from generalities concerning the Servant to particulars, and 52:13—53:12 detail the specifics concerning the Servant.

The Babylonians "afflicted" the *souls* as well as the bodies of the Jewish exiles. They humiliated them, taunting them about the whereabouts of their God, Jehovah; they took their sacred vessles and priests and desecrated them in their pagan country; they forced many of them to perform pagan, idolatrous rituals. They were tortured psychologically as well as being punished physically. We should probably understand the commanded "bow down" as figurative. However, certain Assyrian monuments show vanquished prisoners literally bowing down or lying down on the ground while the conquerors walked on their bodies.

QUIZ

1. How does the "cup of staggering" relate to the coming messianic age?

2. What would "stagger" Zion the most?
3. What is Zion to learn from this?
4. What does the word "therefore" in verse 21 indicate?
5. Give the two possible interpretations of "thou shalt no more drink it again."
6. Were the people of Jerusalem literally "walked" on?

4. EVANGELIZE, CHAPTER 52

a. REDEMPTION

TEXT: 52:1-6

1 Awake, awake, put on thy strength, O Zion; put on thy beautiful garments, O Jerusalem, the holy city: for henceforth there shall no more come into thee the uncircumcised and the unclean.
2 Shake thyself from the dust; arise, sit on thy throne, O Jerusalem: loose thyself from the bonds of thy neck, O captive daughter of Zion.
3 For thus saith Jehovah, Ye were sold for nought; and ye shall be redeemed without money.
4 For thus saith the Lord Jehovah, My people went down at the first into Egypt to sojourn there: and the Assyrian hath oppressed them without cause.
5 Now therefore, what do I here, saith Jehovah, seeing that my people is taken away for nought? they that rule over them do howl, saith Jehovah, and my name continually all the day is blasphemed.
6 Therefore my people shall know my name: therefore they shall know in that day that I am he that doth speak; behold, it is I.

QUERIES

a. Who are the "uncircumcised" and "unclean"?
b. Why does Jehovah say, "What do I here . . .?"
c. Doesn't Israel know God's name? (verse six)

PARAPHRASE

Attention! Alert yourself! You will be strong and beautiful, My True Zion! You will be My holy dwelling place and those who have not made covenant with Me will not, from the day of your establishment, be given entrance. But you must do your part, O True Zion, and shake yourself free from the filth and enslavement of Babylonian paganism. When I deliver you from your captivity, you must return to your royal messianic destiny. I am your Sovereign. When I send you into exile it will be because I exercise My absolute sovereignty and not because someone pays Me to do it. When I redeem you from your exile it will be because I exercise My absolute sovereignty and not because I pay someone to release you. When you went down to Egypt, you went of your own choice and Egypt enslaved you without the right to do so; the Assyrians had no right to take some of you into exile. And now, what do I have in the Babylonian exile—the same thing! Babylon's intent is without moral justification and motivated by wicked rebellion against My sovereignty. The rulers of Babylon are already screaming out their hateful threats and blasphemies. But I am going to save you, O Zion, from Babylon. And when I do reveal My sovereignty in this unequivocal manifestation, true Zion will acknowledge Me as her Savior in a way she has never done before; she will recognize that it is I, Jehovah, who is calling her back to her messianic destiny.

COMMENTS

v. 1-2 Dissociation From Paganism: As before, the prophet is speaking of the future Babylonian exile in the present tense. He is directing the exhortation to his small band of disciples (the "remnant" which shall form the nucleus of "Zion"). This remnant must prepare itself for imminent exile into pagan Babylon. It must strengthen itself by believing what Isaiah is predicting about its Messiah and its messianic role. Zion must commit itself to an adornment of holiness so that when it is taken captive it will be able to keep itself separated from the filth and enslavement of heathenism with which it will be so alluringly surrounded. Zion must not allow the fleeting pleasures of Babylonian ungodliness lure her from her "throne" (her royal messianic queenship).

The aim of this passage is spiritual Jerusalem. That is evident from the prediction that the uncircumcised and the unclean would no more come into her. It cannot be literally or physically intended. Jerusalem has suffered literal invasion and occupation by one uncircumcised culture after another. First the Babylonians, then the Persians, Greeks, Romans, Turks, Mohammedans, Crusaders, Arabs, and even today there are Gentile citizens of Jerusalem. What this passage refers to ultimately is the Israel of God over which the Messiah rules, the church of Christ. Those not in covenant relationship to God through obedience to Christ's gospel (the uncircumcised) and those not purified from sin by the atoning blood of the Suffering Servant (the unclean) will not come into the ultimate Zion, no matter what their genetic ancestry may be—Jew or Gentile. It is interesting to note that Joel predicts, in his messianic conclusion, that "strangers shall never again pass through" Jerusalem (Joel 3:17); and on the other hand Ezekiel, in his portrayal of the glorious messianic era to come, predicts that "aliens" will be given an "inheritance" and be as "native born sons" (Ezek. 47:21-23). It is apparent, therefore, that when the messianic kingdom was to come, people were to become citizens of that kingdom, not as a result of being born a Jew and circumcised in the flesh, but by being reconciled to the Messiah of God through faith. All who are not thus reconciled are "strangers" and "uncircumcised and unclean" and cannot enter spiritual Jerusalem. That is precisely what the New Testament teaches (cf. Rom. 2:28-29; 4:9-25; I Cor. 6:9-11; Gal. 3:1—5:25; Gal. 6:12-16; Eph. 2:11-22; Phil. 3:2-11; Heb. 12:18-29).

God promises to physically deliver Zion from her captors. But Zion herself must make the choices and do the deeds of holiness that separates her from Babylonian wickedness. Verses one and two are saturated with imperatives (commands): "Awake; put on; Shake; arise; sit; loose" are all commands for Zion to act. This is what distinguishes spiritual Zion from genetic Israel—holiness by choice.

v. 3-6 DELIVERANCE FROM PERSECUTION: Jehovah will act to deliver Zion from captivity in a display of divine sovereignty. He will give her up to captivity according to His sovereign plan and rescue her through the same sovereignty. No one will pay Jehovah to exile her—no one will force Him to—and no one will pay Him to rescue her. She will remain in captivity for exactly the time Jehovah assigns (70 years) and she will be delivered.

In verses four and five Jehovah pronounces the guilt of Zion's oppressors—past, present and future. God's sovereign decision to chasten Zion does not relieve her oppressors of guilt. The people of God went down to Egypt of their own choice with Jacob during the famine. And the Egyptians, by their own choice, enslaved and persecuted God's people. Israel's persecutors during Isaiah's lifetime, the Assyrians, were acting by free moral choice—not because they were forced to. "Now therefore, what do I here . . ." may be paraphrased, "Now, what do I have here . . ." in the imminent exile into Babylon? It is the same situation! God will use the exile to chasten the sinful nation of Judah, but at the same time the Babylonians will be held responsible and found guilty. Their captivity of Judah was clearly an unjustified act of aggression. The sovereign God of all mankind declares any nation or people guilty who perpetrate the same acts of unprovoked aggression against other peoples (cf. our comments, *Minor Prophets,* on Obadiah and Amos ch. 1-3). Babylon, like all the other oppressors of Israel, attacked without due cause. Although the sovereign Jehovah may use the wicked assaults of the heathen empires as tools of chastening (cf. Isa. 10:5ff; Jer. 27:1-22, etc.), that does not mean the heathen empires are guiltless for making their own moral choices to "Touch the apple of His eye" (cf. Zech. 2:8) without justifiable provocation. These Babylonians "howl" out harsh orders to their captives (cf. Daniel 1-6) and blaspheme the name of Jehovah continually. What they are doing with God's people is certainly not in agreement with the will of God.

When Jehovah decides, in His own sovereign time-schedule, to deliver Zion from Babylonian captivity (cf. Jer. 27:22; 25:11), then Zion will "know His name." His name is Jehovah (YHWH, "He who causes to be . . .") (cf. Special Study, Vol. II, *O.T. Names for God,* pg. 126f.). Jehovah is the name for "Covenant-God," and here the faithfulness and sovereignty of God to keep His covenant promises is emphasized.

QUIZ

1. What are the "beautiful garments" Zion is to put on?
2. Are we to understand the banishment of the "uncircumcised" literally?
3. Why say the daughter of Zion is to be redeemed "without money"?
4. Why point out that Assyria oppressed Zion "without cause"?
5. What is the name of God that Israel shall know?

b. REVELATION

TEXT: 52:7-12

7 How beautiful upon the mountains are the feet of him that bringeth good tidings, that publisheth peace, that bringeth

good tidings of good, that publisheth salvation, that saith
unto Zion, Thy God reigneth!
8 The voice of thy watchmen! they lift up the voice, together
do they sing; for they shall see eye to eye, when Jehovah
returneth to Zion.
9 Break forth into joy, sing together, ye waste places of
Jerusalem; for Jehovah hath comforted his people, he hath
redeemed Jerusalem.
10 Jehovah hath made bare his holy arm in the eyes of all the
nations; and all the ends of the earth have seen the salvation of our God.
11 Depart ye, depart ye, go ye out from thence, touch no unclean thing; go ye out of the midst of her; cleanse yourselves,
ye that bear the vessels of Jehovah.
12 For ye shall not go out in haste, neither shall ye go by flight:
for Jehovah will go before you; and the God of Israel will be
your rearward.

QUERIES

a. Who is the "messenger" bringing "good tidings"?
b. What is meant by "seeing eye to eye"?
c. Why emphasize that the people would "not go out in haste"?

PARAPHRASE

How lovely will be the Messenger coming across the mountains of this land bringing good news, the good news of peace, goodness and salvation, announcing to faithful Zion, Jehovah has established His sovereign rule among men; the kingdom of God has come! Listen to the voices of your prophets who have been watching and announcing its coming! They are shouting and singing for joy! They see the eventual rule of Jehovah over Zion as surely as if it were right before their eyes! Babylon may ruin you, O Jerusalem, but Jehovah is going to restore you and make you strong, so burst forth into joyous singing. Jehovah is going to unleash His holy power so that the whole world will witness it; His salvation will be revealed to the whole world. So, Zion, when you are delivered from Babylonian captivity in anticipation of the coming kingdom of God, separate yourself completely from all the unholy paganism which has surrounded you there. Do not let your heart be defiled by desiring to cling to the worldliness of Babylon. You are a kingdom of priests to Jehovah and you must be holy unto Him. You will have plenty of time to arrive at the right attitude toward separating yourself from the ungodliness around you. Your exodus this time will not be in haste or in fear, as it was in the days of your forefathers and the Egyptian captivity. The Lord, Your God, will surround you, guiding you and protecting you on every side.

COMMENTS

v. 7-10 PEACE: Apparently we have in this prediction of Isaiah an instance of "shortened perspective." That is, the prophet is predicting the deliverance of Judah from Babylonian captivity and the deliverance of all mankind from sin through the Messiah without mentioning all the history of the scheme of redemption that transpires between the two historical events (cf. our comments on Joel 2:27-28). There is no doubt that the ultimate fulfillment of Isaiah's prediction was to find itself in the Messiah and His gospel (cf. Rom. 10:15). Isaiah's context indicates he is predicting what is going to eventuate with the coming of The Servant. Of course, messengers of the good news that Judah is to be released from her captivity and restored her physical commonwealth in Palestine by the decree of Cyrus will be lovely to behold. The lesson from this miraculous deliverance will be that God rules in the affairs of all men to fulfill His sovereign will. There will be "peace" for a while for Judah. But surely there is more good news involved in this prophecy than a physical deliverance and a physical peace.

The physical deliverance of Judah was the first step in a long series of historical events which were to lead to the coming of the Messiah and the true deliverance, the spiritual salvation, and peace between God and man, (cf. comments on Daniel 9:24-27 for the time-table of historical events between). Ultimately then, "him that bringeth good tidings" is the Messiah. Christ, The Servant, is also The Messenger (cf. Isa. 61:1-2; Lk. 4:16-30; Malachi 3:1-4). The messenger who "prepares the way before" in Malachi 3:1 is unquestionably, John the Baptist. But the "Lord whom you seek . . . the messenger of the covenant . . ." of Malachi 3:1 is the Messiah. Notice what the messenger of Isaiah's prophecy announces: peace—good—salvation—the rule of God—comfort for His people—redemption of Jerusalem. Furthermore, this is to be "seen" by all "the ends of the earth." Surely there is more to God's "salvation" and "comfort" (see Isa. 40:1ff) than a mere temporary deliverance of the Jews from Babylonian captivity. Surely there is more to God's reign than a Jewish nation only superficially submitted to Him in the restored commonwealth under Ezra and Zerubbabel. The post-exilic prophets make it very plain (Haggai, Zechariah, Malachi) that the returned exiles *soon* fell back into their old rebellions against the law of Moses and the rule of God. The salvation, peace and rule of God announced by Isaiah's "beautiful" bearer of "good tidings" is made accessible to all men through Him who came and "preached peace" to those "far off" and those "near" (cf. Eph. 2:11-22). Notice in Romans 10:14-21 how Paul emphasizes the prophecies of Isaiah about the Lord's salvation were *not* fulfilled in a rebellious, physical Israel!

The "watchmen" are probably the prophets and those faithful believers down through the centuries who kept on believing in the coming of the Christ (cf. I Pet. 1:10-12; Heb. 11:13-16; 11:32-40, etc.). These "watchers" put their predictions and hopes into poetic form, song, symbol and type. They did it with great style and emotional expressiveness. For they saw the eventual rule of Jehovah as surely as if it were right before their eyes (cf. John 8:56-58; 12:41), which is what "they shall see eye to eye" means. Even the "return" of Jehovah to Zion is messianic. The crowning glory of Ezekiel's new temple and new city (Ezek. 40-48) is ". . . the name of the city henceforth shall be, The Lord is there." The church is the temple of God's habitation (Eph. 2:21-22).

On account of the absolute certainty that Jehovah is going to eventually send His Messenger with the good tidings of salvation, and on account of the certainty that Jehovah is going to take the first step toward that end delivering the Jews from captivity, the Jerusalem (or Zion) that in Isaiah's day is being "wasted" and "ruined" by pagan oppressors should lift up its spirit and sing of its salvation. This would, of course, take faith because it was not as yet "seen." But that is man's whole relationship to God—faith! That was the problem when the Messiah came to "comfort" His people and "redeem" Jerusalem. Most of the people could not believe it because they could not "see, touch, taste" His deliverance. It is still a problem with so many millions today who want only to be saved physically from trouble and depravation, but not from their sinful rebellion against the revealed will of God!

The salvation of God was "proven"! God's ability to save man and His faithfulness to keep His word was demonstrated visibly, historically and supernaturally. God "bared" His holy "arm" of supernatural power time and again in saving the Jewish people from their enemies. He showed in no uncertain terms to believer and unbeliever alike (read the book of Daniel) that He would deliver those who trusted and obeyed Him. The "arm" of the Lord will consummately be "bared" in the Messiah's death and resurrection (cf. Isa. 53:1ff). God's greatest "power" is the *gospel* which is, fundamentally, the atoning death and justifying resurrection of Jesus Christ. Jehovah showed His power in many and various ways in former ages, but the greatest demonstration of it was in the resurrection of Christ. It was here that God bared His "holy arm" to all the ends of the earth so that all men might see His salvation. God has fixed a day in which he will judge the world, by an appointed man, and He has given assurance to *all men* by raising this man from the dead, and so His message to *all men* everywhere is, repent (cf. Acts 17:30-31). But, you see, the problem is that the "arm" or power of the Lord was revealed in a Suffering Servant (Isa. 53:1) and this, so unacceptable to Jewish presuppositions about the power of Jehovah, is still unacceptable to human presuppositions (cf. I Cor. 1:18-31).

v. 11-12 PURIFICATION: Now we come to the practical application of the prophecy of the coming Messenger and His message. How are these people of Isaiah's day or the people of the Babylonian captivity to relate to a prophecy of something that is so far off in the future? They are to keep themselves from the ungodliness that surrounds them. The temptations to become Babylonianized, to devote their energies to pagan pursuits, will be strong. The temptation to stay in the relative security of the land to which they were exiled and forget they have a messianic destiny to serve will not be easily overcome. Thousands of Jews *did* stay in Babylon! The task of returning to a ravaged land, occupied by hostile people, to struggle through long hard years of rebuilding, was almost overwhelming! Even the temptation to take with them back to Palestine some of the heathen customs and practices that seemed so security-enforcing would seem innocent enough. Yet the command of the Lord is, "depart . . . touch no unclean thing . . . cleanse yourselves." The rule of God cannot be established if the people are unwilling to depart from ungodliness. "Those that bear the vessels of Jehovah" is probably a figurative way of indicating the uniqueness of the Jewish people as a messianic people.

They will have ample opportunity to consider and apply the command of the Lord for separating themselves from their heathen environment. They will not have to make a hasty exodus as their ancestors did in Egypt and so they will not have to take any of the Babylonian baubbles to support them as those under Moses did. These Babylonian exiles will have plenty of time and they will know, by prophecy, exactly how many years they will be spending there. Cyrus will supply them with money to rebuild their commonwealth. And finally, they will not have to tramp the wilderness, constantly fleeing from one enemy after another as their ancestors did. Jehovah promises to surround them with guidance and protection—both front and rear. And so they were protected from those who wanted to thwart their rebuilding (cf. Ezra, Nehemiah, Esther), as they prepared to be the people through whom the great Messenger would come with a revelation of salvation to all the ends of the earth.

QUIZ

1. Why do we call this prophecy of the "messenger" one of "shortened perspective"?
2. Where is the N.T. quotation of this passage and what is the connection?
3. Who are the watchmen and why do they sing?
4. When did Jehovah "bare his holy arm"?
5. Why the command to "depart"?
6. Who are those who "bear the vessels of Jehovah"?

c. REGENCY

TEXT: 52:13-15

13 Behold, my servant shall deal wisely, he shall be exalted and lifted up, and shall be very high.
14 Like as many were astonished at thee, (his visage was so marred more than any man, and his form more than the sons of men,)
15 so shall he sprinkle many nations; kings shall shut their mouths at him; for that which had not been told them shall they see; and that which they had not heard shall they understand.

QUERIES

a. How shall the servant "deal wisely"?
b. In what way was his "visage" marred?
c. How shall he "sprinkle" many nations?

PARAPHRASE

Behold! My Servant shall succeed. He shall be exalted to the highest degree. At first, many will be shocked at the humiliating physical torture and disfigurement he endures—so much more than is possible for others in human form. But his exaltation will be that much more astounding. His success will cause the hearts of many to leap within them. Kings and great men will be awed by His glory. They will see and understand things they could never know before His coming.

COMMENTS

v. 13 AFFIRMATION: Chapter and verse numeration (which came many centuries after the original documents were written) obscures the contextual flow of our present passage; 52:13 through 53:12 should be read as a unit. Making 52:15 the end of a chapter and 53:1 the beginning of another is an unfortunate adumbration which the student of Isaiah's message must be careful to trace out. These verses are all one dissertation on the *success of the Suffering Servant.*

The Hebrew word *yasekkiyl* is the infinitive of *sakal* and may be translated "to prosper; to have success," instead of "deal wisely." This translation would fit the context. The affirmation of Jehovah is that His Servant shall succeed in fulfilling all the predictions made (through Isaiah) of ultimate deliverance, redemption and glorification of Zion. The Servant-Messenger-Messiah of Jehovah will be exalted to the highest degree. Zion has suffered and will suffer much from the days of Isaiah until God comes and establishes His reign among men. Good tidings are beginning to come through the prophets of God. How beautiful will be the feet of the divine Messenger of God who will not only bring the message of salvation and peace but also accomplish it in Himself (cf. 52:7). The mighty Jehovah is going to bare His holy "arm" (power) before all the world (cf. 52:10). Contrary to God's apparent default on His covenant promises to the patriarchs by allowing the Babylonian captivity, the Lord is going to send His Servant and He will succeed in re-establishing Zion in divine power and splendor. This Servant will achieve what He sets out to do. Why is it necessary to affirm the success of the Servant? Because even the Servant's appearance in history will initially be in such a low, humble, unspectacular, humiliating way, most of the world will not believe. He is a manifestation of the *power* of Jehovah! (cf. 53:1ff). But the success of the Lord's Servant will be *extraordinary*. Three Hebrew verbs (*room*—exalted; *nissa*—lifted up; *gavah*—very high) are piled one upon another to emphasize that The Servant will not be defeated in the extreme suffering He will have to undergo (including death).

v. 14-15 AMAZEMENT: Verse 15 is in antithesis to verse 14 and emphasizes the contrast between what the Servant first appeared to be and what He later was acknowledged to be. The "thee" of verse 14 is therefore the Servant-Messiah (not Israel). Men will be shocked at His humble demeanor. He claimed to be the king of the Jews—the Messiah, but He did not in any way fulfill human presuppositions as to messianic royalty. He was slandered, mocked, accused of blasphemy, arrested, unjustly tried and sentenced as a criminal. He was scourged with a Roman whip and physically mutilated more than most human beings ever suffer, placed on a bloody Roman cross and there tortured both physically and psychologically by mocking rabbis, soldiers, and the multitudes. Some were shocked at His extreme disfigurement (cf. Lk. 23:47-49). But the fact of His absolute innocence contrasted with His willing acceptance of the atonement for the sin of the world is what makes his "visage . . . so marred more than any man . . ."

Philippians 2:5-11 expresses it perfectly. The Son of God emptied Himself and took the form of a servant. But God highly exalted Him. As low as His humiliation was, His exaltation was infinitely higher! The Hebrew word *yazzeh* is kin to the Arabic *naza* which means the "springing or leaping of people caused by excess of emotion." *Yazzeh* is from the Hebrew root *nazah* which is usually translated *sprinkle,* but apparently is better translated here, "startle, amaze, cause to jump, scatter." Leupold translates it "startle"; Today's English Version translates "marvel"; New International Version footnotes, "marvel"; RSV is "startle"; most other translations make it "sprinkle." Young comments ". . . he will sprinkle many nations . . . As one who is disfigured, the servant does something for others, in that he performs a purifying rite . . . men regarded the servant as himself unclean and in need of purification, whereas he himself as a priest will sprinkle water and blood and so purify many nations." We prefer the translation *startle* because it seems more appropriate to the intended contrast of the context.

Man will be shocked at His humiliation. But the *goiym* (nations or Gentiles) will be startled at the totally unexpected development events surrounding His humiliation and exaltation will *ultimately* take! The consequences will be world-wide. A church will be born; His disciples will be found even in the household of Caesar! The like of what shall result from the humiliation and exaltation of Jehovah's Servant was never imagined by the great (kings, philosophers, theologians). Never was anyone brought so low; never was anyone raised so high as God's Servant. Emperors, philosophers, rabbis will be awed by His glory. Through Him will come a revelation from God (justification, redemption, sanctification) of things they could never know before His coming, but they would believe, appropriate and experience (I Cor. 2:9).

This text (52:13—53:12) is written in the *predictive present.* It is prophecy, but it is so certain to come to pass it can be written as if it had already happened or was then happening. It is almost as if we were listening to two disciples of Jesus standing on a street-corner in Jerusalem reviewing the things that happened on Good Friday in the light of Easter Sunday and the Day of Pentecost. Isaiah's account is so vivid and was fulfilled so minutely it is little wonder that many of the fathers of the church days of old claim that the account reads as though Isaiah had sat at the foot of the cross.

QUIZ

1. Why emphasize the success of the Servant of Jehovah?
2. Why were men astonished at the marred visage of the Servant?
3. What verses of the N.T. shed light on the humiliation of the Servant?
4. What is the contrast between verses 14 and 15?
5. What is *predictive present?*

SPECIAL STUDY

THE WORD OF GOD, THE ILLUMINATING AGENCY OF THE HOLY SPIRIT IN CONVERSION

by Paul T. Butler

INTRODUCTION

I. QUALIFICATIONS

A. We believe the Scriptures plainly teach that the spoken and written Word of God (the Bible) is the only illuminating agency of the Holy Spirit in the conversion of sinners.
B. This is contrary to the creeds of most major Protestant religious bodies today. They say, in essence:

1. Man, the sinner, has a mind biased and prejudiced by sin and he cannot, therefore, understand the spiritual truths of the Bible until . . .
2. The Holy Spirit acts, directly, irresistibly and apart from the written or spoken Word of God, regenerating man's mind in order that man can understand the written truths in the Bible . . . only then will man be able to believe in Christ and become a Christian.
3. This is individually and subjectively experienced and one cannot be assured of his salvation until he is able to relate such an experience.
4. Those who have never had such an experience, so far as we are able to tell now, are not "elected" to salvation.

C. By our statement in A. above we do not intend to exclude the providential actions of the Holy Spirit.
1. The Holy Spirit may act in providence to bring a Christian and non-Christian together for the purpose of allowing the non-Christian to hear the message of Christ (e.g., Philip and the Ethopian eunuch; Peter and Cornelius, etc.)
2. But in the final analysis, it is the written or spoken Word of God into the sinner's mind and upon his heart that converts and leads him to become a Christian.

II. WHAT WE ARE NOT DISCUSSING IN THIS STUDY

A. We do not wish to discuss here, to any length, at least, the baptism of the Holy Spirit in the miraculous way the apostles were immersed in the Holy Spirit.

B. We do not wish to discuss here the miraculous gifts of the Holy Spirit by which certain people spoke in tongues, prophesied, healed, etc.

C. We do not wish to discuss whether or not people have had particular "religious experiences . . ."
1. That people have had subjective religious experiences is difficult to disprove—at least to the one who

claims such an experience.

2. But whether or not we are to follow what we think those subjective experiences teach, in order to the assurance of salvation, is quite another thing and is contrary to Biblical teaching.

III. ASSUMPTIONS WE MAKE

A. That the Bible is the infallible, inerrant, inspired Word of God and the ultimate and final authority in matters of faith and practice.

B. That we learn all we need to learn on this particular subject from the New Testament.

DISCUSSION

I. JESUS TAUGHT THAT THE WORD OF GOD (WRITTEN AND SPOKEN) ILLUMINATES THE MIND OF MAN UNTO CONVERSION

A. Matt. 11:25-30 . . . only the Son can reveal the Father . . . we must take the Son's yoke upon us and *learn* of Him.

B. Matt. 7:24-27 . . . the wise man is the one who *hears* the words of Christ and *does* them.

C. Matt. 13:1-23; Lk. 8:4-15 . . . the *seed* of the kingdom is *the word* of God sown on the hearts of men. This *word* must be *held fast* in honest and good hearts to bear fruit.

D. Matt. 4:4 . . . Man does not live by bread alone, but by *every word* that proceeds from the mouth of God.

E. Matt. 28:18-20 . . . the great commission is to *teach,* baptize and *teach* all that Jesus commanded the 12 disciples.

F. Lk. 10:21-28 . . . Jesus told a lawyer to do what he *read* in the Law in order to inherit eternal life.

G. Lk. 10:38-42 . . . Mary chose the good portion for she sat at Jesus' feet and *listened* to His teaching . . .

H. Lk. 11:27-28 . . . Jesus said, "Blessed rather are those who *hear* the *word* of God and *keep* it . . ."

I. Lk. 16:19-31 . . . the rich man in Hades was told it would do no good for him to go back from the dead and warn his brothers . . . "They have Moses and the prophets; let them hear them . . . If they do not hear Moses and the prophets, neither will they be convinced if someone should rise from the dead . . ."

J. Lk. 24:13-35 . . . Jesus took special time and effort "beginning with Moses and all the prophets . . . interpreting," for some despondent disciples "all the scriptures" said concerning Himself.

K. John 1:1-18 . . . Jesus, the Incarnate Word of God, "exegeted" God to man; *exegesato* is the Greek word in verse 18, from which we get *exegesis,* but it is translated *declared.*

L. Jn. 5:24 . . . whoever *hears the word* of Christ and *believes* God, who sent Him, has eternal life.

M. Jn. 5:25 . . . whoever *hears* the voice of the Son of God, will live.

N. Jn. 6:63 . . . except men eat the flesh of the Son of man and drink His blood they have no life in them . . . THIS IS TO BE DONE BY HEARING AND DOING THE WORDS JESUS SPOKE, FOR *His words are spirit and life.*

O. Jn. 6:44-45 . . . No one comes unto Christ . . . unless they *learn* from the Father.

P. Jn. 6:69 . . . Peter declared that Jesus has the *words* of eternal life . . ."

Q. Jn. 8:31-32 . . . only those who *continue* in His *word* are His disciples and in doing so they will be made free for it is the *truth* that makes free . . . and only by continuing in *His word* do we *know the truth!*

R. Jn. 10 . . . the sheep follow the good Shepherd only because they *know* the difference between His *voice* (word) and the voice of the hireling.

S. Jn. 11 . . . the *spoken word* of Jesus raised Lazarus from the dead.

T. Jn. 12:44-50 . . . the *words* Jesus spoke will judge men at the last day, and the *commandment* which the Father gave Him *to speak is* eternal life.

U. Jn. 13:12-17 . . . Jesus gave the disciples an example of humble and loving service to one another and then said "If you *know* these things, blessed are you if you do them . . ."

V. Jn. 14:23 . . . Jesus made the *abiding* presence of the Holy Spirit specifically conditioned upon *keeping His commandments.* It must, therefore, be possible for a sinner to come to believe in, and begin to obey Christ before the Holy Spirit abides in him . . . in other words the sinner is converted by knowing, believing and obeying the Word, which is the agency of the Holy Spirit in the sinner's conversion.

W. Jn. 15:3 . . . the disciples were cleansed by the *word* which Christ had already spoken unto them.

X. Jn. 15:1-11 . . . our abiding in Him and His abiding in us is conditioned upon our abiding in His word . . . it is not irresistible.

Y. Jn. 16:1-15 . . . the Holy Spirit was sent to guide the apostles into all truth, etc., and thus, *through their preaching* to convict the world of sin, righteousness and judgment.

Z. Jn. 17:1-26 . . . eternal life is to know the only true God and Jesus Christ . . . this the disciples had because they accepted the *words* which Jesus was commissioned to give them from the Father . . . through His *words spoken* they had joy . . . They were *sanctified* in His *word* which is truth . . . Jesus even prayed for all who should subsequently *believe in Him through the preached word* of the apostles (verse 20).

AA. Jn. 18:37 . . . Jesus said . . . "I have come into the world, to bear witness to the truth. Everyone who is of the *truth hears my* voice."

BB. Jn. 20:30-31 . . . the gospels were written that men might believe and have eternal life.

II. THE ACTS TEACH THAT THE WORD OF GOD (WRITTEN AND SPOKEN) ILLUMINATES THE MIND OF MAN UNTO CONVERSION

A. Acts 2:37-38 . . . when the multitude *heard* the preaching of Jesus they were convinced and obeyed . . . there is no notice that the Holy Spirit illumined their hearts apart from the preaching of the inspired word.
B. Acts 4:4 . . . many who *heard* the preaching of Peter in Acts 3, believed and became Christians.
C. Acts 5:32 . . . the Holy Spirit is given only to those who obey Christ . . . how can one obey Christ unless he has *heard* the commandment of Christ and understood the commandment?
D. Acts 8:34-40 . . . Philip *preached* unto the eunuch Jesus and then the man obeyed.
E. Acts 10:22 . . . Cornelius was directed by an angel of the Lord to send for Peter so that Peter might *preach* to him the gospel in order that Cornelius might hear and believe . . . cf. Acts 10:33; 11:14.
F. Acts 17:29-31 . . . Paul said men should understand that God is going to judge the world and that He wants them to repent simply *from knowing the fact* that Jesus Christ was raised from the dead.
G. Acts 20:18-35 . . . Paul charged the elders of Ephesus to "feed the flock of God" on the word of God as he himself had done . . . and Paul "commended them to God and to the *word of His grace,* which is able to build you up and to give you the inheritance among all those who are sanctified."
H. Acts 26:24-29 . . . Paul presented the *facts* concerning Jesus and appealed to the *writings* of the prophets in hope that Agrippa might become a Christian.
I. Acts 28:23-28 . . . Paul *expounded* the *facts* concerning Jesus all day to a group of Jews, trying to *convince* them about the kingdom of God, etc. some were *convinced,* some were not.

III. THE EPISTLES TEACH THAT THE WORD OF GOD (WRITTEN AND SPOKEN) ILLUMINES THE MIND OF MAN UNTO CONVERSION

A. Rom. 1:16-17 . . . the *gospel* is the power of God unto salvation.

B. Rom. 6:17-18 . . . men are set free from sin by *obedience* from the heart to the *standard of teaching* of the apostles.

C. Rom. 8:6 . . . to set the mind on the Spirit . . . is life . . . the Spirit is revealed in the Word.

D. Rom. 8:13-14 . . . it is by the Spirit that we put to death the deeds of the body and it is by the Spirit we are led . . . the Spirit only does that by revealing His will to us in the Scriptures.

E. Rom. 10:8-17 . . . the word of faith which is in their hearts is the word which the apostles preached . . . all who call upon the Lord will be saved, BUT THEY CANNOT CALL UPON HIM IF THEY HAVE NOT HEARD HIS WORD, BECAUSE FAITH COMES BY HEARING THE WORD OF GOD!!!

F. Rom. 12:1-2 . . . we are to be transformed by the renewing of our mind in order that we may prove what is the acceptable will of God.

G. Rom. 15:18 . . . Paul would win obedience to Christ from the Gentiles by preaching to them the word of Christ . . .

H. Rom. 16:25-27 . . . Paul said that the *preaching* of Jesus Christ was . . . to bring about the *obedience of faith* . . .

I. I Cor. 2:1-14 . . . Paul said that the Spirit of Christ had been given to the apostles . . . and this *Spirit was imparted to the Corinthians in words* . . .

J. I Cor. 15:1-2 . . . the *preached gospel* was what the Corinthians received, that in which they stood fast, that by which they were saved.

K. II Cor. 1:20 . . . all the promises of God find their Yea in Jesus Christ objectively revealed . . . not subjectively.

L. II Cor. 10:3-5 . . . the *preaching* of the word of God has *divine power* and is able to *destroy arguments* and every proud *obstacle to the knowledge of God* and bring every *thought into captivity unto Christ!!!*

M. Gal. 2:20; 3:2; 3:26-27 . . . The Spirit of Christ lives in men and is put on by men through the hearing of faith . . . and faith comes by hearing!

N. Eph. 3:17 . . . Christ dwells in us through faith, and faith comes by hearing.

O. Eph. 1:9-14 . . . those who have *heard the word of truth,* the gospel, have made known to them the mystery of His will and have been sealed with the Holy Spirit.

P. Eph. 3:8-19 . . . Paul was made a minister to the Gentiles to preach to them the unsearchable riches of Christ and make all men see what is the plan of the mystery hidden for ages in God . . . that through the Church thc manifold wisdom of God might now be made known . . .

Q. Eph. 4:11-16 . . . the various offices of ministry (including evangelists) were given to the church to edify the church and bring the church to a mature knowledge of Christ.

R. Eph. 5:17-18 . . . Paul connects being filled with the Spirit directly to first understanding what the will of the Lord is . . .

S. Phil. 4:8-9 . . . Paul said that true, honorable, just, pure, lovely, gracious things were revealed to Christians by the preaching and Christian living of the apostles.

T. Col. 1:27-28 . . . Paul proclaimed and taught Christ to every man in all wisdom so that Christ might dwell in men and they might have the hope of glory.

U. Col. 3:16 . . . Christians are to let the word of Christ dwell in them richly.

V. I Thess. 2:13 . . . Paul said the Christians there received their preaching as the word of God and that this *word* was at *work* in them.

W. II Thess. 1:8 . . . Paul said God would bring vengeance upon all who *do not obey the gospel* . . . an objective standard!

X. II Thess. 2:14 . . . Paul said that men were *called* by God through the preaching of the *gospel.*

Y. I Tim. 4:11-16 . . . Paul told Timothy that by holding to that which he had been *taught* he would *save* both *himself* and his *hearers.*

Z. II Tim. 2:9 . . . Paul speaks of the word of God as not being able to be fettered.

AA. II Tim. 3:16 . . . The scripture is able to completely equip the man of God for every good work . . .

BB. Titus 1:1-3 . . . Paul said the faith of the elect was furthered by the preaching of the word . . .

CC. Titus 2:11-15 . . . Paul said the "grace of God . . . trains us . . ." and we should thus declare it . . .

DD. Hebrews 4:12-13 . . . the word of God is living and active . . . pierces even to the division of the soul and spirit . . . and discerns the thoughts and intents of the heart . . .

EE. James 1:18 . . . "Of his own will he *brought us forth by the word of truth* . . ." Here the word of truth is specifically said to be the agent of the Holy Spirit in the new birth.

FF. I Pet. 1:22-25 . . . "You have been *born anew* . . . *through the living and abiding word of God* . . . that word is the good news which was preached to you . . ." This they did by obedience to the truth. IT CANNOT BE ANY PLAINER THAN THIS THAT THE SPIRIT WORKS THROUGH THE WORD IN REGENERATION.

GG. II Pet. 1:3-4 . . . it is *through a knowledge* of Jesus Christ and through His precious and exceeding great promises that we become *partakers of the divine nature.*

HH. I John 2:3-6 . . . we are sure we are in Him only when we know and keep His commandments.

II. I John 3:24 . . . we abide in Him and He abides in

us when we keep His commandments.

JJ. I John 4:1-6 . . . whoever knows the Spirit of God listens to apostolic teachings and this is the only way man may know the difference between the spirit of truth and the spirit of error.

KK. II John 9-10 . . . anyone who does not abide in the doctrine of Christ does not have God . . . he who abides in this doctrine has both the Father and the Son.

IV. LOGIC TEACHES THAT WE MUST DEPEND UPON THE SPIRIT TO BRING US TO CONVERSION THROUGH OUR RESPONSE TO HIS OBJECTIVE REVELATION OF HIMSELF IN HIS WORD!

A. Alexander Campbell, in *The Christian System* "moral facts are those which either exhibit, develop, or form moral character . . . all the works and words of God are moral facts and truths . . ."

1. The work of redemption is a system of works or deeds on the part of God and Christ which constitutes the most splendid series of moral facts which man or angel ever saw . . .
2. When these moral facts are brought into immediate contact with the mind of man, they delineate the image of God upon the human soul.
3. Testimony is but the channel through which these facts draw the image of God on the heart and character of man.
4. The love of God in the death of Jesus never drew a tear of gratitude or joy from any eye, or excited a grateful emotion in any heart among the nations of our race to whom the testimolny never came. No TESTIMONY, NO FAITH!
5. The quality or value of faith is found in the quality or value of the testimony. If the testimony be valid, OBJECTIVE, and authoritative, our faith is strong and operative. "If we receive the testimony of men, the

testimony of God is *greater* . . ."

6. The power of faith is also found in the power or moral meaning of the testimony, or of the facts which the testimony represents. If by faith I am filled with joy, or sorrow, that joy or sorrow is in the facts contained in the testimony . . . or in the relation of those facts to me. And, if faith purifies the heart . . . this power is in the facts believed.
7. It is neither the faculty of perception, nor the manner of perception, but the things perceived, that excited us to action. It is not the exercise of reflection, but the thing reflected upon. It is not reason itself, nor the exercise of reason, but the thing reasoned upon which affords pleasure or pain—which excites to action—which cheers, allures, consoles us.
8. Even in our volition this is true. It is not choosing, nor refusing; hating, loving, fearing, desiring, nor hoping; IT IS NOT THE NATURE OF ANY POWER, FACULTY, OR CAPACITY OF OUR BEING, NOR THE SIMPLE EXERCISE OF THEM, BUT THE *object or things* UPON WHICH THEY ARE EXERCISED, WHICH INDUCE US TO ACTION, OR INFLUENCE OUR BEHAVIOR!
9. AND SO MY FRIEND WE ARE PURIFIED BY OUR OBEDIENCE TO THE OBJECTIVE TRUTH . . . THE REVEALED, WRITTEN AND SPOKEN TESTIMONY ABOUT THE PERSON AND PROMISES OF JESUS CHRIST BECOME THE OBJECTIVE AGENT WHICH MOVES US . . . WITHOUT AN OBJECT (JESUS) AND AN OBJECTIVE REVELATION OF HIM WE WOULD BE LEFT ONLY TO LISTEN AND FOLLOW THE DECEITFUL WHISPERINGS OF OUR WICKED HEARTS—SEE POINT #V ON PAGE 254.

B. In the religious world today we have many groups, teaching about as many contradictory dogmas, most claiming to be led now or having been led in the past by special direct revelations of the Holy Spirit apart from the received Bible. IF THE HOLY SPIRIT OPERATES ON THE MINDS OF MEN APART FROM AN OBJECTIVE

STANDARD (THE WORD), HOW DO WE KNOW WHICH IS CORRECT?

1. We appeal to such scriptures as Gal. 1:8-9; I John 4:1-6 and assert that there is only one leading of the Holy Spirit today and that is in the infallible, inerrant, objective standard called the Bible, and that only!
2. Don DeWelt says in his book, *The Power of the Holy Spirit,* Vol. I, pg. 31, commenting on Rom. 8:16 . . . "the Spirit himself beareth witness with our spirit, that we are children of God." ". . . The Bible does *not* say that the Holy Spirit bears witness *to* our spirit, thus making it a subjective experience within the Christian. The text *does* say the Holy Spirit bears witness *with* our spirit, thus making it an objective experience without or apart from the Christian. The witness of the Holy Spirit is the New Testament. This is His testimony as to how to become a Christian or child of God, and also how to remain faithful as God's child. We know within ourselves if we have done what the Spirit has said to do in order to become a child of God . . . We then become a child of God, our spirits have agreed with the testimony of the Holy Spirit . . ." when we have done what we are commanded to do in the New Testament. (cf. Jn. 20:30-31; I Jn. 5:13).

V. THE SCRIPTURES TEACH US THAT WE WILL BE DECEIVED BY LISTENING TO THE SUBJECTIVE WHISPERINGS OF OUR HEART.

A. Prov. 16:2 . . . "all the ways of a man are pure in his own eyes, but the Lord weighs the spirit . . ." (cf. also 21:2)
B. Jer. 17:9 . . . "The heart is deceitful above all things, and desperately corrupt; who can understand it? I the Lord search the mind and try the heart . . ."
C. Heb. 3:13 . . . warns that Christians must continually

exhort one another (from the written word) lest their hearts be hardened by the deceitfulness of sin . . .

D. Satan is able to transform himself into an angel of light (II Cor. 11:14); quote scripture (Matt. 4:5-6); perform lying wonders (Rev. 13:11-18); and he is able to enter the mind of man by the power of thought . . . he is a spirit of disobedience, etc.

E. Some examples of people who thought they were doing God's service when following the subjective feelings of their hearts:

   1. The disciples, led by Judas, thought that Mary "wasted" the ointment by pouring it upon Jesus and it could have been sold and given to the poor (Mt. 26:9; Mk. 14:5; Jn. 12:5) . . . THEY HAD TO HAVE AN OBJECTIVE REVEALED TO THEM IN THE WORDS OF JESUS TO STRAIGHTEN OUT THEIR CROOKED SUBJECTIVE THINKING.
   2. Peter thought that defending the life of Jesus against His enemies was the proper thing to do, but it was Satan whispering to Peter (Mt. 16:21-23; Mk. 8:32-33).
   3. Paul said, "I verily thought with myself, that I ought to do many things contrary to the name of Jesus of Nazareth . . ." even to the persecution and killing of Christians (Acts 22:4; 26:9-11; I Cor. 15:9; Gal. 1:13; Phil. 3:6; I Tim. 1:13) . . . he lived in all good conscience in so doing . . . IT TOOK AN OBJECTIVE REVELATION TO PAUL TO STRAIGHTEN OUT HIS THINKING.

5. ATONE, CHAPTER 53

a. SHUNNED

TEXT: 53:1-3

1 Who had believed our message? and to whom hath the arm of Jehovah been revealed?

2 For he grew up before him as a tender plant, and as a root out of a dry ground: he hath no form nor comeliness; and

when we see him, there is no beauty that we should desire him.
3 He was despised, and rejected of men; a man of sorrows, and
acquainted with grief: and as one from whom men hide their
face he was despised; and we esteemed him not.

QUERIES

a. What message was not believed?
b. What is the "dry ground" from which He grew?
c. Why was the Servant a "man of sorrows"?

PARAPHRASE

But when the Suffering Servant comes, who will have believed this message of the exaltation of the Servant from such a state of deep degradation? who will have recognized in this the victorious, powerful "arm" of Jehovah? It was the plan of God that His Servant take the form of man and grow up like a fragile, green plant sprouting from dry and sterile ground. In our eyes there was nothing in Him to make Him attractive as king or Messiah. We saw nothing in Him that made us want Him or want to follow Him as our leader. In fact, we despised Him and rejected Him; He suffered the sorrow of rejection and grief of our unbelief as well as our physical persecutions. We went out of our way to shun Him and ignore Him.

COMMENTS

v. 1 UNBELIEVING: Chapter 53 is still in the *predictive present tense.* It is as if the Servant has come, been rejected, slaughtered and the people of Israel are looking at it all in retrospect! The overall reaction of the nation to Jesus' claims to be the Messiah was scoffing, mockery, rejection and persecution. He gained a few disciples, but at the arest in Gethsemane, they all forsook Him and fled (Mk. 14:50). The nation, as a whole, could not believe that Jehovah was at work revealing His "Arm" in the itinerant Galilean carpenter's son. It was especially difficult for any who had been attracted to Him during His life to believe that He was God's Servant when they gathered at Golgotha and saw His humiliating death, (cf. Lk. 24:13-27). The believing, penitent Jews after their baptism (Acts 2:37, etc.) still marvelled that they could have been so unbelieving. They are represented here by the prophet as continually marvelling as they reflect on their blindness. Twice in the N.T. this very verse of Isaiah's prophecy is quoted as Jesus (Jn. 12:38) and Paul (Rom. 10:16) express shock that the Jews did not believe when Jehovah's Servant came to them.

Is there any question as to the identity of this Suffering Servant of Isaiah 53? Servant of Jehovah, *'ebed Yahweh* in Hebrew is prophesied at least 20 times in Isaiah chapters 40-53. Sometimes it refers to Cyrus, king of Persia; sometimes it refers to the nation of Israel (41:8; 42:19); but most often it refers to the Messiah (42:1-7; 49:1-9; 50:4-9; 52:13—53:12; 61:1-3). The Servant is the same *person* (not nation) previously described in 7:14; 9:6ff; 11:1-5. He is also the "Branch" of 4:2; 11:1; 53:2; Jer. 23:5ff; 33:15; Zech. 3:8; 6:12ff. The inspired authors of the New Testament specifically confirm the following prophecies of the Servant are fulfilled in Jesus Christ; Isa. 42:1-4 fulfilled in Mt. 12:18-21; Isa. 52:13—53:12 fulfilled (or quoted) in Mt. 8:17; Lk. 22:37; Jn. 12:38; Acts 8:32ff; Rom. 10:16. The Servant's *mission* can only be fulfilled by Christ:

1. Birth (Isa. 49:1; 53:2; Lk. 1:31-35)
2. Anointing (Isa. 42:1; 48:16; 59:21; 61:1; Mt. 3:16; Lk. 4:18ff)
3. Ministry (Isa. 49:8-13; Acts 10:36-43)
4. Rejection (Isa. 49:4-7; 53:1-3; Acts 3:13-18)
5. Obedience (Isa. 40:4-7; Phil. 2:5-11)
6. New Covenant (Isa. 42:6; 49:8; 55:3; Mt. 26:26-29)
7. Vicarious death (Isa. 53:4-12; I Pet. 2:22-25)
8. Resurrection (Isa. 53:10-12; Acts 2:24-36)
9. Salvation Offered (Isa. 49:8; 61:2; Lk. 24:46-49)
10. Mission to Gentiles (Isa. 42:1, 6ff; 49:6, 12; 60:3, 9; Mt. 28:18-20)
11. Glorification and Intercession 49:3; 53:12; Acts 2:33-36; Phil. 2:5-11; Heb. 7:24ff)
12. Jesus came to *serve.* (Mt. 20:28; Jn. 12:13-20, etc.)

v. 2-3 UNCIVIL: What Jew in his right mind would ever have dreamed or imagined rejecting his Messiah or Jehovah's Servant in such an odious way as Isaiah predicts? Only the most shameful incivility prompts men to deliberately "hide" from another human being. Yet these verses vividly portray the scandalous hatred the Jews will manifest toward the Incarnate Servant. It is the life-story of the Servant from the cradle to the grave. The Servant's entry into this world was so inglorious; born in Bethlehem (Micah 5:2), of poor parentage, in a stable. When He grew up as a lad in Nazareth He was just like any other lad according to all outward appearances (Lk. 2:51-52) (with the one exception of confounding the scholars at Jerusalem, Lk. 2:41-50).

"He grew up before him . . ." means the Servant grew up in the eyes of Jehovah, or, by the foreordained plan of God, "as a tender plant, and as a root out of a dry ground." Jehovah sent His Servant to the world through the Jews, despised and harassed people by the Roman world of Christ's day. He grew up in Nazareth which was in Galilee (which means, "circuit of the Gentiles"). "Can anything good come out of Nazareth?" (Jn. 1:46) was the attitude toward that infamous village. That the Servant of Jehovah, the Messiah, should come from a carpenter's family would be unthinkable to Jewish theology. A tender, green plant in dry parched ground is regarded with skepticism as to its origin and its survival. So Christ was looked upon.

Among all ancient peoples (even as among some modern advertisers) ideal physique, refined facial features, etc., were considered necessary prerequisites of future greatness, along with "right" parents, "right" birthplace, "right" schools, etc. These verses are not intended to describe Christ's facial features or His physique. They are simply predicting that men would judge Him by that inauspicious human appearance and completely reject Him because of their presuppositions. When Jesus was only a baby, Simeon the aged prophet took Him in his arms and predicted He was the "consolation of Israel and a light unto the Gentiles" but that He would become a "sign that is spoken against," (cf. Lk. 2:22-35). When He was arrested and mocked and tortured by the Sanhedrin, Pilate and Herod, there was no "form or comeliness" in Him that any of the nation desired Him to be king. Why would God plan it that His Servant come into the world in such untoward surroundings? In order to put men into the "refiner's fire." All who beheld His glory through eyes of faith and saw beyond the humiliation of the incarnation that He was the Son of God became sons of God. All who were blinded by their own carnal standards of "comeliness" and judged Jesus by them became "sons of disobedience." God wanted to get at the heart of man, for that is what He judges, not outward appearances.

Jesus was seldom treated with indifference. When He spoke or acted, people either clamored after Him or plotted against Him. But even most of the clamoring of the multitudes was only superficial. It was motivated by fleshly hunger for more "bread and fish" or for instantaneous healing of sicknesses. The Sadducees and Pharisees hated the Servant and plotted His death because He stripped away their facade of orthodoxy and exposed their immoral and rebellious hearts. And, in the end, these pretentious theologians and greedy legalists seduced the carnal-minded multitudes to clamor for His crucifixion! He was despised and rejected of men; forsaken and shunned. The two Hebrew words *makeoyoth* and *kholiy* are literally, "pain" and "sickness," but are translated, "sorrows" and "grief." When people saw that His earthly life was characterized by trouble, pain, rejection, sorrow, poverty, humiliation, absolute honesty and purity, few wanted to have anything to do with Him. Misunderstood by all—even His select disciples and His own human family—He was a "man of sorrows" (see comments on 49:4). How could Jesus have been a "man of sorrows" and yet speak so much of his "joy"? Because the *object* of His joy was beyond this world! (Heb. 12:1ff). All men who live godly in this world will suffer persecution (II Tim. 3:12; Jn. 15:18ff; 16:33), but they may also have joy if the *object* of their joy is beyond this world (Jn. 4:34; 15:11; 17:13, etc.).

What people turned away from the Servant of the Lord for when He was in human form on the earth they still turn away from Him for today—His substitutionary atonement. Some are superficially in agreement with what they think is His pacifistic humanitarianism or His socialistic human-rights stance, but they absolutely will not surrender to the truth that Jesus had to die for their sin. This is what was so unacceptable to the self-righteous Pharisees of Jesus' day. It remains a threat to the self-righteousness of men today!

QUIZ

1. How extensive was the unbelief predicted by Isaiah?
2. Who, alone, could fulfill the predictions of the Suffering Servant?
3. Would it have been a normal thing for the Jews to reject their Messiah?
4. Why did they reject the Servant-Messiah when He came?
5. Why did God foreordain such an inauspicious incarnation for His Servant?
6. What was the fundamental issue over which people turned away from Jesus?

b. SUFFERS

TEXT: 53:4-9

4 Surely he hath borne our griefs, and carried our sorrows; yet we did esteem him stricken, smitten of God, and afflicted.
5 But he was wounded for our transgressions, he was bruised for our iniquities; the chastisement of our peace was upon him; and with his stripes we are healed.
6 All we like sheep have gone astray; we have turned every one to his own way; and Jehovah hath laid on him the iniquity of us all.

7 He was oppressed, yet when he was afflicted he opened not
his mouth; as a lamb that is led to the slaughter, and as a
sheep that before its shearers is dumb, so he opened not his
mouth.
8 By oppression and judgment he was taken away; and as for
his generation, who among them considered that he was cut
off out of the land of the living for the transgression of my
people to whom the stroke was due?
9 And they made his grave with the wicked, and with a rich
man in his death; although he had done no violence, neither
was any deceit in his mouth.

QUERIES

a. How did He bear our "griefs and sorrows"?
b. How did Jehovah lay on Him the iniquity of us all?
c. Did any of His generation consider that he was cut off . . . for the stroke that was due them?

PARAPHRASE

And yet, it was the suffering that should have been ours He suffered; it was our pain He bore. All the time we were thinking that His suffering and humiliation was a sign that He was a blasphemer and God was punishing Him! But He was not a sinner—we were, and it was because of our sins He was wounded and because of our evil that He was willing to be scourged and crucified. Because of His substitutionary punishment for our sins we are vicariously justified and cleansed of iniquity and declared at peace with God. We are the ones who strayed away from The Shepherd. We are the ones who acted like dumb sheep wandering into unsafe and self-destructive pathways. We are the guilty ones, but God laid on Him the guilt of everyone of us. He was treated unjustly and cruelly, but he endured it willingly and without retaliation; He was innocent, and like an innocent lamb that is sacrificially slaughtered, He surrendered to death for us. Like a sheep that submits to being sheared without fighting back, so He did not resist His persecutors. He was tried, sentenced and led away to be crucified when He was completely innocent, and no one cared or understood that He was suffering the penalty that should have been every man's. Paradoxically, He was buried like a criminal but in a rich man's grave. He had done no wrong and had never spoken falsehood.

COMMENTS

v. 4-6 Atoning Grace: Unusual pain, sorrow and grief was equated with unusual guilt in the ancient world. Job's three friends told Job his calamities were punishment from God for his sinfulness (Job 3:7-8; 8:4; 11:6; 15:1-6). The man born blind was stigmatized as a sinner both by the disciples of Jesus and the Pharisees (cf. John 9:1ff.). Jesus *corrected* this concept in Luke 13 by saying that those upon whom the tower of Siloam fell were *not* worse sinners than others but that all calamities were warnings to the world to repent. And the Jews rationalized their prejudice against Jesus by mocking Him as a criminal at His crucifixion. Rather than admit their own ideas about God's Messiah were contrary to the Old Testament, they accused Jesus of blasphemy and pointed to His violation of their traditions and His humble life-style as proof that God was punishing Him for being such a sinner.

But there was nothing wrong with Him. We (all mankind) were the guilty ones. The rejection, misunderstanding, poverty, humiliation, slander He endured should have been ours. He was finally forsaken by God, suffered the second death (Mt. 27:46) and was *made to be sin* on our behalf (II Cor. 5:21; Gal. 3:13). He bore our sins on the tree (II Pet. 2:22-25). The Righteous died for the unrighteous (II Pet. 3:18). Christ did not deserve any of what He suffered. He was hated without cause (Jn. 15:24-25). The great capsulation of the atonement is Romans 3:21-26. The real suffering of the Servant was spiritual, not physical. Many men have suffered physically (perhaps even more torture than crucifxion), but He was innocent, without sin, and actually became sin and suffered spiritual separation (death) from the Father for those who actually deserved it. It is interesting to note that the Hebrew verb *meholal* translated "wounded" means literally *pierced, perforated,* a precise prophecy of the piercing of Christ's body by the Roman soldier (John 19:34-37).

Do verses four and five indicate that the atonement of Christ also provided miraculous healing of physical sicknesses for all mankind? Some modern faith-healers contend that all men who believe in the atonement of Christ may expect God to heal their bodies. T. J. McCrossan in his *Bodily Healing and the Atonement*, pg. 16, says, "Again all Christians should expect God to heal their bodies today, because Christ died to atone for our sickness as well as for our sins." Warren C. Roark, compiler of *Divine Healing,* pub. The Warner Press, Anderson, Ind., 1945, records a statement by a modern advocate of this view, E. E. Byers, pg. 58, "God . . . in the atonement . . . made provision for the healing of man's mortal body so long as he lived in this world." Although honest exegesis must admit that the Hebrew words *makeoyoth* and *kholiy* may literally mean "pain" and "sickness," one must understand they may also be figuratively translated "griefs" and "sorrows." The following considerations make it clear that Isaiah's prophecy of the atonement by the Suffering Servant did *not* mean to include physical healing for *all* believers:

1. The *context* (all important in proper exegesis) indicates the subject is sin, spiritual sickness, not physical sickness. If the atonement made provision for the healing of man's mortal body so long as he lived . . . he would live forever in this world! Death is the cumulative effect of one physical malady or another.
2. In Matthew 8:16-17 a *portion* of Isaiah's prophecy is quoted in connection with Christ's healing of some physical

sicknesses. However, it is highly significant that verse five was *not* quoted by Matthew ("with his stripes we are healed"). Furthermore, Jesus was fulfilling verse four three years before the atonement was made. Verse four was fulfilled in His divine ministry of healing, and not when He hung on the cross. Matthew was simply claiming, therefore, that Christ in performing miracles of healing, was fulfilling what Isaiah prophesied of His healing ministry and not His atonement.

3. There is no statement in the whole Bible suggesting that Christ "bore our sicknesses in his own body on the tree," or that he was made to be "sick, diseased, or possessed with infirmity" for us.
4. The New Testament plainly shows that not all of the healings of Jesus demanded faith in Him. Thus, the efficacy of His atonement could not apply to the healing.
5. The New Testament plainly shows that many people with faith in the atonement of Christ were *not* healed of their sicknesses, including the great apostle Paul!

Some questions on healing in the atonement:

a. If the atonement provides for physical healing, why does not one receive healing at conversion—the place where the efficacy of the atonement is applied?
b. If the atonement provides for physical healing, why do not all believers receive healing? (cf. Paul's "thorn in the flesh" II Cor. 12:7-10).
c. Why is there as large a *percentage* of sickness among believers as there is among unbelievers?
d. Why did Paul prescribe a medical treatment to Timothy for his "oft infirmities"? (I Tim. 5:23)
e. Why are there so many failures among faithful, honest, believing people who so earnestly and diligently seek healing?

THE HEALING MIRACLES OF CHRIST

Case	References	Nature of Malady	Nature of Cure	Comment
Nobleman's son	John 4:46, 54	Sick at the point of death	Healed the same hour	Father believed, but not the son
Impotent man	John 5:1-47	Infirm 30 years; couldn't walk	Made whole at once	No faith, except to walk
Demoniac in the Capernaum Synagogue	Mark 1:21-28 Luke 4:33-37	Possessed spirit of unclean demon	Instantly delivered	No faith indicated
Peter's wife's mother	Matt. 8:14-15 Mark 1:29-31 Luke 4:38-39	Possessed of a "great fever"	Fever left her immediately	No faith required
Many in Capernaum	Matt. 8:16-17 Mark 1:32-34 Luke 4:40-41	Demoniacs, sick, diseased	Instantly healed	No faith indicated
Leper	Matt. 8:1-4 Mark 1:40-45 Luke 5:12-16	Full of leprosy	Heal at once	Had faith; not required
Palsied man	Matt. 9:1-8 Mark 2:1-12 Luke 5:17-26	Palsied, could not walk	Instantly healed	Faith of others

Case	References	Nature of Malady	Nature of Cure	Comment
Man with withered hand	Matt. 12:9-14 Mark 3:1-6 Luke 6:6-11	Hand deformed	Instantly healed	No faith required but to extend hand
Many in Galilee	Matt. 4:23-24 Mark 3:7-12 Luke 6:17-19	All manner of sickness	Instantly healed	No faith indicated
Multitudes	Matt. 12:15-21	Not stated	Healed all	No faith
Blind and dumb demoniac	Matt. 12:22-24 Luke 11:14-15	Possessed a devil; blind and dumb	Healed at once	No faith required
Centurion's servant	Matt. 8:5-13 Luke 7:1-10	Palsied, tormented, and nearly dead	Made whole instantly	No faith of servant
Widow's son of Nain	Luke 7:11-17	Dead	Instantly sat up and spoke	No faith possible
Demoniac	Matt. 9:32-34	Dumb and demoniac	Instantly delivered	No faith evident
Two demoniacs at Gadara	Matt. 8:28-34 Mark 5:1-20 Luke 8:26-40	Possessed legion of devils. Fierce, couldn't be bound	Devils instantly cast out	No faith evident

Case	References	Nature of Malady	Nature of Cure	Comment
The daughter of Jairus	Matt. 9:18-25 Mark 5:34-43 Luke 8:43-48	Dead	Made alive at once	No faith possible
Woman with the issue of blood	Matt. 9:20-22 Mark 5:25-34 Luke 8:43-48	Afflicted 12 years Grew worse, suffered much	Made whole at once	Faith present, but not required
Two blind men	Matt. 9:27-31	Blind	Eyes opened immediately	Faith required
Healing of many	Matt. 14:34-36 Mark 6:55-56	Diseased	Made perfectly whole	No faith required
Daughter of Syrophonecian woman	Matt. 15:21-28 Mark 7:24-30	Demoniac	Made whole instantly	No faith of daughter, but of mother
Many near Galilee	Matt. 15:29-31	Lame, blind dumb, maimed	Healed at once	No faith indicated
Deaf and dumb man	Mark 7:31-37	Deaf with impediment of speech	Healed at once	No faith indicated
Blind man at Bethsaida	Mark 8:22-26	Blind	Saw at once	No faith indicated

Case	References	Nature of Malady	Nature of Cure	Comment
Demoniac child	Matt. 17:14-21	Lunatic, sore vexed; fell in fire and water	Cured that hour	Faith of the father, but not of child
Blind man	John 9:1-41	Blind from his birth	Saw at once	No faith required but to wash
Woman with infirmity	Luke 13:11-17	Bowed for 18 years	Immediately made straight	No faith required
Man with dropsy	Luke 14:1-6	Dropsy	Healed at once	No faith required
Lazarus	John 11:17-46	Dead	Made alive immediately	No faith possible
Ten lepers	Luke 17:11-19	Leprosy	Healed at once	No faith required
Two blind men	Matt. 20:29-34 Mark 10:46-52 Luke 18:35-43	Blind	Saw immediately	No faith required, but present
Servant of Malchus	Matt. 26:47-56 Mark 14:43-52 Luke 22:47-53 John 18:2-12	Ear severed	Ear replaced immediately	No faith required or indicated

Verse six plainly states the healing we receive from His stripes is the healing from sin. Sin is "going astray" (cf. Rom. 3:10-20). Sin is spiritual, psychological, mental sickness that needs healing. Paul calls sin insanity (I Cor. 15:34). Sin is spiritual disorientation. Man was not spiritually created for sin—it is against his spiritual nature. Spiritually, psychologically, emotionally and mentally man deterioriates when he sins. He begins to die, morally and spiritually when he begins to sin. Sin even causes some physical illnesses. Originally, of course, it caused all human illness and death as a constant reminder to man that he was not made for sin (cf. Rom. 1:27—men receive in their physical and psychological selves the "due penalty" for their sins). Jesus came and died and was raised to make us whole. Upon Him was the chastisement that allowed us to regain our innocence (our healing from sin). He takes the guilt and frees us from the deception of Satan's lies that we may come to our right minds (I Cor. 15:34). We still must suffer physical illnesses and death because of Adam's sin, but no longer do we have to suffer spiritual illness and death! Sin is soul-sickness. It fractures, incapacitates, ineverates and destroys the personhood of man. Forgiveness through Christ's atonement heals and saves us and restores us to the wholeness for which God created us.

v. 7-9 ACQUIESCENT GOODNESS: The Lord's servant was utterly innocent and totally submissive. He said nothing to answer the charges of the Sanhedrin (Mt. 26:63); He said nothing to answer the charges of Pilate (Mt. 27:14); He did not answer Herod's questions (Lk. 23:9). Pilate declared Him innocent; the Sanhedrin could bring no true accusation against Him (Jn. 18:19-24). Why did Jesus not argue His case? Would it have persuaded the Jews not to crucify Him even if He had? Jesus' mission as a "lamb" to be slaughtered was unique! He was the Lamb of God to take away the sin of the world (Jn. 1:29)! He was the only Person ever with that mission. His death was preordained. He was the Lamb, foreordained from the foundation of the earth to be slain (cf. I Pet. 1:20; Rev. 13:8; Acts 2:23). He willingly gave up His life, no one took it from

Him (cf. Jn. 10:17-18; 19:11; Heb. 10:1-10; etc.). *We* are not obligated to follow His acquiescent surrender to be illegally executed without reasonable defense. We cannot die for the same reason He died! We should never, of course, take the law into our own hands resisting evil. We must, if the occasion arises, suffer unjust trial and death without personally and individually using force to overthrow crooked judges. But that does not mean we cannot use peaceful, rational means to insist that justice be done. The apostle Paul insisted on correcting injustices (cf. Acts 16:35-39; 25:8-12, etc.); he also wrote that Christians should appeal to their civil governments to uphold justice (Rom. 13:1-7).

The Servant was "cut off" from life in this world (cf. our comments on Daniel 9:24-27 where the same phrase "cut off" is used in connection with the atoning death of the Messiah). And although there were a few plain announcements from Christ Himself that He was to die for the "ransom" of man's sins (cf. Jn. 1:29; Mt. 20:28; Mt. 26:26-29; Jn. 14:1-31; 16:10; 17:11), and many Old Testament types and prophecies (Lk. 24:25-49), none of His contemporaries (not even His own disciples) would accept the doctrine that the Messiah was to die as a substitutionary sacrifice for man's sins. The O.T. has at least four plain prophecies that the Messiah will die (Isaiah 53:1-12; Dan. 9:24-27; Zech. 12:10—13:1; Psa. 22:1-31). Still, even those honest, courageous, Jewish fishermen and tax-collectors who confessed that He was the Son of the Living God, refused to accept the predictions of Jesus Himself that He was to die as a ransom (Mt. 16:21-23; 26:30-35; Mk. 8:31-33; 14:26-31; Lk. 9:43-45; 24:13ff; Jn. 12:27-36 [the crowd said, We have heard from the law that the Christ remains forever—does not die]; Jn. 8:32-36). Isaiah graphically foretells that the Messiah would be slain as if He were a wicked person—a criminal—and yet, paradoxically, He would be buried in a rich man's grave. History records the exact fulfillment of this! Jesus was sentenced as a blasphemer by the Jews, a seditionist by the Romans and executed on a criminal's cross between two thieves. But He was buried in the rock-hewn tomb of the rich man, Joseph of Arimathea.

It is rather astounding that not one of Jesus' own generation comprehended that He was to die an atoning death. Especially since a few of them confessed that He was who He claimed to be, The Son of the Living God. The prophet, overwhelmed by the importance of the substitutionary atonement involved, falls back once more upon it as the only explanation of an outcome so strange. It was the Messiah's own people who had all the revelations of it in their Law and Prophets, and yet they are the ones who, at first totally rejected it; and ever since only a very small minority of Jews will accept it.

QUIZ

1. Why did the Jews "esteem" Jesus as "smitten of God"?
2. Why do we say that the real suffering of the Messiah was spiritual?
3. Do verses four-five indicate Jesus' atoning death also provided physical healing to all believers? Why not?
4. How is sin sickness?
5. Are we to follow Christ's example of acquiescing to death if illegally prosecuted and sentenced? Give examples.
6. How plainly does the O.T. and Christ Himself predict His atoning death?

c. SUCCEEDS

TEXT: 53:10-12

10 Yet it pleased Jehovah to bruise him; he hath put him to grief: when thou shalt make his soul an offering for sin, he shall see his seed, he shall prolong his days, and the pleasure of Jehovah shall prosper in his hand.

11 He shall see of the travail of his soul, and shall be satisfied: by the knowledge of himself shall my righteous servant

justify many; and he shall bear their iniquities.
12 Therefore will I divide him a portion with the great, and he shall divide the spoil with the strong; because he poured out his soul unto death, and was numbered with the transgressors: yet he bare the sin of many, and made intercession for the transgressors.

QUERIES

a. Why did it "please" Jehovah to bruise Christ?
b. How would the Servant be "satisfied" with His travail?
c. What "portion" did the Servant receive?

PARAPHRASE

Although it was God's purpose for the good of man to allow His Servant to be pierced to death and to suffer, when the Servant's death has become expiation for sin, then He will produce a multitude of spiritual descendants. He will then live forever and God's purpose for the good of man will have succeeded because of Him. And when He sees that God's plan has succeeded, He will rejoice with satisfaction. And because He knows and fulfills perfectly Jehovah's plan of salvation, He shall be able to impart righteousness and justification to many people through His atoning sacrifice. On account of His absolute victory over sin and death, He will be rewarded with a glory commensurate with His victory! He will be the greatest among the great. He is the greatest of all because He was servant of all pouring out His life unto death, allowing Himself, though He was sinless, to be made sin for others, putting His sinless innocence down as an offering on behalf of evil and wicked mankind.

COMMENTS

v. 10 PERPETUITY: The Hebrew word *khaphetz* means, "delighted" or "desired" and indicates that the death of the Messiah involved more than a sterile, unfeeling, deterministic plan of an unfeeling God. It is incomprehensible to the finite mind of sinful man how God could "delight" in the death of His Son, but He did. The Hebrew word translated *bruise* is *heheliy* and means to *make painful.* The Isaiah Scroll from Qumran has the word *vyhllhv* which means *that he might pierce him* (see comments on 53:5).

These verses are some of the strongest of the Old Testament on the resurrection or immortality of the Servant-Messiah. The Servant dies, but He also lives on, succeeds and carries out the work of atonement, redemption, justification, sanctification and intercession that the Father has entrusted to Him, just as it was predicted He would do (Lk. 24:25ff). Other O.T. prophecies of the resurrection of the Messiah:

Psa. 16:1-11 --Acts 2:25-33
Psa. 110:1-7 --Acts 2:34-36
Psa. 22:1-31 -----------------------------Mt. 27:46; Mk. 15:34
II Sam. 7:12; Psa. 89:3-4 ---------Acts 13:34 (The enduring throne promised to David's Messiah-Son presupposed victory over death.)
Gen. 22 (Abraham and Isaac; Heb. 11:17-19). Abraham, on Mt. Moriah, participated in a dramatic typical event portraying Calvary and the Empty Tomb. Perhaps Jesus was alluding to this when He said, "Abraham rejoiced to see my day . . . and was glad." Jn. 8:56
Psa. 118:22 (The stone which the builders rejected is become the head of the corner).

There is no doubt that Isaiah 53 is Messianic and that it is predicting His atoning death and resurrection. Philip, by the guidance of the Holy Spirit, interpreted it thusly, Acts 8:26-40.

The resurrection of Jesus Christ from the dead is a well established fact of history:

Proof of the Resurrection of Christ:

1. The historical records, by competent, credible, honest, numerous *eyewitnesses* say the tomb was empty. There is *no* historical testimony or evidence to the contrary. The only explanation is Mt. 28:11-15, soldiers were paid to say His disciples stole the body while the soldiers were asleep. How absurdly incredible!
2. Credible, competent, honest *eyewitnesses* testify they saw Jesus after his death, alive, talking to them, eating fish with them, even saw the nail prints in His hands.
3. The conversion of the enemies of Christianity can only be accounted for by the historical factuality of the resurrection of Christ (Saul of Tarsus; great company of the priests; even some of Caesar's own household).
4. The Catacombs of Rome depict the resurrection of Jesus and testify to the belief in it by first century saints.
5. The existence of the church and its ordinances testifies to the resurrection. The fact of the New Testament itself is inexplicable apart from it.

It is not a question of *could* the resurrection occur or not. It is a question of *did* it occur or not—not a philosophical question, but a historical, scientific question!

Merrill C. Tenney says, "The event is fixed in history, the dynamic is potent for eternity."

Unbelievers say Christ was not raised from the dead—I say prove it! All the reliable evidence we have says He was!

The church began in the city where Jesus' burial was known, among those who could have refuted the testimony of Peter (Acts 2) and proved it false. All they would have to have done was produce the body of Jesus! But 3000 testify that He had arisen and Peter was telling the truth.

There are Imperatives to the Resurrection.

1. There is power in it. The power of Christianity is not in the esthetic value of great cathedrals, somber ritual and tradition, nor emotionalism but in the *historical fact* of the

resurrection of Christ.

a. Gives hope that is living (I Pet. 1:3)
b. Brings joy unspeakable and full of glory (I Jn. 1:1-4)
c. Sanctifies and purifies (I Jn. 3:3; Acts 17:32)
d. Gives power to evangelism (Acts 4:33)
e. Gives stedfastness (I Cor. 15:58)

2. There is only one alternative to the resurrection. That is a life of eating, drinking, for tomorrow we die (I Cor. 15:12-19—15:32).
3. But, if Christ is raised from the dead, and we shall be also, then:
   a. The Bible is God's Word!
   b. Heaven and Hell are real places!
   c. Man will live forever, one place or the other!
   d. A man's sins may really be forgiven!
   e. The plan of salvation in the N.T. is the only valid one!
   f. Christ is coming again!
   g. There is only one church, the universal body of Christ which consists of all who believe in Christ, are repenting of their sins and have been immersed in water in obedience to His command!
   h. No one will be saved who is not a member of that church!

The resurrection of Christ makes all the above imperative! There is no middle ground on any of that because His resurrection establishes beyond any question His deity and His authority!

The Servant shall produce "seed" or descendants. He shall have a family, but it will be a spiritual family (cf. Rom. 9:8; Gal. 3:15-20; 3:23-29). So, it is in being lifted up He will draw men unto Him (cf. Jn. 3:14-15; 8:28; 12:32). He shall fall into the ground like a grain of wheat and die, and then bear much fruit (Jn. 12:23-26). And the *khephetz* (delight) of Jehovah shall succeed through His efforts. The delight of Jehovah is, of course, His eternal plan for the redemption of man! What wonder, what unsearchable grace, that Jehovah's delight should be the salvation and regeneration of a planet full of wicked rebels. But more wonderful, His Son should come to this planet in the form of a man and willingly submit to humiliating death allowing Himself, though absolutely innocent, to become sin on man's behalf!

v. 11 PLEASURE: The Servant will have "travail of . . . soul" (cf. 49:4ff). But He will be "satisfied." For the joyous reward that was set before Him, He could endure the cross (cf. Heb. 12:2). He will look back from His enthronement at the right hand of the Father and see that He has succeeded in accomplishing the once-for-all-time redemption and regeneration of the Father's creation (man and cosmos). As Young points out, the suffix on the Hebrew word *beda'etto* is difficult of interpretation. Is the suffix subjective or objective—that is, is Isaiah speaking of the knowledge that the servant himself possesses or of knowledge of the servant on the part of others? We think the context is emphasizing the successfulness of the Servant Himself and that it is through His own incarnation (human experience) that He performs His work of justification. It was through the experience of obedience as a Son that He became the author of eternal salvation unto all them that obey Him (cf. Heb. 5:7-9; Phil. 2:5-11). The righteous servant (*tzaddiyk 'aveddiy*) will make many righteous (*yatzeddiyk*). He makes it possible for us to become the righteousness of God in Him (II Cor. 5:21). This was the "grace that was to be ours" which the prophets prophesied (cf. I Pet. 1:10-12). He bore our iniquities and became a "curse for us" (cf. Gal. 3:13).

v. 12 PORTION: On account of the Servant's victory over sin, Satan and death, Jehovah will exalt Him above every other man. The exaltation of the Servant of Jehovah is clearly predicted by the prophet earlier (Isa. 49:7; 52:15). When the Servant made purification for sins, he was enthroned at the right hand of the Majesty on high (Heb. 1:3-4). When He ascended, He took captivity captive (Eph. 4:8) and dispensed His gifts according to His will and purpose for the ongoing of the kingdom of God here on earth. The Servant whom the Jews crucified, God made both Lord and Christ (Acts 2:36). There is no other name under heaven given among men by which we must be saved (Acts 4:12). The reason for this exaltation is summarized in the statement, "because he poured out his soul unto death." "Worthy is the Lamb that was slain to receive power, and riches, and wisdom, and strength, and honor, and glory, and blessing" (Rev. 5:12).

A whole volume could justifiably be written on this chapter alone. Perhaps the most intriguing question about Isaiah 53 is: "If the New Testament is so clear about its fulfillment in Jesus Christ, why do the majority of Jews not see and understand it?" A few references to The Servant of Jehovah in Jewish literature, both ancient and modern, may provide a partial answer to this question:

Jewish Apocrypha and The Suffering Servant concept:

The apocalyptic literature of the Jewish apocrypha are such books as I Enoch, The Sibylline Oracles, The Testaments of the XII Patriarchs, the Psalms of Solomon, II Esdras, II Baruch and others. They were written in the years 165 B.C.—100 A.D.

In a book entitled, *The Method and Message of Jewish Apocalyptic,* by D. S. Russell, pub. Westminster, we learn, "There is no serious evidence of the bringing together of the concepts of the Suffering Servant and the Davidic Messiah *before* the Christian era." Mr. Russell continues, "The Targum (Jewish Targums are rabbinical interpretations of the O.T.) on Isaiah 53 has often been alluded to, but it cannot be the Suffering Servant Isaiah predicted. The Messiah presented in this Targum is one who will triumph over the heathen and all the enemies of God's people! The suffering he has to endure is minimal and devoid of all vicariousness. In fact, it is hardly suffering at all, for it consists simply in the exposure of himself to those dangers he will have to face in the coming struggle with the heathen before his final victory is assured. There is *no* mention of an *atoning death—no* reference to a *suffering and dying Messiah.*

II Esdras and II Baruch (cir. 90 A.D.) use the word "servant" to describe the Messiah from the seed of David. However, there is no suggestion of a suffering Messiah, or an atoning death. He is not killed by enemies or disease—he simply ceases to exist. The reference to his death is with the same casualness as any human death. He establishes his kingdom, dies, and presumably will rise with other humans at the general resurrection of the people of God."

Modern Jews:

1. A Jewish woman doctor, recounting her conversion to Christ in a book called *Pursued:*

   While recuperating from illness she began reading a Bible. She read Isaiah 53. She was forced to acknowledge it must be talking about the Messiah. But then she said she refused to accept the consequences of that passage for her Messiah. Suddenly she realized that she was reading from the KJV, "A Protestant Bible! Of course, it was slanted to sound that way. I went to sleep that night, confident I had caught the gentiles at a not-too-clever trick."

   But then she read it in a Jewish Bible and it was basically the same message!

2. "Chapters 52-53 (of Isaiah) and other chapters contain the prophecies concerning the 'suffering servant' which the Christian church later interpreted as referring to Jesus, but which, *in Jewish tradition, refer to the people of Israel,"* pg. 151 from, *The International Jewish Encyclopedia,* by Rabbi ben Isaacson and Deborah Wigoder, compiled and produced in Israel for Prentice-Hall.

3. *History of the Jew,* by Heindrich Graetz, pub. The Jewish Pub. Soc. of America, 1893, in chapter entitled "Messianic Expectations and Origins of Christianity," indicates the idea of a *suffering* Messiah was completely foreign to Jewish thinking.

It it not difficult now to understand the "rebuke" Peter had for Jesus (Mt. 16:22) when Jesus predicted His death!

4. *Non-Messianic Interpretations:*
   a. Most prevalent among Jewish writers is that Isaiah 53 means *the nation of Israel.* Some say *empirical* Israel; some say *ideal* Israel; some say the *pious remnant* of the true Israel.
   b. Isaiah 53 means the *prophetical order*—i.e. the collective body of the prophets . . . as the sacrificial victim taking upon itself the sins of the people.
   c. Isaiah 53 means *an individual* (Hezekiah, Isaiah, Josiah, but most frequently, Jeremiah), but a *human* individual. Some said, an *unknown* sufferer (sounds like the apostles first answer to Jesus at Cesarea Philippi, Mt. 16).
5. Aaron Kligerman, in his book, *Old Testament Messianic Prophecy,* pub. Zondervan, paperback, thinks there were some Jewish interpretations which believed the Suffering Servant was to be the Messiah. He refers to *Yalkut* and *Rambam* which are Talmudic and Midrashic literature of the days of Maimonides (cir. 1135-1204 A.D.). These are so obscure, however, they are not worth considering as having direct reference to the Messiah as an individual. They could be understood in any of the categories listed above. Furthermore, they are of such late date they are probably concessions to Christian interpretations of Isaiah 53.

Jews are not alone in disavowing the biblical doctrine of the substitutionary atonement. Bishop G. Bromley Oxnam, former head of the World Council of Churches says in his book, *A Testament of the Faith,* pg. 144, Boston, 1958;

> "We hear much of the substitutionary theory of the atonement. This theory to me is immoral. If Jesus paid it all, or if He is the substitute for me, or if He is the sacrifice for all the sin of the world, then why discuss forgiveness? The books are closed. Another has paid the debt, borne the penalty. I owe nothing. I am absolved. I cannot see forgiveness as predicated upon the act of some one else. It is my sin. I must atone."

It is not trite to repeat that Philip, by the guidance of the Holy Spirit, applied Isaiah 53 to the atoning death and justifying resurrection of Jesus Christ. It is difficult to see how one may claim to be a disciple of Jesus and contradict this doctrine!

QUIZ

1. How do these verses teach the resurrection of Jesus Christ?
2. Is the resurrection of Christ historically valid?
3. What "knowledge" of Himself was involved in the Servant's justifying work?
4. Why do you think the Jews will not accept Jesus Christ as the fulfillment of Isaiah 53?

EXAMINATION

CHAPTERS FORTY-NINE THROUGH FIFTY-THREE

DEFINITION

(Define the following words or phrases as they were discussed in the comments.)

1. *Israel*
2. *acceptable* time
3. *Sinim*
4. *graven* on palms
5. face like *flint*
6. *monster*
7. *cup* of staggering
8. *sprinkle* man nations
9. *griefs* and *sorrows*
10. *wounded*
11. *pleased, pleasure*
12. *bruised*

MEMORIZATION

Surely he hath _____ our griefs, and carried our _____; yet we did esteem him _____, smitten of God, an _____.

But he was ______ for our transgressions, he was ______ for our iniquities; the chastisement of our ______ was upon him; and with his stripes we are ______. All we like sheep have gone ______; we have turned every one to his own ______; and Jehovah hath laid on him the ______ of us all. (53:4-6)

EXPLANATION

1. Explain the prediction that the Messiah would experience frustration.
2. Explain how the Messiah was to *become* a covenant.
3. Explain why the Servant (Messiah) was to be "as one who was taught."
4. Explain how O.T. people could have God's law *on their heart.*
5. Explain how the cup of staggering was taken out of Jerusalem's hand.
6. Explain how Christ bore our griefs and sorrows in His death.
7. Explain why Isaiah 53 does not teach divine healing for today.
8. Explain why the Messiah would be satisfied with the travail of His soul.
9. Explain why the majority of the Jews did not accept Jesus as the Servant.

APPLICATION

(In its context every scripture has one meaning—the author's intended meaning. How may the following be applied in the believer's life?)

1. Is there an application for overcoming frustration in our own human experience from the Messiah's overcoming?
2. How may we apply the proofs we have that God bared His holy arm in Jesus Christ?

3. Does the humiliating entrance and exit of the Messiah in history apply to modern man's relation to God?
4. Does the personal refusal of Christ to defend Himself at His illegal trial and death mean Christians must never defend themselves? Why?
5. How can modern men accept and apply the death of a Jewish man (Jesus) nearly 2000 years ago for the atonemen of their personal sins?
6. Are there any definitive manifestations of God's *love* in this section that may contradict the allegation that the God of the O.T. is *only* a God of wrath?
7. Are there any teachings in this section which may be applied to the idea that there is salvation for the world *only* in Jesus Christ?

SPECIAL STUDY

THE RIGHTEOUSNESS OF GOD AS MANIFESTED BY THE PROPHETS

by John Butterman

INTRODUCTION

I. God is Righteous in Judging His People

1. God is the judge over all the earth
   a. From the beginning in the Hebrew community the judges were acting on behalf of God (Deut. 1:17)
   b. It was unthinkable that he would act unfairly (Gen. 18:25)
2. God is the fountain of justice
   a. Everything he does may be relied upon as just (Deut. 32:4; Zeph. 3:5)
   b. God's equity as judge will be seen most clearly "in the day of the revelation of the righteous judgment of God" (Rom. 2:5)

   c. Man's righteousness is defined in terms of God's judgment
3. God is impartial in his dealings
   a. The prophet Amos called for a similar righteousness in men (Amos 5:15, 24)
   b. Inflicting retribution is an element of the righteousness of God (Isaiah 61:2)
   c. If in a world of unrighteousness, righteousness is to be established, God himself must become the indicator and protector of the oppresssed
   d. God's righteousness is manifested in his defense of those who have no helper (Psalms 10:14; 72:12)

II. God is Righteous in Protecting His People

1. In his rescue of them from Egypt
   a. The victories which accomplished this are described as the righteous acts of God (Judges 5:11; I Sam 12:7)
   b. The pharaoh himself acknowledged that the ten plagues were evidence of God's righteousness (Ex. 9:27)
2. In his redemption of his people from exile
   a. God showed his righteousness by this deliverance
   b. This righteousness is closely associated with salvation (Isaiah 45:8; 46:13; 51:5-6)
3. In his redemption of his people from sin
   a. The messianic king is just and having salvation (Zech. 9:9)
   b. The Gospel is the power of God unto salvation to everyone who believes; in it is revealed the righteousness of God

MAIN THOUGHTS

I. The Prophets Revealed the Righteousness of God

1. Man has no righteousness of his own
   a. It hurts to be told that man's righteousness is but a filthy rag in God's sight

b. How futile to try to establish our own righteousness by our own works (Isaiah 64:4)
c. The human heart is deceitful and desperately wicked (Jer. 17:9) and therefore cannot produce righteousness acceptable to God
d. The garment of our own self-righteousness is our pride (Isaiah 64:9)
e. Man must turn from his own self-righteousness to Christ who was made unto us righteousness (Isaiah 45:8, 24; 46:12-13; 54:17)

2. God provided for man what he could not do for himself
   a. A way to return to Zion
      (1) He will come and save you (Isaiah 35:4)
      (2) There shall be streams in the desert (Isaiah 35:6)
      (3) The highway shall be called the Holy Way (Isaiah 35:8)
      (4) The ransomed of the Lord shall return (Isaiah 35:10)
   b. A river shall flow from the sanctuary
      (1) Everything will live where the river goes (Ezek. 47:9)
      (2) This river will enable trees to grow with fruit for food and leaves for healing (Ezek. 47:12)
   c. A fountain shall be opened
      (1) To cleanse the inhabitants from sin (Ezek. 13:1)
      (2) To cleanse them from all uncleanness
   d. A well of salvation will be opened
      (1) To draw the water of life from
      (2) To proclaim that his name is exalted

3. The prophets revealed the righteous One
   a. His revealed birth
      (1) "Behold, a virgin shall conceive, and bear a son, and shall call his name Immanuel" (Isaiah 7:14)
      (2) "For unto us a child is born, unto us a son is given" (Isaiah 9:6)
   b. His revealed ministry
      (1) Beyond Jordan, in Galilee . . . the light shined

(Isaiah 9:1-2)
- (2) The Lord shall suddenly come to his temple (Malachi 3:1)
- (3) Sent to the lost sheep of Israel (Ezek. 37:11; Jer. 50:6)
- (4) The Spirit of the Lord is upon me (Isaiah 61:1)
- (5) The eyes of the blind shall be opened (Isaiah 42:7)

c. His revealed death
- (1) They weighed my price thirty pieces of silver (Zech. 11:12)
- (2) He opened not his mouth (Isaiah 53:7)
- (3) They shall smite the judge of Israel with a rod (Micah 5:1)
- (4) He was wounded for our transgressions (Isaiah 53:5)
- (5) He was numbered with the transgressors (Isaiah 53:9)
- (6) He made intercession for the transgressors (Isaiah 53:12)
- (7) They shall look upon me whom they have pierced (Zech. 12:10)
- (8) It shall come to pass on that day, that I will make the sun go down at noon, and I will darken the earth on a clear day (Amos 8:9)
- (9) He would make his grave with the rich (Isaiah 53:9)
- (10) He gave his back to smiters (Isaiah 50:6)
- (11) He poured out his soul unto death (Isaiah 53:12)

d. His revealed resurrection
- (1) Thy dead men shall live together . . . they shall arise (Ezek. 37:7-10)
- (2) Those that sleep in the dust of the earth shall awake (Dan. 12:2)
- (3) In the third day he shall raise us up, and we shall live in his sight (Hos. 6:2)
- (4) I will ransom them from the power of the grave (Hos. 13:14)

II. The Christ Brought the Righteousness of God

1. Unrighteous man is totally incapable of making himself righteous enough to be accepted by God
2. Jesus brought righteousness to man
   a. "By his knowledge shall my righteous servant justify many" (Isaiah 53:11)
   b. "The righteousness is of me, saith the Lord" (Isaiah 54:17)
   c. "Unto the Son, God said . . . a scepter of righteousness is the scepter of thy kingdom (Heb. 1:8)
   d. "To declare his righteousness . . . that he might be just (right) and the justifier (the one who puts right) of him which believeth in Jesus" (Rom. 3:25-26)
   e. He (Jesus) is righteous (I John 2:29)
3. Jesus was qualified to become our righteousness
   a. Because he was just and right in all his ways and witness, ever obedient to his righteous Father
   b. Because he was never crooked in his dealings with others
   c. Because his life was never out of the least fraction from the plumbline of truth and morality
4. Jesus brought the justice of God
   a. "Of the increase of his government and peace . . . upon the throne of David . . . to establish it . . . with justice" (Isaiah 9:7)
   b. "Behold thy king comes . . . he is just" (Zech. 9:9)
   c. "I judge and my judgment is just" (John 5:30)
   d. Peter claims him to be just:
      (1) "You denied the Holy One and the Just" (Acts 3:14)
      (2) "Christ . . . the just for the unjust" (I Pet. 3:18)

III. The Believers are Constituted the Righteousness of God

1. The sinner through believing is constituted the righteousness of God
   a. The devil cannot call in question the fact that God is

"just and the justifier of him who believes in Jesus" (Zech. 3:2)

b. So we can rest secure and serene in the confidence that
   (1) Christ is our peace—who can disturb it?
   (2) Christ is our hope—who can destroy it?
   (3) Christ is our righteousness—who can tarnish it?

2. Man's righteousness came by *someone* not *something*
   a. Even him who possessed Lordship (Mark 12:36-37)
   b. Righteousness is not earned, it is imputed to man
   c. Daniel speaks of the wise turning many to righteousness (Dan. 12:3), which means they are brought to God who alone can justify them
   d. Such righteousness is said to be reckoned or imputed, and put to the account of a guilty sinner accepting God's terms of salvation, Isa. 55:1ff.
   e. It is reckoned unto man on the ground of Christ's finished work
3. Divine righteousness can only become ours by faith in Christ
   a. By his knowledge shall the righteous one, my servant, make many to be accounted righteous; and he shall bear their iniquities (Isaiah 53:11)
   b. In his days Judah will be saved, and Israel will dwell securely. And this is the name by which he will be called: "The Lord is our righteousness" (Jer. 23:7)
   c. The righteousness of God by faith (Rom. 3:26; 4:6; II Cor. 5:21)

CONCLUSION

I. God's Righteousness is Shown in His Saving of His People

1. The prophets revealed it
2. In Christ he is now doing it
3. His people are no longer a restricted race but include all who believe (Rom. 2:28-29)
4. "As many as call upon the name of the Lord shall be

saved" (Joel 3:32; Acts 2:38-39)

II. God's Righteousness Declares Righteous Those Who Believe in Jesus

1. God justifies those who have faith in Jesus (Rom. 3:22)
2. It is the righteousness of God that is imparted to man, not man's own self-righteousness that he is to seek after (Phil. 3:9)

III. God's Righteousness of His People is Based on Redemption Brought by Christ

1. Men are justified by his grace as a gift, through the redemption (Rom. 3:24)
2. It is a righteousness through forgiveness, based on the blood of Christ (I John 1:7, 9)
3. God put Christ forward as an expiation by his blood to be received by faith (Rom. 3:25)
4. This was to show God's passing over sins aforetime (Rom. 3:24)
5. It was to prove in the present time that He himself is righteous and that he justifies him who has faith in Jesus (Rom. 3:26)

IV. God's Righteousness Provides Manifold Blessings

1. The righteous are blessed with prosperity: "Say you to the righteous, that it shall be well with him: for they shall eat the fruit of their doing" (Isaiah 3:10)
2. The righteous are surrounded by divine favor: "For thou, Lord, will bless the righteous; with favor will thou compass him as with a shield (Psalm 5:12)
3. The righteous experience deliverance from affliction: "Many are the afflictions of the righteous, but the Lord delivereth him out of them all" (Psalm 34:19)
4. The righteous enjoy peace, quietness, and assurance: "And the work of righteousness shall be peace; and the effect of righteousness, quietness and assurance forever" (Isaiah 32:17)

V. God's Righteousness Provides Hope in His Glory.

1. The time is coming when the heavens will delcare his righteousness.
2. When the Sun of Righteousness appears with healing in his wings (Malachi 4:2) accompanied by all the heavenly saints, what a glorious consummation that will be of his work on our behalf.
3. The ultimate blessing of righteousness by faith is eternity with Him who is our righteousness. This is the glad hope of the righteous (Malachi 3:17-18).
4. "Hope of righteousness" is the sight of the righteous One himself, who promised to return for his own (John 14:3).

VIII. COMMUNION THROUGH GOD'S COVENANT CHAPTERS 54 - 59

A. WED TO THE LORD IN COVENANT RELATIONSHIP CHAPTER 54

1. RECONCILED

TEXT: 54:1-8

1 Sing, O barren, thou that didst not bear; break forth into singing, and cry aloud, thou that didst not travail with child: for more are the children of the desolate than the children of the married wife, saith Jehovah.
2 Enlarge the place of thy tent, and let them stretch forth the curtains of thy habitations; spare not: lengthen thy cords, and strengthen thy stakes.
3 For thou shalt spread abroad on the right hand and on the left; and thy seed shall possess the nations, and make the desolate cities to be inhabited.
4 Fear not; for thou shalt not be ashamed: neither be thou

confounded; for thou shalt not be put to shame: for thou
shalt forget the shame of thy youth; and the reproach of thy
widowhood shalt thou remember no more.
5 For thy Maker is thy husband; Jehovah of hosts is his name:
and the Holy One of Israel is thy Redeemer; the God of the
whole earth shall he be called.
6 For Jehovah hath called thee as a wife forsaken and grieved
in spirit, even a wife of youth, when she is cast off, saith
thy God.
7 For a small moment have I forsaken thee; but with great
mercies will I gather thee.
8 In overflowing wrath I hid my face from thee for a moment;
but with everlasting lovingkindness will I have mercy on
thee, saith Jehovah thy Redeemer.

QUERIES

a. Who is the "barren" one?
b. Why "enlarge" the place of her tent?
c. When did God "forsake" her?

PARAPHRASE

When the Suffering Servant of God accomplishes His work, O Zion, My covenant people you will sing and shout for joy. You have not been able to produce spiritual offspring; you have been like a childless woman. You have been cast off by your Husband-God because you sinned against Him, but through the reconciling work of the Messiah you shall have more children than you had when you were married. Prepare yourself to accept the expansion of God's kingdom beyond your present nation because through the Messiah, God is going to establish a kingdom that stretches to the ends of the earth. The offspring that shall be given you through the Servant will include people from every nation on the earth. The Servant will also take away the humiliation of your present barrenness. You will not suffer the reproach of spiritual barrenness again, because the God who created you is also your Husband. The Faithful Covenant God, Jehovah—the Holy One of Israel—The Sovereign, Omnipotent God of all creation—He is your Redeemer. This is the God who has promised to betroth you to Himself through the Servant, even though He has forsaken you and cast you off because of your unfaithfulness. I will cast you off into captivity for only a short time, but My mercy extended to you through the Servant will be great. In a flood of wrath I will turn away from protecting you for a short time, but I will love you and be kind to you forever through the Servant.

COMMENTS

v. 1-4 Repopulated: The result of the Suffering Servant's redemptive work (52:13—53:12) shall be a prolific spiritual offspring. He is to "bring many sons to glory" (Heb. 2:10-13). That is why Zion (God's faithful remnant in the O.T. which will become His church in the N.T.) is told to "break forth into singing." The physical descendants of Abraham (cf. Gen. 12:1-3; 17:2-8, etc.) did not produce spiritually as they should have. Most of his offspring turned to idolatry and ungodliness. Jerusalem, the "holy" city, was barren of spiritual children except for a small remnant of faithful (cf. Isa. 8:16). But when the Servant shall have completed His work Israel shall produce spiritual offspring prolifically (cf. Gal. 3:29). Jerusalem cannot produce because God, her Husband has forsaken her on account of her sins. She will be given over to captivity for a season. But the time will come when she will produce more children than a woman who had never been forsaken (cf. Isa. 49:18-26; 51:1-3; Zech. 2:1-5; Hosea 1:10-12). She will produce a "great multitude which no man could number, from every nation, from all tribes and peoples and tongues . . ." (Rev. 7:9).

Inasmuch as the "new" Jerusalem (the Messiah's kingdom, the church) is to produce an innumerable offspring, she will need to "enlarge" her "tent." Jehovah instructs the people of Isaiah's day to stretch their faith to accept an expanded concept of the Messiah's kingdom. God is going to extend covenant relationship to more than Jews; He is going to include "the nations." Ezekiel's vision of the glorified temple, land, city and priesthood (Ezek. 40—48) is a graphic, figurative prophecy of the immense enlargement which will be necessary for the coming messianic kingdom. Ezekiel's "temple" was never intended to be literally built. It is hyperbole. The *terumah* ("most holy place" RSV, Ezek. 48:12) measures about 2500 square miles, nearly twice as large as the whole area of geographic Judea! The rebuilt temple (Ezek. 40:2) of Ezekiel was 500 reeds (4500 square feet), larger than the literal Jerusalem of Ezekiel's day or our day. Ezekiel's exaggerated temple, land and city are visionary predictions of the "enlargement" of the messianic age. Micah predicts, "A day for the building of your walls! In that day (the messianic age) the boundary shall be far extended . . ." (Micah 7:11f).

Jehovah's people are to take comfort in the fact that their redemption draws nigh. The finished work of the Servant is now on the prophetic horizon (Isa. 53), therefore, Zion need no longer look upon her temporary captivity and "indignation" with hopelessness. She shall forget all her shame when the Servant comes and takes her shame upon Himself. The reproach associated with barrennesss will be forgotten when she begins to produce spiritual children through the gospel. She will then be the church of Christ "without spot or blemish" (Eph. 5:25-27).

v. 5-8 REUNITED: Through the Servant, Jehovah will reclaim His "wife." Jehovah will be reunited, remarried to His people in a new covenant relationship (cf. Isa. 56:6-8; Jer. 31:27-34; Ezek. 37:24-28; etc.). The Old covenant will pass away and be remembered no more (cf. Jer. 3:15-18). They must remember that the prophet Isaiah is speaking the promise of Almighty God. They must find their reasons for singing and shouting and for overcoming their shame and hopelessness in the fact that these are promises of Jehovah, the Holy One of Israel, the God of the whole earth! Jehovah will call back His forsaken wife (cf. Ezek. 16:53-63; Hosea 1:10-12; 2:14-23; 3:1-5), through the messianic covenant. The Lord will forsake Zion for only a short time (during the "indignation"; see our comments, *Daniel,* Dan. 8:19; 11:36, College Press) compared with the time He will show His great mercy to Zion. The "indignation" will last only 600 years (from the captivities until the Christ). But Jehovah will show *everlasting* lovingkindness to Zion.

The interesting thing about this passage in which the Lord refers to His reconciliation to His "wife" is that it is to include the "nations" (*goiym,* Gentiles). The Gentiles will be called into the new covenant relationship and be a part of the "bride of Christ." Although the prophets predicted it and the Christ taught it, many of the Jews could never accept it. It took even some of the apostles a few years to understand and accept it (cf. Acts 10, 11, 15; Gal. 2, etc.).

QUIZ

1. What is the basis for Zion's singing and shouting?
2. Where in the Prophets do we have a visionary picture of the "enlargement" of Zion to receive the messianic multitudes?
3. What is the basis of Zion's being able to forget her shame?
4. How long did God forsake her?

2. REGALED

TEXT: 54:9-17

9 For this is as the waters of Noah unto me; for as I have sworn that the waters of Noah shall no more go over the earth, so have I sworn that I will not be wroth with thee,

nor rebuke thee.

10 For the mountains may depart, and the hills be removed; but my lovingkindness shall not depart from thee, neither shall my covenant of peace be removed, saith Jehovah that hath mercy on thee.

11 O thou afflicted, tossed with tempest, and not comforted, behold, I will set thy stones in fair colors, and lay thy foundations with sapphires.

12 And I will make thy pinnacles of rubies, and thy gates of carbuncles, and all thy border of precious stones.

13 And all thy children shall be taught of Jehovah; and great shall be the peace of thy children.

14 In righteousness shalt thou be established: thou shalt be far from oppression, for thou shalt not fear; and from terror, for it shall not come near thee.

15 Behold, they may gather together, but not by me: whosoever shall gather together against thee shall fall because of thee.

16 Behold, I have created the smith that bloweth the fire of coals, and bringeth forth a weapon for his work; and I have created the waster to destroy.

17 No weapon that is formed against thee shall prosper; and every tongue that shall rise against thee in judgment thou shalt condemn. This is the heritage of the servants of Jehovah, and their righteousness which is of me, saith Jehovah.

QUERIES

a. What do the "waters of Noah" have to do with this text?
b. Why mention her "stones"?
c. How shall their righteousness be from Jehovah?

PARAPHRASE

Your redemption from captivity and salvation through the coming Servant is certain. The covenant relationship through the Servant is as sure as the covenant I made in the days of Noah when I swore that the waters would no more destroy the earth. So I have now sworn to turn away My anger from you through the atoning work of the Servant. In fact, My covenant through the Servant is even more certain than that! Even if the mountains and hills and the earth pass away, My covenant of reconciliation in the Servant shall never pass away. O you helpless and oppressed Zion, I am going to make you beautiful. I will lay your foundations with sapphires, your towers with rubies, your gates will be built of stones that shine and glow like fire and I will build your walls with precious stones of all kinds. All of your children shall have the privilege of being taught by God Himself. He will come directly from heaven to earth in the flesh. He will bring great peace and prosperity to all your children. You shall be vindicated and declared righteous, O Zion, and you shall be delivered from spiritual oppression and fear; the terror of guilt and judgment shall never come to you again. You will survive all your enemies even though they may conspire to destroy you; they do so against My will and I will destroy them. I create and control those who build weapons; I also create and control those who use weapons against My people. I will not let any weapon or any army completely destroy My Zion. There will be no accusation permitted to stand against you then, because your righteousness shall be imputed to you from Me. This is what I am going to give you, Zion, says the Lord.

COMMENTS

v. 9-10 PERMANENCE: The future reconciliation promised in 54:1-8 is, of course, predicted on the condition that Zion will enter into covenant relationship with Jehovah through the Suffering Servant who is to come. This covenant relationship will be as intimate and precious as a marriage; for that, in fact, is what it will be—the Lord married to His bride (the church) Zion. In the verse before us now, the *permanence* or *certainty* of that relationship is declared. When the Lord predicts that He will enter into a covenant of reconciliation with Zion, it is as certain to come to pass as His promise not to destroy the world by a flood again.

God's covenant sign to Noah was the rainbow. God's covenant sign of reconciliation was the resurrection of Jesus Christ from the dead. The Jews of Jesus' day were not satisfied by the evidence of His miracles that He came to fulfill the covenant promises made through the prophets. Jesus told them that *one* great sign would be given them (the sign of Jonah; Mt. 12:38-42; Lk. 11:29-32) confirming that He was the Messenger of the Covenant (cf. Mal. 3:1-4). The writer of Hebrews said that when God desired to demonstrate the immutability of His promise of covenant reconciliation, He "interposed" (*emesiteusen,* Gr., Heb. 6:17) with an oath. What God actually did was "interpose" *Himself* as that oath, incarnate in Jesus Christ. All the promises of God find their verification, validation, confirmation and authentication ("Yes" or "Amen") in Christ (cf. II Cor. 1:18-20). The new covenant is one of a "living hope" by the resurrection of Jesus Christ from the dead (I Pet. 3:3-5). The surety of God's new covenant does not originate subjectively within man. It does not have its basis in man's ability to earn surety through self-righteousness. The surety of God's reconciliation is in God's objective, historical "interposition" in the death and resurrection of Jesus Christ. We appropriate it by faith and may experience it subjectively, but its certainty is in its objectivity and historicity! The confirmation of God's new covenant is even more certain than the confirmation of the covenant made to Noah. Mountains and hills, heaven and earth, rainbows and clouds may pass away (and most certainly will), but Christ conquered death and lives forever. The Word of God, confirmed by the resurrection of Christ, abides forever (Mt. 5:17-20; 24:35; I Pet. 1:22-25). God through Isaiah, is promising Zion that she shall be cast off for a little while but she will be reconciled to Him later (through the Servant) in an eternal marriage. He has sworn it will come to pass. God does not lie. His word is sure!

v. 11-12 PRECIOUSNESS: When this "marriage" takes place between God and His new Zion, the bride (the church) will be regaled in beauty. The old Zion, having degraded itself with idolatry and paganism (Jer. 18:12-17, etc.), is about to be taken captive and made a "byword" among the nations. The old Zion will suffer shame, humiliation and mocking. The old Zion will be loathed as a harlot (cf. Ezek. 16:1-52), but Jehovah will restore her fortunes and make her the beautiful, new Zion (Ezek. 16:53-63).

The Hebrew word *puk* in verse 11 is translated "fair colors" but might be more accurately translated "antimony" because the Hebrew word apparently refers to a mineral powder used as an eye pigment (cf. II Kings 9:30) which was also mixed with a liquid to make a cement or paste in which stones or jewels might be set. This *puk* would make a setting that would enhance the beauty of the jewels. That is the point of the passage. *Peniyniym* is the Hebrew word for *rubies* (they are red); *sappiyriym* are *sapphires* (they are blue-green); *aekeddakh* is Hebrew for *carbuncles* (they are also brilliant red) and the word more literally means simply, *sparkling.* The new Zion will be beautiful and precious. Peter must have had this in mind when he wrote I Pet. 2:4-10! Christ's church is precious and pure (Eph. 5:25-27). The best human words available to John to describe the extravagant beauty of the New Jerusalem (Rev. 21:9-21) were words describing jewels and precious stones. Of course, the "precious stones" will be purified, sanctified Christians who are "living stones" in whom the Spirit of the living God abides (cf. Eph. 2:19-22).

v. 13-17 PROTECTION: The phrase, ". . . taught of Jehovah" is quoted by Jesus (Jn. 6:45) in His sermon on The Bread of Life. It is therefore a prediction of the Messiah. Isaiah was predicting the Incarnation! Jesus Christ was "the bread come down out of heaven." The new Zion would be established and continually sustained by "eating" the incarnated Bread from Heaven. The new Zion would have the privilege of being taught directly by God in the flesh. The old Zion had only "divers portions and divers manners" of God's revelation through the prophets (Heb. 1:1), but in the messianic age the new Zion would be spoken to by God Incarnate in the Son. Anyone taught by Jesus is taught by God Himself.

The protection God is promising Zion here is essentially spiritual. It should be clearly understood by any student of the New Testament that Christians are never promised complete deliverance from wars, sicknesses, trials and tribulations. All who live godly in this world will suffer persecution (II Tim. 3:12). The prophets never promised the Jewish people a time when they would be free of physical tribulation on this earth. The promise that Zion shall be "far from oppression" is a promise of freedom from spiritual oppression (guilt, fear of judgment). The new Zion will be founded in righteousness (cf. Isa. 2:1-4; 9:6-7; 11:1-16, etc.). The imputed righteousness of God because of the atoning death of Christ will free the new Zion from guilt and fear of judgment. The Lord will protect His church and the gates of eternal death shall never prevail against it because Christ will partake of flesh and blood and destroy the power of the devil which is the fear of death (cf. Heb. 2:14-18; Isa. 25:6-9). In verses 15-17 the prophet clearly predicts that Zion will suffer physical attacks as well as judgmental accusations (probably referring to the chief slanderer himself, the devil), but none of it shall prevail against God's new Zion. God is the Creator of everything and everyone. He is able to control all His creation and use it to fulfill His ultimate purpose which is the redemption of those who come into covenant relationship to Him through the Servant. And He will do so! Zion's future righteousness cannot be gainsaid. The accuser of all mankind cannot hurt God's new Zion with his accusations. The heritage of new Zion shall be the perfect righteousness of God Himself, which God has given her by His grace through His Servant. The Hebrew word *tsedek* is able to be translated righteousness or justness. The meaning in this text apparently has more of the flavor of justification, vindication or exoneration. God's new Zion will be cleared of all guilt and be given God's righteousness through her covenant marriage in the Servant.

QUIZ

1. Upon what is the future reconciliation of Zion to the Lord predicated?
2. How certain is the Lord's promise of reconciliation toward Zion?
3. What is the sign of that reconciliation?
4. How did God swear an oath of that reconciliation in the New Testament?
5. How does Isaiah speak of the future beauty of new Zion?
6. How will God vindicate and justify and protect the new Zion?

B. WORD OF THE LORD IS BOND AND BOUNDS OF COVENANT, CHAPTER 55

1. EVIDENCE

TEXT: 55:1-5

1 Ho, every one that thirsteth, come ye to the waters, and he
that hath no money; come ye, buy, and eat; yea, come buy
wine and milk without money and without price.
2 Wherefore do you spend money for that which is not bread?
and your labor for that which satisfieth not? hearken diligently unto me, and eat ye that which is good, and let your
soul delight itself in fatness.
3 Incline your ear, and come unto me; hear, and your soul
shall live: and I will make an everlasting covenant with you,
even the sure mercies of David.
4 Behold, I have given him for a witness to the peoples, a
leader and commander to the peoples.
5 Behold, thou shalt call a nation that thou knowest not; and a
nation that knew not thee shall run unto thee, because of
Jehovah thy God, and for the Holy One of Israel; for he hath
glorified thee.

QUERIES

a. Why offer water, wine and milk for no money?
b. What are the "sure mercies of David"?
c. Who is going to call the unknown nation?

PARAPHRASE

Attention, Come to the water of life everyone who is thirsting for righteousness; it will be given to you freely. You may obtain refreshment, joy and nourishment and you will need no money because it will come to you by the grace of God. Why do my people spend all their lives trying to buy satisfaction for their souls from that which can never satisfy? Listen to Me and obey My word and you will be filled with goodness and your soul will be satisfied. Pay attention to what I am saying to you, Zion, be obedient, and you shall have eternal life for I am preparing to make an eternal covenant with you which shall prove My faithfulness and fulfill all the promises I made to your forefather, David. Look! I have promised My Servant for a herald of good news to the whole world; He will be the King and the Prophet I promised. And you, Zion, will call to share the kingdom of God with you a people which you formerly considered outside the kingdom of God. Yes, people from Gentile nations will hasten to make themselves members of Zion motivated by the glorious redemption of Jehovah through the Holy One of Israel. That will result in the glory of God being manifested in Zion!

COMMENTS

v. 1-2 FAVOR: Redemption has been predicted and explained as occuring in the Suffering Servant (ch. 53). The invitation has been extended for participation in that redemption through covenant relationship (ch. 54). Now the bond and bounds of that covenant relationship is declared to be in the word of Jehovah which is faithful and powerful. All who realize their need of the substance of life are invited to come and receive freely. In Palestine where water-wells were few and far between and where water had to be purchased for money, this would be an exceptionally arresting figure of speech! Water, wine and milk are used throughout the O.T. as figures of spiritual blessings. The same elements are used in the N.T. by Christ and His apostles to portray the blessings of God's grace. The point of these verses is that God's provision of redemption through the Servant shall be by *grace.* Peter makes it plain that the O.T. prophets predicted salvation by grace (I Pet. 1:10-12). Paul's treatise to the Romans declares that justification before God is by faith. Paul, of course, knows that our salvation is by grace (Eph. 2:1-10), but it is faith that gives us access into that grace (Rom. 5:2). And Paul said the O.T. prophets (and the O.T. law) bore witness to salvation by grace through faith (Rom. 3:21-26). Water is figurative for salvation (cf. Isa. 12:3; 35:7; 41:17-18; 49:10; Psa. 42:1; 36:9; Jer. 2:13; 17:13; Ezek. 47:1-12; Zech. 13:1; 14:8; Jn. 4:7-26; 7:37-38, etc.). Wine is figurative for exhilaration and enjoyment (cf. Isa. 26:6-9, etc.). Milk is figurative for nourishment (cf. Isa. 7:22; 60:16; Joel 3:18; I Cor. 3:2; Heb. 5:12; I Pet. 2:2, etc.). It was not astonishing to the Jews that Jehovah would be gracious to them. What was astonishing to many was that He would grant them mercy without their having earned it. Most of them rationalized that they earned whatever graciousness God would shower upon them. Actually the Law was intended to teach Israel that she could never, by human merit, earn her justification before the Holy One of Israel. Israel should have known from the Law that her salvation rested in the unmerited favor of Jehovah. But Israel for the most part, was too wrapped up in her self-righteousness. She was spending herself, exhausting herself in trying to earn righteousness through keeping laws and traditions. That is a vain quest! Attempting to attain justification before God by human goodness is frustratingly impossible and only compounds the human dilemma of guilt. The only solution that will satisfy the human soul is faith in the vicarious, substitutionary atoning death of Jesus Christ. That solution cannot be reasoned out; it cannot be explained by anything within the human experience, because it is supra-human; it is supernatural. It can only be believed. Believed, of course, on the basis of the historical verification and validation of its efficacy by the resurrection of Jesus Christ from the dead. The resurrection is the only fact that makes the cross of Christ (His atoning death) believable! This is predicted in ch. 53 (see our comments there). The exhortation of the prophet here is for Zion (true believers) to focus its attention on the promises of God that they may have salvation by *grace.* All attempts to be saved any other way will fail!

v. 3-5 FIDELITY: Next, the prophet calls upon Zion to give its attention to the promise of Jehovah that He is going to verify His fidelity in a future covenant relationship which will be everlasting. The future covenant will not become obsolete like the old covenant which has a stated termination (cf. Jer. 3:15-18; Jer. 31:31-34, etc.), or fulfillment. The future covenant will be eternal; it will bring into being the "sure mercies of David" (the promise of an eternal king to sit upon David's throne for ever) (cf. II Sam. 7). This is fulfilled, according to the inspired apostle Paul, in the atoning work of Jesus Christ. "What God promised to the fathers . . ." He fulfilled by raising Jesus Christ from the dead and proclaiming through Jesus the forgiveness of sins (cf. Acts 13:32-40). The atonement is the promise (Isa. 53), and God's *faithfulness* to keep His promise of atonement through Jesus was *verified* once and for all by raising Jesus from the dead! The empirically demonstrated everlasting life of Jesus validates God's non-empirical promise to remove our guilt, if we believe and accept God's covenant terms. The forgiveness of our sins is not *based* on our feelings, but upon empirical verification of the faithfulness and sovereignty of God, the Son. When we acknowledge and trust in that verified faithfulness, then we may have a legitimate experiential *feeling* of guiltlessness.

Inasmuch as the apostle Paul quoted (or paraphrased) Isaiah

55:3 in Acts 13:34, and plainly indicates it was fulfilled in the death and resurrection of Jesus Christ, we must look upon this whole chapter of Isaiah as messianic. Therefore, the "him" of 55:4 is the Messiah (the Servant) who has been given as a "witness to the peoples, a leader and commander to the peoples." The Hebrew word translated *leader* is *nagiyd* which means *prince* and is the same word used in Daniel 9:25-26 (see our comments there). The word *metsaveh* is Hebrew for *commander* and comes from *mitsvah* or *commandment.* Thus the one to be given for a witness to the nations will be a ruler and a commandment-giver (cf. Isa. 54:13). This probably refers to the twofold messianic office of King-Prophet. In Isaiah 53, the Servant makes intercession and thus becomes the Messiah-Priest. Zion must be apprised of the fact that Jehovah's future eternal covenant will be validated by The One who is Prophet-Priest-and-King. Futhermore, Jehovah's covenant will be secured by this One for all peoples!

Since the Servant comes through Zion, she will be given the privilege of "calling" nations she formerly "knew not" in covenant relationship. Nations that "knew not" Zion in covenant relationship shall, when the Prophet-King-Priest comes, "run" to her because Jehovah is who He is and will have verified that His covenant is universal through the work of the Messiah (cf. Isa. 2:3-4; 19:16-25; 45:14; 45:22-25; 49:12; 60:3-6; 66:18; Zech. 8:20-23; Lk. 24:47). It was in the same Jewish synagogue in Antioch of Pisidia where Paul quoted Isaiah 55:3 that he also told the recalcitrant Jews that the covenant of the Lord was for the Gentiles to whom he would thenceforth go and preach (Acts 13:42-52).

QUIZ

1. What is the main point of verses one and two?
2. How do men have access to the grace of God?
3. How much does the O.T. say about the grace of God?
4. What is the only thing that makes the atoning aspect of the

death of Christ believable?
5. How do we know this context points to the Messiah?
6. How did Jehovah establish the faithfulness of His promises?
7. In what sense will Zion call a nation it does not know?

2. EXTENT

TEXT: 55:6-13

6 Seek ye Jehovah while he may be found; call ye upon him while he is near:
7 let the wicked forsake his way, and the unrighteous man his thoughts; and let him return unto Jehovah, and he will have mercy upon him; and to our God, for he will abundantly pardon.
8 For my thoughts are not your thoughts, neither are your ways my ways, saith Jehovah.
9 For as the heavens are higher than the earth, so are my ways higher than your ways, and my thoughts than your thoughts.
10 For as the rain cometh down and the snow from heaven, and returneth not thither, but watereth the earth, and maketh it bring forth and bud, and giveth seed to the sower and bread to the eater;
11 so shall my word be that goeth forth out of my mouth; it shall not return unto me void, but it shall accomplish that which I please, and it shall prosper in the thing whereto I sent it.
12 For ye shall go out with joy, and be led forth with peace: the mountains and the hills shall break forth before you into singing; and all the trees of the field shall clap their hands.
13 Instead of the thorn shall come up the fir-trees; and instead of the brier shall come up the myrtle-tree: and it shall be to Jehovah for a name, for an everlasting sign that shall not be cut off.

QUERIES

a. Why does Isaiah exhort his audience to seek Jehovah?
b. Why mention the word of God here?
c. How do mountains and hills sing?

PARAPHRASE

Believe what the Lord says about His Servant and His covenant, O Zion, and seek Him in faith while the opportunity to do so is still yours. Those who are rebelliously and wickedly pursuing lives of worldliness, assuming that the Lord's covenant promises are not going to come to pass had better forsake their unbelief and turn back to Jehovah. Trust in the faithfulness of Jehovah is the only source of mercy for the sinner; and that mercy will be abundant. You may not understand all I am saying about My Servant and His covenant of grace, but that is because my thoughts are not completely reducible to human experiences and concepts, says the Lord. My sovereign program and plan of redemption through My Servant and His Covenant is beyond human wisdom. But just as rain and snow falling from heaven have life in themselves and are the source of life for physical vegetation on the earth, so My Word has spiritual life in it. When I promise forgiveness only through My Servant and His covenant it shall be so. My word will produce eternal life through an eternal covenant. Do not think that the imminent captivity of Zion by Babylon is going to stop My promises from coming to pass. Your redemption from captivity by My sovereign purpose will eventuate in an everlasting covenant of joy and peace for Zion. Indeed, even nature itself shall ultimately be redeemed through My sovereign word. When this covenant is fulfilled it will be a sign that will last forever, a reminder of what I, Jehovah, have done.

COMMENTS

v. 6-7 REPENTANCE: The favor (grace) and the faithfulness (verified in the work of the Servant) of Jehovah's promised everlasting covenant is appropriated through repentance in accordance with the revealed word of God. Great numbers of the people in Isaiah's day were choosing to believe that Jehovah was not, indeed, could not, ever make good on bringing to pass His glorious promises to the fathers. The rich and powerful really did not want God to interfere with their worldliness. They wanted Jehovah to get out of their lives (cf. Isa. 30—31). The prediction of the Suffering Servant (Isa. 52:13—53:12) was unacceptable then as later. So Isaiah's exhortation to Zion is, "Believe what the Lord says about His Servant and His covenant and turn to Him while you still have the opportunity to do so!" Many of them would die in the captivity that was coming. If they did not turn in faith and repentance to the promises of Jehovah of atonement through the Servant, they would die in their sins. Isaiah believed and saw the glory of the Christ (Jn. 12:38). If he could, why couldn't other Jews of his day? Because they chose to pursue a worldly scheme of salvation. They chose to believe in idolatry or alliances with foreign military powers. Isaiah calls upon his people to change their minds and forsake their wicked ways, and to put their confidence in God's promises that He will work out their salvation through His Servant. Before they can claim His promise of pardon, they must make up their minds they want it. They must choose. If they choose to trust God's way of salvation, they may find it in His salvation.

v. 8-11 REVELATION: The sovereign plan of God for the redemption of the world is beyond the experience of man. That God Himself could become incarnate and live a perfect life (without sin in a fleshly body) and then willingly allow Himself to be "made sin" on sinful man's behalf so that man might be given an imputed righteousness which man does not deserve, is incomprehensible to man because man has no experiential base from which to comprehend such an event. The cross is a stumbling block to Jews and foolishness to the Greeks (cf. I Cor. 1:18—2:15; see also Special Study, "The Wisdom of God," pgs. 309-322). God's plan to redeem man through The Servant and His New Covenant is a challenge to the pride of man who believes he can secure his own salvation by his own wisdom. Therefore, man refuses to accept God's plan because God's plan is beyond man's wisdom. But that is just the point—God's plan is a revelation. Habakkuk had this problem. He could not understand why God would punish the Jews by the Chaldeans. But God told Habakkuk, in effect, "I do not ask, Habakkuk, that you understand it, but that you believe it and accept it!" The apostle Paul quoted from Habakkuk in Romans 1:16-17. The gospel of God cannot be understood by man, it must be simply believed and accepted.

There is, however, a tangible point of contact between the incomprehensible, unsearchable mind of God and the mind of finite man. That is the revealed word of God. If man will believe the word of God and conform his actions to the covenant terms of God's revealed word, he shall have redemption. The word of God is authenticated and validated by supernatural proofs seen by eyewitnesses and transmitted in human language under the direction of the Holy Spirit of God. So faith in the revelation of God is not a subjective leap without an objective basis. And God promises that His word is dynamic—it is *living* (Heb. 4:12-13). His revealed word is the *source* of our spiritual life, (cf. John 6:63; I Pet. 1:22-25; James 1:18, 21, etc.). God's word produces life like the rain and snow produces vegetation. That is one of the evidences upon which we may base our faith in God even though we may not understand His ways. We see His word produce goodness and life. Man believes many things he does not fully understand (electricity, gravity, personality, atomic structure and behavior). Man believes and acts upon those principles because of objective evidence he has seen to establish their reality. So, man can believe and act upon the revealed precepts and principles of God in the Bible, even though he may not understand them.

The point of these words of Isaiah is to encourage the Jews

of his day that covenant relationship to God in the work of the Servant may not be completely comprehensible, but this relationship has as its bond the historical deeds of God for evidence and has as its bounds, the propositional (verbal) revelation of God in human language. Covenant relationship to God is through the Servant according to the precepts of God's written word. Anything less than that is too little; anything more is too much. God has spoken through Isaiah and the other prophets that He is going to fulfill His covenant in the Servant. God's word will accomplish that for which it is sent!

v. 12-13 REJOICING: The graphic picture of the whole creation rejoicing at Zion's redemption in these verses may be hyperbolic description of release from the Babylonian captivity. Contextually, however, it is a figurative description of the rejoicing the whole creation is going to enter into when the whole creation is redeemed through the work of the Servant (cf. Rom. 8:18-25). When that redemption which the Servant accomplished is finally consummated at the creation of a new heavens and new earth there will be cosmic jubilation. Paradise will be restored and the curse which brought thorns and thistles upon the original earth (Gen. 3:17-19) will be removed. It is through the work of the Servant that man's dominion over creation has been *potentially* regained *now* (cf. Heb. 2:5-9). Isaiah, by the Spirit of God, saw all this. No wonder he burst forth into such beautiful hyperbole! All of this shall cause the name of Jehovah to be exalted forever and ever.

QUIZ

1. How is the favor of God appropriated?
2. Were people of Isaiah's day capable of believing and turning to the promise of atonement through the Servant?
3. Why are God's ways beyond man's comprehension?
4. May we believe something we do not understand?
5. Is belief a "leap in the dark"? Why not?
6. What is the ultimate goal of the rejoicing mentioned in vv. 12-13?

THE WISDOM OF GOD

OBC Chapel Sermon

by Paul T. Butler

". . . For Jews demand signs and Greeks seek wisdom, but we preach Christ crucified, a stumbling block to Jews and folly to Gentiles, but to those who are called, both Jews and Greeks, Christ the power of God and the wisdom of God . . ." I Cor. 1:22-24

"He (Christ) is the source of your life in Christ Jesus, whom God made our wisdom, our righteousness and sanctification and redemption . . ." I Cor. 1:30

INTRODUCTION

I. WHAT IS WISDOM?

A. Some ancient philosophers believed man was incapable of wisdom that it was only attainable by God (Socrates). In fact, Socrates said the wise man will not seek wisdom.
   1. Yet, most men have continued to seek wisdom; and all of their own.
   2. Many of the ancients were driven to despair, cynicism and hopelessness because they could never find wisdom.
   3. THEY LEARNED A LOT OF THINGS, BUT THEY COULD NEVER FIND WISDOM.

B. Solomon (in Eccl.) probably tried every human source available and concluded that the hope of finding wisdom was vain!

C. Because wisdom is, as one modern philosopher has said, "Whatever else wisdom may be, it is in some sense an understanding of life." Abraham Kaplan, in *The Pursuit of Wisdom, The Scope of Philosophy*, pub. Glencoe Press, pg. 16. "Wisdom is a matter of seeing things— but *as they are, not subjectively.*"

II. MAN'S TROUBLE WITH WISDOM

A. He has been deceived by the devil that wisdom may be found in knowing evil as well as good.
B. God, man's creator, plainly told man that wisdom was in truth, goodness, humility, righteousness, holiness, purity.
C. But the devil, Gen. 3, convinced man that if he would partake of the forbidden, he would be as wise as God knowing both good and evil!
D. The biggest lie of all is, of course, that man is wise if he dispenses with God. Wisdom is found in freedom from any and all divine meddling in man's attempt to enjoy life.
E. Modern philosophy (from Nietzsche on) delcared the death of God and began to construct utopia on earth through science, politics, education and economics, and psychology.
F. But the "wisdom" of man brought on economic depression, war, illiteracy, exploitation, pollution, and on and on.

H. G. Wells, a believer in the sufficiency of science, had earlier prepared blue prints for Utopia, entitled his *last* book, *Mind at the End of its Tether* and said, "Homo sapiens, as he has been pleased to call himself, is played out."

Others are saying, "Man is a useless passion." "Meaning is found in meaninglessness." "There is no meaning to life."

DISCUSSION

I. POWER OF THE WISDOM OF GOD

A. It destroys false wisdom which enslaves and destroys people and society.

1. We have seen through Francis Schaeffer's films the power of the Word and Wisdom of God moving through societies and cultures, redeeming society and individuals.
2. The wisdom of God redeems, regenerates and transforms men and reunites them with their Creator for the blessed end for which He created them (Heb. 2).
3. It converted Pharisees, publicans, harlots, cruel soldiers, pagan philosophers and politicians.
4. It changed homosexuals, thieves, murderers, drunkards, fornicators and liars in the decadent city of Corinth into people after the image of Christ (I Cor. 6:9-11).
5. In the late 1700's the mutineers on the British ship, Bounty, landed on Pitcairn Island in the South Seas. With some of the native women they established a settlement which rivaled Sodom and Gomorrah for its iniquity. Sometime later while rummaging through a sailor's chest, the sole survivor of the mutineers, Alexander Smith, came across a Bible. He made it the textbook and standard of conduct for the community. When an American whaler landed there in 1808, the crew found an ideal commonwealth governed by Smith. No illiterates, thieves, liars, drunkards, profaners, adulterers, or murderers cast their stigma on the community, but righteousness and its fruits of happiness blossomed everywhere. A single copy of Scripture transformed that tropical cesspool into a moral paradise.

What has human wisdom, separated from God done for the world? It has created a Nietzsche and a Hitler, a Marx and a Stalin.

Human wisdom, separated from God, decays, degenerates and destroys! It destroys humanness, socialness and nature!

Take all the military force, economic wealth, erudite philosophy, theology aristocracy, cultural refinement and put it all together in one human system and you still do not have power worthy to be compared with the transforming power of the wisdom of God, incarnated in Jesus and inscripturated in the Bible!

TAKE IT IN YOUR HAND, LEARN IT WITH YOUR MIND, RECEIVE IT INTO YOUR HEART AND PROCLAIM IT WITH YOUR LIPS AND LIFE!

B. It builds and sustains Life as God intended Life for man.
   1. It restores man to fellowship with His Creator; puts man in harmony with his fellow man; puts man in harmony with creation.
   2. Man learns where he came from; what his reason for existence is; and what his destiny is.
   3. The wisdom of God explains history; gives purpose and solves the fragmentation of life without God.
   4. All the experiences of human life (suffering, pain, evil, joy, goodness, truth, falsehood, ugliness) are inexplicable, frustrating and maddening without the Word of God. All human experience is epitomized and sanctified and explained in the life of the perfect human, Jesus.
   5. Christ has given us an example that we should follow in His steps (I Pet. 2). He came and partook of our nature to bring many sons to glory (Heb. 2).

A real note found by a real policeman:

"To anyone in the world who cares. Who am I? Why am I living? Where am I going? Life has become stupid and purposeless. Nothing makes sense anymore. The questions I had when I came to college are still unanswered and now I am convinced that there are no answers. There can only be pain and guilt and despair here. My fear of death and the unknown is far less terrifying than the prospect of the unbearable frustrations, futility, and hopelessness of continued existence."

Glancing at the lifeless, sheet-draped form on the bed, the officer shrugs his shoulders heavily and turns away. For him it is routine—just another suicide. For the ambulance crew it is routine—just another DOA. And, tragically, it is becoming all too routine all over America, especially on college campuses.

In contrast:

Charlie Powell was student body president of the University of California at Berkeley during the Free Speech Movement and at the height of that crisis made a decision for Christ. Looking back, he said, "for the first time in my life I began to see that, if Jesus Christ were really the person He claimed to be, then He had the answers to my problems as student body president as well as in my own personal life."

C. It produces unity among believers in the kingdom of God.

1. It is interesting that Paul says it is the wisdom of God alone which brings unity and on the other hand the practice of unity gives evangelistic power to the gospel (1:17).
2. If ever the world is to be convinced of Christ's saving power, the unity of believers will have a great deal to do with it!
3. And yet churchmen and theologians keep insisting on trying everything under the sun to promote unity except the Word of God!
4. The church at Corinth was trying many things to make the congregation a happy, unified, successful,

respected congregation—BUT WHAT THEY WERE DOING WAS CAUSING MORE DIVISION THAN UNITY.

a. Forming parties and groups following famous men

b. Showing off how much more sanctified they were than others by comparing miraculous gifts

BUILDINGS, BUDGETS AND BANQUETS . . . PROGRAMS, PROMOTIONAL GIMMICKS AND ENTERTAINMENT ARE NOT UNITY, NOT PROOF OF UNITY, NOR CAN THEY SUSTAIN UNITY. Those things are sometimes good and useful as means, but are also sometimes harmful . . . I've seen more division and fighting over buildings, budgets and programs than I care to recollect.

I've seen church people come to church "fellowship" dinners and separate themselves from other members and never speak because of unconverted hate and unforgiveness!

ONLY THE POWER OF THE CONVERTING WISDOM OF GOD WILL BRING UNITY.

II. PROPOGATION OF THE WISDOM OF GOD (Its transmission to men)

A. The wisdom of God cannot be reduced to and bound by human wisdom!

1. Not in human art, not in human music, not in human sermons!
2. None of these dare claim the inspiration or verbal inerrancy of the Holy Spirit!
3. The primary reason for this is that the wisdom of God—the redemptive program of God—is outside human experience. That a sinless, Incarnate God, should willingly die for a sinful world, is humanly inexplicable.
4. Not only that, it is moral outrage to human pride. THIS IS THE MAIN CAUSE FOR UNBELIEF . . . FOR RESISTANCE TO THE WORD AND WISDOM OF GOD.
5. I've quoted so many times in my class, the little excerpt from Bishop Oxenam in Baker's *Dictionary of Theology* article on Atonement, "The doctrine of

the atonement to me is immoral. . . . That someone else should atone for my sins is immoral. . . . they are my sins, I will atone for them."

6. Of course, through human forms of expression we may point people toward, and motivate them toward the wisdom of God found in His Word, but it is still the plain, uncluttered, Word of God that does the begetting of the Spirit . . . not our eloquence, or expertise.

HUMAN SERMONS, HUMAN MUSIC, HUMAN ART, HUMAN METHODS, COME AND GO, BUT THE WORD OF GOD ABIDES FOREVER!

B. The wisdom of God is undiscoverable—it *has* to be revealed.

1. God is a Person, an objective person, just like I am a person and you are persons, but God is infinite, omnipotent and omniscient, while I am finite.
2. Now finite man cannot even know the mind of another finite person unless that mind is revealed to him either by directly talking and acting in one another's presence or by communicating through writing to one another.

   If I should want to know what a man's mind is on some subject, I have to let him tell me. I can't ask anyone else; I can't guess; I can't find it within myself subjectively.

   Almost every time we say, "I just have this feeling that this is what God wants me to do," it is usually what we want to do. . . . It is presumptuous to say, "I just have this feeling that this is what so-and-so would want me to do."

   HOW MUCH MORE PRESUMPTUOUS FOR US TO SAY, "I HAVEN'T REALLY SEARCHED THE SCRIPTURES ABOUT THIS, I JUST FEEL LIKE IT HAS GOD'S APPROVAL!"

   NOW THE QUESTION IS, "WHO HAS KNOWN THE MIND OF THE LORD . . ."

THE NATURAL MAN DOES NOT RECEIVE THE MIND OF CHRIST . . . THAT IS, THE NON-APOSTLE, DOES NOT RECEIVE THE MIND OF CHRIST, IN A REVELATORY MANNER.

All Calvinistic commentaries, I know, say I Cor. 2:14-16 to the unconverted man not able to understand spiritual things . . . that is contextually erroneous as well as unsuited to the teaching of the Bible as a whole.

How can the invitation be to "whosoever will" if one must wait for the miracle of Holy Spirit quickening of the mind before we can understand the gospel message? What is the point of preaching if we must preach and then hope the Holy Spirit will quicken the mind apart from the Word so the man may understand?

THE POINT IS THAT ONLY THE APOSTLES RECEIVED THE REVELATION OF GOD, THE MIND OF GOD, TO TRANSMIT TO ALL MANKIND FOR ALL AGES!

David Lipscomb paraphrases: "Who of you uninspired hath known the mind of God, so as to be joined together with Him? But we inspired men so understand him that we are united in him in teaching his will, we are laborers together with God."

The whole trend and meaning of the chapter is that none could know or teach the will of God by human wisdom. They were dependent upon the revelation made by God's Spirit through the apostles for a knowledge of His will, and only through receiving this could any become co-workers with Him in saving men.

THERE IS ONLY ONE WAY TO TEST THAT WHICH CLAIMS TO BE THE MIND OF CHRIST. . . . DOES IT AGREE WITH APOSTOLIC REVELATION. . . . I Jn. 4:1-6

It is one thing to say, "I am persuaded by historico-grammatical study that this is what the biblical author has revealed to be the mind of God. . . ." and quite another thing to say, I've put it before the Lord and He revealed to me that I should do this or that.

C. The wisdom of God is revealed only through the apostles,

but in human terms . . . in human words

1. The will, the mind, the Person of God came in flesh. Jesus was the Incarnate God, and the Incarnate Holy Spirit. ALL THE FULLNESS OF THE GODHEAD DWELT IN HIM BODILY!
2. He was the Word of God, Jn. 1:1-18, in human form.
3. The words He spoke were the words of God, the mind of God, the wisdom of God.
4. The words He gave the apostles after He ascended back into heaven, through the work of the Holy Spirit, are just as powerful in redeeming and saving and regenerating as they were when He was here in the flesh. . . .
5. Jn. 6:63; II Pet. 1:3-5 . . . through this word (promises) we are made partakers of the divine nature; II Tim. 3:16-17, they may make the man of God complete! I Jn. 3:24, they complete our fellowship with Christ.

THE WORD OF THE SPIRIT THROUGH THE APOSTLES IS THE SAME WORD AS THE INCARNATE WORD. . . . IT HAS THE SAME AUTHORITY. IT HAS THE SAME POWER!

WE NEED NO FURTHER REVELATIONS FROM THE HOLY SPIRIT! WE DON'T EVEN NEED ANY MORE MIRACLES TO CONFIRM THAT IT IS THE WORD AND WILL AND MIND OF GOD!

Some will say, "There is no power in the words on this printed page of the Bible, the power is in the Person. . . ."

Be careful of such statements. Of course, we do not worship a book, but you can no more separate the words on the Bible's pages from the Person than you can separate the words of any man from his person! THE WORD OF CHRIST IS THE MIND OF CHRIST, THE WORD IS THE POWERFUL, ENERGIZED AGENT OF THE HOLY SPIRIT IN CONVERSION AND SANCTIFICATION!

By the word, Paul begat the Corinthians. The word is the incorruptible seed. The word is implanted. Sanctify them in the truth, thy word is truth. If we abide in His commandments we abide in Him and He in us. Man does not live by bread alone, but by every word that proceeds from the mouth of God. The word that I have spoken to you is Spirit and life. The miracle of regeneration occurs through the Word.

WE HAVE LOST RESPECT FOR THE AUTHORITY AND POWER OF THE WORD. . . . Jesus said, "All authority . . . etc., Go and make disciples . . . teach them to observe whatsoever I have commanded you . . ."

THERE IS AN INSIDIOUS GRASPING FOR HUMAN AUTONOMY IN CHRISTENDOM TODAY THAT IS JUST AS UNBELIEVING AS THAT RATIONALISTIC HUMANISM OF A CENTURY AGO . . .

IT IS SUBJECTIVISM . . . HOW I FEEL . . . MY EXPERIENCE . . . RATHER THAN WHAT DOES THE BIBLE SAY! You see that evaluates the Bible by my feeling or my experience rather than evaluating my feeling-experience by what the Bible actually says.

Full Gospel Business Men's International lead article claims the whole movement built first on the experiences, testimonies, of alleged, extra-biblical workings of the Holy Spirit . . . and what the Bible says follows that second in importance.

A missionary's paper points out how some of the Pentecostals in Chile teach their people that much study of the Bible is a sin. They are opposing the work of Christ and the Bible correspondence work because they declare that the Holy Spirit will teach them without having to read or study the Word of God!

This leads some to believe that God does all our thinking and deciding for us. We don't even have to decide. But that would keep us immature, moral runts.

III. PURPOSE OF THE WISDOM OF GOD, I Cor. 3-4

A. To build the temple of God by begetting Christians through the gospel and by edifying them through the apostolic doctrine.

1. The purpose of the wisdom of God is NOT:

a. To erect a brain-washed, psyched, structured, non-thinking American corporation!

THE KINGDOM OF GOD IS A COMMUNITY OF

OBEDIENT BELIEVERS STRUCTURED ACCORDING TO SCRIPTURE, BUT UNSTRUCTURED WHERE THE SCRIPTURES DO NOT SPEAK AND FREE TO THINK AND GROW MORALLY AND SPIRITUALLY INTO THE IMAGE OF CHRIST!

b. To form a society through which man may build a physical, material utopia on this present earth! THE GOSPEL IS PRIMARILY TO REGENERATE MINDS AND SAVE SOULS IN SPITE OF PHYSICAL CIRCUMSTANCES. . . . Of course, Christian love wants to relieve physical suffering and wherever it can it should. But first priority is preaching the Word.

c. Just to Christianize society to save a human culture. THE WISDOM OF GOD IS TO CALL OUT AND SAVE FROM ALL DYING CULTURES, "A PEOPLE OF HIS OWN WHO ARE ZEALOUS FOR GOOD DEEDS."

d. To make men famous. WHEN MEN USE THE PULPIT TO GAIN PERSONAL FAME AND FOLLOWING, THEY EMPTY THE CROSS OF ITS POWER (I Cor. 1:17). HUMAN BEINGS HAVE A TENDENCY TO THINK OF THE CHURCH AND HER LEADERS AS THEY DO HUMAN LEADERS! PAUL FOUGHT THAT IN CORINTH AND EPHESUS, AND ROME, AND COLOSSAE AND THESSALONICA AND EVERYWHERE HE WENT.

B. To make men truly wise through humility
   1. I Cor. 3:18-22. "Let no one deceive himself. If anyone among you think that he is wise in this age, let him become a fool that he may become wise."
   2. Humility is the queen of virtues.
   3. PRIDE IS THE CAUSE OF UNBELIEF. Unbelief is not because God hasn't given enough evidence. We don't need more evidence, we need MORE HUMILITY.

IF YOU LEAVE THESE CLASSROOMS KNOWING THE BIBLE AND KNOWING HOW TO PREACH IT . . . BUT PROUD AND ARROGANT . . . YOU DO NOT HAVE THE WISDOM OF GOD!

C. To teach man how to live (I Cor. 3:6) according to the scripture

1. Not to go beyond what is written
2. Dean Seth Wilson has a little printed essay entitled, "What the Bible Does Not Say About a Christian's Life and Conduct."

   He asks, "Is there any part of life on which the Bible has no teaching?"

   He answers, "No!"

   There are precepts and principles in the Bible to cover every aspect of human life. ". . . all things that pertain to life and godliness . . ."

CONCLUSION

I. THE VILLAGE THAT LIVES BY THE BIBLE

November, 1960, *Reader's Digest*:

Soldiers in 1945 found this village which had been formed from two men converted by a missionary who left them a Bible and a hymn book. "Picking their way through the Bible, the two converts had found not only a Person on whom to pattern a life, but sound precepts on which to to base their society. . . . Nurtured on this Book a whole generation had drawn from it their ideas . . . the result was plain to see. Shimabuku for years had had no jail, no brothel, no drunkenness, no divorce; there was a high level of health and happiness. . . .

The soldiers attended a worship service and observed the lives of the people for a few days.

A seargent whispered to his lieutenant, "So this is what comes out of only a Bible and couple of old guys who wanted to live like Jesus! . . . then, with a glance at a shell hole, he murmured, "Maybe we're using the wrong kind of weapons to make the world over!"

II. THE WISDOM OF GOD IS POWERFUL: THE WORD OF GOD IS POWERFUL BECAUSE IT IS THE REVELATION OF THE WISDOM OF GOD

A. If you think words and ideas are not powerful, think of

what Adolph Hitler did with lies, words. Marx and Lenin have captured more than two-thirds of the total population of the world with false ideas expressed through words.

B. The gospel is infinitely more powerful than all those put together.

A. Campbell said, "The work of redemption is a system of work, or deeds, on the part of Heaven, which constitute the most splendid series of moral facts which man or angel ever saw. . . . When these facts are understood, or brought into immediate contact with the mind of man, as a moral seal or moral prototype, they delineate or stamp the image of God upon the human soul."

Mr. Campbell goes on to point out that it is through the preaching of the gospel and through man's obedience to the scriptures (the revelation of the works and deeds of God) that the image of God is stamped upon the soul of man and through no other means.

"The love of God in the death of Christ never drew a tear of gratitude or joy from any eye, or excited a grateful emotion in any heart among the nations of our race to whom the testimony never came." (*The Christian System,* pg. 90-102. "Fact, Testimony, Faith, Feeling.")

III. BUT THE INFINITE POWER OF THE WISDOM OF GOD IN THE GOSPEL WILL PRODUCE NOTHING IF IT IS NOT PROCLAIMED. . . . Leaven will not make bread if it is not put into contact with the lump.

THAT IS WHAT OZARK BIBLE COLLEGE WAS FOUNDED TO DO. . . . FILL MEN AND WOMEN WITH ALL THE FULNESS OF CHRIST IN WHOM ARE HIDDEN ALL THE TREASURES OF WISDOM AND KNOWLEDGE AND SEND THEM FORTH TO DECLARE THE WISDOM OF GOD TO A FOOLISH AND DYING WORLD!

THAT IS WHAT FACULTY AND STAFF HAVE DEDICATED THEIR LIVES TO. . . . THAT IS WHAT PEOPLE SUPPORT THE COLLEGE FOR. . . . THAT IS WHAT WE HAVE RECRUITED YOU FOR. . . . IF YOU HAVE COME FOR ANY OTHER REASON THAN THAT, YOU

ARE SHORT OF THE MARK.

I SAY TO YOU IN THE WORDS OF EDWARD JOHN CARNELL:

"IF IT IS TRUE THAT JESUS CHRIST DIED ON THE CROSS TO SAVE SINNERS, HAVE WE ANY RIGHT TO SAY THAT WE LOVE SINNERS IF WE FAIL TO CONFRONT THEM WITH THIS TRUTH? AND WHERE CAN WE FIND A DIVINELY VALIDATED ACCOUNT OF THIS TRUTH APART FROM SCRIPTURE? IN SUM, WE CAN EXPRESS NO HIGHER LOVE TO LOST HUMANITY THAN TO PREACH THE GOSPEL IN THE PRECISE FORM IN WHICH GOD HAS BEEN PLEASED TO REVEAL IT!"

C. WORLDWIDE IS THE INVITATION TO COVENANT RELATIONSHIP, CHAPTER 56

1. DISTINCTIONS DESTROYED

TEXT: 56:1-5

1 Thus saith Jehovah, Keep ye justice, and do righteousness; for my salvation is near to come, and my righteousness to be revealed.

2 Blessed is the man that doeth this, and the son of man that holdeth it fast; that keepeth the sabbath from profaning it, and keepeth his hand from doing any evil.

3 Neither let the foreigner, that hath joined himself to Jehovah, speak, saying, Jehovah will surely separate me from his people; neither let the eunuch say, Behold, I am a dry tree.

4 For thus saith Jehovah of the eunuchs that keep my sabbaths, and choose the things that please me, and hold fast my covenant:

5 Unto them will I give in my house and within my walls a memorial and a name better than of sons and of daughters; I will give them an everlasting name, that shall not be cut off.

QUERIES

a. Why single out the sabbath as a mark of righteousness?
b. How could a foreigner join himself to Jehovah?
c. Why would a eunuch be worried that he was a "dry tree"?

PARAPHRASE

This is what the Lord says, I am soon going to establish My covenant of salvation by grace through the Suffering Servant. It is your responsibility to enter into My covenant by doing justice and righteousness. Blessedness for all men shall be found in keeping My covenant according to My terms. All the former distinctions that hindered foreigners and eunuchs from full covenant relationship will be abrogated when My salvation through the Servant becomes a reality. So the Lord says, Let the foreigners and eunuchs be faithful in keeping My covenant terms out of a heart that chooses to do so, and I will give them a relationship to Me of much more value than any earthly blessing or reputation; I will give them an eternal reputation of blessedness.

COMMENTS

v. 1-2 COVENANT ESPOUSED: On the basis of the Suffering Servant's atonement and the offer of a new covenant relationship through His accomplishment, the emphasis is now put on man's espousal or choice of that covenant. Jehovah's salvation is "near"! In His salvation, His righteousness will be revealed (cf. Rom. 1:17; 3:21-26). Logically, then, those who choose the benefits of His righteousness must accept the responsibility of such a choice which is to *do* righteously. Those who want the results of righteousness must practice righteousness! Practicing righteousness can be *clearly defined!* Doing what God's revealed covenant terms say is right and refraining from what God's covenant says is evil is practicing righteousness. The apostle John amplifies this principle in his writings (John 14:15, 21, 23; 15:10; I Jn. 2:3-6; 2:24; 3:19-24; 4:6; 5:1-3, etc.). In our text here, Isaiah uses the "sabbath" as an example of man's obligation to keep God's covenant according to God's terms. Next to circumcision, the sabbath was the central sign of the covenant (cf. Ex. 31:13ff; Ezek. 20:12ff). This does not mean the sabbath day was to be a commandment of the New Covenant which the Messiah would establish. *Sabbath* is used in a number of messianic prophecies to exemplify the prediction that members of the future messianic kingdom would be covenant-keepers instead of covenant-breakers like the Jews of the days of the prophets (cf. Isa. 66:22-23; Ezek. 44:24; 45:17; 46:3). Sabbath-day keeping in the New Covenant dispensation is definitely abrogated as a law of God since the O.T. ordinances were "nailed" to the cross (cf. Col. 2:13-15; Heb. 9:10; 10:1, etc.). Sabbath-keeping is, at best, merely a matter of opinion in the New Dispensation (cf. Rom. 14:1-12; Col. 2:16-23). The use of the sabbath by Isaiah in this messianic text is a clear example of "times-coloring" in prophetic literature. How is a prophet 700 years removed from the messianic age to communicate the idea of sincere covenant-keeping to his audience? He must do it in terminology and practices contemporary with his own dispensation and age. Therefore, he idealizes the concept of covenant-keeping with one's sincerity in keeping the sabbath!

v. 3-5 CONTEMPTIBLE EXALTED: Foreigners (*nakerily,* Heb.) and sojourners (*ger,* Heb.) might become citizens and members of the covenant people but they were prohibited from participating in full fellowship with the people of the land (cf. Ex. 12:43-49; Lev. 16:29; 17:12; 18:26; 22:10; 25:35; 25:40; Num. 15:15; 16:29; 19:10; 35:15, etc.). Eunuchs were also barred from the temple of God (Deut. 23:1). Naturally, when they heard Isaiah's magnificent predictions of the glorious messianic age to come they would assume "second class citizenship" to be their lot in that age also. Taking the case of the eunuchs first the Lord says they shall have an inheritance in the messianic kingdom in spite of the fact that they could produce no progeny. In the Jewish mind messianic inheritance was tied directly to the land and tribal inheritances. If a man could produce no offspring he had ho hope in the messianic future. But there will be no such limitations or hindrances to full favor in the messianic age. If men will keep God's covenant in the new dispensation and *choose* what pleases the Lord, they will be brought into God's house in full fellowship. Outward observance is not sufficient (Mt. 5:17—6:18; Jn. 4:21-24; Mt. 15:1-19), the new covenant will be written on the *heart* (Jer. 31:31-34). In the messianic kingdom there will be no distinctions as to race, physical perfection, economic or educational status (cf. Gal. 3:23-29). All will be full-fledged sons of the covenant, descendants of Abraham according to faith, heirs of the promises of God (Eph. 2:11-22, Rom. 8:12-17, etc.). We have a specific example of the fulfillment of this in the baptism of the Ethiopian eunuch (Acts 8:26-40). Here is one eunuch indeed who has a name that is far more honored than it could have ever been by a long line of illustrious descendants. The primary reason for restrictions about sojourners and eunuchs in the O.T. was ceremonial uncleanness. But those who shall choose the covenant terms of the Messiah and keep them shall be cleansed of all defilement (ceremonial and moral) (cf. Zech. 12:10—14:21; Mal. 3:1-6; etc.).

QUIZ

1. What salvation is predicted as "near"?
2. Why the exhortation to keep justice and do righteousness?
3. Is sabbath-keeping a literal requirement for the messianic age?
4. What is "times-coloring"?
5. What status did foreigners and eunuchs have in relationship to the O.T. covenant?
6. How does Isaiah's promise to the eunuchs here fit in with N.T. doctrines?

7. Cite an example of a eunuch in N.T. times being accepted into Christ's covenant.

2. DOERS ARE DISCIPLES

TEXT: 56:6-8

6 Also the foreigners that join themselves to Jehovah, to minister unto him, and to love the name of Jehovah, to be his servants, everyone that keepeth the sabbath from profaning it, and holdeth fast my covenant;
7 even them will I bring to my holy mountain, and make them joyful in my house of prayer: their burnt-offerings and their sacrifices shall be accepted upon mine altar; for my house shall be called a house of prayer for all peoples.
8 The Lord Jehovah, who gathereth the outcasts of Israel, saith, Yet will I gather others to him, besides his own that are gathered.

QUERIES

a. How can these "foreigners" be brought to God's holy mountain?
b. Who are the "others" of verse eight Jehovah will gather to Himself?

PARAPHRASE

When My new covenant is established by the Servant, many Gentiles will love the Lord and join themselves to Him and serve Him through obedience to the terms of the Servant's covenant. I, the Lord, will bring them to Zion and cause them to partake of all My blessings there; I will also allow them to minister to Me in Zion. Indeed, My new house shall be the

the house of worship for all nations. The same Lord who gathers the believing scattered ones of Israel will gather others from all the Gentile nations to join the gathered of Israel.

COMMENTS

v. 6 GODLY: Already there has been an abundance of predictions from Isaiah that Jehovah will join foreigners (Gentiles) to Zion in the coming messianic age. There are also a number of predictions that these New covenant citizens will become ministers in the New dispensation (cf. Isa. 60:3, 7, 10; Isa. 66:18-23; Zech. 14:16-19, etc.). These ungodly foreigners will "love" the name of Jehovah and keep His covenant ordinances (the new covenant). The foreigners, excluded from the covenant of Israel because of ceremonial and moral uncleanness, will be accepted because they love the name of Jehovah and choose to become His, taking His name as theirs (cf. Isa. 43:1-5). Every member of the new covenant is a priest (minister) (cf. I Pet. 1:5, 9; Heb. 13:15-16).

v. 7-8 GATHERED: Jehovah will not necessarily bring foreigners to the literal hill of Moriah where the Jewish temple stood. He will bring them to Zion (Heb. 12:22ff), the N.T. church (cf. Isa. 2:1-4). The following descriptive phrases, ". . . prayer . . . joyful . . . sacrifices accepted . . .," point to full covenant membership for foreigners. Gentiles will be restored to loving fellowship with the Creator through the Messiah and His new covenant. The Messiah's sacrifice (once for all, cf. Heb. 10:1-18) will atone for all men's sins. God's new house, Zion, will be for men of all nations (Eph. 2:11-22) a house of prayer (cf. Mk. 11:17) because the Messiah will cleanse God's house of those who profane it.

That Jehovah would someday give full covenant membership to Gentiles should not have been such an unlikely thing to the Jews. Verse seven is quoted by Jesus in Mark 11:17. Verse eight is quoted by Jesus in John 10:16. Yet, when Jesus stood and read Isaiah 61:1-2 and applied it to God's mercy extended to Gentiles, even in O.T. times, they wanted to kill Jesus for it. The following excerpts illustrate the incorrigible obstinacy of the Jewish theologians to accept the predictions of their prophets that Jehovah would accept the Gentiles into full covenant relationship:

THE JEWISH VIEW OF GENTILES
(*Everyman's Talmud,* p. 66 & 371)

'Kill the best of the Gentiles! Crush the head of the best of snakes!' (Mech. to xiv, 7; 27a).

'Gentiles are addicted to licentiousness' (Jeb. 98a). The Rabbis were revolted by the low standards of conduct they saw practised around them and were thankful for the finer ideals which their religion offered them. A prayer, composed to be said on leaving the House of Study, reads: 'I give thanks before Thee, O Lord my God and God of my fathers, that Thou has set my lot among those who sit in the House of Study and the Synagogue, and hast not set my lot with those who frequent the theatres and circuses; for while I labour to inherit Paradise, they labour for the pit of destruction' (p. Ber. 7d).

The Holy One, blessed be He, clears Himself with respect to the gentile nations by giving them their reward for the minor precepts which they observed in this world so as to judge and sentence them in the World to Come, that they may have no plea to make and no merit can be found on their behalf' (Tanchuma Kedoshim I).

'R. Eliezer declared, "No Gentiles will have a share in the World to Come; as it is said, 'The wicked shall return to the nether-world, even all the nations that forget God' (Ps. ix, 17); 'the wicked' refers to the evil among Israel." R. Joshua said to him, "If the verse had stated 'The wicked shall return to the nether-world and all the nations,' and had stopped there, I should have agreed with you. Since, however, the text adds, 'that forget God,' behold, there must be righteous men among the nations who will have a share in the World to Come" '(Tosifta Sanh. xiii. 2). That the righteous of all peoples will inherit the bliss of the Hereafter is the accepted doctrine of Rabbinic Judaism.

"The daughter of an Israelite may not assist a gentile woman in childbirth, since she would be assisting to bring to birth a child for idolatry." (Mishnah, A.Zar. 2.1)

Isaiah is not the only prophet to predict Gentile acceptance; see also Amos 9:11-12 (Acts 15:12-21); Micah 4:2; 7:15-17; Zech. 8:20-23; 9:9-10; 14:16-21. The point of Isaiah's remarks here seems to be that *anyone* who loves the name of Jehovah and keeps His covenant terms will be acceptable (cf. Acts 10:34-35). Doers are disciples!

QUIZ

1. How could Gentiles become "ministers" (priests)?
2. What do the words "prayer, joyful, sacrifices" point to for Gentiles?
3. Where does Jesus quote the verse about "house of prayer"?
4. Where does Jesus quote verse eight?
5. How adamant were Jews that Gentiles should not be allowed standing before God?

3. DUMB DOGS DENOUNCED

TEXT: 56:9-12

9 All ye beasts of the field, come to devour, yea, all ye beasts in the forest.

10 His watchmen are blind, they are all without knowledge; they are all dumb dogs, they cannot bark; dreaming, lying down, loving to slumber.

11 Yea, the dogs are greedy, they can never have enough; and these are shepherds that cannot understand: they all turned to their own way, each one to his gain, from every quarter.

12 Come ye, say they, I will fetch wine, and we will fill oursevles with strong drink; and tomorrow shall be as this day, a day great beyond measure.

QUERIES

a. Who are the "dumb dogs"?
b. Were the "shepherds" of Israel actually drunkards?

PARAPHRASE

Come like wild beasts, all you pagan nations, and devour this helpless people of Mine, says Jehovah. The watchmen of this people are blind to unbelief and covenant-breaking which is crippling them. The men who are supposed to be spiritual leaders of My people are like stupified dogs; they should be barking the alarm, but they do not because they have sated themselves with self-indulgence so they lie around lazily sleeping and dreaming. These so-called spiritual leaders are like greedy dogs that never get enough. They are like shepherds who cannot seem to understand that an enemy is about to attack their flock because they are completely engrossed in their own selfish pursuits of making money and they are oblivious to the needs of the flock. Not only are they profligates themselves, but they are busy trying to seduce others into their debauchery. They are advocating deliberate drunkenness in order to blot out any concern or responsibility for the spiritual problems facing Israel.

COMMENTS

v. 9 DESTRUCTION: This section (v. 9-12) connects to the main topic under consideration—Covenant Relationship. This section focuses on the major reason Isaiah was having such a difficult time getting the majority of his countrymen to renew their messianic relationship with Jehovah. The spiritual leaders were corrupt. Because the nation of Israel had defaulted on its theocratic uniqueness, by dividing into two warring nations (Israel and Judah) and by assimilating idolatry, God was letting her suffer the due penalty of her error in her own body-politic. She tried to deceive pagan empires with treaties and alliances, pitting one against another. Israel exchanged her covenant relationship with the omnipotent Jehovah for vain and destructive covenants with God-opposing nations. Now those empires are poised to wreak destruction upon her (cf. Jer. 12:9; Ezek. 34:5, 8). The figure of speech under which Isaiah here delineates the nations which were enemies of God's people is "beasts" and is used elsewhere in Scripture for the same identification (cf. our comments, *Daniel,* College Press, pgs. 259-260; see also Revelation 13:1ff where Rome is symbolized as "beasts").

v. 10-12 DRUNKENNESS: The "watchmen" (spiritual leaders such as priests and judges) of Israel were blind. Isaiah refers to spiritual blindness which is a deliberate blindness; a blindness of the heart by choice. The spiritual leaders of Israel refused to acknowledge the dangers that were everywhere apparent to men of faith like Isaiah. Micah, (Micah 1:5) a prophet-contemporary of Isaiah, put his finger on the root cause of the sin of both Israel and Judah when he pointed to the capital cities of both nations as the place where corruption began and was at its worst. When the political and spiritual leadership of a nation is decadent, it does not take long for corruption to filter down into the entire fibre of the whole nation at grass-roots levels. Those who would aspire to positions of such leadership have a responsibility beyond their own personal lives—they have a responsibility to those who look to them for leadership in character as well as function.

Isaiah calls the leaders "dogs"! Dogs are mentioned about 40 times in the scriptures. They were not the friendly, domesticated dogs we know in the Western world today. They were half-wild, with some mixture of jackal or wolf, thin from want of food and ill-natured, which roamed the streets or sometimes traveled with the nomadic shepherds of Palestine, (cf. Job 30:1, etc.). The apostle Paul uses "dogs" to symbolize the vicious Judaizers who were always trying to attack him and the church (cf. Phil. 3:2ff). Here, however, the "dogs" have lost their alertness and activeness because they have sated themselves on self-indulgence. They are mute! They just cannot get up the energy to bark. They really do not care to bark. No warning will come from these "critters" Every farm-boy has seen an illustration of this in the old hound who has filled himself with food and has gone off to lie down in the shade of a tree, hardly opening an eye when someone approaches—he just doesn't care. The whole picture is one of devotion to self-enjoyment and satisfaction and neglect of duty.

These "dogs" (leaders of the nation) are greedy gluttons. They are never satisfied. They must always have more. They are interested only in their own gain. Nothing will bring the downfall of a nation more rapidly than selfish hedonism in its leadership. When public servants serve only themselves, they set the same moral tone for the whole populace. The leaders of Israel preyed upon the flock (cf. Ezek. 34:1-10). They exploited and abused their constituents until the whole nation was sapped of its economic and moral fibre. Then the nation collapsed without the will to reform its morals, resist its enemies or return to the Lord. These leaders encouraged one another and the whole nation to drunkenness, (cf. Isa. 5:11, 22; 24:9—28:7; 29:9; Isa. 24:20; 51:21; Micah 2:11; etc.) Rather than face the reality of the consequences of their careless indulgence, they advocate an alcoholic stupefication that will anesthetize their reasoning ability. Thus they will create for themselves a fool's paradise, saying, ". . . tomorrow shall be as this day, great beyond measure . . ."

QUIZ

1. How does this text connect to the previous discussion of Covenant Relationship?

2. Why does Isaiah use "beasts" to refer to pagan nations?
3. Why is it so dangerous for a nation's leadership to become drunkards?
4. Why is the word "dogs" so appropriate for the leaders of Isaiah's day?
5. Why the encouragement by the leaders for all the people to become drunkards?

SPECIAL STUDY

WHAT IS TO BE DONE CONCERNING FALSE TEACHERS AND TEACHING

Compiled by Paul T. Butler

1. Beware of them (be on the lookout for). (Matt. 7:15)
2. Know them (by their fruits, their works and doctrines). (Matt. 7:16)
3. Beware of their leaven-like doctrines. (Matt. 16:5-12) (cf. Gal. 5:9)
4. Follow God's word even when the teachers may be hypocritical or partisan. (Matt. 23:1-3) (cf. Phil. 1:15-18)
5. Let them alone. (Matt. 15:13-14)
6. Even if their doctrines are a result of centuries of national heritage, we must follow divinely revealed truth. (John 4:24)
7. Must not hear the voice of hirelings if we want to remain in the One true fold. (John 10)
8. We must follow only those who keep the word of the apostles. (John 15:20; 17:20)
9. We must follow only those who strive for unity. (John 17:21-23)
10. We must cautiously resist any teaching lest we be found fighting against God. (Acts 5:38-39)
11. We have apostolic precedent for debate with false teachers to defend truth. (Acts 6:8-10; 9:28-29; 10:1-18; 11; 13:6-12)
12. We are not to resist evil opposers to the point of reckless and foolhardy throwing away of our life. (Acts 14:1-7)

13. Their doctrine must be investigated in the light of revelation by the leaders of the church and the true doctrine preached polemically (Acts 15:1—16:5) in churches.
14. When they oppose and blaspheme the truth we should refuse to continue with them. (Acts 18:6) (cf. Matt. 7:6)
15. Separate the disciples from those who speak evil of the Way. (Acts 19:9)
16. Those sincere believers who have not learned and are not teaching the complete revelation need to be taught privately. (Acts 18:24-28; 19:1-7)
17. Elders are to "take heed"; "feed"; "watch"; "admonish with tears night and day"; "commend the flock to God's word" as *preventive polemics.* (Acts 20:28-32)
18. Opinions are not necessarily false teaching until someone makes them laws. (Rom. 14:1—15:7)
19. Mark them—turn away from them in their devisive doctrines. (Rom. 16:17)
20. Those who claim to be prophets or teachers must acknowledge the apostles' letters as divine revelation. (I Cor. 14:37-38)
21. We are not to be "yoked together" with those who teach falsely or live falsely. (II Cor. 6:14-18)
22. Beware of their abilities to fashion themselves into angels of light and ministers of righteousness. (II Cor. 11:13-15)
23. They are to be anathematized. (Gal. 1:6-9) (They anathematize themselves.)
24. Rebuke publicly ("to the face") in some instances. (Gal. 2:13-14)
25. Stand fast in freedom of the gospel (do not be bound by false laws added to it). (Gal. 5:1)
26. If a brother trespass in false teaching we are to seek his restoration in a spirit of gentleness. (Gal. 6:1-5)
27. We are to grow up in faith to prevent being "carried away by false teaching." (Eph. 4:11-16)
28. We are to speak boldly the truth in love—each member of the body fulfilling his part in this speaking of the truth.

(Eph. 4:15-16)

29. Not to be partakers (associate) with them (Eph. 5:6-11) and to prove all things by bringing God's revelation to shine upon them—we are to expose false teachings.
30. We are to redeem the time by learning and understanding what the will of the Lord is in order to *prepare* for combating falsehood. (Eph. 5:15-18)
31. We are to recognize that we wrestle against supernatural power (Eph. 6:10-18)—and we must arm ourselves with truth, righteousness, the gospel, faith, salvation, and the sword of the Spirit, with prayer—we must be wise as to Satan's devices. (II Cor. 2:11)
32. We are to pray for knowledge to prove what is excellent. (Phil. 1:9-10)
33. Mark them and beware of false teachers. (Phil. 3:2, 17-19)
34. Take heed and beware of philosophies of men. (Col. 2:8)
35. Let no man judge us in matters of expediency. (Col. 2:16)
36. Train ourselves to answer false teachers. (Col. 4:6)
37. Declare the gospel in face of great opposition and beware of those who preach to please men. (I Thess. 2:1-6)
38. We are not to be ignorant. (I Thess. 4:13)
39. We are to prove all things—hold fast to the good. (I Thess. 5:21)
40. We are to strengthen one another with pure doctrine. (I Thess. 4:18)
41. Withdraw from every brother that does not abide in apostolic doctrines. (II Thess. 3:6)
42. Have no company with disobedient (II Thess. 3:14)—but admonish like a brother.
43. Charge false teachers to refrain from their teaching. (I Tim. 1:3-4)
44. Paul delivered two unto Satan who, through their blasphemy and apostasy, had "shipwrecked the faith." (I Tim. 1:19-20)
45. Preachers are to expose the hypocrisy and demonical nature of false doctrines. (I Tim. 4:1-6)
46. Refuse profane doctrines. (I Tim. 4:7)
47. Evangelists are to train themselves in the Word to withstand

these false doctrines. (I Tim. 4:11-16)

48. We are to shun those who do not agree with sound doctrine and who have a morbid craving for controversy. (I Tim. 6:3-11)
49. We are to "fight the good fight" and withstand false doctrine. (I Tim. 6:12)
50. We are to turn away from false teachings and "guard" the truth. (I Tim. 6:20-21)
51. Charge brethren in the sight of the Lord not to strive about words. (II Tim. 2:14)
52. Shun profane babblings. (II Tim. 2:16-17)
53. Refuse foolish and ignorant questionings. (II Tim. 2:33)
54. Correct in spirit of meekness those that oppose themselves. (II Tim. 2:25)
55. Turn away from false teachers. (II Tim. 3:1-5)
56. We are to imitate the apostles in their dealings with false teachers—to teach, correct, reprove, instruct. (II Tim. 3:10-17)
57. We are to preach constantly, reproving, rebuking, exhorting. (II Tim. 4:1-5)
58. We are to exhort in sound doctrine, convict (show them for what they really are) the gainsayers. (Titus 1:9)
59. The mouths of false teachers *must be stopped.* (Titus 1:11)
60. The false teachers are to be reproved sharply. (Titus 1:13)
61. Shun foolish questionings. (Titus 1:9)
62. A factious man is to be refused after a first and second admonition. (Titus 3:10)
63. We are to exercise our senses to discern good and evil. (Heb. 5:11-14)
64. We are to obey elders as those who watch for our souls. (Heb. 13:17)
65. We are to pray for divine wisdom to guard against demonical wisdom. (James 1:5)
66. We are to grow in grace and knowledge of Jesus lest we be carried away. (II Peter 3:17-18)
67. We are to remember that God's word foretells false teachers arising. (II Pet. 3:1-7)

68. We are to take heed to what the apostles have warned about false teachers. (I John 2:18-25)
69. Believe not every spirit but prove (test) each teacher. (I John 4:1-6)
70. Test teachers as to how they listen and heed the apostolic doctrine. (I John 4:5)
71. We are not to fellowship with false teachers (II John 5-11)—we are not to receive them into our home nor give them greeting (those who deny the deity of Jesus Christ).
72. We are to contend (agonize) earnestly for the faith which is once for all time delivered unto the saints. (Jude 3)
73. Remember that false teachers have been prophesied. (Jude 17)
74. We are to build ourselves up in faith, pray in the Spirit, keep ourselves in love (Jude 20, 21) as a method of combating false teaching.
75. On some who are teaching falsely not of perverse nature but out of doubt, we are to convince in an attitude of mercy. (Jude 22, 23)
76. Try those who claim apostolic authority to teach. (Rev. 2:2)

D. WEARINESS TO WICKED WHO BREAK COVENANT WITH THE LORD, CHAPTER 57

1. SORCERY

TEXT: 57:1-5

1 The righteous perisheth, and no man layeth it to heart; and merciful men are taken away, none considering that the righteous is taken away from the evil to come.
2 He entereth into peace; they rest in their beds, each one that walketh in his uprightness.
3 But draw near hither, ye sons of the sorceress, the seed of the adulterer and the harlot.

4 Against whom do ye sport yourselves? against whom make ye
a wide mouth, and put out the tongue? are ye not children
of transgression, a seed of falsehood,
5 ye that inflame yourselves among the oaks, under every green
tree; that slay the children in the valleys, under the clefts of
the rocks?

QUERIES

a. Who are the "sons of the sorceress"?
b. Were the Israelites really "slaying" children?

PARAPHRASE

These insensitive, indulgent leaders of Israel have produced a whole nation of uncaring people. These are times when good men are being destroyed and dying and no one seems to care or wonder why. Most do not realize that when the good man dies he is being taken away from these calamitous times. When the good man dies he enters in to a peaceful rest from the trials of this life. But you followers of sorcery and idolatry, prepare yourselves to face the wrath of Jehovah. Who are you making fun of? Who are you mocking with your impudent face-making? You are the sinners, aren't you? You passionately indulge in the sexual orgies of idol worship in the groves of terebinth trees and let your children be slain as human sacrifices in the rocky valleys of Palestine, do you not?

COMMENTS

v. 1-2 THE RIGHTEOUS: The problem Isaiah addresses here has been a problem for mankind ever since the Fall—why is it that the wicked seem to prosper and the righteous suffer? Of course, it is a problem only because of faulty perspective.

History looked at from the human perspective (limited to the past and the present; limited to this world and this life only) does seem to substantiate the idea that it "does not pay" to be good. But history seen from the divine perspective (by faith in the revelation of God about the past, present and future) says quite the opposite. The righteous man may *perish* (*'avad* in Hebrew which means "destroy") and the world evaluates it as something to be shunned. But the prophet of God says when the righteous man dies it is far from a tragedy for he is taken away from the evil to come. That is, the righteous man is delivered from the trials and tribulations of this world (cf. Rev. 7:14-17; 14:13; Psa. 116:15). Hosea, a contemporary of Isaiah, writes of the social chaos in the northern Ten Tribes (Israel) (cf. Hosea 4:1ff). No doubt the same kind of injustice and destruction was being directed against the righteous in the southern kingdom (Judah). Micah, also a contemporary of Isaiah, speaks of the ungodliness of Judah (cf. Micah 2:8-11; 3:1-3; 6:6-16; 7:1-6). Micah agrees with Isaiah that "the godly man has perished from the earth . . ." (Micah 7:2). The Hebrew word *yanuhu* is translated *rest* and has the connotation of "repose" (relaxation, ease). It is more precise than the usual Hebrew word for rest which is *shavath* ("sabbath"). Isaiah likens this rest unto sleep in the "bed." The word *shalom* at the first of the verse indicates the utter peacefulness which death brings to the man who "walks" in righteousness (cf. Dan. 12:10-13). Even if the righteous man must walk through the valley of the shadow of death, he will dwell in the house of the Lord forever (cf. Psa. 23). The wicked covenant breakers of Isaiah's day have it all wrong! They are self-deceived. They think the righteous have come to an untimely death because of their stubborn faithfulness to keep God's covenant. But it is the wicked covenant breakers who shall suffer!

v. 3-5 THE RIOTOUS REBROBATES: Thus the prophet arraigns the riotous leaders whom he had just characterized as "dumb dogs" (cf. 56:9-12). These leaders and their followers (which was the majority) are now characterized as "sons of the sorceress."

The Hebrew word used here for *sorceress* is *'onenah* which means literally "one who divines by the clouds." All "divining, soothsaying, magic, astrology" was prohibited by Mosaic law (cf. Ex. 22:18; Deut. 18:9-15). In the passage in Deut. 18:9-15 Moses categorizes the pagan practices as:

1. *me'onen* — one who bewitches with the evil eye; a cloud diviner
2. *menahesh* — an enchanter; snake-charmer; mesmerist; hypnotist
3. *mekasheph* — mutterer of incantations; ventriloquial whispers as under the influence of the spirits of the dead
4. *khover* — one who inflicts a spell by weaving magical knots
5. *'ov* — lit. means "bottle" indicating something like one who pretends powers over genii
6. *yidde'oniy* — a wizard; one who interprets the ravings of a medium
7. *doresh 'el-hammethiym* — a necromancer; one who calls up the spirits of the dead

Moses placed Moloch-worship at the head of his list, probably to show the integral connection between the practice of magic and idolatry. Making their children "pass through the fire" (human sacrifice) was more intimately connected with soothsaying (delving into the future) and magic than any other practice of idolatry. See Isaiah 8:19; 44:25 and Ezekiel 21:21 for more on this. Men have, ever since Eden, been possessed with the desire to penetrate the future and to manipulate its course. History clearly demonstrates that such power is not within the realm of the natural abilities of man. Men therefore have always attempted to gain the help of beings (departed dead, demons, Satan, angels, etc.) supposedly possessing such knowledge and power. But this is strictly forbidden by God and His word. By faith in God and obedience to His word men may know all (past, present and future) that pertains to life and godliness (cf. II Pet. 1:3-4).

The majority of people in Isaiah's day no longer sought the

word of God but had turned to "wizards" (cf. Isa. 8:16ff). This inevitably led to the other abominable practices of paganism and idolatry—adultery, fornication, and human sacrifice. They were an impudent, scornful, profane people (cf. Ezek. 2:1-7; 3:1-11, etc.). They were making malicious sport at someone else's expense—probably the poor and the righteous; they were making impudent gestures with their faces, sticking out their tongues in derision. This showed their real character. They proved their falseness by these actions. They mocked the righteous man who died an untimely death, but they were really profaning themselves!

Isaiah's generation was as sick as our generation. The Hebrew word *hannechamim* means literally, *violently, passionately,* but is translated, *inflame yourselves* in verse five. They indulged in the violent, passionate, sexual orgies among the terebinth (*'elim*) trees. The *terebinth* is related to the pistachio trees. In Palestine it grows sometimes as high as 40 feet and spreads its branches, with their thick, dark-green foliage, over a wide area (cf. II Sam. 18:9ff). The same Hebrew word is sometimes translated *oak* and sometimes *green tree.* It was the tree that provided the "groves" in which the pagans practiced their idolatry and adultery (cf. Deut. 12:2; I Kings 14:23; Jer. 2:20; 3:6, 13; 17:2; Hos. 4:13ff; Ezek. 6:13, etc.). The worst of the idolatrous practices was child sacrifice. This was often carried out in the Valley of Hinnom, within sight of the Temple of God (cf. Jer. 32:35; Ezek. 26:26-31). "In the valleys" suggests the many rocky valleys of Palestine walled on each side by "clefts of the rocks." Archaeologists have uncovered earthen jars containing the bones of sacrificed infants from various cities and villages of ancient Palestine, confirming the statements of the prophets. Ed. J. Young points out that the description "in the valleys, under the clefts of the rocks" is certainly "not applicable to Mesopotamia . . ." Another piece of the cumulative evidence that the latter portions of Isaiah were written by the prophet Isaiah who lived in Palestine *before* the Babylonian captivity, and not by some unknown post-exilic "Deutero-Isaiah."

QUIZ

1. What is the problem with the righteous dying Isaiah deals with in this text?
2. Is it a tragedy when the righteous man dies?
3. How many different kinds of "sorcerers" might have practiced in Palestine?
4. What kind of sorcerer did Isaiah name in verse three?
5. How were Isaiah's people demonstrating their profaneness?
6. How intense was their indulgence in idolatry?
7. What bit of evidence do we have for the authorship of Isaiah here?

2. SENSUALITY

TEXT: 57:6-10

6 Among the smooth stones of the valley is thy portion; they, they are thy lot; even to them hast thou poured a drink-offering, thou hast offered an oblation. Shall I be appeased for these things?

7 Upon a high and lofty mountain hast thou set thy bed; thither also wentest thou up to offer sacrifice.

8 And behind the doors and the posts hast thou set up thy memorial: for thou hast uncovered thyself to another than me, and art gone up; thou hast enlarged thy bed, and made thee a covenant with them; thou lovedst their bed where thou sawest it.

9 And thou wentest to the king with oil, and didst increase thy perfume, and didst send thine ambassadors far off, and didst debase thyself even unto Sheol.

10 Thou wast wearied with the length of thy way; yet saidst thou not, It is in vain; thou didst find a quickening of thy strength; therefore thou wast not faint.

QUERIES

a. What is the portion called "among the smooth stones"?
b. Where is "behind the doors and the posts"?

c. How could they be "wearied" and yet find "quickening of strength"?

PARAPHRASE

You stupid people. You go down into the valleys and take the stones worn smooth by the rains and winds and make them your gods. You have declared that these rocks are the focus of all your existence. You worship rocks with wine and grain offerings. Do you think this is acceptable to Me, the Living God? You have not allowed any obstacle to deter you from entering into the gross sexual immoralities connected with your idolatry. You laboriously carry your beds up steep mountains and set them there to aid in your indulgence. Up there you also haul all your offerings and sacrifices. The scripture plaques that are supposed to be where they can be seen on the door-posts of your homes you have deliberately hidden behind the posts. You have done this because you have committed yourselves to total intimacy in idolatry and immorality. You take off your clothes and climb into your large beds up among the groves of the hills along with those prostitutes you have paid to have sexual intercourse with you. This is your consuming passion, Israel! You spared yourself no trouble in developing these abominable practices as your way of life. A long time ago you sent merchants and envoys to pagan kings trading your goods for their gods. You continued to go out of your way to make yourself more and more comfortable to heathen practices. You allowed yourself to be debased with a rottenness like that of the grave in order to practice your immorality. All this made you physically and psychologically weary but you never admitted the stupidity of it all because you found a certain intoxicating, exhiliration in your rebellious immorality. So, you kept it up!

COMMENTS

v. 6-8 PRESENT: The depravity of the rulers and leaders infected the whole nation. The "smooth stones" of the valley apparently are to be linked to the idolatry being practiced. Perhaps they were using these "smooth stones" to build altars (which in itself was forbidden; not even to Jehovah was an altar to be built anywhere except in Jerusalem) to pagan gods. They might have been using the "smooth stones" to chisel into images of Molech or other idols. The question of Jehovah through His prophet is, almost incredulous, "Do you actually believe this is acceptable to Me, the Living God!?" Worshiping rocks!? The worship of Molech (in Hebrew the word means, "governing"), god of the Ammonites, was best noted for its gross sexual orgies and sacrifice of children. It was already forbidden by Moses (Lev. 18:21; 20:1-5); allowed by Solomon to please his foreign wives (I Kings 11:7); principally worshipped in the valley of Hinnom (Gehenna) (II Chron. 33:6). The words Moloch, Molech, Milcom (I Kings 11:5) and Malcam (Zeph. 1:5) are all variations of the same image. (See *Minor Prophets,* by Clinton Gill, College Press, pgs. 22-38; and Ezek. 16:20; 23:37-39; Jer. 7:9-11, 31; 19:4-13; Psa. 106:35-42; for further information on the worship of Molech.)

Setting up a bed upon a "high and lofty mountain" indicates extensive and elaborate preparations were made by the Hebrews in order to engage in these Canaanite fertility-cult practices. There were special groves of trees, well-kept flower gardens and elaborately furnished "temples" high up in the hills of Jehovah's holy land where the men and women went to "worship" at the throne of flesh. Great amounts of labor and money were spent building and maintaining these whore-houses. The worship of flesh is not dead! Great amounts of labor and money are expended today to build and maintain modern sophisticated whore-houses. The Anglo-saxon fertility cult has its groves, prophets, priestesses, publishing-houses, and "temples" today in both America and Great Britain.

One might wonder how the Hebrew people could ever succumb

to such gross depravity. They had the Law of Moses. They even copied some of those Laws and fastened them to the door-posts of their houses so they might be reminded constantly of Jehovah's presence and His revealed will. Verse eight tells the tragic story! These people had deliberately taken these "memorials" of scripture off their door-posts and hidden them "behind" the posts. Out of sight, out of mind! The Hebrew people had long ago rejected the word of God (II Kings 17:19; II Chron. 36:16; Amos 2:4, etc.). Incredibly, the books of the Law of the Lord had even been lost at one point in Judah's history (cf. II Kings 22:8ff). These people had prostituted themselves to pagan gods. What they were doing was no accident. It was not because they had been socially deprived, or because they were born in a "ghetto." They voluntarily chose to "uncover" themselves to another. This is a figurative description of the intimacy with which they joined themselves to their idols. They really gave themselves to idolatry; they "married" their pagan gods ("made . . . a covenant"). That is not unique. People today "marry" their possessions, their jobs, their recreation. These Jews "loved" their idol-beds (orgies). They were not forced into idolatry.

v. 9-10 PAST: Judah's past history was replete with instances of her kings and leaders going to pagan kings for help in bringing idolatry into the land of Jehovah (cf. II Kings 16:10ff; II Chron. 28:22ff; Isa. 30:1ff; Amos 5:25-27, etc.). Ezekiel's graphic parody of Judah's idolatry (spiritual adultery) pictures the nation, the bride of Jehovah, as an adulterous nymphomaniac! She did not play the part of a normal prostitute accepting pay for her adultery. She went after her lovers, paying them to practice spiritual harlotry with her (Ezek. 16:23-34)! Judah could not invent enough idolatry on her own—she had to send ambassadors to other nations to copy their idolatry for themselves. *Sheol* symbolized the grave, the place where human flesh rots. Graves were associated with that which was "unclean" according to the Mosaic Law. Isaiah declares Judah "debased" herself even unto rottenness, corruption and death by joining herself so intimately and wholly to idolatry.

Judah expended great effort, millions of shekels, and willingly allowed herself to be humiliated before pagan kings in her insatiable lust for idolatry. Judah "wore herself out" running after every opportunity to engage in it. Prophets likened Israel's pursuit of idolatry to a "wild ass" in heat (cf. Jer. 2:23-24; Hosea 8:9ff). Pursuing idolatry as Judah did was expensive, exhausting and debasing, but she never would admit the obvious: "It is vain." As a matter of fact, she found a certain intoxication and exhiliration in it. Sin and rebellion is inticing because it intoxicates with a *false* sense of *power.* Man in rebellion against God falsely assumes an exhilirating sense of sovereignty. His brain, intoxicated with this false sovereignty, is philosophically and psychologically addled and he will not admit the stupidity of his rebellion. He floats in a fantasy-land of philosophical inebriation like the drunkard. He has a false sense of "strength." This was Judah. She would not admit the stupidity of idolatry (cf. Isa. 44:9-20) because she was inebriated with the indulgent pleasure and false sovereignty she felt in practicing it.

QUIZ

1. What were the people doing with the "smooth stones"?
2. What was involved in the worship of Molech?
3. To what pains did these people go to practice their idolatry?
4. Would the Hebrew people reject the Law of Moses?
5. To what extent did Judah go after idolatry?
6. What is so invigorating about sin and idolatry?

3. STUPIDITY

TEXT: 57:11-13

11 And of whom hast thou been afraid and in fear, that thou liest, and hast not remembered me, nor laid it to thy heart?

have not I held my peace even of long time, and thou fearest
me not?
12 I will declare thy righteousness; and as for thy works, they
shall not profit thee.
13 When thou criest, let them that thou hast gathered deliver
thee; but the wind shall take them, a breath shall carry
them all away; but he that taketh refuge in me shall possess
the land, and shall inherit my holy mountain.

QUERIES

a. What "righteousness" did Judah have to declare?
b. When would Judah cry?

PARAPHRASE

Israel, what has preoccupied you and possessed you? Who has so impressed you that you have so thoroughly devoted yourself to that which is false? Why have you forgotten Me? Apparently you no longer fear Me because I have withheld My hand of judgment so long from you. Let Me tell you that I am soon going to show you, in no uncertain terms, what I think of your alleged righteousness. I am also going to show you that the idols you have made for yourself are not gods at all. Then you will cry out for deliverance but I will say, Let your idol-gods deliver you. They will be proven to be absolutely useless. They will disappear like a feather in a windstorm. In that time of trial, the person who puts his trust in Me will be able to look forward in hope that I will fulfill My promises to the faithful.

COMMENTS

v. 11 ENTRENCHED: The Hebrew word *da'agethe* is translated *afraid* but more properly means *anxious* or *preoccupied*. The word *thyire'yi* is from the root *yera'* and is translated *fear;* it is the most generic word for *fear* in Hebrew and generally means *reverential fear*. These people were not trembling with a paralyzing terror; they were just totally preoccupied with worshipping their idols and all the false living that went with it. They were living a lie and had totally committed themselves to it. This was a result of their breaking covenant with Jehovah. It was stupidity. And Jehovah was about to expose that stupidity. They were so thoroughly engrossed in their plunge into self-indulgence they did not remember Jehovah. How quickly men forget!

The goodness of God in "holding His peace" and withholding His judgments did not cause them to remember Him in thankfulness. They were not moved by His grace to repent. Their selfish, twisted minds rationalized that they were getting away with their wickedness. Israel had wanted to "be like the nations" for a long time (cf. I Sam. 8:4ff). For centuries she had preoccupied herself with the approval of men. When that consumes a nation or a man, Jehovah is forgotten. You cannot be a friend of the world and a friend of God (James 4:4).

v. 12-13 EXPOSED: All the time the Hebrews were engaging in idolatry they were also maintaining a facade of righteousness by offering sacrifices in the temple and by observing certain Sabbath regulations (cf. Amos 8:4-6; Isa. 1:10-15, etc.). But Jehovah will not "hold His peace" forever. He will soon come forth in judgment upon this people and then their sham righteousness will be exposed. The world will see then just where Israel has put its trust. Jehovah will demonstrate that all their pretended righteousness was unacceptable to Him. Not only that, He will expose once and for all the impotency of the idols they worshipped. Their enemies (Assyria and Babylon) will come in succession and attack them, destroy their cities and carry them away into exile. Their enemies will also carry their idol-gods away on horseback. Their idol-gods will not deliver them from their enemies. Their enemies will mock their idols, their temple, their worship and even Jehovah. Of course, Jehovah will not be mocked. He will eventually destroy their enemies also. When the Hebrews cry out for deliverance, they will see clearly that idols are not gods. What misery and wretchedness is in store for the one who has been so thoroughly preoccupied and possessed by idol-mania. Despair, frustration, shame and guilt will be his end.

To the contrary, the one who has listened to the prophets of God and trusted Jehovah's word will find blessedness. The Hebrew word *khoseh,* translated *refuge,* means *confidence, trust,* or *flee to for safety.* The man whose preoccupation is to seek the approval of the Lord will find fulfillment, satisfaction and hope in the ultimate blessings of God. This is the man who keeps covenant with Jehovah.

QUIZ

1. What kind of fear did the people have?
2. What was false about them?
3. Why had they forgotten Jehovah?
4. What was God going to do about their sham righteousness?
5. What is the character of the man who receives Jehovah's blessing?

4. SMITING

TEXT: 57:14-19

14 And he will say, Cast ye up, cast ye up, prepare the way, take up the stumbling-block out of the way of my people.
15 For thus saith the high and lofty One that inhabiteth eternity, whose name is Holy: I dwell in the high and holy place, with him also that is of a contrite and humble spirit, to

revive the spirit of the humble, and to revive the heart of
the contrite.
16 For I will not contend forever, neither will I be always wroth;
for the spirit would faint before me, and the souls that I
have made.
17 For the iniquity of his covetousness was I wroth, and smote
him; I hid my face and was wroth; and he went on backsliding in the way of his heart.
18 I have seen his ways, and will heal him: I will lead him also,
and restore comforts unto him and to his mourners.
19 I create the fruit of the lips: Peace, peace, to him that is
far off and to him that is near, saith Jehovah; and I will
heal him.

QUERIES

a. What is the "stumbling-block" in the way of His people?
b. Whose spirit would "faint" before Him?
c. Who is the one "far off" to whom peace is declared?

PARAPHRASE

And it will be said by the Lord, Build up a roadway, Build up a roadway; make a way that is prepared for My people. Take every obstacle over which they might stumble out of their way. This is the declaration of The High and Lofty One who dwells beyond time and space in eternity and who is Absolute Holiness. This One says, I dwell in the realm of Absolute Holiness beyond time and space, but I also dwell in people who are of a broken, penitent and humble spirit. I am the One who supplies the power to regenerate the broken and humble hearted. I have smitten My people time and again, but I will not smite forever (in fact, I am working toward a peaceful reconciliation with those who will be reconciled), for if I smote them forever and did not provide a way of reconciliation then all mankind would perish—all the souls I have made. It was on account of My people's greed and defrauding of one another that I smote them. Time after time I withdrew My presence and protection from them but they went right on rebelling and turning away from Me to their own devices. Yes, I have been fully aware of Israel's rebellions, yet, I will accomplish My work of reconciliation and offer Israel healing by My grace. I will offer Myself to Israel for leadership and I will restore blessings to her I promised her long ago. The work of reconciliation and its proclamation will come from Me, says Jehovah, I will accomplish and proclaim peace to everyone in the world who will accept it—to Israel who has been in special covenant relationship to Me and to all the Gentiles who have not. This reconciliation will heal all who accept it of the sickness of their rebellion.

COMMENTS

v. 14-15 RELIEVED: Although the Lord has recounted the sorceries, sensualities and stupidities of Israel and although He has smitten them in the past (and will smite them again in the captivities), He *now* addresses Himself to the future reconciliation He is going to accomplish through the Servant which will begin in the restoration from the captivity and be offered to all mankind through covenant relationship. Jehovah will command, "Build a roadway, build a roadway . . ." The Hebrew words *sollu sollu* are from the root word *salal* which means "heap up" as in building up a road-bed. In rescuing His people from captivity (the first and imperative step toward messianic fulfillment) Jehovah commands their captors not merely "let my people go," but "Put your hand to the task, O captors of My people, and assist them by working for their return to their land!" And thus it was so! Cyrus and the Persians contributed financially and in other ways to return the Jews to Palestine (cf. Ezra, chapters 1-6). The Persians also removed a number of "stumbling-blocks" (Hebrew *mikeshol,* "obstacle") from the way of the Jews.

It is the omnipotent Jehovah, the high and lofty One who has decreed this redemption of those He will soon smite in captivity. Jehovah is God without beginning and end. He dwells in absolute unendingness ("eternity"). He sees all things at once. There is no time with Him. Thus He is able to talk about Israel's captivity and redemption all at the same time. The same *perspective* is available to human beings through *faith* in Jehovah. This is hope in the midst of trouble. Jehovah is about to make "the Valley of Achor (Trouble) a door of hope" (cf. Hosea 2:15; II Cor. 1:3-11). Jehovah is also absolutely holy (righteous, pure, true, just, faithful). He keeps His word. What He is and says is always good. And, although He dwells in the high and holy place, He also dwells with men who are of a contrite and humble spirit—for that is good. The Hebrew word *daka'* means literally, *bruise, break in pieces, crush, contrite.* Men who wish to be filled with the goodness God can supply must first of all be poor in spirit (cf. Mt. 5:3-9; Psa. 34:18; 51:17; Isa. 66:2). The Hebrew word *shephal* means, *made low, depressed, thrown down, sit down low, humbled.* The Lord could not dwell with the nation as it was during the days of the prophets for it was haughty (Isa. 2:11, 17; 3:16; 10:33; 24:4; Ezek. 16:50; Zeph. 3:11; Micah 2:3). He exhorted them to be humble (Micah 6:8). The Lord cannot dwell in a church that is haughty either (Rev. 3:17, etc.). How is it that the Lord requires humility and contrition in order to dwell in the human heart on the one hand and then on the other hand promise to "revive the spirit of the humble"? In this case, of course, the Lord is not going to "revive" haughtiness. He is going to regenerate. What a man boasts in determines his state of aliveness. If he boasts in himself, he is dead because human power is impotent. If he boasts and trusts in the Lord he is humbled but he has hope because he shall receive an imputed exaltation—an imputed righteousness and eternal life. And, of course, the only way an *imputed* exaltation can be received is by faith in the One who is alone able to impute it—God! That is why David was a "man after God's own heart." In his contrition and humility David cried out, "Create in me a clean heart, O God, and put a new and right spirit within me . . ." (Psa. 51:10).

Jehovah is going to smite His people in captivity in order to make it possible for those who will to be contrite and humble. Then He is going to redeem them and revive them and form a faithful remnant from among them through which to bring to fruition His ultimate redemptive work in the Suffering Servant.

v. 16-19 REASON: The reason for the smiting and the reviving is now proposed. If He should contend *forever* there would be *no* redemption for anyone! All have sinned. All deserve eternal punishment. But, amazing grace, God has a divine plan by which He will offer salvation to those who will accept it. He will punish sin in His Son, thereby justifying His holiness and at the same time justifying those who believe (cf. Rom. 3:21-26)! Man's salvation originates absolutely in the *grace* of God! Had it not, all "spirits would faint" before Him and all the "souls that He made" would perish.

Certainly, for the iniquity of man's covetousness God was, by His very nature, moved with wrath and condemnation. The question is not, "How could a good God send anyone to Hell? . . ." the question is, "How could a good God send a sinner to Heaven?" He could not. Therefore, He worked out a way to make sinners good enough to go to Heaven. The Hebrew word *batsa'* is translated "covetousness" and means *unjust gain, to spoil, to plunder, to defraud.* It was this deliberate, often violent defrauding of one's fellow man that moved Jehovah through the centuries to smite Israel. Still she kept on "turning away from" Him (Heb. *shovav*) or "backsliding." To turn away from God is to go backwards. Many men have thought that turning away from God and the Bible was to advance. But history has proved over and over that turning away from God and the Bible is regression for humanity.

Now the purpose of God's smiting is to "heal." This healing is a spiritual healing—a healing of the inner man (cf. Isa. 19:22; 53:5; Hosea 5:13; 6:1; 14:4; Jer. 17:14; 30:17, etc.).

God, the divine surgeon, had to use drastic, radical "surgery" to heal Israel, for she resisted it adamantly (cf. Jer. 6:14; 8:11; 15:18, etc.). The healing process began with the smiting at the captivity, continued through the rescue from captivity and the "indignation" of the post-exilic centuries, and was finally accomplished in the Servant through whose "stripes we are healed," (Isa. 53:5ff). And that is precisely, we believe, the relationship of verse 19 to this context, inasmuch as it appears to be fulfilled in Acts 10:36 and Ephesians 2:17. God's healing was reconciliation of Himself to man (Isa. 53:1ff). Reconciliation (healing) in the plan of the God of all mankind was ultimately to be provided for all men. Thus, when peace (reconciliation) was declared to those near and to those afar, it was done in the completed work of the Messiah. Again, the missionary call rings forth from the "Gospel prophet of the O.T."

QUIZ

1. What does the term "Cast ye up . . ." imply about the Hebrew return from captivity?
2. Why stress the nature of God here?
3. Why emphasize that God dwells in the contrite and humble hearted?
4. How does God "revive" the humble hearted?
5. Why did God have to "smite" Israel to heal?
6. Who all are to be recipients of God's healing?
7. Where is the fulfillment of verse 19?

5. SEETHING

TEXT: 57:20-21

20 But the wicked are like the troubled sea; for it cannot rest, and its waters cast up mire and dirt.
21 There is no peace, saith my God, to the wicked.

QUERIES

a. Why are the wicked like the sea?
b. Is there really no peace to wicked people?

PARAPHRASE

But the wicked are never healed in the inner man because they are filled with a restlessness of soul that keeps boiling up within them like the sea whose waves never stop rolling in, bringing up filth and muck. There is no secure feeling of being at peace with the wicked.

COMMENTS

v. 20 CONSCIENCE: The contrite and humble man will be healed. He will be healed in the inner man where the conscience dwells. He will receive, by grace, through faith, an imputed righteousness—a cleansed conscience. But the wicked man's conscience is like the constantly rolling sea. It is *never* completely at rest. It may be calmed at times, but it is forever boiling and churning and more often than not it is casting up all the mire and muck thrown into it. The wicked, said Calvin, ". . . are terrified and alarmed by conscience, which is the most agonizing of all torments and the most cruel of all executioners." Luther said, "Conscience is a savage beast and a devil . . . There is nothing which so much disturbs the peace or causes so much unrest as a frightened heart. It turns pale at the flash of lightning and at the rattle of a leaf." From the St. Louis Post-Dispatch of September 22, 1941 comes the following story:

> Seven years of tortured nights, when he awakened screaming at the specter of the man who had befriended him and whom he had killed, have ended for Harold Malmberg.

Malmberg, 27 years old, died yesterday in the Nebraska Penitentiary hospital from poison he swallowed three days before, Warden Neil Olson said. During his seven years, Malmberg "was a model prisoner," who never complained and did not seek parole, Olson added. But he could not face his conscience.

Malmberg had few nights of peace after he shot Russell Goodwin three times in 1934 and left him beside the road to die, after Goodwin, a traveling salesman, had picked up the hitchhiking youth. In prison he had nightmares in which the man he admitted murdering "came back every night to sit on his bed and talk to him," the warden explained.

In the daytime, Malmberg was "a jovial sort who did the tasks required of him cheerfully and well."

While he steadfastly refused to tell what he had swallowed, doctors labored continuously over Malmberg from the time he was discovered ill early Friday morning until he died. The poison apparently had been stolen from the prison photographic darkroom where he worked.

Malmberg consistently denied he intended to kill Goodwin when he ordered the salesman out of his car at pistol point. The jury did not accept his pleas of insanity, and the Des Moines, Iowa, youth was sentenced to life imprisonment.

Man may escape the punishment of human courts and judges. His evil deeds may be kept in absolute secrecy from everyone else. He may carry them with him to the grave, but he cannot hide himself from his conscience, nor can he escape from its tormenting judgment. Every man must live with his own conscience, and woe to him whose conscience has become his judge and executioner. Be assured of this, "If our hearts (conscience) condemn us, God is greater than our heart" (I Jn. 3:20-21).

v. 21 CONFLICT: A guilty conscience may become a frightful tormentor and a source of intense agony and distress leading to mortal sorrow and, sometimes, even suicide if the sense of guilt cannot be removed effectively. A guilty conscience may even prove disastrous to the physical and mental health of an individual. The wicked, unfaithful, covenant-breaker can never have security, peace of mind and soul.

The point of these last two verses is to make a sharp contrast between the "healing" that will come to those of contrite and humble hearts and their turning to the Lord and His promises to be eventually accomplished in the Servant, and the wicked who refuse healing and reconciliation. The guilty conscience can only be healed through imputed righteousness. The cleansing of the conscience can only come by grace through faith in the substitutionary atonement of Christ (cf. I Jn. 1:8-9; 2:1-6; Heb. 9:14; 10:19-22; I Pet. 3:21). One of the important reasons there are certain actions required of men for entrance into covenant relationship with Christ (faith, repentance, immersion in water) is to provide man a series of overt actions and a point of reference in time to which he may relate his inner, invisible spiritual person with the cleansing of his conscience. In other words, man needs such reference points by which to express his faith and experience access into the grace of God (cf. Rom. 5:1-2). It is in our obedience to the word of God that we have assurance of the purification of our souls (cf. I Pet. 1:22-23).

QUIZ

1. How is the contrite and humble man healed?
2. Have you experienced the truth of verses 20-21 in your conscience?
3. Have you experienced the cleansing of your conscience?
4. How are we assured, what is the source of our assurance, that we may have our conscience cleansed?

E. WHOLENESS TO THE WISE WHO KEEP CONVENANT WITH THE LORD, CHAPTER 58

1. HEARKEN

TEXT: 58:1-5

1 Cry aloud, spare not, lift up thy voice like a trumpet, and declare unto my people their transgression, and to the house of Jacob their sins.
2 Yet they seek me daily, and delight to know my ways: as a nation that did righteousness, and forsook not the ordinance of their God, they ask of me righteous judgments; they delight to draw near unto God.
3 Wherefore have we fasted, say they, and thou seest not? wherefore have we afflicted our soul, and thou takest no knowledge? Behold in the day of your fast ye find your own pleasure, and exact all your labors.
4 Behold, ye fast for strife and contention, and to smite with the fist of wickedness: ye fast not this day so as to make your voice to be heard on high.
5 Is such the fast that I have chosen? the day for a man to afflict his soul? Is it to bow down his head as a rush, and to spread sackcloth and ashes under him? wilt thou call this a fast, and an acceptable day to Jehovah?

QUERIES

a. Why is the prophet not to "spare" in his crying?
b. How could they "smite" on a fast day?

PARAPHRASE

Shout this message to the whole nation. Do not relent when they try to justify themselves. Shout clearly to the nation this warning so the wise will acknowledge their sin and hypocrisy. Most of the people go right on tramping into the courts of the Temple daily as if they really were sincere in knowing My will. They pretend they are concerned about righteousness and obeying My commandments. On the one hand they say they want Me to give them holy guidelines for living because they enjoy doing them. And on the other hand they say, Why should we afflict our souls in fasting and obedience since it appears Jehovah is not taking notice of our righteousness and rewarding us?

Hearken to what I have to say, says the Lord: I know exactly why you fast! The truth is that you are not really afflicting your souls in penitence when you fast. You use your fasts to indulge yourselves in carnal pleasures and to defraud the poor and powerless. You do not prepare your mind and heart to worship God when you fast. Your indulgence and oppression cause you to bicker and fight one another when you are pretending to fast! Do you actually think this is the kind of fasting I have commanded? Is this what you think I call "afflicting one's soul"? Do you think by such an outward show of extreme humiliation (bowing yourself double like a reed and lying down on a bed of sackcloth and ashes) that you can hide your hypocrisy? Is this what you call fasting? Do you believe I will accept your hypocrisy?

COMMENTS

v. 1-3a HAUGHTINESS: Isaiah is told to cry a "throaty" call. The Hebrew words *kera' vegaron* mean literally, *call with the throat.* The *Jerusalem Bible* translates, "Shout for all you are worth." Apparently the Lord knew there would be a few in Judah who would hearken to the prophet's call and wisely repent. There were some who would become covenant-keepers. Presently, however, the majority of people were covenant-breakers. Not only so, they were hypocrites as well. The Hebrew word *thakhesek,* translated *spare not,* means *do not withhold.*

The point is that Isaiah is not to hold back declaring the hypocrisy of the majority even when they may appear to be righteous by their great show of religiosity or their attempts to justify themselves (as in verse three) or by their threats against the prophet himself. Isaiah is to become a *shophar* (ram's horn or trumpet, the instrument used to sound a warning).

For the most part, the nation went right on, day after day, haughtily tramping into the courts of the Temple (cf. Isa. 1:12ff), pretending to seek Jehovah and pretending to find satisfaction in obeying His appointed fast days. Publicly they have a finely practiced facade of not being caught disobeying the rituals and ordinances of the Law. They have put on an ostentatious show. Then they reasoned that Jehovah should reciprocate with goodness toward them (material goodness, no doubt) and judgments upon their enemies. It appears they think they have fooled God with their outward show and now expect Him to reward them accordingly. They took pleasure in their religiosity because they had deceived themselves into thinking Jehovah's righteousness could be compromised by their hypocrisy. They believed they could have their sin and Jehovah's blessing at the same time. But obviously, Jehovah had not responded to their sham-fasting as they had expected. He had not healed the social depravity of the day; He had not removed the growing threat of Assyrian or Babylonian invasion of their country. They had so thoroughly calloused their own consciences they blamed Jehovah for what was very evidently about to befall them. They accuse God of insensitiveness, of carelessness and unconcern. Usually, the hypocrite plays his part so well, he fools himself more than anyone else. These haughty hypocrites had so deceived themselves they were incredulous that God should not be impressed with their self-righteousness!

v. 3b-5 HYPOCRISY: Now Jehovah exposes the hypocrisy of their religiosity. Jehovah makes it plain that He does indeed know what they are doing! They are not fasting to afflict their souls. While they pretend to fast, they are really indulging in their favorite occupation—making money. The Hebrew words *'atzevyekem negoshu* are from root words that literally mean, *grieve* and *oppress* respectively, but translated *labors* and *exact* respectively. Obviously, these people were not gathering at fasts to grieve and oppress their own souls so they must have been plotting business deals that would grieve and oppress one another or the poor.

A word about fasting may be in order here. The Hebrew word used for *fast* in the Pentateuch is *'innah* and means literally *to afflict* (the soul) (cf. Lev. 16:29). The Hebrew word most often used after the Pentateuch (and not used in the Pentateuch) is *tzum* meaning literally *to abstain.* Both words are used in verse three. Actually, fasting was commanded in the Law of Moses only once (Lev. 16:29) and that on the Day of Atonement. Apparently, the Hebrew people amplified this command and extended it to most any time of sorrow or need for repentance. The nation and individuals were capable of fasting with proper motives (cf. I Sam. 7:6; II Sam. 1:12; Judg. 20:26; I Kings 21:12-29; Psa. 109:24; Jer. 36:9; Esther 4:1-3; 4:16; Neh. 1:4). The Jewish people who came back from the captivities had doubts about the efficacy of so many fasts and inquired of the prophets and priests whether they should keep them all or not (cf. Zech. 7:1-6; 8:13). In Isaiah's day these fasts were being exploited for mercenary purposes.

The fasts, rather than providing an opportunity for men to abstain from worldly pursuits, afflict their souls and concentrate on God's holiness, provided opportunities for them to haggle, strive, contend, argue and even physically strike one another over profiteering. Leupold visualizes these verses: "The prophet follows them to their place of assembly on a fast day. There, off in a corner, two men are not evaluating their own conduct and that of their nation; they are not seeking the face of God in true repentance. They are carrying on a business transaction. Or . . . while they are publicly engaged in holy exercises, at home the laborer who is working for them is slaving under heavy burdens and is being oppressed."

Rhetorically the Lord asks, Do you think this is the kind of fast I would approve? Their humility was mockery. The long, tender rush was easily bent double without breaking and furnished a graphic figure for the bent-over false humility of these hypocrites. Jesus described the false humility of the fasting hypocrites of His day as *skuthropos* (Greek for *sad, dejected, sullen, morose*). Jesus said the hypocrites of His day made their normal faces to disappear (*aphanizousin,* Gr.) so they might put on faces (*hopos phanosin*) of fasting, (Mt. 6:16-18). These men of Isaiah's day were extreme in their pretentions even to spreading under themselves a "bed" of sackcloth and ashes. But none of it fooled God! Let every man who reads this be forever impressed with this—God is not mocked! Religious ritual (no matter how scriptural and orthodox and correct) if it is coerced, "psyched," or played-at, if the heart is not right, is an abomination to God! We cannot put on a sad face and fool God; we cannot put on a happy face and fool God; we cannot put on *any* face and fool God!

QUIZ

1. How emphatic is Isaiah to be in crying his message to the nation?
2. What made these people continue to haughtily pretend to worship Jehovah?
3. What made them criticize God for not being aware of their religiosity?
4. What was fasting originally instituted for?
5. How were these people profaning the matter of fasting?
6. What should we all learn about pretending from this passage?

2. HOLINESS

TEXT: 58:6-12

6 Is not this the fast that I have chosen: to loose the bonds of
wickedness, to undo the bands of the yoke, and to let the

oppressed go free, and that ye break every yoke?
7 Is it not to deal thy bread to the hungry, and that thou bring the poor that are cast out to thy house? when thou seest the naked, that thou cover him; and that thou hide not thyself from thine own flesh?
8 Then shall thy light break forth as the morning, and thy healing shall spring forth speedily; and thy righteousness shall go before thee; the glory of Jehovah shall be thy rearward.
9 Then shalt thou call, and Jehovah will answer; thou shalt cry, and he will say, Here I am. If thou take away from the midst of thee the yoke, the putting forth of the finger, and speaking wickedly;
10 and if thou draw out thy soul to the hungry, and satisfy the afflicted soul: then shall thy light rise in darkness, and thine obscurity be as the noon-day;
11 and Jehovah will guide thee continually, and satisfy thy soul in dry places, and make strong thy bones; and thou shalt be like a watered garden, and like a spring of water, whose waters fail not.
12 And they that shall be of thee shall build the old waste places; thou shalt raise up the foundations of many generations; and thou shalt be called The repairer of the breach, The restorer of paths to dwell in.

QUERIES

a. Why exhort them not to "hide" from their own flesh?
b. What is "putting forth of the finger"?
c. How would they "raise up foundations of many generations"?

PARAPHRASE

To the contrary, I do have standards for the kind of fasting that is acceptable to Me. If you will afflict your souls and truly repent, you will cease to oppress your fellow man and make every effort to free the oppressed from any unfair exploitation they may be under. If you will feed those who are hungry, give shelter to the outcast and the needy stranger, clothe those in need of something to wear and remember to minister to the needs of your own family, then you will be repenting as I wish you to do. When you do these things, the glory of God's goodness will burst on your nation like the suddenness and brilliance of the morning sun. Your land will be cured of its chaos and wickedness rapidly. The glory of the Lord will completely surround you, protecting and sustaining you as in the days of old. Then you will be able to call upon the Lord and He will be able to answer. No longer will you be rebelling against Him and running from Him, but you will find Him and He will come to you.

Let Me repeat for emphasis, If you put an end to all the oppression, stop making contemptuous gestures and slanderous words toward people—and if you turn in sympathy to the hungry and feed them and help all who are in need, then the darkness around you now will turn to goodness and truth as bright as the noon-day sun. The Lord will guide such a people every day and will bring life and health to them. Such a people will blossom with righteousness and produce the fruit of justice and give life to all about them like an ever flowing spring in an oasis. If you people will do this you will produce offspring that will build back the messianic nation that was once founded and is now in ruins. What you build, as a result of such repentance, will lay a foundation upon which many generations of the future may be able to build the messianic kingdom. You will be known as the people who repaired the ruined walls of God's redemptive "city" and as the people who restored the way that leads to man's salvation.

COMMENTS

v. 6-9a REPENTANCE: God promises wholeness to those who will keep His covenant. But Judah needs to repent before it can meet God's standards of holiness. That is, the nation must change its direction theologically (repenting of idolatry) and morally (repenting of social transgressions). This has to be done individually, of course. If Judah will keep her covenant with the Lord as He wishes her to she will "loose the bonds of wickedness, unto the . . . yoke . . .," feed the hungry, clothe the naked, etc. The word "fast" in verse six may be used generically to mean the total relationship of man toward God which would be covenant relationship. Micah's prophecy gives an excellent parallel to Isaiah; they were, after all, contemporaries. Micah, chapters 1-3, document the atrocious sins of the powerful against the weak; chapters 4-5 promise the messianic destiny of the Jews; chapters 6-7 announce to the people of Micah's day what they must do to cooperate with Jehovah in that destiny. The essence of covenant-keeping, according to Micah, is not spectacular religious ritual or sacrifice but simply being Godlike in the everyday, mundane relationships with both God and man. Micah puts it this way, "He has showed you, O man, what is good; and what does the Lord require of you but to do justice, and to love kindness, and to walk humbly with your God" (Micah 6:8).

It should not be strange to the people of Judah that one of their prophets would exhort them to care for the poor. The Law of Moses was very clear on caring for the poor (cf. Deut. 14:28—15:18). The Law of Moses was also explicit as to responsibilities toward one's own flesh and blood (family relationships). In such areas as training and discipline of children, levirate law of provision for in-laws, divorce, inheritance laws, etc., the Law is plain. It seems almost incredible that people should have to be reminded to take care of their families, yet even in the New covenant scriptures Christians are admonished, "if any one does not provide for his relatives, and especially for his own family, he has disowned the faith and is worse than an unbeliever" (I Tim. 5:8). The Pharisees, rather than "honoring" their fathers and mothers by financial support in their old age, declared their assets "Corban" (devoted to God and unavailable for "social security" support). And the Pharisees were *very* religious people who were certain that they, above every one else, were covenant people of Jehovah!

If the people will repent (change) and turn back to the instructions of God in the Law of Moses, God promises three distinct changes will take place in their society: (a) "Healing" of the wounds and sicknesses of society will take place suddenly and brilliantly like the morning sun. In the land of Palestine, the sun seems to come up instantaneously, not gradually, as in lands with an abundance of trees and other things to block the horizon. (b) The righteousness they practice will be a source of safety and security for life and at the same time Jehovah will give His glorious providential safety and security. Judah will be *surrounded* by a security of righteousness. (c) Repentance will also bring renewed access to God. Jehovah cannot countenance a kingdom in rebellion. Man is created with a free will and the freedom to choose his spiritual Sovereign. If man wishes God to be his Sovereign, man must conform to the Sovereign's rule. As long as man rebels against the sovereignty of God, he cannot (because he does not want) have access to God. Jehovah will answer all who surrender to His sovereignty and call upon Him.

v. 9b-12 RESULTS: There are grander and more gratifying results to add to the nation if it repents. The qualification is restated, but still the same: repentance. Evidently the "putting forth of the finger" was a kind of derisive, contemptuous pointing of the finger (cf. Prov. 6:13). It is listed here in connection with "speaking wickedly" and must have reference to slander or unjust accusations. God says men must repent of that. It is graphic evidence of a hateful heart—one that would despise the hungry and have no compassion on the afflicted.

But look at the promised results of repentance: (a) continual guidance of Jehovah who is absolute truth, absolute justice, absolute righteousness. To the individual who repents will come a personal satisfaction of the soul like the desert nomad's thirst is satisfied when he finds a cool, shady, bubbling spring of water. There will come personal wholeness and spiritual integration like a man feels physically when he is young and strong and in the prime of health. (b) The man who repents and keeps God's covenant will also produce something for the benefit of others. He will become like a "watered garden" and a "spring of water, whose waters fail not." Jesus said His disciples would become "rivers of living water" (cf. Jn. 7:37-39). The disciples of Jesus are to become salt of the earth and light of the world (cf. Mt. 5:13-16). (c) The man who repents will build the kingdom of God. Obviously, the rebuilding work of those who repent here is the rebuilding of the people's covenant relationship to Jehovah in order that they may fulfill their messianic destiny and form the kingdom of God on earth (the church). Repairing literal walls and building literal foundations can in no way be the goal of this prophecy. Its only goal is to encourage the people of Isaiah's day to be instruments of Jehovah as He reaches toward the establishment of New Israel. And the church was founded on a generation of covenant-keeping Hebrews in the first century A.D. when the gospel was obeyed first in Jerusalem, then in Judea, then in Samaria and then in the uttermost parts of the earth.

QUIZ

1. What is the word "fast" used for generically in verse six?
2. What does the Law of Moses have to say about treatment of the poor?
3. What does God promise to do for the nation and the individual who repents?
4. How does covenant-keeping enter into this section?
5. What may the individual enjoy personally as a result of his repentance?
6. What may the individual produce for the benefit of others by repentance?

3. HERITAGE

TEXT: 58:13-14

13 If thou turn away thy foot from the sabbath, from doing thy pleasure on my holy day; and call the sabbath a delight, and the holy of Jehovah honorable; and shalt honor it, not doing thine own ways, nor finding thine own pleasure, nor speaking thine own words:
14 then shalt thou delight thyself in Jehovah; and I will make thee to ride upon the high places of the earth; and I will feed thee with the heritage of Jacob thy father: for the mouth of Jehovah hath spoken it.

QUERIES

a. Why is the sabbath so important?
b. How will they "ride" upon the high places?

PARAPHRASE

You people must stop kicking around My sabbath day and wiping your feet on it as something that can be desecrated by exploiting it for your own greedy gain. You must cherish My sabbath as that which is exquisitely precious, that which you delight in and honor. You must honor My sabbath by ceasing to take the day to concentrate on your own indulgence and talking of everything but Me. If you will take this attitude toward My sabbath and cherish Me, then I will exalt you and make you conquerors. I will give you the spiritual birthright which I promised to your ancestor Jacob. That will sustain you for all eternity. These are the words of Jehovah the omnipotent God!

COMMENTS

v. 13 DEVOTION: The Hebrew word *oneg* (v. 13) or *te 'annag* (v. 14) is translated *delight* but means literally, *delicate, exquisite, luxurious.* The Lord is insisting that His people *cherish* His sabbath. They are presently trampling it under foot, so to speak, as of no more value than something to wipe their feet on. It is being used as a day for planning self-indulgence. They are gathering on God's holy day, a day set aside to think and talk of Him, to talk of making money and plan ways to circumvent His Law (Amos 8:5).

Why is the Sabbath so significant? It was the one condition or requirement that could provide a covenant-keeping relationship that would bring the Hebrew closer to Jehovah than any other. The Sabbath was instituted and set aside as holy unto the Lord long before the Mosaic law. It was consecrated from the beginning of creation. It was given as a type and symbol of the cessation from labor (or rest) into which one enters when entering into covenant relationship provided by Christ. In other words, the old sabbath was an experience symbolic of the Christian experience. The sabbath rest "remaining" in Hebrew 4:9-10 was "being entered" by the "ones believing" (Gr. *oi pisteusantes,* present tense) of Hebrews 4:3. In other words, the one who believes Christ and becomes a Christian does (present tense) enter the *rest* God symbolized by the old sabbath day (cf. also Mt. 11:28-30). Of course, the Christian's present *rest* will some day be finally and ultimately consummated in the new heaven and new earth when he will cease from his labors (cf. Rev. 14:13, etc.). That is why proper relationship to God for those of Isaiah's day be expressed by proper attitude toward God's sabbath day! It had to do with all that God was going to do in salvation and redemption in the Messiah and His kingdom.

v. 14 DOMINION: Proper attitude and action toward God's revealed will (in this case the Sabbath law) logically results in proper attitude and action toward the personhood of God. If a man cherishes God's laws (Psa. 119:1ff), he will cherish

God. Actually the relationship is cyclical. We must first cherish God in order to cherish His law. But the more we cherish His law, the more we will cherish Him! The more we luxuriate in God and His will, the "higher" we will "ride"! The phrase, ". . . make thee to ride upon the high places of the earth . . ." symbolizes victory, conquest, dominion. If we have faith as a grain of mustard seed (cf. Lk. 17:5-6) we can do mighty, victorious, conquering things. The mustard seed means qualitative, not quantitative. It is not a *small* or *big* faith that counts but a *living, producing, working* faith (like a seed has life and production in it). To that kind of faith God will fulfill His promises of victory. It may not be the kind of victory measured by worldly standards; it may not be *physical* victory or dominion in this life. Physical victory in this life was what the majority of the Jews anticipated from the glorious promises of their prophets (e.g., Isa. ch. 60-66). But God intended to give those who were faithful victory and dominion over sin and death through the Messiah. The "heritage of Jacob" was, of course, the birthright. The birthright was a physical thing that had to do with perpetuation of the Hebrew family's inheritance of land and goods through the eldest son. But it had as its ultimate goal the preservation of a people whose destiny was messianic! The birthright was really a spiritual thing. It was to result in the redemption of the whole human race through a human family from a particular human nation.

The promises of verse 14 may find a temporary fulfillment in the return of the Jews from the captivities, but like all other promises concerning the Jewish people and their land and their nation, the ultimate fulfillment was in the "seed" (singular) (cf. Gal. 3:16ff), the Christ and the New Israel (Gal. 6:16). The redemption of man will be consummated when God restores man to the dominion man was given at creation which Christ earned for man (cf. Heb. 2:5-18).

QUIZ

1. What attitude does God want the people to take toward His sabbath?
2. Why?
3. What does one's attitude toward the law of God have to do with one's attitude toward God?
4. How will God give man dominion?
5. What is the "heritage" of Jacob?

F. WRATH OF THE LORD UPON COVENANT DESPISERS, CHAPTER 59

1. THEIR CRIMES

TEXT: 59:1-8

1 Behold, Jehovah's hand is not shortened, that it cannot save; neither his ear heavy, that it cannot hear:
2 but your iniquities have separated between you and your God, and your sins have hid his face from you, so that he will not hear.
3 For your hands are defiled with blood, and your fingers with iniquity; your lips have spoken lies, your tongue muttereth wickedness.
4 None sueth in righteousness, and none pleadeth in truth: they trust in vanity, and speak lies; they conceive mischief, and bring forth iniquity.
5 They hatch adders' eggs, and weave the spider's web: he that eateth of their eggs dieth; and that which is crushed breaketh out into a viper.
6 Their webs shall not become garments, neither shall they cover themselves with their works: their works are works of iniquity, and the act of violence is in their hands.
7 Their feet run to evil, and they make haste to shed innocent blood: their thoughts are thoughts of iniquity; desolation

and destruction are in their paths.
8 The way of peace they know not; and there is no justice in their goings: they have made them crooked paths; whosoever goeth therein doth not know peace.

QUERIES

a. Why bring up the subject of the people's salvation here?
b. With what "webs" did the people hope to "cover themselves"?
c. Why do they not know the "way of peace"?

PARAPHRASE

Look! The reason My great redemptive plan has to be delayed by a period of chastening for you is not because My power or My willingness is insufficient. You are the reason, O Israel. You are in rebellion against all I want to do for you and through you. Your rebellion and sin has built a wall of unwillingness and rejection. As long as you are determined to continue in your wickedness, you will not see Me as I am. Yes, it is because you have your hands in every conceivable practice of wickedness there is (murder, thievery, convenant-breaking, slander) that you cannot receive My purpose for you. No one practices justice in legal suits or tries cases honestly. People are building this society on moral impotence and falsehood. They spend most of their time plotting wickedness and their plots produce violence. Poisonous seed is produced by these snakes like the eggs of a viper. They build traps for one another like a spider weaving webs. They produce poisonous offspring and everyone who partakes of their wickedness is poisoned also. They think that their subtle "webs" will provide a covering or escape, but the evil of their hearts is clearly seen in what their lives produce. They do not merely stumble into sin, they eagerly race one another to kill and maim the innocent.

They dream and think and plan wickedness all day and all night. They haven't the slightest desire for real peace in this society. They prefer to live crooked and devious lives and when anyone prefers that he is an enemy of justice and peace.

COMMENTS

v. 1-4 BARRICADED: In chapter 58 Jehovah tells the people the virtues which would prepare them to be covenant-keepers and to carry out His messianic plans. But these people are so thoroughly entrenched in sin and rebellion against God's program of righteousness and holiness they must be repeatedly warned of the wrath that comes to those who despise His covenant. These first verses of chapter 59 are a graphic description of Judah's adamant hostility against God's way and her passionate wantonness for wickedness. Isaiah is describing here the conditions during the reign of the most wicked king Judah ever had—Manasseh. Manasseh came to the throne in 687 B.C. as a boy of 12 and was seduced by a powerful group of priests, noblemen and false prophets to reintroduce the idolatry of his ancestors (Ahaz, et al). Judah's prophets (Isaiah and Micah) predicted the wrath of Jehovah which had earlier fallen (722 B.C.) upon Israel. Manasseh outstripped all his ancestors in wickedness, (cf. II Kings 21:1-17; 23:11-14; II Chron. 33:1-20). He instituted a reign of terror and persecution against Jehovah's true prophets unequaled in the history of all Israel (cf. *O.T. History,* Smith and Fields, College Press, pg. 647-650). Isaiah was probably executed during that persecution.

Judah and Jerusalem had been saved from her enemies when Hezekiah paid heed to Isaiah's message from the Lord (cf. chapters 36-39). But now she has, through the leadership of the vilest king she has ever had, committed herself to a path of rebellion which will lead inexorably to captivity. Undoubtedly, there were plain indications to the nation that it was in danger of foreign invasion and captivity. Manasseh was taken captive and imprisoned by Esarhaddon, king of Assyria, in 673 B.C. It appeared that the whole nation would soon suffer the same fate. Whether the people were asking for Isaiah's advice or not, he was giving it. He states unequivocally that they had barricaded themselves from God and He could not help them. The Lord has the power to save them from their enemies if they will turn to Him and trust Him. But as long as they choose paganism, depend upon themselves and heathen allies, He cannot and will not help them. God made man and gave man the sovereignty of his own will. He gave man the awesome freedom to make his own sovereign choices with the attendant responsibility of the consequences of those choices. When man chooses to rebel against the revealed will of God, man willingly separates himself from God's redeeming, saving power. Of course, man is never able to separate himself from God's judgmental power. Men perish because they *refuse* to love the truth (II Thess. 2:9-12). Men scoff and follow their own passions because they deliberately ignore God's truths (cf. II Pet. 3:1-7). Men will not come to the light because they love darkness (Jn. 3:19-21). Men do not come to God because they do not want to be shepherded by Him (Jn. 10:1-39). Men do not come to God because He tells them the truth and they had rather listen to the devil (Jn. 8:39-47). When men build such walls of their own between themselves and God. His only alternative (in the light of man's freedom to exercise his own sovereign will) is to give man up to a base mind and improper conduct (cf. Rom. 1:18-32). When God is forced to give rebelling man up, man must save himself and man cannot do that! Man cannot save himself from nature, from death, from men more powerful than he, and last, but most important, man cannot save himself from his own conscience!

The prophets of God (Isaiah and his contemporaries, Amos, Hosea and Micah) have promised a glorious salvation for God's people and an even more glorious messianic future. Recent circumstances (the wickedness, increased tribute to Assyria, Manasseh's capture, etc.) have brought on fear, chaos and bitterness. Judah is complaining with sarcasm that the God of Isaiah is not fulfilling His promise. They are apparently preaching that Jehovah has no power to save them (advocating at the same time that power for rescue will come from their idols and alliances with the heathen). The nation is in a mess. The easiest explanation is to blame God for it (cf. comments 50:1-3).

God is not to blame. Their hands are filled with blood. Their lips have spouted lies. They have destroyed themselves. God has never lied to them. He has never defaulted on one of His promises. He has not cheated them, robbed them, murdered them. He can save them, but not in their condition. Should God save them, allowing them to continue in wickedness, He would be a partner in their wickedness and thus dishonest, unjust, unholy, unrighteous reducing Himself to moral impotency and consigning Himself and these people to an endless hell! God cannot be God and condone a kingdom in rebellion. If He is to rule in perfect righteousness and holiness He must rule a kingdom of citizens who have willingly surrendered to His sovereign will.

Isaiah's description of the depravity of society in Judah is similar to Hosea's description of Israel's wicked anarchy in an earlier day (before 722 B.C.) (cf. Hosea 4:1—5:15). There was no truth, no justice, no goodness in the land. There was murder, lying, slander, robbery, vain revelry and adultery. Manasseh was eventually returned to Judah. His imprisonment in the city of Babylon apparently caused him to repent, and he instituted a religious reform in the land. God's judgment of Judah was postponed for about a hundred years (until 606-586 B.C.). Manasseh's reform was only superficial. Underneath a veneer of orthodoxy was a deep-seated wickedness sown by Manasseh when he was a younger man. Eventually, Judah returned to this wickedness and God's word says it was because of Manasseh's earlier seduction of the nation (cf. II Kings 24:3; Jer. 15:4). The student should read the first 23 chapters of Jeremiah's prophecy as a record of the consequences of Manasseh's leading Judah into idolatry and sin.

v. 5-8 BARBAROUS: The *adder* is *tziphe'oni* in Hebrew and

describes the most poisonous of all serpents, or fiery serpent. The Hebrew word for *viper* is *'ephe'eh* and is from the root word which means *whisperer* or *hisser.* Isaiah is emphasizing to his disciples the lethal danger of flirting with the majority of people in his day. Most men in the prophet's generation were like deadly poisonous snakes. He also likened them unto cunning spiders. Poisonous snakes lay eggs which incubate poisonous embryonic snakes. Anyone who eats of the fruit (eggs) of that poisonous society will die of the same poison. Even those who try to "crush" what that society produces shall be slain by the "snake" that comes from the egg. Most spiders use their webs as snares and hiding places ("cover"). This evil generation will be trapped by their own webs and instead of being able to hide in their webs will be exposed by them. The violent consequences of their deeds are plain to everyone. The decadence of that generation is manifested in the fact that no one really cared. It is difficult to believe that people would "run" with "haste" to shed innocent blood. But even among God's people there were "syndicates" or "mobs" of organized criminals, incredibly enough, among the priests (cf. Hosea 6:9). There is no restraint in the doing of evil. Jeremiah said they "trooped" to the houses of harlots (Jer. 5:7-8); they "lurked" like trappers lying in wait to ensnare men and women (Jer. 5:25-28). They gave their minds to dreaming, thinking, planning, plotting and preparing for wickedness all day and all night (cf. Hosea 7:4-7). They were like the wicked people of Noah's day whose "every imagination of the thoughts of their heart was only evil continually . . ." (Gen. 6:5).

They did not know the "way of peace." The Hebrew word *shalom* is translated *peace* but means primarily, *soundness, wholeness, well-being, prosperity, health, goodness.* In all of the following scriptures the word *shalom* is in the original text: (Psa. 122:7; 35:27; 73:3; Job 9:4; 22:21; I Kings 9:25; Deut. 27:6; Josh. 8:31; Gen. 29:6; 37:14; 43:27; II Sam. 18:28; II Kings 4:23, 26; 5:21, 22; 9:11). In II Sam. 11:7, David asked Uriah concerning the *shalom* of Joab and the *shalom* of the people and the *shalom* (peace?) of the war. In each instance here we have a graphic illustration of the usage of the word *shalom* being primarily, *well-being, prosperity, wholeness, integrated-goodness.* In Deut. 27:6 and Josh. 8:31 the word *shalom* is translated "uncut" stones. Only whole, sound, perfect (in the sense of uncut) stones were to be used for altars. The people of Isaiah's day did not know the way to *soundness, wholeness, prosperity,* (*shalom*). They thought they did! Apparently they believed security, well-being, prosperity would result from copying their pagan neighbors and worshipping in the fertility cults of idolatry. They felt secure in allying themselves politically, militarily and economically with pagan empires. Moral crookedness, social injustice and exploitation, compromise with pagan unbelief always leads to spiritual, moral, physical and social disintegration. Sin fractures; it does not produce wholeness. Man was not made for sin; he was made for righteousness. Falsehood disorients, divides, alienates, deranges; truth solidifies, integrates, consolidates and frees. Faith in God and Christ makes *whole* (Mt. 9:12; Mk. 2:17; Lk. 5:31; Mk. 5:34; Lk. 8:48; 17:19; Jn. 5:6, 14). Peace (*shalom*) is a prominent feature of the messianic kingdom according to the prophets (cf. Isa. 2:4; 9:6; 11:6; Ezek. 34:25; Micah 4:2-4; Zech. 9:10, etc.). Ephesians 2:11-22 is a vivid illustration that the *eirene* (*peace*) of the New Testament church is of the same essence as the *shalom* of the Old Testament; that is, *wholeness, integration, unification, well-being, soundness.*

Materialism, sensuality, carnality and idolatry leads to "foolishness, faithlessness, heartlessness and ruthlessness." It leads to barbarity! (cf. Rom. 1:30).

QUIZ

1. Who was primarily responsible for the wickedness described by Isaiah here?
2. How does man "separate" himself from God's saving power?
3. Why cannot God save men in rebellion?
4. Why liken the majority of his generation to snakes?

5. What is peace?
6. What is the way of peace?
7. What does all this indicate about the meaning of peace in the N.T.?

2. THE CONSEQUENCES

TEXT: 59:9-15a

9 Therefore is justice far from us, neither doth righteousness
overtake us: we look for light, but, behold, darkness; for
brightness, but we walk in obscurity.
10 We grope for the wall like the blind; yea, we grope as they
that have no eyes: we stumble at noonday as in the twilight;
among them that are lusty we are as dead men.
11 We roar all like bears, and moan sore like doves: we look
for justice, but there is none; for salvation, but it is far off
from us.
12 For our transgressions are multiplied before thee, and our
sins testify against us; for our transgressions are with us,
and as for our iniquities, we know them:
13 transgressing and denying Jehovah, and turning away from
following our God, speaking oppression and revolt, con-
ceiving and uttering from the heart words of falsehood.
14 And justice is turned away backward, and righteousness
standeth afar off; for truth is fallen in the street, and uprightness cannot enter.
15 Yea, truth is lacking; and he that departeth from evil maketh
himself a prey.

QUERIES

a. Who is the "we" doing the pleading for "light"?
b. Is the confession of wickedness sincere?

PARAPHRASE

Yes, it is on account of our crimes that our nation is in such a state of chaos. There is no justice or righteousness in our society. It is no wonder that this generation which has expected light finds nothing but darkness and ignorance. It is no wonder we grope and grasp at things like blind men; no wonder we stumble around wounding ourselves like blind men in broad daylight; no wonder we are like a nation of dead corpses. Our whole nation is filled with confusion and turmoil and some people run around like bears roaring at the agitation they are suffering. Others go moaning like troubled doves. This disordered and disturbed society looks everywhere for justice and salvation but they never find it. There is no way this society can deny the multiplicity of its sins. Our sinfulness manifests itself to us in the consequences we are suffering. We know we are a sinful, disobedient people, rebelling against the Law of Jehovah. We have deliberately turned away from Him, we have advocated oppression of our fellow man and revolt against our leaders and we are a nation of liars. Injustice is the order of the day; justice has been completely perverted. Righteousness is unheard of in this country; truth is dead in the wicked streets of the cities and honesty and fairness could not come into this society if it wanted to because it is banned. Indeed, there is no truth here, it is all falsehood, and the man who tries to quit his wickedness becomes an outcast and a hunted man!

COMMENTS

v. 9-11 CONFUSION: The first part of chapter 59 is Jehovah's indictment. In 59:1-8 the Lord, speaking through Isaiah, tells Judah that He knows their sin. This section (59:9-15) is an evaluation of Judah's predicament from man's (Isaiah) perspective. It is, as it were, Isaiah concurring with the Lord's indictment. It cannot be a penitent confession of sin by the nation of Judah. The attitude of the populace grew *more* and *more rebellious and not penitent* as evidenced clearly by Jeremiah and Ezekiel. Isaiah says, in effect, "Lord, You are correct! This nation is filled with confusion because of its sin." The stupefying effect of the rejection of God's truth is seen in their clamoring, roaring, moaning for light and salvation while at the same time clamoring for more and more wickedness. They were like disoriented blind men groping, feeling, grasping for some object by which they might find their way. The way is there but they cannot see it because they have deliberately chosen not to see it. One is reminded of King Zedekiah who when faced with the consequences of his disobedience to God, sent for Jeremiah the prophet and asked, "Is there any word from the Lord?" (Jer. 37:17). Jeremiah had been preaching the "word from the Lord" for at least 23 years (Jer. 25:3)—why had Zedekiah been unable to find the way for 23 years? Why all of a sudden roar and moan for salvation, Zedekiah? Because he had come to the "end of his rope." He could no longer solve his problems by himself.

The nation of Judah was fast approaching the end of its rope. Isaiah recognized it. Many of the people, however, had not yet admitted it. Not until they had been violently dragged off into pagan captivity and had gotten their fill of idolatry did they confess their own helplessness and turn to God for salvation.

The interesting thing in our text here is the incongruity of moaning for salvation while running to evil and making *haste* to shed innocent blood (59:7). But what they are doing is nothing new. Israel did the same thing during the wilderness wandering, during the period of the Judges, during the period of the Seleucids and during the Roman occupation and the days of Jesus. Nation after nation has acted in the same stupid way—moaning for light while increasingly practicing darkness and roaring for salvation while continuing to enslave itself with falsehood and wickedness. This senseless paradox fits certain segments of our own society and our own country. Some Americans run around roaring for liberty while burning and looting and shedding innocent blood. Others moan for truth in politics and religion while cheating on their income tax, stealing their neighbor's wife, violating every law they can without getting caught. People want their sins but they do not want the consequences. Judah was no different from every other generation.

v. 12-15 CONFESSION: As we stated earlier, this is not so much a confession of repentance as it is an admission, on Isaiah's part, that the Lord is correct about His charge against Judah. Even if this does represent a confession of sin by the nation, it is one thing to confess one's sins and another thing to repent of them. Sin and its consequences may even be regretted and still not repented of. Judas regretted betraying Christ but did not repent—he hanged himself.

As a matter of fact, it would be difficult for a nation as saturated with wickedness as Judah was *not* to be aware of its sin! The consequences of sin are usually apparent even to the sinner himself. When the consequences of sin are felt more by the society as a whole than by the individual sinner it is easier to admit the sin and the consequences, than it is when those consequences cause individual catastrophe. Individual sinners profiteering from their sin without any privations or calamity may hypocritically bemoan the sins of others in their society and go right on sinning themselves.

Apparently these verses are the righteous moanings of Isaiah the prophet concurring with God that Judah is a wicked nation. The depravity of the entire society was plainly evident. Anyone could see the nation had deliberately turned away from Jehovah and had become idolatrous. Anyone could see there was no truth anywhere in that nation; not in government, not in business, not in religion! Truth had fallen dead in the streets. Honesty and uprightness was not permitted. Any man who tried to give up his wickedness made himself a victim, a prey! He became a hunted man! Could any society become that wicked! Jeremiah was told to "run through the streets of Jerusalem . . . to see if he could find a man, *one* who does justice. . . ." (Jer. 5:1). Jeremiah, only some 80 or 90 years removed from Isaiah, found the people of Judah *totally* committed to wickedness. Not only so, they loved it that way (Jer. 5:30-31); they could not be shamed (Jer. 6:15); no one repented of wickedness (Jer. 8:5-6); and Jeremiah was told *not* to pray for that people (Jer. 7:16-17; 11:14; 14:11; 15:1). Yes, a society can become that wicked! And it happens to any nation when its preachers do not proclaim the word of the Lord and when its rulers transgress God's commandments (cf. Jer. 2:7-13).

QUIZ

1. Why are these verses probably not to be considered as a penitent confession of the nation of its sins?
2. How is it possible for a people to bemoan the consequences of their sins and yet keep on sinning?
3. Did Israel ever do this before? When?
4. Why is it nearly impossible for a society not to be aware of its sins?
5. How far into wickedness did the nation go as recorded by Jeremiah?

3. THE CURE

TEXT: 59:15b-21

15 And Jehovah saw it, and it displeased him that there was no justice.

16 And he saw that there was no man, and wondered that there was no intercessor: therefore his own arm brought salvation unto him; and his righteousness, it upheld him.

17 And he put on righteousness as a breastplate, and a helmet of salvation upon his head; and he put on garments of vengeance for clothing, and was clad with zeal as a mantle.

18 According to their deeds, accordingly he will repay, wrath to his adversaries, recompense to his enemies; to the islands

he will repay recompense.
19 So shall they fear the name of Jehovah from the west, and
his glory from the rising of the sun; for he will come as a
rushing stream, which the breath of Jehovah driveth.
20 And a Redeemer will come to Zion, and unto them that turn
from transgression in Jacob, saith Jehovah.
21 And as for me, this is my covenant with them, saith Jehovah;
my Spirit that is upon thee, and my words which I have
put in thy mouth, shall not depart out of thy mouth, nor
out of the mouth of thy seed, nor out of the mouth of thy
seed's seed, saith Jehovah, from henceforth and for ever.

QUERIES

a. Why did Jehovah wonder that there was no "intercessor"?
b. When is Jehovah going to "come" as a "rushing stream"?
c. Who is the "Redeemer" to come to Zion?

PARAPHRASE

The Lord saw all this depravity and it excited His wrath that there was nothing being done to bring justice and righteousness to the nation. The Lord also saw that there was no one strong enough or good enough to intercede with salvation and it appalled the Lord. So the Lord is going to take it upon Himself to intercede with His own power and His own righteousness and bring salvation to His covenant people. The Lord will dress Himself in the armor appropriate for the battle (righteousness, salvation, vengeance and zeal) and He will conquer His enemies and punish them, no matter who they are, according to what they deserve. All over the world those who were His enemies will fear Him because He will overwhelm the world with His Spirit like a flood overwhelms the land when it is sent from heaven. Jehovah will come as a Redeemer to the Zion that has turned from transgression, He says. I, even

I, am their covenant, says Jehovah. And when I become their Redeemer, their Covenant, My Spirit will abide with them through their receiving My word and obeying My word and proclaiming My word forever.

COMMENTS

v. 15-18 MEDIATION: These last verses form a fitting climax and summation to the two sections entitled, *Salvation Through God's Servant* (ch. 40-53) and *Communion Through God's Covenant* (ch. 54-59). In this text (59:15b-21) the prediction that God Himself will become the atoning Intercessor and that God in The Spirit will Himself become the Covenant is summarized.

What the Lord God saw in the wickedness of Isaiah's generation agitated His heart. The Hebrew phrase is *ra'—be'ayin* which is translated in the KJV "*. . . it was evil in His eyes . . .*" but means more precisely, *"it excited His displeasure . . ."* The point is that what Jehovah saw not only excited His displeasure but it also moved Him to compassion as is evidenced by the subsequent plans to intercede Himself for salvation to those who will accept His covenant. Jehovah's agitation of spirit here is similar to that of Jesus at the graveyard in Bethany when He groaned and wept over the death of Lazarus (caused by sin) and the trying of the faith of Mary and Martha (cf. Jn. 11).

The Hebrew word *maphegi'a* is translated *intercessor.* It means literally, *to strike upon or against,* or *to assail anyone with petitions.* In Ruth 1:16 it is translated *urge* or *beg.* It is the word used in Jer. 7:16; 27:18; Job 21:15; Gen. 23:8; Isa. 53:12 (of the Servant) and in Jer. 36:25. When the Lord saw the wickedness and lostness of Judah, He also saw that there was no man interested or capable of petitioning Him on their behalf. They were all sinners, even Isaiah ("undone" Isa. 6:5). Who will intercede, who will stand between their wickedness and lostness and the just vengeance of Jehovah? He will! God interposes Himself in the Incarnate Servant (cf. our comments on Isa. 45:23; 53:12; 54:9). God's own "arm" brought salvation (comments on "arm" see Isa. 40:10; 51:5; 52:10; 53:1). God upheld His own absolute faithfulness by imputing or supplying His righteousness to unrighteous man through the incarnated intercession of Himself! He accomplished both a vindication of His justness and the justification of those who believe through the vicarious, substitutionary atonement of Christ (cf. Rom. 3:21-26).

See our comments on Isaiah 53:1-12; 55:1-5; (and Daniel 9:24-27 in *Daniel*, by Butler, College Press) for extended discussion of God's imputed righteousness.

It was the *zeal* of the Lord who sent Him into this world as the incarnate Son clothed in righteousness, salvation and judgment (justice). See comments Isaiah 9:6-7. It was *zeal* for God's "house" that consumed Christ (Jn. 2:17).

These words of Isaiah may have been intended initially to predict the salvation of Judah from the Babylonian captivity by the intercession and mighty arm of Jehovah. As we have already seen, however, the release from captivity had a much more glorious goal (the messianic redemption) as its ultimate fulfillment. And these words of Isaiah are no less messianic-oriented! Indeed, Jehovah delivered Judah from exile and recompensed her Gentile captors ("the islands"). But He also judged all earthly kingdoms when He established His own eternal kingdom through the work of the Messiah as we have already pointed out. By the death and resurrection of Jesus Christ God demonstrated with all the finality and absoluteness He could that the kingdoms of this world were judged. The great apostle Paul makes that the authentication of the world's judgment in Acts 17:30-31; I Cor. 15:20-28; Col. 2:14-15, etc. These words of Isaiah, then, point ultimately to the Messiah and His kingdom.

v. 19-21 MEMBERSHIP: The *mediation* (intercession) provided by God also provides *membership* or communion with God through covenant relationship. And that is precisely what this whole section of Isaiah (ch. 54-59) is all about. The "isles" of the Gentiles, from the west and east will fear Jehovah's name and His glory. Jehovah's name and glory will flood the world ("as a rushing stream"). The Hebrew word *ruakh* is translated *breath* (v. 19), but is more generally translated *spirit. Ruakh* is the same word that is translated *Spirit* in verse 21. It would make more sense to us to translate the word *spirit* in verse 19. Thus the name and the glory of Jehovah that floods the world will be by the power of His Holy Spirit as He converts Gentiles and Jews through the preaching of the gospel of Christ.

The Hebrew word *goel* is translated *redeemer.* The original meaning of the word was *to demand back,* or *to extricate.* In Leviticus 25—27 the word signifies the liberation of property from a mortgage against it or a vow against it by payment or exchange. In cases of poverty, where no payment was possible, the nearest of kin was made responsible for performing the work of redemption. Thus a kinsman came to be called by the name *goel,* (cf. Num. 5:8; I Kings 16:11; Ruth 2:20; 3:2; 3:9, 12, etc.). Jesus is our *goel* (kinsman) (see Heb. 2:10-18). That this message is messianic is well established by its quotation in Romans 11:26-27. "All Israel" in Rom. 11:26 is the New Israel (Gal. 6:14-16) the church of Christ. The salvation of "all Israel" is accomplished when the Redeemer redeems both Gentiles and Jew in one body (cf. Eph. 2:11ff) and that is the intent of Isaiah 59:15b-21 and Romans 11:26-27! *Goel* is a favorite theme of Isaiah (Isa. 35:9; 41:14; 43:1, 14; 44:6, 22, 23, 24; 47:4; 48:17; 49:7, 26; 51:10; 52:3; 62:12; 63:4). The Redeemer comes to redeem those who wish to be redeemed and express that wish in a voluntary "turn from transgression."

Two Hebrew pronouns are side by side at the beginning of verse 21; *'eni zo'th* would read literally, "I, this very One," am covenant for them. God interposed Himself with an oath. He, Himself became covenant. All the promises of God find their "Amen" in Him (II Cor. 1:20-21). His life (atoning death and justifying resurrection) became the New covenant (Mt. 26:26-29). To partake of Christ's life is to partake of His Spirit (Jn. 6:52-63). To partake of Christ's word is to partake of His life and His Spirit (Jn. 14:21-23; Acts 2:38; 5:32; II Pet. 1:3-5; see comments in *The Gospel of John*, by Butler, College Press, chapters 14-17). The Spirit of Christ dwells in man through faith (Eph. 3:17); faith comes by hearing and obeying the Word of Christ (Rom. 10:17). The exclusiveness of the instrumentality of the Word in the dwelling and working of the Spirit is emphasized even here (59:21). The Spirit of God was in the prophets (I Pet. 1:10-12) but He functioned through their preaching. The Spirit of God was in the apostles, but He functioned through their preaching. The Spirit of God is in Christians, but He functions through their printing or preaching the Word which the apostles preached and printed and left for the salvation of the world. The apostolic message is the *only* message of the Spirit; He has no further word for the world! He will not function in the life of any one in the world except through the instrumentality of the apostolic Word. Covenant relationship to God has always been made available exclusively through the instrumentality of a revealed Word. God has always limited the delivery of His Word to a few selected individuals in order to preclude the possibility of deception (I Jn. 4:1-6). God has always authenticated His messengers by signs and wonders (Heb. 2:1-4). Once the messengers have been authenticated and the message has been delivered in human language and committed to the printed page, anyone claiming to have a revelation of the Spirit beyond that message is a false messenger! All that is needed for the rest of the world to come into covenant relationship is that the completed, perfected message of the Spirit be passed on by printing or preaching from one generation to another.

The covenant accomplished by the Redeemer and inscripturated by the Spirit will last forever. It will never need updating, changing or superceding. It will need simply to be passed on from generation to generation. It is for the whole world so long as the world shall last!

QUIZ

1. How do these last verses fit in with what has been written in Isaiah 40-59?
2. What all is involved in the excitation of God's displeasure?
3. What is an intercessor? Why did God have to intercede?
4. Give as many reasons as you can why this points ultimately to the Messiah.
5. Who is the Redeemer in verse 20, according to Romans 11:26?
6. What does the Spirit of God have to do with covenant? and how?

EXAMINATION

CHAPTERS FIFTY-FOUR THROUGH FIFTY-NINE

DEFINITION

(Define the following words or phrases as they were discussed in the comments.)

1. *enlarge* your tent
2. *waters* of Noah
3. *leader* and *commander*
4. *foreigners*
5. *watchmen*
6. *rest*
7. *sorceress*
8. *Moloch*
9. *terebinth*
10. *covetousness*
11. *afflicted* our soul
12. *adder* and *viper*
13. *peace*
14. *intercessor*

MEMORIZATION

Ho, everyone that thirsteth, come ye to the ______, and he that hath no ______; come ye, buy, and ______; yea, come, buy wine and ______ without money and without price.

Wherefore do ye ______ money for that which is not ______? and your labor for that which ______ not? hearken diligently unto me, and eat ye that which is ______, and let your ______ delight itself in fatness. Incline your ______, and come unto me; ______, and your soul shall live: and I will make an everlasting ______ with you, even the sure ______ of David. (55:1-3)

EXPLANATION

1. Explain how Jehovah used *marriage* to describe His relation to His people.
2. Explain how unique, in a Hebrew dispensation, it is to speak of all being taught by the Lord. Explain how Jesus quoted this passage in John's Gospel.
3. Explain how God could teach salvation by grace in the O.T.
4. Explain the relationship of God's everlasting covenant with His promised mercy to David.
5. Explain how foreigners minister to Jehovah.
6. Explain why there is no peace to the wicked.
7. Explain Isaiah's emphasis on keeping the Sabbath.
8. Explain how man's sin separates him from God.

APPLICATION

(In its context every scripture has one meaning—the author's intended meaning. How may the following be applied in the believer's life?)

1. Do people today still need to understand that God offers salvation by grace, not by earned merit?
2. Is it still necessary today to teach what Isaiah does about God's word being above man's thoughts or ways?
3. Is it necessary today to stress keeping covenant with God

as Isaiah did?
4. May we apply the Hebrew meaning of peace to the Christian experience?
5. Is there any application of the believer's "marriage" to God to human marriage?
6. What application for the N.T. age may be made concerning the lethargy of the religious leaders of Isaiah's day?
7. May we apply the attitude expressed by the sinners of Isaiah's day of "weariness" with sin, to any attitudes of sinners today?
8. Is the admonition of Isaiah against the hypocrisy in fasting and worshiping relevant for the church today? How may his admonition be applied?

IX. ZION—THE ZENITH, CHAPTERS 60 - 66

A. REWARD OF ZION, WEALTH OF THE NATIONS CHAPTER 60

1. GLORY

TEXT: 60:1-7

1 Arise, shine, for thy light is come, and the glory of Jehovah is risen upon thee.
2 For, behold, darkness shall cover the earth, and gross darkness the peoples; but Jehovah will arise upon thee, and his glory shall be seen upon thee.
3 And nations shall come to thy light, and kings to the brightness of thy rising.
4 Lift up thine eyes round about, and see: they all gather themselves together, they come to thee; thy sons shall come from far, and thy daughters shall be carried in the arms.
5 Then thou shalt see and be radiant, and thy heart shall thrill and be enlarged; because the abundance of the sea shall be turned unto thee, the wealth of the nations shall come unto thee.

6 The multitude of camels shall cover thee, the dromedaries of
Midian and Ephah; all they from Sheba shall come; they
shall bring gold and frankincense, and shall proclaim the
praises of Jehovah.
7 All the flocks of Kedar shall be gathered together unto thee,
the rams of Nebaioth shall minister unto thee; they shall
come up with acceptance on mine altar; and I will glorify
the house of my glory.

QUERIES

a. When does Zion's light come?
b. How is the "abundance of the sea" turned to her?
c. Where is Nebaioth?

PARAPHRASE

Do not let the coming captivity prostrate you Zion. Stand up, be stedfast and faithful and begin to be a light to the dark world. The glorious light of God is shining on you—the grandeur, splendor and righteousness of Jehovah is being given to you. It is still night and darkness to the heathen nations around you, but you are going to be light for the whole world when Jehovah gives you His glory. You will become a reflection of God's truth and love that will be seen by people from all over the world. The Gentiles will be attracted to your glory and come to it; great and famous rulers will humbly come to bask in the splendor of your majesty. Look around you, Zion, from all directions people of every nation and tribe and tongue are coming to you; they are all bringing others to you with the tenderness and compassion a foster-parent shows its adopted child. You will see all this and it will make you radiate joy and gratitude. Your heart will be thrilled and swell with excitement toward the Gentiles coming to you. This will be your attitude because you will recognize that God is giving you, in these who are coming, the true wealth of the islands and coastlands—believers! Multitudes of people will make their way to you, Zion; people from every direction will come bringing their most precious possessions as gifts and they will testify to the majesty and power of Jehovah. Even your inveterate enemies from Mesopotamia and Idumea will be accepted by Me and by you and they will join you in ministering and worshipping Me. The Lord will make His house more glorious than ever when He brings people from all over the world into it.

COMMENTS

v. 1-5 LIGHT: It has been our purpose to show the student of Isaiah the logical progression of the prophet's message. In the first 35 chapters Isaiah has declared that Israel's salvation is not in any human programs; neither self-righteousness nor idolatry nor military alliance with the heathen will save her. In chapters 36-39 Isaiah inserts parenthetically a record of an historical event which demonstrates precisely what he is preaching; that Israel, God's covenant people, can only be saved and reach her messianic destiny through faith in Jehovah by keeping covenant with Him. Finally, in chapters 40-66, Isaiah will prophesy and typify the grand climax of God's program for the redemption of the whole world through the Servant and Covenant relationship to Him. The last section, with which we now begin to deal, predicts the glorious consequence of Zion's appropriation of the Servant's work by Covenant-communion. Zion will enjoy Reward, Regeneration and Rest, among other blessings. Zion is going to be made "whole" (see our discussion of the word *shalom/peace* on 59:8) because she will have given to her a covenant of peace or wholeness (cf. 54:10) when the Servant becomes peace/ *shalom* for her (cf. 53:5).

In anticipation of this wholeness (peace) Zion is told to arise and shine. The future glory of Zion is so certain (although it is centuries away from accomplishment by the Messiah) Isaiah speaks of it as if it had already come. The remnant of Judah will be prostrated in exile along with the unbelievers of the nation. It will be a temptation for the remnant to despair and give up hope that God will ever keep His promises made to their forefathers (Abraham, Jacob, Moses, David). But Isaiah says, "Stand up, stand fast in your witness as those who believe God will keep His covenant. Let your messianic light shine, for God has promised, and it will come to pass!"

The "light" which comes upon Zion is the "glory" of Jehovah. That cannot be anything less than the Messiah. Christ was the effulgence of the glory of God and bore the very image of His substance (cf. Heb. 1:3). Jesus was the Word become flesh and men beheld His glory, glory as the only begotten from the Father (cf. Jn. 1:14). The Word was the life and the light of men (Jn. 1:4). The Hebrew word *kevod* is translated *glory.* The fundamental root meaning is probably *weight* or *heaviness,* conveying the idea of some external, physical manifestation of dignity or preeminence of majesty. But the word as it is most widely used means, "the exhibition of the *excellence* of the subject to which it is ascribed." In other words, *character* is the chief element of glory. Concerning God it is the display of His divine attributes and perfections of righteousness, power, truthfulness, faithfulness, mercifulness, justice, compassion, love, etc. Some of the *glory* of God may be seen in a limited way in nature (cf. Rom. 1:18-23; Acts 14:15-18, etc.).

Zion is to have the excellence of the character of Jehovah "rise" upon her. The glory of God is to be imputed to Zion through the Servant and made available for appropriation through the New Covenant. Zion will not earn His glory. The Servant comes to earn God's glory for Zion. Zion simply receives it by exercising faith through covenant conditions.

She is to reflect His glory. Darkness covers the earth. All nations (including Israel) fall short of the glory of God (cf. Rom. 3:9-26; esp. 3:23). But the people who walk in darkness will see a great light (cf. our comments 9:1-7). The Light of the World came to Zion and made her a kingdom of light (cf. Jn. 8:12-20; 12:46; Eph. 5:8; Col. 1:12-13; I Thess. 5:5; I Pet. 2:9; Rev. 2-3). The letters of the apostle Paul to churches predominantly Gentile confirm the prediction of Isaiah 60:3 that "nations shall come to thy (Zion's) light." Great and powerful rulers and men of reknown were attracted to Zion's glory (see comments 49:7).

The Hebrew word *'amanah* is translated *carried* but means more literally, a *foster-father* or *foster-nurse* who has a child in safe keeping. What it means in verse four is that the Gentiles shall bring children safely to Zion (cf. comments on 49:22-23). Zion is exhorted to look even now in faith down through the centuries from Isaiah's day to the messianic glory and behold Gentiles coming to her from all directions of the earth. This vision compares to the one given the seven churches of Asia Minor by the apostle John when he recorded the spectacle of the redeemed "which no man could number" from every nation, from all tribes and peoples and tongues standing before the throne (Rev. 7:9).

The Hebrew word *nahare* is translated *radiant* in verse five. It is from a root which means *to flow, to run.* Zion's reaction to the Gentiles coming to her for the glory of Jehovah which she has will be that of effervescent joy. She will *radiate* a bubbling excitement because she sees the promises of God being fulfilled that "in her seed shall all the nations be blessed." The word *phakhad* means to *tremble with joy* and is thus translated *thrill.* The picture Isaiah paints of Zion is of the messianic age when she has realized she has become the instrument of God for the salvation of the world and is one of excitement. Zion's heart trembles, swells, pumps and jumps with excitement as she realizes she is engaged in divine, eternal, cosmic redemptive history as a colaborer of Almighty God (cf. Acts 11:18; 15:3; 19:10, etc.). Zion is caused to tremble with joy because she sees that there are Gentiles who are precious in character and that there are Gentiles worthy of becoming jewels in the crown of a Jewish apostle (cf. Phil. 4:1; I Thess. 2:19). The "abundance of the sea" is the wealth of the islands and coastlands (Gentile territories). What is the wealth of a nation? It is its people, especially regenerated, redeemed people. These are the people who produce goodness, truth and beauty in any nation or society. These are the people who serve humanity without selfish motives. Zion sees that she possesses that which is the wealth of the world after all—people being conformed to the image of Christ.

v. 6-7 LAUDATION: As Keil and Delitzsch point out: "The prophet, indeed cannot describe even what belongs to the New Testament in any other than Old Testament colors, because he is still within the Old Testament limits." In other words, Isaiah is depicting the spiritual prosperity of New Testament Zion (the church) in terminology of his own times. The picture Isaiah draws is that of multitudes of people from the fartherest reaches of civilization uniting in praise and honor to Jehovah. Midian was a son of Abraham from Keturah (Gen. 25:1-6) and Ephah was a son of Midian. Midian and his descendants claimed the land east of the Jordan river and the Dead Sea, southward through the Akabah and including the southern and eastern parts of the peninsula of Sinai. Sheba was the oldest son of Jokshan (Jokshan was also a son of Abraham by Keturah). His descendants probably became what is called the kingdom of Sheba or the Sabeans. The Queen of Sheba who visited Solomon was from this people. These far distant peoples shall contribute their wealth to Zion and they shall come to Zion and proclaim the praises of Jehovah. Kedar was the second son of Ishmael (a son of Abraham by Hagar, the handmaiden of Sarah), (cf. Gen. 25:13), whose descendants lived in the desert between Syria and Mesopotamia. Nebaioth is mentioned always in connection with Kedar or the descendants of Ishmael (Gen. 25:13; 28:9; I Chron. 1:29) and is regarded by most as identical with the Nabataeans. It is interesting to note that all these are descendants of Abraham, but alien to the original covenant which was administered exclusively through the only son of Abraham by Sarah—Isaac. Yet, when the promise was given to Abraham, before Isaac's birth, it included blessedness to "all nations" through that "singular" seed (cf. Gal. 3:16).

These Gentiles are going to be acceptable! Their offerings (worship) will be acceptable and their ministry will be acceptable. As Young says, "The picture here given is that of Gentiles converted to Christ who bring all that they have and devote it to His service."

These desert nomads (Midian, Ephah, Sheba, Kedar, Nabataeans) were all enemies of the Jews for centuries. They are even today, racial, geographical and political enemies. The only way these people could ever become united in praising Jehovah and be accepted as worshippers and ministers of Jehovah is through the reconciliation that is in Christ Jesus (cf. Eph. 2:11-22; II Cor. 5:16-21, etc.).

These verses indicate that Jehovah is going to send His "Light" (the Messiah) to glorify Zion and make available to her the wealth of the world. In other words God is going to demonstrate, once and for all, that His redemptive people (the church) are the focal point of the cosmos. Everything in His creation is to glorify Zion. Sooner or later, ultimately, inevitably God will use everything He has created to serve for the glorification of the redeemed. The apostle Paul said as much in I Cor. 3:21-22: ". . . all things are yours . . . whether . . . the world or life or death or the present or the future . . . all are yours." Everything that is good and eternal and abiding of God's is the birthright of His Son, and Christians are joint heirs with Him. The "house" of God is going to be made more beautiful than it has ever been when He adorns it with the "wealth" of the nations (Gentiles beautiful in character) (see comments 56:7).

QUIZ

1. Can you trace the logical progression of Isaiah's book and include this section?
2. Why does Isaiah see a necessity to exhort his people to "Arise" and "shine"?
3. What is the "light" or "glory" that is to come upon Zion?

4. What will be Zion's reaction to "nations" coming to her light?
5. What is the wealth of the nations?
6. What would be necessary for the nations listed in verse six-seven to unite with Zion in praising the Lord.

2. GAIN

TEXT: 60:8-14

8 Who are these that fly as a cloud, and as the doves to their windows?
9 Surely the isles shall wait for me, and the ships of Tarshish first, to bring thy sons from far, their silver and their gold with them, for the name of Jehovah thy God, and for the Holy One of Israel, because he hath glorified thee.
10 And foreigners shall build up thy walls, and their kings shall minister unto thee: for in my wrath I smote thee, but in my favor have I had mercy on thee.
11 Thy gates also shall be open continually; they shall not be shut day nor night; that men may bring unto thee the wealth of the nations, and their kings led captive.
12 For that nation and kingdom that will not serve thee shall perish; yea, those nations shall be utterly wasted.
13 The glory of Lebanon shall come unto thee, the fir-tree, the pine, and the box-tree together, to beautify the place of my sanctuary; and I will make the place of my feet glorious.
14 And the sons of them that afflicted thee shall come bending unto thee; and all they that despised thee shall bow themselves down at the soles of thy feet; and they shall call thee The city of Jehovah, The Zion of the Holy One of Israel.

QUERIES

a. What are the "clouds" and "doves" of verse eight?
b. How would it be possible for "foreigners" to build Zion's walls?
c. How would the nation that did not serve Zion perish?

PARAPHRASE

There are shadowy forms on the prophetic horizon drifting inexorably in our direction; they are like homing pigeons or doves going straight for their nests. Who are they: They are ships coming from all over the world bringing all those Gentile sons of Zion who have been waiting so long in darkness to find her. These ships of the prophetic future are bringing the real wealth of the world to Zion. They have been attracted to Zion because God has made her beautiful by giving her His redemptive glory and they want to be made a part of that beauty also. Yes, Gentiles are going to be participants in forming the future Zion; Gentiles will be co-laborers and fellow-citizens of that messianic city. Even some of the rulers of Gentile peoples will become citizens and serve the new Zion. I, Jehovah, am about to destroy the present city of Jerusalem, but I will in mercy also restore a remnant and through them eventually build the everlasting Zion. Access to the new Zion will be open as long as there are people deciding they want to take up citizenship. Nations from the ends of the earth will contribute their best and greatest resources to the new Zion; people great and small shall become willing captives of this glorious city. Those peoples and individuals who do not willingly surrender to Zion will perish. The attitude of many peoples toward you Zion, My dwelling place, will be reverence and a desire to give the best of their possessions to beautify you. Those who have been Zion's enemies will become willing citizens, humbling themselves and believing that what Jehovah has said about her belonging to Him is true. They shall willingly confess that you are Mine, that I dwell in You and that I am God.

COMMENTS

v. 8-12 CITIZENS: Zion now "arisen" and awake to what God has been trying to communicate through the prophet begins to see "dimly" certain shadowy cloud-like forms of the prophetic ingathering of the world to herself. Isaiah has repeated and repeated the message. Like the inexorable movement of clouds and the magnet-like homing of doves the prophet's visions of masses of humanity coming to Zion has finally caught on in the mind of the remnant. So they ask, "Who are these . . .?" The answer comes back immediately, "They are the isles!" (see comments on 11:11; 20:6; 23:2, 6; 40:15; 41:2, 5; 42:4, 10, 12; 49:1; 51:5). *Tarshish* was the great-grandson of Noah (Gen. 10:4), and considered to be the progenitor of a people along the western coastlands and islands of the Mediterranean. *Tarshish* is also conjecturally believed to be a form of the name of Tartessus, an ancient city located on the southern or eastern coast of Spain (see comments, *Minor Prophets,* Jonah 1:3, pg. 225, Butler, College Press). Tarshish probably represents the fartherest known reaches of traveled or commercialized civilization of that age. These people so long in darkness waited for Jehovah to manifest Himself and reveal a way back to His presence (cf. 42:4). The prophet has repeatedly predicted that some day their waiting will be over. When that day comes, they will fly inexorably and directly to God. The reason given for that flight is that Jehovah will have "glorified" Zion. That is, of course, the redemptive work of the Servant and the New Covenant available to all peoples.

Foreigners "building the walls" of Zion is definitely a messianic figure of speech (cf. Amos 9:11-12 with Acts 15:16-17; see also Jer. 31:4-6 and attendant context; Jer. 33:7-26; Micah 7:11-17; Isa. 19:16-25). Paul wrote to the Gentiles in Ephesus that they were a part of the New dwelling place of God (Eph. 2:11-22). In the New Zion all members will be "ministers"—even Gentiles. There will be no special priesthood—all members of the New Covenant will be a holy priesthood (cf. I Pet. 2:5, 9; Heb. 10:19ff). All who come to New Zion (Heb. 12:22-24) will offer sacrifices as ministers and priests (cf. Heb. 13:15-16). God, in His wrath against the wickedness of Old Zion, destroyed it (not only in the Babylonian exile, but centuries later [forever] when Old Zion rejected its Messiah [70 A.D.]). But God is going to build a New Zion by grace (favor) because the Messiah came and earned God's grace for man. The Messiah's merited favor will be made available not only to the Jew but to the Gentile also. Gentiles will be included in the New "building."

Access to New Zion will be constant. Access to New Zion will be for everyone who wishes it. The Holy Spirit, through His Word, and the Bride (the church—New Zion) say "Come" to all who will (cf. Rev. 22:17). Of course, the invitation will not always be offered for men to become citizens of the New Zion. But those who will not willingly enter Zion in this life would not enter it in the next life either (cf. Lk. 16:29-31). This is really the point of Isaiah's statement that Zion's gates are open continually; the idea is ready access for all who wish. There shall be no danger to those in New Zion that the gates will have to be shut and barred. There will be continual freedom and peace in New Zion. The members of Zion will be continually "bringing in the sheaves" (the wealth of the nations).

One very forceful reason for concluding the Zion here is New Zion (the church) is that all who "will not serve" her shall "perish." As Young puts it, "It is obvious that this prophecy does not fit the time of the restoration from exile . . . What nations at that time perished because they did not serve the empirical Zion?" There have been nations through the centuries, and there are nations now, not only refusing to serve literal Zion but making her serve them and they have not perished. Literal Zion as Jehovah's dwelling place perished in 70 A.D. (cf. Mt. 24:37-39; Lk. 13:34-35; 19:41-44). The Hebrew word *kharav* is translated *wasted* and means basically *destroyed by drying up.* What tragic *waste* all the potential resources, and wealth of those nations and peoples who will not surrender to the New Zion!

v. 13-14 COMELINESS: The place of God's dwelling (New

Zion) will be exalted above all that is on the earth—both of nature and men. It is going to be made glorious and preeminent. Everything in creation will be made available to glorify her (art, music, learning, literature, thoughts, emotions). The greatest powers opposing her will be humbled (cf. Matt. 16:18; Col. 1:15-20; 2:14-15; Heb. 2:5-18). Many of the powerful forces and peoples opposing Zion will become converts to her. Formerly they ridiculed and scoffed at her—but they will penitently call her what she very evidently is: The (only) city of Jehovah, The Zion (Citadel or Sanctuary) of the Holy One of Israel. In Old Testament times it appeared Zion could be despoiled, humbled and obliterated by war, seige and death. But Zion's Eternal King came (the Messiah) in a space-time historical event and conquered death forever! This is the message of the book of Revelation. The Lamb has come and conquered death by resurrection and is now worthy to reveal (open the scroll) that New Zion (the church) is unconquerable! New Zion is the citadel of eternal safety.

QUIZ

1. Why does Zion see "clouds" and "doves" (verse eight)?
2. How do the "isles" bring their sons to Zion?
3. Why do we say "foreigners building" Zion's walls is a messianic term?
4. What is the meaning of the continual "opening" of Zion's gates?
5. How does verse 12 help determine this is a messianic passage?
6. Why will Zion's enemies bow down to her?

3. GOODNESS

TEXT: 60:15-22

15 Whereas thou hast been forsaken and hated, so that no man passed through thee, I will make thee an eternal

excellency, a joy of many generations.
16 Thou shalt also suck the milk of the nations, and shalt suck
the breast of kings; and thou shalt know that I, Jehovah,
am thy Saviour, and thy Redeemer, the Mighty One of Jacob.
17 For brass I will bring gold, and for iron I will bring silver,
and for wood brass, and for stones iron. I will also make
thy officers peace, and thine executors righteousness.
18 Violence shall no more be heard in thy land, desolation
nor destruction within thy borders; but thou shalt call thy
walls Salvation, and thy gates Praise.
19 The sun shall be no more thy light by day; neither for
brightness shall the moon give light unto thee: but Jehovah
will be unto thee an everlasting light, and thy God thy glory,
20 Thy sun shall no more go down, neither shall thy moon
withdraw itself; for Jehovah will be thine everlasting light,
and the days of thy morning shall be ended.
21 Thy people also shall be all righteous; they shall inherit
the land forever, the branch of my planting, the work of my
hands, that I may be glorified.
22 The little one shall become a thousand, and the small one a
strong nation: I, Jehovah, will hasten it in its time.

QUERIES

a. What does Isaiah mean by Zion sucking "the milk of the nations"?
b. Why would Zion need only Jehovah for light?
c. How does the "little one" become a "thousand"?

PARAPHRASE

Zion, you have been laughed at and scoffed at by the world because it never believed what you proclaimed about your God. You have also been despised for your hypocrisy and profligacy. Although you have been mocked and shunned by the world,

I am going to make you so exalted and majestic for all eternity you will be an object of rejoicing for millions. You shall be fed and grow into beautiful maidenhood from the life and vitality that comes from the nations of the world. Kings and great leaders of these nations shall become part of that food that shall be given you. When this comes to pass you will compare the experience with the predictions I have made in My Word and you will know that I, the God of the Jews, am the only God there is! Only the best will be good enough for you Zion. You will be built with that which is superior and precious instead of that which is inferior. Failing, faltering human rulers will no longer be needed in Zion because I will put Peace and Righteousness upon her throne. There will be no more violence in her midst. Desolation and destruction will be banished from within Zion. My Salvation and My Praise will protect her like walls around a city. She will no longer be dependent upon mere reflections of My Glory for her light, but she shall have the ultimate origin and source of all Light, My Person, illuminating her forever. There will never again be sadness or grief with Zion. Her citizens will all be made righteous and they shall all be given the eternal inheritance I promised them and this will cause all the world to see My glory. From a small and insignificant remnant Zion shall grow into an innumerable multitude of people forming a universal kingdom. I, Jehovah, will accomplish this according to My time schedule of the world's history.

COMMENTS

v. 15-17 Riches: The time came when the "glorious land" (Palestine) and the "holy" city (Jerusalem) was an object of ridicule and mockery. After Assyrian invasion of Israel in 722 B.C. and the deportation of the ten northern tribes (and the immigration of foreigners into the unoccupied territory) came the Babylonian invasion of Judah (606-586 B.C.). Nebuchadnezzar destroyed the Temple, tore down most of Jerusalem's walls and took the people back to Babylon as prisoners of war. The land of Palestine became inhabited by a nomadic people from the deserts and mostly pagan. The beautiful homes and luxuriant vineyards and productive farms of the Jews were allowed to deteriorate. The city of Jerusalem remained in a semi-ruined state until 70 years later when Nehemiah received word that it was in ruins (Neh. 1:1-4), and got permission to return and rebuild it. For two generations caravans, travelers and soldiers passed by Palestine and by the city of Jerusalem, wagging their heads and "hissing" (whistling) at the devastation. This was what God predicted (cf. Jer. 18:16; 19:8; 25:9, 18; 29:18; Lamentations 2:15-16; Micah 6:16). The world not only hissed at the land of Palestine, it also mocked the Jewish people. They had (until idolatry became so prevalent) claimed their God, Jehovah, was the only true God and that He was all-powerful. They also claimed He was righteous and holy. But they had become pagan themselves and were conquered by those they held in contempt as ignorant heathen. Suddenly they were mocked and shunned and despised. This was precisely predicted (Deut. 28:15-46, esp. 28:37).

From these despicable depths, however, God promises to rescue a remnant and form a New Zion which He will exalt and magnify eternally. The Hebrew word *ge'on* is translated *excellency;* it means *to grow up, to increase, to be lifted, exalted, majestic.* The Lord is going to make the New Zion majestic and an object of rejoicing for succeeding generations (millions of people).

The interesting phrase in verse 16, "Thou shalt also suck the milk of the nations," is a graphic figure of speech to portray the New Zion as a hungry nursing child feeding on the choicest products of the nations of the whole world. This has already been commented on in 60:11. There have been the Augustines, Justin Martyrs, Pascals, Gladstones, Lincolns, Agassizes, Miltons, Handels, *ad infinitum,* "the milk of the nations" which have sustained Zion. There have been the millions and millions of "little" people, the "salt of the earth" people, the real jewels of each generation and nationality which have also come to Zion. The fact that great and small, rich and poor, literate and illiterate, weak and powerful may come together in a kingdom of peace redounds to the glory and praise of Jehovah who created Zion. The church itself is undeniable, empirical evidence of the existence of God. Verse 17 is a continuation of the idea that God is going to build New Zion from only the best of everything. There will be no inferior materials in building His New dwelling place (the church). There will be no more need for human rulers in New Zion (human rulers were oppressive and inferior) because she shall be ruled by Peace (see comments on 59:8 for "peace") and by Righteousness. In the church of Christ there are no positions of human rulership—only servanthood. Elders, deacons and evangelists are not rulers—they are slaves, ruled over by the Prince of Peace and the King of Righteousness. The Hebrew word *Jerusalem* means *righteousness-peace.*

v. 18-22 RIGHTEOUSNESS: As important to the goodness Zion is to have as riches, is righteousness. Citizens of New Zion are not belligerent; they do not retaliate (they leave justice to be done by the proper authority); they do not war and fight against one another (Mt. 5:7, 9; Mt. 5:21-26; 38-42; I Cor. 6:1-8; Eph. 5:25-28; James 4:1-12; I Pet. 2:13-25, etc.). Citizens of New Zion have conformed their thinking and acting to the image of God's Son, Jesus Christ, and there is no violence in Zion. The New Zion is the only Zion of which this can be said. It certainly cannot apply to any literal, physical Zion or Jerusalem! The reason there is no violence in New Zion is that she is walled about by Salvation and Praise. Jesus pointed out to some men in His day that the kingdom of God had suffered a history of violent men wanting to take God's kingdom from Him and use it for their own violent purposes (cf. Mt. 11:7-15), but (the inference is) His coming to establish His rule as King would stop all that.

Some commentators think verses 19-20 refer to the heavenly-consummation when heaven and earth shall have passed away and there is no more sun or moon (cf. Rev. 21:23; 22:5). Isaiah does not actually state here that the sun and moon will be done away, but merely that it is no longer to give light to Zion by day. It is possible that this is merely a figure to predict that all light (mental and spiritual illumination) except Divine Light will be excluded from the New Zion. The *menorah* (lampstand) in the Tabernacle in which only that oil made according to Divine formula could be burned typified the fact that in the Lord's dwelling place only Divine Light was to shine. Instructions concerning the Tabernacle also prohibited the Jews from allowing sunlight, moonlight or any other light to shine inside the tent. Jesus was the Light (Jn. 1:4; 8:12; 9:5; 12:46). The gospel is the Light (Acts 26:23; II Cor. 4:4; Eph. 5:8; I Thess. 5:5; I Pet. 2:9; II Pet. 1:19; I Jn. 1:5, 7; 2:9, etc.). Malachi predicts the "sun of righteousness shall rise, with healing in its wings" (Mal. 4:2) which we believe to be a messianic prophecy. God's city will be changed from a physical, geographical Zion which has a physical sun to a spiritual, universal Zion which will have a spiritual Light.

Isaiah was directed to "comfort" Israel with the prediction that her "warfare is ended" (cf. Isa. 40:1ff, see comments there). Chapters 60-66 are amplifications of that prediction. When New Zion is created, the days of mourning for God's people will be over (cf. comments Isa. 25:6-9).

The crowning characteristic of New Zion will be the righteousness of her citizens. This is possible only because God has provided a satisfactory atonement and imputed His righteousness to Zion's citizenry (cf. comments 53:11). Zion's citizens, declared righteous, must by righteous living be faithful to their calling, however, or they will not remain citizens. In other words, there is an imputed righteousness and a lived righteousness. The one who is justified and saved will do righteousness (cf. I Jn. 3:4-10). Anyone born of God cannot go on sinning (deliberately). This is the correct understanding of the present tense Greek verb *poiei* in I John 3:9, and the present tense participle *poion* in I John 3:8. Present tense in Greek means *continuing action.* Citizens of Zion hunger and thirst after righteousness. As John says, ". . . let no one deceive you . . . the one continuing to do righteousness is righteous . . . the one continuing to do sin is of the devil . . ." Ultimately, of course, we will be saved forever by God's imputed righteousness for we sin even after accepting by faith the grace of God (I Jn. 1:8; 2:1-2 was written to Christians). But if we repent (change our minds) and determine not to continue in a particular sin but rather keep His commandments, we are faithful citizens of Zion and we shall receive our inheritance. We are the human offspring of our earthly parents by their grace, so to speak, and we remain in the grace of our mothers and fathers only so long as we choose to be faithful to them. We are joined to our earthly spouse by his or her grace, but we remain in the love of that grace only so long as we are faithful.

When God's people are faithful and live righteously, God is glorified. And Zion's population is increased when God is glorified. The phrase "The little one shall become a thousand . . ." apparently means that the Lord will take the foolish, weak, and despised and confound the wise and powerful (cf. I Cor. 1:18-31). God will take what the world says can never become anything and give it increase and glory (cf. Micah 5:2); even Bethlehem of Ephrathah small among the claims of Judah will produce the Messiah, Jehovah will not follow man's timetable. He has His own seasons and times in His great redemptive work (cf. Daniel 9:20-27, see our comments there, College Press). The Lord fixes all times and seasons in His own authority (cf. Acts 1:6-7; Dan. 2:20-23). And the Lord will create New Zion "in its time." Its time was, of course, in the days of the kings of the fourth kingdom (cf. Dan. 2:44); the Day of Pentecost (Acts 2:1ff). The creative work of Zion's incarnate King began on a Sunday, as He mounted a colt, the foal of an ass, and rode toward physical Zion declaring Himself the prophesied King of Zechariah 9:1-10 coming to establish spiritual Zion.

QUIZ

1. When was Jerusalem "hated"?
2. What does the term "excellency" mean?

3. What is the "milk of nations"?
4. Which Zion would experience the cessation of violence?
5. Are verses 19-20 speaking literally or figuratively?
6. What are the two aspects of righteousness the people of Zion shall have?
7. What was the time Jehovah chose to create New Zion?

B. REJOICING OF ZION, CHAPTER 61

1. FREEDOM

TEXT: 61:1-4

1 The Spirit of the Lord Jehovah is upon me; because Jehovah hath anointed me to preach good tidings unto the meek; he hath sent me to bind up the broken-hearted, to proclaim liberty to the captives, and the opening of the prison to them that are bound;
2 to proclaim the year of Jehovah's favor, and the day of vengeance of our God; to comfort all that mourn;
3 to appoint unto them that mourn in Zion, to give unto them a garland for ashes, the oil of joy for mourning, the garment of praise for the spirit of heaviness; that they may be called trees of righteousness, the planting of Jehovah, that he may be glorified.
4 And they shall build the old wastes, they shall raise up the former desolations, and they shall repair the waste cities, the desolations of many generations.

QUERIES

a. Who is "me" in verse one?
b. What is the "year of Jehovah's favor"?
c. How shall the "desolations of many generations" be rebuilt?

PARAPHRASE

The Servant says, The Sovereign God will send Me in all the fulness of His Sovereign Spirit because His mission for Me is to deliver the message of the good news of redemption. The Spirit of God upon Me will be the sign that I come with His authority. My mission is to heal men who have been broken in heart and spirit by sin, to declare liberation for all those who have been made prisoners of sin and to announce that the time Jehovah has set in His schedule to be gracious and conciliatory toward sinful man has arrived. Yes, I am to be sent to comfort and strengthen all who are mourning in Zion for spiritual help. I am going to give them a crown of beauty in exchange for the ashes of affliction they have had to suffer, anointing of My Spirit for joy in exchange for their mourning; I am going to wrap them in divine praise and take away their heaviness of heart. I am going to do this so that My New Zion may be established and stabilized like firmly rooted trees. After I have done this no winds or storms of affliction shall uproot them. The ancient house of Israel which for hundreds and hundreds of years has been in ruin and disarray will be rebuilt by these people whom I will liberate from the prison-house of sin.

COMMENTS

v. 1-2 MESSAGE: The "me" of verse one can be none other than the Servant of Jehovah, the Messiah. We have divine sanction for that verified by the Servant Himself in the synagogue of Nazareth (Lk. 4:21). Jesus read these verses from the scroll of Isaiah and applied them directly to His own incarnate ministry by saying, "Today this scripture has been fulfilled in your ears." The Greek *peplerotai* is perfect tense for *has been fulfilled* and would read more literally, *has been and is continuing to be fulfilled.* From the moment Jesus was born until the Christian dispensation shall close and the gospel cease to be preached, what Isaiah wrote in these verses is being fulfilled. And the Servant is the source of it all. The Hebrew reads, *ruach adonay yehoih,* or literally, *spirit of Lord Jehovah. Adonay* is the Hebrew word which suggests Judge or Master. It is like *kurios* in Greek. *Yehoih* is translated *Jehovah* and suggests Covenant-Revealer. This combination of divine character was the *ruach* (Spirit) which was upon Jesus. God gave His Spirit to Jesus without measure (Jn. 3:34). The reason Jesus needed this full anointing of the Godhead was His mission to a world of rebel prisoners enslaved by a supernatural devil. God anointed Jesus with the Holy Spirit (Acts 10:38) so that in Jesus dwelt all the fulness of the Godhead bodily (Col. 1:19; 2:9). To anoint (the Hebrew word *mashah* is anoint and is the word from which we get Messiah) meant to crown as king—to give authority. Jesus' authority to proclaim "good tidings from heaven" was demonstrated by the miracles and signs confirming His deity. He demonstrated He had authority on earth to forgive sins by making the lame to walk and giving sight to the blind and raising the dead.

The Hebrew word for *meek* is *'anah* and means *afflicted, oppressed, ravished, miserable, poor.* This is an excellent word to describe those who know they are in need of help. It indicates the kind of person who would be glad to hear good news from God. Jesus pronounced a blessing upon those who were "poor in spirit" (Mt. 5:3-12). *Brokenhearted* is from the Hebrew *shavar* meaning *fractured, distressed, sorrowing.* This is why the Servant is sent to those who are mourning—sin has fractured their lives—they are disintegrating. Jesus was sent to bring them wholeness and to "bind them up."

The Servant came to announce *liberty* to the captives and release to those who were *bound.* The Hebrew word for *liberty* is *deror* and was used in connection with the Year of Jubilee (Lev. 25:10; Ezek. 46:17, etc.) when bond-slaves were set free and land taken in payment for debts was returned to its original owners. The Mosaic "Year of Jubilee" was evidently intended to typify the messianic time. Christ came to "bind" our jailor (the devil) and free us (Mt. 12:25-30; Heb. 2:14-15;

I Jn. 3:8-9; Rev. 20:1-6). We have allowed Satan, by choosing sin, to imprison us in falsehood, lawlessness, fear and selfishness. The Servant of God sets us free from that prison (see Special Study on "Liberty Is Not License"). The Hebrew word for Jubilee is *yovil,* from *yaval,* which means, *protracted sound of the trumpet,* signifying that a very important, "once-in-a-lifetime" announcement is about to be made.

Of course, most of the Jews expected Jesus in the synagogue at Nazareth (Lk. 4:16-30) to interpret this physically. That was the traditional interpretation of the rabbis (see comments on Isa. 53). When Jesus talked of "food" they wanted bread and fish; when He talked of "wholeness" they wanted limbs restored; when He talked of "freedom" they wanted foreign rulers driven from their land. But circumstances are not what constitute the Kingdom of God—it is character, (Rom. 14:17).

Hebrew *qara* means *proclaim, call out, shout, cry, summon.* The Servant became The Prophet, The Apostle. He was sent not only to live a godly life and to do miraculous things; He was sent to *preach* and *teach* the will of God for every other individual in the world. That was really His fundamental mission—accomplishing atonement and preaching the gospel. His miracles were simply means to that end. The Hebrew word *ratzah* is translated *favor* (or *acceptable*) and means *delightful, pleasurable, gracious.* The Servant came to announce the precise time God chose in His divine schedule of redemption to accomplish His grace toward man. In the *fulness* of time God sent forth His Son . . . (Gal. 4:4). The Servant of the Lord was anointed to "summon" all men to the "year" (or appointed time) of the Lord's pleasure or conciliation. And the day of *vengeance* was part of the Servant's announcement. All through the O.T. prophets, in highly figurative language, God promises (in the "last days" of the O.T. dispensation) He is going to defeat His foes in one great battle (Joel 2:30—3:21; Ezek. 38:1—39:29; Zech. 9:9—10:12; 12:1-14; 14:1-21; etc.), and give His people victory. That great battle was at *Calvary* and the great victory over Satan was there and at the *empty tomb.* The principalities and powers were "triumphed over publicly and shamed" at the cross (Col. 2:15); when He ascended on high He led captivity captive (Eph. 4:8). Of course, the final and consummate vengeance of God will come at the end of this "year" of grace (end of the Christian dispensation, which are the *last days,* or end of all ages, I Cor. 10:11). But this "year" is the only "year" God has sent His Servant to announce. Now is the *acceptable* time . . . *Today* is the day of salvation! (cf. II Cor. 6:1-2). The defeat of God's enemies and His victory is the source of *comfort* for Zion. The Hebrew word *nakham* (translated *comfort*) is very appropriate here for it means *consoled, eased, freed.*

v. 3-4 MISSION: The Hebrew word *phe'er,* translated *garland,* means more precisely, *an ornamental headdress,* or *adorning tiara.* The Servant-Messiah accomplishes more than conquest—He brings coronation to His people (cf. Rom. 8:31-39). He makes it possible for believers to "sit with Him in the heavenly places" (Eph. 2:6). His followers are crowned and reign with Him over death and all other circumstances. (cf. I Cor. 5:9-13; Heb. 11:7; I Cor. 3:21-22; Rev. 5:10). The Servant anoints His followers with "the oil of gladness" by the anointing of the Holy Spirit (cf. II Cor. 1:21; I Jn. 2:26-27) which is the indwelling presence of the Holy Spirit and the "down payment" on the believer's future inheritance (cf. Eph. 1:14). The *ma'eteh* is from the root *'ataph* meaning *to cover for protection,* or, *cloak, veil.* A man may, so to speak, wrap himself in his human moods as a defense mechanism. Human moods and emotions are no protection; they are capricious, vulnerable to circumstances and temporal. Instead of human moods which are so manipulative and conducive to despair, the Servant will wrap His followers in a protective cloak of praise. If our lives are wrapped in praise to Jehovah we are protected from the manipulative capriciousness of human emotions which are so subject to circumstances. The object of our heart's desires and hopes is The Almighty, Never Varying, Always Faithful God and so we do not ever need to despair (cf. II Cor. 1:8-11). The Servant will dress His people up richly like the father dressed the prodigal son when he returned home (cf. Lk. 15:22-24). All the despair and heaviness will be forgotten when the Messiah brings God's sons home! The Messiah will give His followers beauty (righteousness) and stability (trees, planting of Jehovah) (cf. Psa. 1:1-3). The messianic people are going to be established as God's people and nothing can "snatch them out of the Shepherd's hand" (cf. Jn. 10:27-28). No human, no spiritual power, no circumstance can take away their beauty. All this, of course, brings glory to the one so clothed, but ultimately to the One doing the dressing. The real glory went to the father of the prodigal because he exhibited such mercy, love and forgiveness.

The Servant's followers will build up the ancient ruins. The house (tabernacle, dynasty, family) of David was in ruins. David's house was the house of messianic destiny. David's throne was the throne reserved for the Messiah. But those who were sitting on David's throne in the days of the prophets scorned and usurped its messianic destiny. They violently rebelled against God's purposes for this throne of David and had brought it to shame and ruin. Amos predicted that the house of David (tabernacle of David) would be rebuilt (Amos 9:11-12). Amos' prophecy was fulfilled when the Gentiles were brought into the messianic kingdom (the church) (cf. Acts 15:12-21). We have already commented on this "rebuilding" (cf. Isa. 59:10, etc.). The church is built as a dwelling place of God in the Spirit (Eph. 2:22); Christians are living stones built into a spiritual house (I Pet. 2:4-8).

QUIZ

1. What proof do we have that this is a messianic prophecy?
2. What character is suggested in the "Spirit" by which the Servant is anointed?
3. Who are the "meek"?
4. What kind of liberty will the Messiah bring?
5. What is the "garment of praise"?
6. How will the Messiah's followers rebuild the ruins of generations?

2. FORTUNE

TEXT: 61:5-7

5 And strangers shall stand and feed your flocks, and foreigners
shall be your plowman and your vinedressers.
6 But ye shall be named the priests of Jehovah; men shall call
you the ministers of our God: ye shall eat the wealth of the
nations, and in their glory shall ye boast yourselves.
7 Instead of your shame ye shall have double; and instead of
dishonor they shall rejoice in their portion: therefore in their
land they shall possess double; everlasting joy shall be unto
them.

QUERIES

a. Why emphasize so much the subjugation of "foreigners"?
b. Why promise that New Zion's citizens would be priests?

PARAPHRASE

Amazing but true, many of those who are now your enemies, alienated against you, will, in the days of the messianic Jubilee, become subjects of the New Kingdom of Zion and join with you in service to Jehovah. All of you together will be anointed as priests and ministers of Jehovah. Those former enemies who become members of New Zion will be the most precious thing their nations have and they will aid in the ongoing of Zion and their coming will bring fame and honor and blessing to you. The fact that Jehovah will conquer and make citizens of Zion of those who once opposed and mocked Him will replace whatever shame you once knew with twice as much glory and honor and blessing. And Zion will be glad and happy forever because of this.

COMMENTS

v. 5-6 JOINING: The Hebrew word *zarim* is translated *strangers* and means, *loathed-ones, barbarians, enemies, excluded-ones. Ben-nekar* is Hebrew for *sons of the alien* or *sons of the foreigner.* When the Messiah-Servant came crying aloud the time of the messianic Jubilee (the time of the Lord's pleasure), those who had been excluded, alienated from covenant relationship to Jehovah were to be given an invitation to join the chosen people in serving and ministering to Him. Jesus in the synagogue at Nazareth apparently closed the scroll of Isaiah before He read beyond verses one and two of this chapter. He did not read the verses now under consideration, but He implied them in His reference to the mercy shown by Jehovah to two Gentiles (Lk. 4:23-27) in the remainder of His sermon!

Paul's statement to the Gentiles in Ephesians 2:11-22 is certainly the fulfillment of this. Isaiah is replete with predictions that the nations (*goiym*) will be included in the messianic age as God's people (Isa. 2:1-4; 19:23-25; 25:6-12; 56:6-8; 60:10-14, etc.).

The Jewish Apocrypha (non-canonical writings) however, reflect the humanistic, materialistic interpretations of such prophecies as those of Isaiah here concerning God's purposes for the Gentiles in the messianic age. These apocryphal writings show a *liberal* attitude of the Jewish mind toward the Gentiles during a time of relative freedom and peace for the Jews in the days of the Maccabeans, but an intensifying *bitterness* and *hatred* for the Gentiles as the oppression of Rome increased until the days of Jesus and the hotheaded *Zealots* and *Sicarii* eventually stirred up the rebellion and insurrection that brought about the destruction of Jerusalem and the Jewish nation in 70 A.D.

According to I Enoch 10:21, (written about 164 B.C.), all the Gentiles will become righteous and offer to God their adoration and worship. In the Sibylline Oracles III (written about 150 B.C.), the Gentiles will make their way in procession to God's Temple there to ponder his law and supplicate the Eternal King (716ff; 725ff); from every land the Gentiles will bring frankincense and gifts to the house of the great God and in the coming messianic kingdom they will have a share in the blessings that it brings. However, in II Baruch (written after 90 A.D.), it is written: "My Messiah . . . will both summon all the nations, and some of them he will spare and some of them he will slay. These things therefore will come upon the nations which are to be spared by him. Every nation which knows not Israel, and has not trodden down the seed of Jacob, shall indeed be spared. And this because some out of every nation will be subject to thy people. But all those who have ruled over you, or have known you, shall be given up to the sword (II Baruch 72:2-6)."

But the bitterness of the Jews toward the Gentiles finds its fullest expression in Similitudes of Enoch and II Esdras (both written in the first century A.D.). They teach that all Gentiles who dwell upon the earth, at the time of the messianic age, will bring to the Elect One gifts and presents and tokens of homage, but these will be of no avail; they will be destroyed and banished from the face of the earth and will perish forever and ever. D. S. Russell says in *The Method and Message of Jewish Apocalyptic,* pub. Westminster, pg. 303, "The bitterness . . . expressed by the writer of II Esdras against the Gentiles is to be understood against the background of persecution which the Jewish nation as a whole had to suffer, first in the time of the Seleucids and then in the time of the Romans. It reflects the troubled years following the capture of Jerusalem in A.D. 70 and is in keeping with the trend in Judaism generally. From this time forward, and especially from the close of the first century A.D., the harsher view prevailed and the universalism of the earlier years was gradually replaced by that spirit which could be satisfied only with the annihilation of all the other nations of the earth."

In the light of these apocryphal views, which were undoubtedly the views of the majority of the Jews in Jesus' day, we may well understand the extreme animosity generated toward Jesus when He interpreted chapter 61 of Isaiah to mean the Gentiles were to be accepted and blessed in the messianic kingdom! The traditional interpretation the people of the synagogue in Nazareth expected to hear was that the Gentiles would at least become literally the conquered slaves of the Jews. That Saturday crowd expected to hear Isaiah 61 interpreted to mean God's people would someday kill most of the Gentiles and those not killed would become slave laborers (like the ancestors of the Jews had been in Egypt) and put to work building a rich, prosperous Jerusalem and Palestine which would become the capital city of the world.

What God meant in Isaiah 61 was, of course, just the opposite of the common Jewish concept. Many of the Jews learned this with great difficulty but rejoiced once it became apparent that it was the will of Jehovah (cf. Acts 9:1-16; 10:34-43; 11:18; 13:44-52; 15:12-21; Gal. 2:11ff, etc.).

The Hebrew word for *priests,* is *kohenyim* from the root word *kahan,* meaning, *to stand, to prepare, make ready, adjust*—thus to *officiate* as one who readies or adjusts something. The word translated *ministers,* is *sharethey* and means, *to wait upon, to serve, to attend;* it is applied only to the Levites in the O.T. Law. The concept that *all* Jews, (let alone a kingdom of Jews and Gentiles) would become priests and ministers to Jehovah was revolutionary! It is essentially a prediction that the Law of Moses will be abrogated in the messianic age! Only those of Levi could be priests and ministers according to the Mosaic covenant. It took the major portion of the book of Hebrews in the N.T. to convince Jewish Christians of the first century that Jesus (from the tribe of Judah) could be a priest (after the order of Melchezidek). *All* of Messiah's people are priests—even Gentiles (cf. I Pet. 2:4-5; Rev. 1:6; 5:10; 20:6). Access, intercession, offering will be the vocation of *all* members of the New Zion (Heb. 10:19-25; 13:15-16; Rom. 12:1-2).

The Hebrew *heyl goiym* could be translated *host* or *army of the Gentiles.* The wealth or riches of any nation is not its gold or diamonds, but its *people.* It is the character of the people that make any kindgom what it is. God predicts through His prophets that the future "Israel" (N.T. church, Gal. 6:16) will "feed on" the best of all nations (cf. Obadiah 17, 21; Micah 7:11-17; Zech 14:16-21; Isa. 19:16-25; 60:10-18; 66:12-21). Many of those who came into the N.T. church were not what most nations would consider their best (I Cor. 1:26-31), but they were people who could repent and be made into the image of Christ and were really the jewels of creation (cf. Phil. 4:1; I Thess. 2:19-20).

v. 7 JOY: The Hebrew word *bashettekem* is from the root *bash* which means, *disappointment, confusion, ingnominy, disgrace.* When the Jews were sinning the prophets called on the pagan nations to look at them and see if there had ever been a nation on earth so disgraceful (cf. Jer. 2:10-12; 18:13; 23:14, etc.). The nations of the Gentiles could not "hold a candle" to the Jews of the days of Isaiah, Jeremiah and Ezekiel! The Gentiles mocked, derided and held in contempt everything Jewish. When they were taken into captivity the Assyrians and Babylonians hissed at them for they had claimed to be invincible because Jehovah was with them. The Jews suffered much indignity and reproach living in "unclean" heathen lands as prisoners. But Isaiah predicts a time (when the Messiah comes) when all these indignities shall be turned into exaltation and joy. The Messiah will take away all "uncleanness" and "disgracefulness." Of course, it would *not* be relief from national, cultural shame, but spiritual disgrace and spiritual uncleanness would be taken away. One is reminded of the glorious predictions of the messianic relief made by the father of John the Baptist (by the direction of the Holy Spirit) when he (Zechariah) spoke of the mission of his own son, the way-preparer (Lk. 1:67-79). Everlasting joy is a promise to be fulfilled only in the Messiah's kingdom (cf. Isa. 35:10; 51:11; Jn. 15:11; 16:22, 24; 17:13; Rom. 14:17; 15:13; Gal. 5:22; I Jn. 1:4, etc.).

QUIZ

1. What would have been the common interpretation of Isaiah 61:1-7 in Jesus' day?
2. Why is calling citizens of New Zion priests so revolutionary?
3. What will the everlasting joy of Zion have as its object of gladness?

3. FAME

TEXT: 61:8-11

8 For I, Jehovah, love justice, I hate robbery with iniquity; and I will give them their recompense in truth, and I will make an everlasting covenant with them.

9 And their seed shall be known among the nations, and their offspring among the peoples: all that see them shall acknowledge them, that they are the seed which Jehovah hath blessed.

10 I will greatly rejoice in Jehovah, my soul shall be joyful in my God; for he hath clothed me with the garments of salvation, he hath covered me with the robe of righteousness, as a bridegroom decketh himself with a garland, and as a bride adorneth herself with her jewels.

11 For as the earth bringeth forth its bud, and as the garden causeth the things that are sown in it to spring forth; so the Lord Jehovah will cause righteousness and praise to spring forth before all the nations.

QUERIES

a. What is the "truth" in which Jehovah will recompense?
b. Whose "seed" shall be known among the nations?
c. Why use the illustration of a "bridegroom" and "bride"?

PARAPHRASE

I am Absolute, I am Faithful-Yaweh, and so justice is My very nature. I despise injustice and wickedness and so I will faithfully reward My people by delivering them from their wicked oppressors and My pledge of this shall be in an everlasting covenant which I will establish with them. The citizens of New Zion shall be uniquely recognizable and even famous wherever they are all over the world. It will be so simple to identify the godly that everyone who sees them will recognize and acknowledge that Almighty God has blessed them. Zion will be filled with joy and she shall continually offer happy praise to God for His goodness. God has wrapped Zion in the grace of His righteousness and salvation and made her as beautiful and admirable as a bridegroom in his wedding suit or a bride wearing her precious jewelry. Just as surely as the earth produces fruit when seeds are sown in it, so the fruits of righteousness and praise will sprout from the "seed" of New Zion sown by Jehovah among the nations.

COMMENTS

v. 8-9 RENOWN: Zion will one day rejoice because she shall be made famous. The reason she shall be made famous, however, will not be due to her own merit but because God is who He is: He is by nature absolutely just and faithful. God will deliver Zion from her enemies because He loves justice and hates iniquity and therefore must vindicate His absolute sovereignty by destroying iniquity and rewarding loyalty. The loyalty Jehovah will reward will be that of the sinless Servant; but the Servant will impute His perfect meritorious obedience (Heb. 10:5-10) to all who by faith and covenant-keeping become citizens of the New Zion. The Lord's primary goal is the vindication of His Name (cf. Ezek. 29:9, 14, 22, 44; 36:21, 22, 23, 32; 38:16, 23; 39:7, 8, 25-29). It is imperative that Jehovah's absolute sovereignty and absolute faithfulness be proven and vindicated. Man's salvation depends on God's faithfulness, not his own (see comments, Isa. 48:9-11).

The word *'emeth* is translated *truth* and is from the Hebrew root *'aman* (same as Greek and English *amen*). The word means *firmness, faithfulness, stability, fidelity, verity.* The idea in verse eight is that God is going to prove His fidelity by keeping His promise to destroy Zion's enemies because they are wicked. This demonstration of Jehovah's absolute faithfulness will, in turn, move men of all nations to happily come into covenant relationship with Jehovah. All this will be accomplished when Jehovah makes an *everlasting covenant* with man. Thus once again we conclude these scriptures are prophetic of the New Zion, the church. It was at the cross and the empty tomb that God destroyed the power of all the enemies of man (cf. Lk. 1:67-79; 2:29-35; Jn. 12:27-33; 16:11; Rom. 8:31-39; Col. 2:14-15; Heb. 2:14-15, etc.).

The Hebrew word *berith* is the word for *covenant.* It is from the Hebrew root word *barah* which means literally *to cut,* or *to choose, to select.* Its fundamental idea is "chosen" "separated" or that which distinguishes a "selected" people. God's salvation and blessings are available always *within a covenant.* A covenant, by its very nature, demands choice, or selection, and that requires conditions and terms. The everlasting covenant (or "new" covenant Jer. 31:31ff) has conditions and terms men must choose if they wish its blessings. Christ is the *new* covenant (cf. Mt. 26:26-29; Heb. 8:6; 12:24; 13:20). He is the resurrection and the life, whoever *lives* and *believes* in Him shall never die (Jn. 11:26). Paul, the apostle, spoke of the new covenant relationship as "being *in* Christ" (cf. Rom. 12:5; I Cor. 15:22; II Cor. 1:21; 3:14; 5:17; Gal. 3:27; Eph. 3:6; etc.). The everlasting covenant is predicted in many places in the O.T. (cf. Isa. 55:3; Jer. 32:40; Ezek. 16:60-63; 37:26, etc.).

The "seed" and "offspring" of New Zion will be renowned among the Gentiles. The people of the Messiah (Christians) were known throughout the Roman world of the first century (and ever after) for their faith, obedience and love (cf. Acts

2:47; 4:13, 33; Rom. 16:19; I Thess. 1:8-10; Philemon 4-7; I Pet. 4:4). Pliny the younger wrote "the believers met regularly early in the morning to worship Christ as a divinity. They insisted on a strict code of ethics; to abstain from fraud, theft, and adultery, never to lie, nor to default on an obligation. At the end of the assembly they ate a common meal and then adjourned." John Noble (prisoner of the Russians for 12 years) received the admiration and respect of the Russian prison guards for his Christian life. Isaiah means to stress how different the people of the Messiah will be from the heathenish behavior of the Israel of his day or the paganism of the world in general (cf. Jn. 13:35). The goodness and blessedness and joy of the lives of the citizens of Zion will be acknowledged (perhaps even grudgingly respected) by the whole world. The Messiah's people are "blessed with *every* spiritual blessing in the heavenly places" (Eph. 1:3).

In verse ten, New Zion is rejoicing in the Lord because the Lord has clothed her in salvation and righteousness. The church is all dressed up like someone waiting for a wedding! (cf. Eph. 5:25-27; Rev. 19:6-10). The people of the Messiah partake of the glory of the Messiah by being made partakers of His nature (II Pet. 1:3-4) which is done by abiding in His Will (Jn. 15:1-11). New Zion partakes of her King's nature gradually, progressively, "from one degree of glory to another" (II Cor. 3:17-18). New Zion must never forget that her beauty is relative to and dependent upon partaking of her Lord's righteousness and salvation. New Zion has no beauty of her own. She is clothed by Someone else! So all her boasting or rejoicing is directed to the Source of her glory (cf. I Cor. 1:29-31; Gal. 6:14-16).

As surely as the earth produces when seeds are sown in it, so the Lord will produce righteousness and praise to spring forth all over the world. Isaiah affirms the faithfulness of Jehovah to keep His word. God's word always produces—it always comes to pass! (Isa. 55:10-11). The existence of God and His faithfulness has been demonstrated in thousands of supernatural, historically-eyewitnessed events. Many of these events were predicted hundreds of years before they occurred. But most finally and ultimately God has proved His absolute veracity and trustworthiness in the resurrection of Jesus Christ from the dead. Death, the ultimate enigma, the ultimate obstacle, has been defeated. It has been swallowed up forever (Isa. 25:8). He kept His word! In spite of dungeon, fire and sword, God saved a remnant of Judah and brought the Messiah into the world. Babylon could not stop His word from being fulfilled; Persia, Greece, Rome—they could not stop it! Not even the death of the Messiah upon a Roman cross could stop His word.

Now the Lord works slowly, estimated by our finite, limited experience. But He works certainly! Some, in fact a majority of men, may scoff (II Pet. 3:1-10), but one day this victorious, living Messiah is coming back for His dressed-up bride. What righteousness and praise that will call forth from New Zion (the bride) whose citizens are from every tribe and tongue and people on the face of the earth. Every knee *will* bow and every tongue *will* confess that Jesus Christ is Lord, to the glory of God the Father!

QUIZ

1. What does the nature of God have to do with our salvation?
2. What is a covenant?
3. What is man's relationship to God's covenant?
4. Has verse nine been fulfilled?
5. What is the source of Zion's beauty?
6. How do we know God's word is sure?

LIBERTY IS NOT LICENSE

Gal. 5:13; I Pet. 2:16

INTRODUCTION

Bob Iverson tells of the man who went to one of the new style worship services in which a "rock and roll" record was being played at ear-shattering levels (Rolling Stones now hold Guiness record of decibels 120 . . . SST Concorde is 130 decibels at take off). When he asked the young man in charge why such noise, the youth replied that this was an expression of "doing one's own thing." The older man, then, did "his own thing" by getting out his pocket knife and destroying the amplifier.

This illustrates the human problem of knowing and practicing freedom or liberty.

I. NO SUCH THING AS ABSOLUTE FREEDOM FOR MAN

II. TRUE FREEDOM

A. Is when human beings recognize their limitation and obligations

B. Is always relative and relational. It is relative to the will of the Absolute Creator and in relation to knowing and abiding in His will and fellowship with other human beings.

C. True freedom is:

1. Legacy
2. Not license
3. Liability

DISCUSSION

I. LIBERTY IS OUR LEGACY

A. Christ came to free mankind.

1. "Truly, truly, I say to you, every one who commits sin is a slave to sin. The slave does not continue in the house forever; the son continues forever. So if the Son makes you free, you will be free indeed." Jn. 8:34-36
2. "If you continue in my word, you are truly my disciples, and you will know the truth, and the truth will make you free." Jn. 8:31
3. The most important freedom Christ gives is freedom from falsehood. He reveals the real, abiding, saving, edifying TRUTH about who God is, who man is and how life is to be lived. YOU SEE, THE DEVIL LIED TO EVE AND ADAM ABOUT THAT AND HAS DECEIVED MOST OF MANKIND SINCE. . . . MAN ACTS ACCORDING TO WHAT HE BELIEVES. WHEN THE DEVIL DECEIVED MAN INTO BELIEVING AND DOING A LIE, HE ENSLAVED MAN WITH GUILT, FEAR AND SELFISHNESS.

B. The real hindrance to true freedom is not God's Law (His Will) BUT GUILT, FEAR AND SELFISHNESS.
   1. These are the elements Satan uses to keep men in bondage (Heb. 2:5-18) etc.
   2. Freedom comes only by faith in Christ's atonement, His priesthood, and His Lordship.

C. Christ frees us from sin.
   1. Sin is lawlessness.
   2. The devil's subtle lie is that freedom is found in rebellion . . . that we cannot really be free if we are going to let God tell us what is right or wrong.

      What most people do not realize is that if we don't let God tell us then we let the devil tell us! And he lies. You see, man, limited to this world cannot determine right or wrong, reality or unreality, for that has its basis in what is beyond our finite existence—only supernatural sources know ultimate truth.
   3. Christ frees us from the slavery of lawlessness.
   4. If you want an example of the slavery of lawlessness read Rom. 1:18-32.
   5. He also frees us from the guilt and penalty of sin.

D. Christ frees us from fear.

1. It is through guilt and the fear of death and the judgment the devil keeps men enslaved to him.
2. Christ paid our penalty, died and rose again and we who are in covenant relationship with Him do not fear death.
3. We are not driven by a motive of fear of failure to keep God's law . . . that is a never-ending, never-attaining bondage.
4. We are forgiven, freed, adopted sons and now serve willingly from love.
5. By faith the law of love is transformed into the love of law and almost in proportion as the law is loved, it ceases to be felt as law at all, but privilege and blessing!
6. THE LOVE OF GOD MASTERS THE CHRISTIAN, AND THE MASTERY OF LOVE IS FOUND TO BE PERFECT LIBERTY.

E. Christ frees us from inordinate love of self.

1. L. H. Marshall in his, *The Challenge of N.T. Ethics,* says, "Jesus attributes all moral evil to the self-will that knows not the rule of God," page 31.
2. Selfishness enslaves us. We become incapable of growth; we become unteachable, impenetrable, unloving.
3. Selfishness destroys creativeness, the ability to appreciate and enjoy.
4. The selfish person imprisons himself, fetters himself, hinders himself more than any man who has ever been imprisoned in any concentration camp.

II. LIBERTY IS NOT LICENSE.

A. God has objectively, judicially and propositionally freed me.

God has emotionally, willingly loved me when I was unlovely . . . and He did it in such a way that it breaks my rebellious heart . . . and I love Him.

1. Loving Him is not something I can produce without an adequate cause. "We love because he first loved us" (I Jn. 4:19).
2. Jesus commanded His disciples to love others as He loved them. Perfect love has its origin and reproduction in the divine Lover.
3. Our love is a rebound—a reaction—a response.
4. Love is both a motive and a force operating on the human will.
5. Love moves a person to want to do something.

B. The love of Christ constrains me, but constrains me from what or to do what?
1. Love is not self-defining.
2. Even in the Garden of Eden—in innocence, man's liberty and freedom could only be enjoyed and expressed within divine guidelines.

   Before man had ever been deceived by falsehood, God told man what to do to love his Creator.
3. The creaturely nature of man forbids absolute license.
4. God must be allowed to tell us how to love and what to love.

C. Liberty is not self-defining.
1. C. S. Lewis in *Mere Christianity,* page 39:
   "What Satan put into the heads of our remote ancestors was the idea that they could 'be like gods'—could set up on their own as if they had created themselves—be their own masters—invent some sort of happiness for themselves outside God . . . The reason why it can never succeed is this. God made us: invented us as a man invents an engine. A car is made to run on gasoline, and it would not run properly on anything else. Now God designed the human machine to run on Himself. He Himself is the fuel our spirits were designed to burn, or the food our spirits were designed to feed on. There is no other. That is why it is just no good asking God to make us happy in our own way without bothering about His will."

2. Anything God forbids He does so to free us from anything which is not His nature.

   Anything God commands He does so to create in us the divine nature.

D. Liberty is found in order. God is order. Our lives must operate within order and discipline.

1. An ancient writer of Athens illustrated the consequences of license and disorder this way:

   A farmer, not wishing to take the time and effort to sort his harvest, threw into his granary barley and wheat and peas together. But then, when he wanted barley bread or wheat bread or pea soup, he had to pick them grain by grain, instead of having them separately stored and easily accessible.

2. In 1776 George Mason wrote this statement into the Virginia Declaration of Rights:

   ". . . the blessings of liberty can (not) be preserved to any people but by a firm adherence to justice, *moderation, temperance,* frugality, and *virtue,* and by frequent recurrence to fundamental principles."

   Edmund Burke, British statesman 1727-1797, said: "(Liberty) cannot exist unless a controlling power on the will and appetite is placed somewhere; and the less there is within, the more there must be of it without."

4. Discipline is not antagonistic to liberty. License is not proof of freedom. The test of the greatness of liberty is the extent to which we can obey self-imposed law.

5. As Christians we are free to move responsibly within an orbit as wide as the revealed will of an all-knowing, all-loving, all-true, all-holy God.

A study in 1968, entitled "Studies in Self-Esteem," of young men from homes where parents demanded high standards of behavior and performance and where firm discipline was a fact . . . findings . . . suggest . . . the development of independence and self-reliance is fostered by a well-structured, demanding environment rather than by largely unlimited permissiveness and freedom to explore in an unfocused way. (See *Education In America,* by G. Charles Roche, III, pub. Fee, p. 142.)

III. LIBERTY IS LIABILITY.

A. Booker T. Washington, in his book, *Up From Salvery,* describes the scenes among the blacks on the night of the proclamation of their freedom. "There was no sleep that night. . . . All was excitement. . . . Early in the morning we were all sent for. The proclamation was read and we were told that we were free and could go when and where we pleased. . . . There was great rejoicing, followed by wild scenes of ecstasy. But the wild ecstasy did not last long. . . . The great responsibility of being free seemed to take possession of them. . . . Now that they were liberated, they found possession of freedom to be much more serious business than they had anticipated . . ."

B. Freedom is never free! There is always a price that those who would possess it must pay. The price of freedom is responsibility. Those who demand freedom but are not willing to pay this price, seek, not freedom, but license.

C. One man illustrates it as like the fundamental law of economics: "There is no such thing as a free lunch . . . there are no moral bargins in freedom. Liberty has a price—it is responsibility."

   1. A generation of young adults fed existentialism in education, art, and modern rock music, pursues the self-defeating course of aspiring to freedom while seeking to evade responsibility.

D. Liberty demands self-mastery.

   "During a Fritz Kreisler concert, a young violinist sat enthralled. 'Ohhh,' she sighed, 'what I would give to have such finger dexterity, such mastery, such freedom!' Later she told the incomparable Kreisler that she would give her life to play as he did. The violinist looked at her compassionately, then said, 'But, my dear, *I did.*' "

E. The man who has not accepted the liability and paid the price to discipline himself has narrowed his freedom. A man who cannot deny himself, cannot choose.

More advance in rank in USN, more liberty—*but* more responsibility.

More Christian maturity, more liberty—*but* more responsibility.

F. Liberty is a capacity, a potentiality.

1. We are freed by Christ to make possible the reaching of that capacity, that potentiality for which we were made . . . that beautifully free, purposeful, harmonious person, Christ demonstrated in the flesh it was possible to be!
2. Liberty is in being . . . not in things or circumstances!
3. The difference between a baby making random movements in his crib and the beautiful balance and coordination of a Willie Mays or Jack Nicklaus is the discipline and self-mastery and growth it takes to reach the potential.
4. The difference between a show-off, infantile, immature church of Christ in Corinth, and one that truly serves and ministers and reflects the gospel of Christ, is the discipline and self-mastery those Christians would exercise in the liberties Paul declared they had as Christians.
5. Liberty is not license.

Paul wrote: "All things are lawful, but not all things are helpful. All things are lawful, but I will not be enslaved by anything."

"All things are lawful, but not all things build up." True liberty is having self-mastery to do what is right and good when we don't "feel" like it!

"Let each of us please his neighbor for his good, to edify him. For Christ did not please himself . . ."

HOW DID CHRIST, THE FREEST, MOST LIBERATED PERSON EVER TO LIVE UPON THIS EARTH, KNOW SUCH LIBERTY? He found it surrendering self to the will of the Father as revealed in God's Word.

Liberty cannot survive in a vacuum. Jesus illustrated this with His parable of the unclean spirit who returns to his house to find it swept and put in order, but empty, and goes and gets seven other spirits more evil than himself and re-occupies the liberated, but empty, dwelling place!

CHRIST HAS LIBERATED US *for* SERVICE. HE HAS LIBERATED US TO LIBERATE OTHERS. LIBERTY IS NOT JUST TO ENJOY . . . IT IS TO USE! AND TO USE FOR HIS GLORY! LIBERTY IS NOT SELF-INDULGENCE, BUT SERVICE.

A famous poet once said, "I have on my table a violin string. It is free. I twist one end of it and it responds. It is free. But it is not free to do what a violin string is supposed to do—to produce beautiful music. So I take it, fix it in my violin and tighten it until it is taut. Only then is it *free* to be a violin string."

Each of us is free, if we choose, to be an untightened, unhampered piece of violin string and flop around or lie around and produce nothing. Or we are free, if we choose, to be tightened, constrained and tuned by the will of the Master and only then are we *free* to be what He can make us and produce what we were made to produce.

C. REGENERATION OF ZION, CHAPTER 62

1. NEW NAME

TEXT: 62:1-5

1 For Zion's sake will I not hold my peace, and for Jerusalem's sake I will not rest, until her righteousness go forth as brightness, and her salvation as a lamp that burneth.

2 And the nations shall see thy righteousness, and all kings thy glory; and thou shalt be called by a new name, which the mouth of Jehovah shall name.

3 Thou shalt also be a crown of beauty in the hand of Jehovah

and a royal diadem in the hand of thy God.
4 Thou shalt no more be termed Forsaken; neither shall thy
land any more be termed Desolate: but thou shalt be called
Hephzi-bah, and thy land Beulah; for Jehovah delighteth in
thee, and thy land shall be married.
5 For as a young man marrieth a virgin, so shall thy sons marry
thee; and as the bridegroom rejoiceth over the bride, so shall
thy God rejoice over thee.

QUERIES

a. How could Zion's salvation be like a burning lamp?
b. How is Zion to be a "crown" in the hand of Jehovah?
c. What is "Hephzi-bah"?

PARAPHRASE

For the sake of Zion, I dare not remain silent. For the sake of My holy city, I dare not remain inactive. It has come time for Me to act on her behalf again so that men may not think I have become powerless or defaulted on My promises toward her. I will act historically and supernaturally so that what I do toward her salvation will be as unmistakable as the bright sunshine and a burning lamp. What I am going to do in justification of My people will be so radically different from anything I have ever done before these people will have to be called by a new name, which comes directly from the mouth of God. When God totally remakes His people they will be so glorious they will sparkle and dazzle in God's hand like a jewel-covered diadem. My people will no longer be called Forsaken or Desolate; they shall be called God Is Pleased With Her and Happily Married, because Jehovah will be pleased with her and He will marry her. Just like a young man eagerly takes possession of a virgin when he marries her, so God's people will be eagerly possessed by Him. Just as a groom is delighted with his bride, so God will delight in His people.

COMMENTS

v. 1-3 APPEARANCE: Jehovah dare not remain *khashah* ("silent") or *shakat* ("inactive") any longer in relationship to Zion. Apparently this "inactivity" and "silence" toward Zion has to do with the long period between the O.T. and the N.T. when there was no God-sent prophet and no specific supernatural action from Him. Of course, God providentially sustained Israel during the intertestamental period. Daniel predicted that He would (Dan. ch. 10-12). But Jehovah dare not allow this period of Jewish "indignation" go on longer lest His enemies think He has no more concern for them.

So Jehovah will not rest again until He has made Zion so righteous her splendor and glory will be as blindingly evident as the sun in the heavens or a lamp shining in pitch darkness.

What God is going to do in glorifying Zion, the whole world shall see. And it shall be so totally different from what Zion has been before she shall have to be called by a new name. Everything about her will be new; old terminology will be inadequate. This wholly *new* Zion is predicted by other prophets (Jer. 3:15-17; 33:16; Ezek. 48:35). This prophecy was fulfilled when God's New Covenant people began to be called "Christians" (cf. Acts 11:26). It was fitting that those "married" to Christ should be called "Christians" (cf. Jn. 3:31-36; Eph. 5:21-33; Rev. 19:6-8; 21:2; 22:17, etc.). The Hebrew word *shem* is the word for *name.* It means literally, *a mark, fame, reputation, monument.* God was going to do something so radical to Zion she would henceforth be distinguished by a completely new *mark!* She would have a "new" commandment and live by a "new" love (Jn. 13:34-35). Of course, there were many *names* by which New Covenant believers were known; e.g., "the way" (Acts 24:14), "saints" (I Cor. 1:2), "brethren" (Gal. 1:2), "church of God" (I Cor. 1:1-2) and others.

Notice, the crown of beauty is not on the head of Jehovah, but in His hand. Zion, the church, is a work of His hands and He now beholds the work which contributes to the glory that is already His. The "woman" (Rev. 12:1-2) which we take to represent the covenant people of God (in both Old and New Testaments) has a crown upon her head. The church is the "crowning" accomplishment of God through the redemption of the Son. Recreation glorifies God even more than creation!

v. 4-5 APPELLATION: The point of the name-change appears to be focused on the changed relationship of God toward His people. He will no longer call them *'ezuvah* (Forsaken) or *shemamah* (Desolate). God will eventually call His people *khephzi-bah* (My Delight is in Her) and *be'ulah* (Married). These name-changes may have initial application to God's redemption of Judah from Babylonian captivity. However, their ultimate goal is the changed relationship in the New Zion (the messianic kingdom-church). One is reminded here of Hosea's prophecy of changed relationships and changed names (Hos. 1:8—2:1; 2:14-23). Hosea's prediction definitely found its fulfillment in the New Covenant church (cf. Rom. 9:25-26; I Pet. 2:10). It may be of interest to know that the Hebrew word *be'ulah* (married) comes from the root word *ba'al* which means, *to have dominion, to be lord over, to possess.*

The emphasis on marriage as descriptive of the new relationship stresses the fact that God's concern for His people is not one of mere duty; it is deeper than that—it is love. Just as a young man eagerly possesses (marries) his bride, so Jehovah will join Himself intimately to His people. He makes a covenant of love with His bride (the church) to protect her, sustain her, live with her and give her the honor of His name. He will lavish upon her the best of everything He has—even His own Son to atone for her sins.

QUIZ

1. Why must Jehovah not remain silent any longer about Zion?
2. When was Jehovah silent toward Zion?
3. Why was it necessary to rename Zion?
4. What is the probable fulfillment of the "new name"?

5. How do we know the name-changing refers to the messianic kingdom?
6. Why illustrate God's relationship to New Zion as a marriage?

2. NEW NOURISHMENT

TEXT: 62:6-9

6 I have set watchmen upon thy walls, O Jerusalem; they shall never hold their peace day nor night: ye that are Jehovah's remembrancers, take ye no rest.

7 and give him no rest, till he establish, and till he make Jerusalem a praise in the earth.

8 Jehovah hath sworn by his right hand, and by the arm of his strength, Surely I will no more give thy grain to be food for thine enemies; and foreigners shall not drink thy new wine, for which thou hast labored:

9 but they that have garnered it shall eat it, and praise Jehovah; and they that have gathered it shall drink it in the courts of my sanctuary.

QUERIES

a. What is a "remembrancer"?
b. Why bring up the subject of grain and wine?

PARAPHRASE

I will set sentries all around you, O City of Righteousness and Peace; they will be constantly vigilant crying out warnings and directions. I will also establish intercessors within you, Zion, and instruct them that they are to continually offer supplications and intercessions and prayers of thanksgiving for your establishment throughout the earth. Jehovah has sworn by His own Self, the most powerful oath there is, saying, I will not permit your enemies to plunder you and take away from you what is rightfully yours anymore. What is yours by right of inheritance you shall have and enjoy because you shall be forever in My presence.

COMMENTS

v. 6-7 PROTECTION: Watchmen were sentinels standing watch upon the tops of walls and in watch-towers of ancient cities to cry out warning at the approach of the enemy. The term is also used figuratively to denote men especially commissioned by God to preach and proclaim the Law of God to His people (cf. Ezek. 3:17; 33:1-9; Isa. 56:10, etc.). God promises that the "watchmen" in New Zion will be alert, constant and adept. They will not be like the watchmen of Isaiah's day, satiated, filled with wine, loving to lie down and slumber (56:10). The watchmen of New Zion will declare the whole counsel of God, night and day, with tears (cf. Acts 20:17-35). Shepherds of the flock will be always on guard protecting against "grevious wolves" (false teachers and false doctrines). Faithful ministers of the gospel and elders and teachers of the church are her watchmen. They can never afford the false luxury of holding their peace for Zion's enemy, like a roaring lion, seeks whom he may devour. Not only shall Zion have faithful watchmen, she shall also have persistent "remembrancers." The Hebrew word *hammazkirim* is literally, *those who remind.* The idea is that New Zion will have those who are constant in prayer, supplicating God on her behalf. Jesus taught constant, persistent prayer as a characteristic of the citizen of the messianic kingdom (cf. Lk. 11:5-14; 18:1-8). The point of Jesus' parables is not that we can wear God down until He gives in because we have prayed so long and so eloquently, but that if an exasperated friend or a grouchy old judge will answer the pleading of someone in need, *how much more* will our Father who is really *anxious to help,* answer us speedily?! The first century church was in constant prayer because its leaders (apostles, elders, evangelists) were men of constant prayer (I Thess. 5:16-18).

The main thing to be "remembered" and that which is to be kept constantly before God in prayer is the "establishment" of New Jerusalem as a praise in the earth—evangelism. Jesus instructed His disciples to pray for laborers for the harvest (cf. Mt. 9:37-38; Lk. 10:21; Jn. 4:35, etc.). Going into all the world to make disciples was our Lord's parting words to the church (Mt. 28:18-20; Lk. 24:44-53; Acts 1:8). Prayer for the evangelization of the world must be constantly upon the heart and lips of New Zion.

v. 8-9 PROVISION: Jehovah has allowed Jerusalem's enemies to plunder the land. Specifically Assyria and Babylon invaded Palestine and looted harvest field and city shops. Even the Temple was ravaged by Babylon and its vessels carried off. Israel's inheritance was wrested from her. But it shall not be so with New Zion. Her inheritance is incorruptible and eternal —one that does not fade away (I Pet. 1:3-5). Nothing in the seen or unseen world can separate New Zion from her inheritance (Rom. 8:31-39). Ancient Zion's glory was transient but New Zion's is eternal (cf. II Cor. 4:16—5:5). Once again Isaiah puts New Zion's future glory in terminology comprehensible to ancient Zion (agricultural terms).

New Zion will enjoy the constant presence of the Lord. She "eats and drinks" at the Lord's Table. She has been invited to a feast (see Isa. 25:6-12 and Special Study, *RSVP, Come To the Feast*).

QUIZ

1. Who are the watchmen in New Zion?
2. What is their function?
3. What should New Zion be constantly in prayer for?
4. Why can New Zion's inheritance not be plundered?

3. NEW NATURE

TEXT: 62:10-12

10 Go through, go through the gates; prepare ye the way of the people; cast up, cast up the highway; gather out the stones;

lift up an ensign for the peoples.
11 Behold, Jehovah hath proclaimed unto the end of the earth, Say ye to the daughter of Zion, Behold, thy salvation cometh; behold his reward is with him, and his recompense before him.
12 And they shall call them The holy people, The redeemed of Jehovah: and thou shalt be called Sought out, A city not forsaken.

QUERIES

a. What is an "ensign"?
b. When were they called "The holy people"?

PARAPHRASE

Zion you must get out of the middle of heathenism, separate yourself once and for all from such a life, and build your highway toward the City of God as He is preparing it for you. Your mission is to become, as it were, a flag or signal toward which people from all over the earth may be drawn to find God. Listen, this is what Jehovah has announced to the whole world; Zion, your salvation is surely coming, and all the blessings and judgments promised in connection with that salvation are coming also. When this great salvation comes Zion's citizens will be acknowledged as holy, separated unto the Holy God, purchased by Jehovah. Zion will at last be what she was intended to be, Sought Out, A City Not Forsaken.

COMMENTS

v. 10-11 SEPARATED: The admonition to Judah here is that she prepare to separate herself from paganism in order that she may become the remnant through which Jehovah will build

New Zion (the redeemed messianic church). Judah will soon go into captivity. There she will be surrounded by the idolatry and carnality with which she is so enamored in her own land. It will be a great temptation to all of the Jews to compromise the truth of God's revelation and take up with paganism to the extent that when the time comes to return to Palestine and restore the Jewish commonwealth they will all decide to remain in Babylon (see our comments 48:20-22). These verses are similar to 40:3-4 and 57:14.

God had placed the Hebrew people in Palestine so they might be a sign and witness to all the heathen world around them of the Only Righteous, Omnipotent, True God (cf. Ex. 19:5-6; Ezek. 5:5ff). Israel was to be *masas* (*ensign*) or standard, flag, banner, sign, token, by which the world was to be attracted to her God. But she "showed pirate colors"—she demonstrated more paganism than the pagans (Ezek. 5:5ff; Jer. 18:13, etc.).

Now the Lord is calling her back to her divine mission and predicting that there will be a remnant who will choose to fulfill this mission and eventually form New Zion (the church) which will draw people from all nations to her.

Jehovah will accomplish Zion's redemption. He will pay the price. He will conquer her most powerful enemies, sin and death (in the Messiah). But Zion must exercise her will and accept that salvation by faith, repentance and obedience to the covenant terms. Repentance and faith requires an obedient turning away from sin, separating oneself deliberately and willingly from all that God prohibits and living deliberately and willingly what God commands. Covenant terms for New Zion involves obedience in baptism (immersion in water), Acts 2:38; 8:12-13; 8:38-39; 10:47; 16:15; 16:33; 18:8; 22:16; Rom. 6:1-6; Gal. 3:26-27; Col. 2:12; I Pet. 3:21, etc.). Zion is also to announce to the world the proclamation that God has accomplished salvation. With acceptance of God's proffered salvation comes the rewards of all spiritual blessings in the heavenly places (Eph. 1:3; 2:6). With rejection of God's proffered salvation comes the recompense of judgment (cf. II Thess. 1:8-9).

v. 12 SANCTIFIED: When Zion separates itself from paganism and accepts the Lord's salvation, she shall be acknowledged as *holy.* It will be apparent to the whole world that she is dedicated, set-apart, and belongs to the Lord of Glory, author of Life and Righteousness. This is what the church of Christ is for—a testimony of the Holy God. She is to fulfill what God intended for Israel (Ex. 19:6). The world is to acknowledge that members of New Zion consider themselves *purchased* (redeemed) by Almighty God. Zion is to testify that her citizenship is in heaven and that she has no abiding place here—she is a city of sojourners whose destiny is the Eternal Jerusalem where God dwells forever and ever.

QUIZ

1. Why is Zion admonished to "go through the gates"? What gates?
2. What must Zion do concerning the salvation offered by Jehovah?
3. What will the New Zion fulfill that Old Zion did not?

D. RESTLESSNESS OF ZION, CHAPTERS 63 - 64

1. PREDICTED VINDICATION

TEXT: 63:1-9

1 Who is this that cometh from Edom, with dyed garments from Bozrah? this that is glorious in his apparel, marching in the greatness of his strength? I that speak in righteousness, mighty to save.
2 Wherefore art thou red in thine apparel, and thy garments like him that treadeth in the winevat?
3 I have trodden the winepress alone; and of the peoples there was no man with me: yea, I trod them in mine anger, and

trampled them in my wrath; and their lifeblood is sprinkled upon my garments, and I have stained all my raiment.
4 For the day of vengeance was in my heart, and the year of my redeemed is come.
5 And I looked, and there was none to help; and I wondered that there was none to uphold: therefore mine own arm brought salvation unto me; and my wrath, it upheld me.
6 And I trod down the peoples in mine anger, and made them drunk in my wrath, and I poured out their lifeblood on the earth.
7 I will make mention of the lovingkindnesses of Jehovah, and the praises of Jehovah according to all that Jehovah hath bestowed on us, and the great goodness toward the house of Israel, which he hath bestowed on them according to his mercies, and according to the multitude of his lovingkindnesses.
8 For he said, Surely, they are my people, children that will not deal falsely: so he was their Saviour.
9 In all their affliction he was afflicted, and the angel of his presence saved them: in his love and in his pity he redeemed them; and he bare them, and carried them all the days of old.

QUERIES

a. Who is the one "who speaks in righteousness"?
b. What is the "year of my redeemed"?
c. Who is the "angel of his presence"?

PARAPHRASE

Who is this majestic figure I see approaching Zion from the direction of Edom. He has on royal robes and strides along in a grand and stately march. He answers, I am the One who vindicates Zion, the One who is Zion's Saviour. But why are your robes stained all over with red as if you had been tramping grapes in the winevat? He answers, There was no one capable or willing anywhere to do what I have done so I have had to do this mission all by myself. What I have been doing is enforcing My threats of wrath and anger by utterly destroying the enemies of My people. That is the blood of My enemies staining My garments! I have done this because the allotted time for punishment to be meted out has reached its fulfillment in My divine program of redemption. When this time came, I looked for someone to join with Me in this work of judgment but there was no one and I was disturbed. So I did the work of destroying the enemy alone. When I executed My anger upon My enemies, I made them reel and stagger with the destruction. The cup of their wrath which they made others drink, I filled up with My wrath and made them drink until they died of it.

In all of this judgment upon Zion's enemies the compassion of Jehovah is manifest toward Israel and I will therefore praise Him and proclaim His lovingkindness with all that is within me. It is also evident in this great deliverance through judgment that Jehovah has saved Zion to make of her a people who will not deal falsely but will be righteous and just. God Himself experienced affliction when His people were afflicted and so He sent Himself to save His people. Personally affected as He was by His love and compassion for them, He personally entered into the salvation and redemption of His people all the years of their past history and He will take a personal hand in their future salvation and redemption.

COMMENTS

v. 1-6 CONQUEST: The prophet sees "Someone" coming from the direction of Edom (southeast of the Dead Sea) with "dyed" garments. The Hebrew word is *khamutz* and means, *highly colored,* indicating royalty or affluence. The remainder of verse one indicates the approaching One is majestically divine since He is One that "announces vindication" (*davver tzedakah* in Hebrew) and is "mighty to save." Later, the prophet praises Jehovah for His lovingkindnesses as expressed in the judgments upon Zion's enemies. The unrecognizable figure coming from Edom is Jehovah. Bozrah was the ancient capital of Edom. For a discussion of Edom and its relation to the Israelites, read our comments in *Minor Prophets,* pub. College Press, pg. 117-118. The Edomites were inveterate enemies of Israel. They rejoiced with spite-filled hearts at any misfortune befalling the Jews. Edom participated in every opportunity that came their way to plunder Jerusalem and Judah, selling Jewish captives into slavery and killing them unmercifully (cf. Obadiah 1-14; Isa. 34:5-15; Ezek. 35:1-15). Many of the prophets predicted the judgment of God upon the Edomites. Edom is often mentioned as typical or representative of *all* the ungodly powers that oppose Jehovah's redemptive work through Israel. We believe that is the case here also. The picture here is of Jehovah's judgment of all that opposes His messianic program.

The Hebrew word *'adom* is translated *red* and is the same word we apparently translate *man* and *Edom.* The garments of the One approaching are splattered with *red* like a man who has just come from tramping in the winevat and has splattered red grape juice all over his clothing. This red is the "lifeblood" of his enemies (cf. v. 3). A similar picture is painted by John the apostle as he portrays the judgment of God upon the Roman empire in Revelation 19:13.

Lest someone get the idea that Edom's downfall (and that of any other nation for that matter) is a matter of chance, or that it might have been averted if other circumstances had fallen just right, Jehovah emphasizes that He *alone* brought it about. The One approaching (the Lord) had trodden the "winepress" alone. He had no assistance, not only because no one else would be adequate for the task, but also because He needed no one else! The emphasis of this whole passage is that Jehovah is *personally* involved in and responsible for the deliverance, salvation and redemption of Zion—even to the destruction of her enemies. In a prior statement (Isa. 59:16) the Lord emphasizes the same ideas. The Lord has everything needful for Zion's messianic destiny exactly scheduled in history and He carries it out according to His own righteous pleasure. The "day" of His vengeance was in His own heart and the "year" of His "redeemed" comes precisely according to His timetable, (cf. Isa. 61:1). The Lord sets times and seasons (Dan. 2:20-23); He deposes and sets up kings and kingdoms to fit His own plans (Dan. 5:18-21); He has a definite time schedule for the messianic nation to bring forth the Messiah (see comments Dan. 9:24-27). He has the power in His own "arm" to bring salvation to His people and needs no other assistance (cf. Isa. 40:10; 51:5; 52:10; 53:1 for comments on "arm"). The Lord made His enemies *drunk* with His wrath. This is a figure of speech indicating two ideas. First, His enemies have caused the Jews to "drink" their cup of wrath in plunder and slavery; Jehovah will recompense these enemies with His own cup of wrath filled to the brim. God is not mocked; whatever a nation sows, that shall it reap, double! Second, when Jehovah's enemies are made to drink His cup of wrath, they will stagger and reel under it as drunken men reel (cf. Isa. 29:9; 49:26; Rev. 17:6; 18:3-7, etc.). God's wrath is *perfect;* it is complete and lacks nothing.

v. 7-9 CELEBRATION: Zion, through the prophet Isaiah, is led to rejoice in Jehovah's judgment of her enemies. It is not sadistic for those who love righteousness to praise God when He judges and defeats evil. The Bible insists that an Omnipotent, Absolutely Holy and Just God must, by His very nature, ultimately uphold and give complete victory to truth, holiness and justice. He must, on the other hand, bring about complete defeat and incarceration of evil. That is why He made Hell! God intends to accomplish those objectives through two means. First, He will make available an opportunity and a way for all human beings, who so choose, to be declared righteous (by Jesus' blood) and to grow into the image of His own righteous nature (through faith and obedience to His revealed New Covenant). These, He will save and give Life everlasting. Second, He creates an everlasting penitentiary (Hell) where He will ultimately defeat and imprison all those who choose against His will and desire to live in rebellion against Him. Now a part of recreating in His own righteous image those who choose that Life by surrender to His will is that they shall also hate evil and love good (cf. Isa. 1:16-17; Prov. 8:13; Amos 5:15). Heaven and the saints are told to rejoice over the fact that God destroyed the "harlot," "Babylon" (the city of Rome and the Roman empire) with blood, war, pestilence, fire, destruction and torments (cf. Rev. 17-18, esp. Rev. 18:20 and 19:1-8)! A person who cannot hate evil, cannot love good! The uniqueness of Jesus' fleshly nature was that as a man He "loved righteousness and hated lawlessness" (Heb. 1:9) and thus was the Perfect Man!

Thus in these verses it is a mark of the righteousness and godliness of Zion that she praise God and speak of His lovingkindnesses in response to His wreaking vengeance upon those who despise Him, rebel against Him and oppress His people. He vindicates His holiness, He upholds His absolute justness and He delivers His people and vindicates their faith in Him. If He cannot thus vindicate man's faith in His absolute holiness and justice and righteousness, then His faithfulness is compromised and there is no hope in worshipping Him as opposed to any other god!

God is true! Those who wish to be known as His children must be true. They must rejoice at the defeat of evil and the establishment of righteousness because this is the absolute truth. Those who oppose good and rejoice in evil cannot be His children because that is the ultimate falsehood. In addition, His sons will act upon their choice and *do* righteousness. Those who claim to be His children will not deal falsely. A citizen of Zion cannot *say* he stands for righteousness and *refuse to do* it. That is falseness (cf. I Jn. 2:3-6; 3:4-10). God cannot save the declared rebel and He cannot save the pretending servant; the pretender is as much a rebel as the declared one!

There is a difficult problem with the opening phrase of verse nine. The modern, vowel-pointed Hebrew text reads, *bekal-tzaratham l'o tzar,* or, "In all their affliction he was *not* afflicted." The ancient Hebrew text was strictly consonantal (without vowel-points). There is a consonantal text known as *Kethiv,* or, "written" which acquired a standing of sacredness and prohibited any scribe from tampering with it. It could not be changed. But the Massoretes (cir. 950 A.D.), a group of Hebrew scholars, produced a text which preserved traditional readings in variance with the "sacred" *Kethiv;* this was called *Qere,* or, "to be read." The *Qere* was a text with the "traditional" variant consonants out in the margin. Because the vowels, being added later, did not have the sacredness of the consonants, the Massoretes felt it was proper to put the vowels for the marginal consonants (*Qere*) with the old consonants in the text (that is, with the *Kethiv*). This, of course, resulted in some impossible forms. The problem in verse nine is that the Kethiv text has *l'o* while the Qere text has *lo.* Young advocates the adoption of the *Qere* reading which would make the phrase read, "In all their affliction, there *was* affliction to him." Keil and Delitzsch say, "The Masora actually does reckon this as one of the fifteen passages in which *lo* is to be read for *l'o.*" The *Qere* reading of *lo* certainly fits the context better and suits the concept already expressed concerning the suffering Servant (cf. Isa. 53:4-6; 53:10-11). The context indicates that when His people suffered affliction from their oppressors, God Himself felt that affliction and acted in judgment. That is no strange teaching in the Bible. The experiences of Hosea were indicative of the feelings God experienced toward a nation of people who had spurned His love (cf. Hos. 1:2-3; 3:1; 11:1-4, etc.). Our God feels—He is not a robot or a stoic, impassive, insensitive Idea. Jesus proved God feels (cf. Jn. 11:33-35).

Another interesting phrase in verse nine is, "and the angel of his presence saved them . . ." The Hebrew word translated *presence* is *panaym* which means literally, *face* or *person.* The word *male'k* is *angel* and means *messenger.* God promised to send the *messenger* of His *face* or *person* to His people (Ex. 23:20-23) and actually did send to them this messenger (Ex. 14:19; Num. 20:16). He is the Lord's messenger (Ex. 33:14, 15) and is actually the Lord Jehovah Himself (Ex. 33:12). Keil and Delitzsch say, "This mediatorial angel is called 'the angel of His face,' as being the representative of God, for 'the face of God' is His self-revealing presence (even though only revealed to the mental eye); and consequently the presence of God . . . is called directly 'His face' in Deut. 4:37 . . . and 'my face' in Ex. 33:14-15, by the side of 'my angel' in Ex. 32:34, and the angel in Ex. 33:2, appears as something incomparably higher than the presence of God through the mediation of that one angel . . ." Young says, "The angel of His face is the angel who is His face or in whom His face is made clear. In him the Lord is Himself present." When the Lord said He would send His angel to slay 185,000 Assyrian soldiers (Isa. 37:36) it is reported that the Lord Himself did the deed (cf. Isa. 10:12; Isa. 10:33-34).

The next section (63:10-14) indicates the judgments over Zion's enemies here declared (63:1-9) were past judgments upon which Zion might base her trust in Jehovah for deliverance from the Babylonian captivity which was apparently inescapable as Isaiah was writing these words. But, as the next section indicates, Zion is having difficulty believing that Jehovah will work for her deliverance as He did in days gone by.

QUIZ

1. Why is the One appearing to Isaiah's vision coming from Edom?
2. What could be a different translation of the word "righteousness" in verse one?
3. Why does this One coming have "red" on his garments?
4. Why stress that this One has trodden the winevat alone?
5. Is it proper for Zion to speak of God's lovingkindness in connection with judgment and vengeance?
6. How is God afflicted when His people are afflicted?
7. What is the relation of this angel to Jehovah?

2. PRAYER FOR VICTORY

TEXT: 63:10-14

10 But they rebelled, and grieved his holy Spirit: therefore he was turned to be their enemy, and himself fought against them.
11 Then he remembered the days of old, Moses and his people, saying, Where is he that brought them up out of the sea with the shepherds of his flock? where is he that put his holy Spirit in the midst of them?
12 that caused his glorious arm to go at the right hand of Moses? that divided the waters before them, to make himself an everlasting name?
13 that led them through the depths, as a horse in the wilderness, so that they stumbled not?
14 As the cattle that go down into the valley, the Spirit of Jehovah caused them to rest; so didst thou lead thy people, to make thyself a glorious name.

QUERIES

a. Upon whom did Jehovah turn to be an enemy?
b. Who remembered the days of old?
c. When did they "rest"?

PARAPHRASE

In spite of all the times God vindicated His people by saving them from their enemies in past times, they have grieved His Holy Spirit by rebelling against His commandments. Because of their rebellion He had to become their enemy and must now fight against them. Now they are remembering those days gone by when Moses delivered God's people and they are crying out, Where is the One who brought our ancestors through the Red Sea with shepherds like Moses? Where is the One who put His Holy Spirit within them? They are also saying, Where is the One whose glorious power parted the Red Sea in the path of our ancestors and vindicated His name forever when Moses lifted up his rod? Where is the One who guided them through the bottom of the Sea? Like horses galloping easily through a desert cleared of all obstacles, our ancestors never slipped or stumbled walking through that Sea's rocky bottom. Just like cattle that go easily and safely down to graze in the wadis, the Spirit of Jehovah gave our ancestors rest. That is the way You led our ancestors, Lord, and Your name then was made glorious. Where are you now, Lord?

COMMENTS

v. 10 RESISTING HIS SPIRIT: Although the Lord has given the prophet a vision of His power and faithfulness to destroy Zion's enemies and uphold her when she trusts Him (63:1-9), Zion seems bent on not believing and acting upon it (63:10-14). Therefore the Lord is going to give Zion over to humiliation, destruction and captivity (63:15-19).

The Hebrew word *maru* is translated *rebel* and is the strongest word for that circumstance, meaning literally, *to revolt.* Their revolt *pained* or *sorrowed* the Holy Spirit; in Hebrew *'itzevu 'eth-ruach kadesho.* In Ex. 23:20-21 Jehovah said to the people, "Behold, I send an angel before you, to guard you on the way and to bring you to the place which I have prepared. Give heed to him and hearken to his voice, do not rebel against him, for he will not pardon your transgression; for my name is in him." However, the people rebelled from the time they left Egypt (Ex. 17:1ff; 32:1ff), and they continued their rebellion until God finally took them out of their land and into captivity. The third Person of the Godhead was actively involved in the program of redemption in the Old Testament (see Special Study, "The Holy Spirit In Old Testament Times," pages 458-462). Young sees in this chapter all three Persons of the Godhead: "Thus, . . . there is a distinction of the three persons of the Triune God: He (Yahweh), the angel of His presence and the Spirit of His holiness. In the history of the chosen people each Person of the Trinity was active." The point of this verse (10) is that the people whom Jehovah chose to co-operate with Him in redeeming the whole world forced Him to be their enemy because they revolted and afflicted His Holy Spirit. Jehovah is against them because they are against Him. He must vindicate His holiness and justice now upon the chosen people. He is giving them up to chastening in Mesopotamia for 70 years. The writer of the Hebrew epistle in the N.T. exhorts, ". . . do not harden your hearts as in the rebellion" (Heb. 3:7-19). The Lord had to turn from being "afflicted with their affliction," to "fighting against them" because that was what He said He would do if they rebelled against Him. The Lord keeps His promises!

v. 11-13 REMEMBERING HIS SPIRIT: The subject of "remembered" could be either Jehovah or Zion. It appears Zion would fit the context better. With the downfall of Jerusalem and the Babylonian captivity imminent, Zion (the people of Judah) is *remembering* (and evidently praying for a return of) the Holy Spirit of God in power and deliverance as He did through Moses at the crossing of the Red Sea. If the Holy Spirit of God could part the waters of the Red Sea, can He not now deliver them from Babylon? The phrase, "where is he that put his holy Spirit in the midst of them?" is interesting and perhaps should give us pause to rethink our concept of the activity of the Holy Spirit in the Old Testament age. The Hebrew word *kerev* is translated midst; the usual word for midst is *tok. Kerev* is unique and means *inward part, inwards, bowels;* hence, *the heart. Kerev* is the word in I Kings 17:22 where "the soul of the child came *into him* again." Did God's Spirit indwell the believer of the O.T.? Could it be that God put His Holy Spirit in the hearts of the people as He was leading them in the exodus from Egypt—and there they grieved Him? One N.T. passage appears to preclude the possibility of the Spirit dwelling in believers of the O.T. age. John notes, "But this spake he of the Spirit, which they that believed on him were to receive; for the Spirit was not yet given; because Jesus was not yet glorified" (Jn. 7:39). Note, however, the word *given* (in Jn. 7:39) is a supplied word—it is not in the Greek text. Does this indicate that the Spirit was not yet for *everyone* who believes (including Gentiles)? or does it mean that the Spirit was *not yet given at all* (not even for Jews) until after Jesus was glorified? The latter has been the traditional interpretation. If the latter interpretation is to be followed, what is one to do with the apostle Paul's clear statement that, ". . . if any man hath not the Spirit of Christ, he is none of his . . ." and, ". . . if the Spirit of him that raised up Jesus from the dead dwelleth in you, he that raised up Christ Jesus from the dead shall give life also to your mortal bodies through the Spirit that dwelleth in you" (Rom. 8:9-11)? If eternal life and resurrection from the dead necessitates the Spirit of God dwelling in man, and if the Spirit was *not* given at all until Christ was glorified, how do we account for the eternal life apparently granted to Abraham, Isaac and Jacob (Mt. 8:11; Lk. 13:28; 16:23, etc.). How could Abraham be justified by faith without receiving the Spirit of God also by faith (Rom. 4:2-9; Gal. 3:6-7; Jas. 2:23)? How could the beggar be borne to Abraham's bosom if the beggar did not have the Spirit of God (Lk. 16:22)? How could Moses and Elijah be transfigured with Christ in glorified appearance without having the Spirit of God (Mt. 17:1-5; Lk. 9:30-31, etc.)?

The only resolution of this dilemma appears to be to recognize that the Spirit of God was certainly *in* men of the Old Testament (Enoch, Abraham, Moses, Elijah, David and the prophets, cf. Num. 27:18; Psa. 51:11; 143:10, etc.). Rotherham says on Psa. 51:11, "David . . . had enjoyed the presence of the Holy Spirit, or he could not have prayed, *Take it not from me.* Was that Spirit, not hallowing, as well as illuminating and revealing? Can we really enter into the undercurrent of this psalm, without perceiving that a hallowing Divine *Presence* had lain at the roots of the writer's spiritual life; . . . By how much soever this is clear, by so much also must it be clear that the Evangelist (John) spoke *comparatively* when he said (Jn. 7:39) that the Spirit could not be given until Jesus was glorified." (*Studies In The Psalms, Vol. I,* by J. B. Rotherham, pub. College Press, pg. 352).

B. B. Warfield in his *Biblical and Theological Studies,* (pub. The Presbyterian and Reformed Publishing Co., 1952), says, "The Spirit of God, in the Old Testament, is not merely the immanent Spirit, the source of all the world's life and all the world's movement . . . . He is as well the indwelling Spirit of holiness in the hearts of God's children."

We submit that the message of the Messiah was therefore, that the Spirit of God was *not* come *in His fulness* until Jesus was glorified and redemption was completed. After the redemptive work of God was completed through the Son, the indwelling presence of the Spirit would give man a greater, more strengthening participation in the inheritance God had stored up for believers. The New Covenant is certainly better, far surpassing and the fulfillment of the Old. The New is enacted upon better promises. But it would seem to us that the Spirit of God was in those saints of old who were justified and thus given eternal life (historically accomplished at the death of Christ, Heb. 9:15-17; Rom. 3:21-26), which they appropriated by faith. Perhaps it was a matter of "good, better and best" as pictured in the following chart. Or, perhaps the Spirit of God was given to the O.T. saints "on credit" or "retroactively" to guarantee their resurrection to eternal life much as their forgiveness was "on credit" (cf. Heb. 9:15). One thing is certain, having the Spirit of God is necessary to being raised from the dead!

Be that as it may, the point of this passage is to portray the frustration of the people over the impending captivity. It appears to them as if God's Spirit has deserted them and that God Himself does not care that His name will be debased if He does not save them as He saved their ancestors. He led their ancestors across the bed of the Red Sea as easily and swiftly as a horse runs through a desert where all the obstacles have been removed. Why does He not do that now?

Was not The Spirit of God in the saints of old
in order to keep them from eternal death? (Rom. 8:9-11)

YES

Perhaps in lesser degree of companionship.

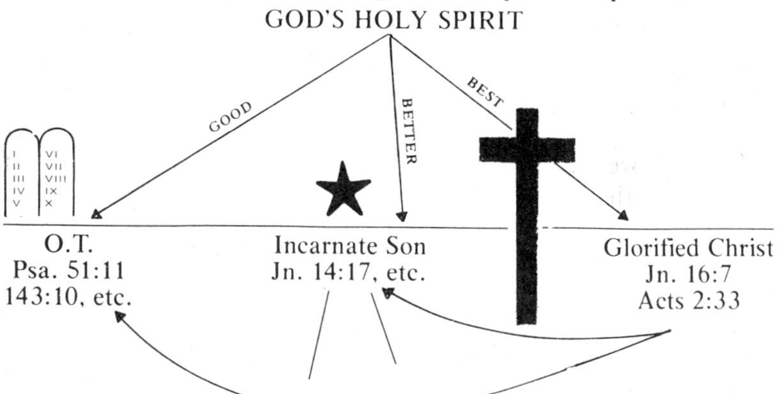

Or, perhaps the Holy Spirit was theirs in promise before
Jesus was glorified and theirs in fact, retroactively,
after His glorification (like forgiveness, Heb. 9:15f).

v. 14 Resting In His Spirit: The people remember that their ancestors were led by the Spirit of God into the land of Canaan like contented cattle are led securely and easily down into the wadis to graze. The Spirit of God was the *cause* of their *nukh* ("rest, settling down, having repose, abiding") in Canaan. Now they are wondering why He cannot cause them to remain in their land. Could it be that their prayer is not really a penitent prayer but a selfish one? Could it be that they want Jehovah to deliver them *in* their rebellion and not *from* it—as so many of us are prone to want to be saved in sin and not from it? On the other hand, perhaps this is a prediction of the prayers of penitence the people will offer down in Babylon when they have had time to consider their sins and truly repent. Perhaps this is prophecy! When they have truly repented (cf. Dan. 9:3-19) God will hear their prayer (Dan. 9:20-23) and return them to their land to fulfill their messianic destiny (Dan. 9:24-27).

QUIZ

1. When did God's people rebel? How long?
2. Did God put His Holy Spirit in people in the Old Testament?
3. Have you thought through the teaching of the Bible on the Holy Spirit as thoroughly as you would like? (We suggest C. C. Crawford's two-volume work entitled, *The Eternal Spirit, His Word and Works,* pub. by College Press.)
4. Do you think the prayer of the people here is a penitent prayer?

3. PETITION OF VICTIMS

TEXT: 63:15-19

15 Look down from heaven, and behold from the habitation of thy holiness and of thy glory: where are thy zeal and thy mighty acts? the yearning of thy heart and thy compassions are restrained toward me.
16 For thou art our Father, though Abraham knoweth us not, and Israel doth not acknowledge us: thou, O Jehovah, art our Father; our Redeemer from everlasting is thy name.
17 O Jehovah, why dost thou make us to err from thy ways, and hardenest our heart from thy fear? Return for thy servants' sake, the tribes of thine inheritance.
18 Thy holy people possessed it but a little while: our adversaries have trodden down thy sanctuary.
19 We are become as they over whom thou never barest rule, as they that were not called by thy name.

QUERIES

a. Why did they think they had to call upon God to "look"?
b. Why does Abraham not know the nation?
c. What time reference is involved in verse 18?

PARAPHRASE

Lord, where have You gone? Lord, are You oblivious to our predicament? Look down from where You sit on Your transcendently glorious and holy throne and give attention to our situation. Where is all the eagerness and power You used to show us now? Apparently You are deliberately keeping Your love and pity from us! You are the only Father we have with enough power to save us from the impending captivity. Yes, Abraham and Jacob were our earthly fathers, but they are not able to redeem us or save us; You, Jehovah, are our only Everlasting Father. Why have You disowned us? Why have you prevented us from wandering away from You and prevented us from hardening our hearts toward You? Come back, Lord, for the sake of those who serve You and help us, for we are the people of Your possession. We, your holy people, have possessed the land so briefly; our enemies are making us a dispossessed and dispersed people by taking over Your land. Lord, You are treating us as if You had never been our Sovereign and as if we had never been Your people.

COMMENTS

v. 15-17 DISOWNED: The Hebrew word *shamayim* is plural for *shamah* which means *high, heavenward, height.* The word is always in the plural form in the O.T. God most often manifested Himself from the direction of the sky in the O.T. and the Hebrew thought of the sky (or beyond) as the place of Jehovah's habitation. Actually, due to the limitations of human language (which is limited by human experience) designating the *heavens* as God's habitation is about as accurate as any man can be. The point seems to be that these people feel Jehovah is so utterly transcendent, dwelling in such absolute holiness (separation from this world) He is disowning His creatures. The petition is that He will look down from His high and lofty place and give attention to their predicament.

Based upon the historical record of Jehovah's dealings with their ancestors (Genesis, Exodus, et al.) He was eager, zealous and arduous in delivering, guiding and sustaining their nation in centuries past. But suddenly, it appears, Jehovah has deliberately *restrained* (withdrawn) His zeal for their nation. It is their assumption that Jehovah does not even care about them anymore. How could they get that idea? Jehovah repeatedly told them of His love and care through the prophets. But their accusation that Jehovah was deliberately insensitive to their needs was based upon their carnal concept of what their need was and their carnal ideas as to how God should act toward them. They believed their imperative need was to be delivered from those who would take them into captivity. They believed God should act in supernatural, judgmental power *now* upon their enemies as He had done in the past. Man has always had the tendency (ever since the devil taught him in Eden to do so) to blame God, or someone else, for the consequences of his own faults and failures. Judah has been indulging in false religion which induces false ethics which results in social disintegration; she has been playing the dangerous game of international intrigue and politics which results in war and invasion; now she is blaming God for her predicament. Judah suggests that Jehovah has defaulted on His Fatherhood! Acknowledging that He is the only Father capable of saving their necks, the implication is that He is unwilling now to act as their Father. He has disowned them! There is no disavowal of their ancestry to Abraham and Jacob here—the point is the contrast between human fathers and Supernatural Father. An emergency has arisen and now they need their heavenly Father; they did not seek Him before (cf. Isa. 8:19-22; 30:9-11; 58:2-5; 59:1-3, etc.). The Hebrew word *tate'enu* is from the *Hife'iyl* stem which denotes causative manner and is thus translated *make us to err* in verse 17. Certainly God does not *force* man to sin. God does not even cause man to sin in the sense that He makes man's choice for him. Of course, man very often *accuses* God of making him sin, or being the cause of his sin. That is the way of rebellion, dishonesty, lawlessness and devil-mindedness! Man may be even more subtle (as we have given it in our paraphrase) and blame God for *not preventing* him from sinning! It is the old cliche, "If God is a good God, why does He permit evil to happen?" The Lord tried every way possible consistent with the free will of man to keep man from wandering into rebellion and lawlessness. Judah, by the use of the *hife'iyl* stem, has betrayed her moral dishonesty in trying to blame God for her wandering and hardening of heart against Him. In one sense of the word God must, by the fact of man's freedom to choose, allow man to either choose that which will soften his heart and bring him to walk in God's way, or, choose that which will harden his heart and lead him to wander away from God's way. But God will also make the ultimate sacrifices to furnish man with every opportunity to make the right choice; He will send His Spirit in His word through the prophets, leaders and kings; and finally in His Son He will Himself atone and offer a New covenant.

God has not disowned His people. He is about to demonstrate, through the captivity, just how much He owns them. The child who is not chastened has no real father (cf. Heb. 12:1-11). So, our Father-child relationship to God depends upon our perspective. These people of Judah could not look upon their impending captivity as the chastening of a loving Father (which is what it was revealed to be by Hosea, Isaiah and others). They looked at it through carnal eyes, not eyes of faith. Looking thus, they charged God with desertion!

v. 18-19 DISPOSSESSED: In these two verses the people are dangerously near impuning the honor of the Lord. They complain that although God gave them the land of Palestine and built them a Temple, they had lived in it only a brief time (from appoximately 1400 B.C. to 600 B.C.) and now it was about to be invaded by enemies and they would be dispossessed. So the Lord appears to them unable to maintain His people in His land and keep His Sanctuary standing. The time in which the Lord maintained His people in His land by His sovereign power was so relatively short (800 years), it hardly seems worthy of calling it a "rule." The length of time in which the Hebrews were called "the people of Jehovah" seems so short it is as if they were never His people at all. They are saying, in essence, Lord if Your name is ridiculed because of our being taken from our land, it is your fault. Their attitude is if God does not help them *now* and on their terms, He cannot blame anyone but Himself. How often all men are tempted to evaluate their circumstances through the dying eyes of carnal-mindedness and blame God for them. May it not be so in New Zion!

QUIZ

1. Where did the Hebrews believe God dwelt?
2. Is there a better location to suppose God abides?
3. Why do these people think God has disowned them?
4. Why are they now calling on Him to act like a Father when they did not before?
5. Does God *make* men err?
6. Can God demonstrate in their captivity that He is their Father? How?
7. What seems to be their accusation against God in verses 18 and 19?

SPECIAL STUDY

THE HOLY SPIRIT IN OLD TESTAMENT TIMES

by Ron Fisher
Great Lakes Bible College

INTRODUCTION:

There is a wealth of teaching in the Bible with respect to the person and work of the Holy Spirit. He is said to do what only persons can do. He can speak, teach, search, reveal, lead, and forbid (I Tim. 4:1; John 14:26; I Cor. 2:10; Acts 16:6, 7). He has the faculties of a person-mind, knowledge, affection, and will (Rom. 8:27; I Cor. 2:11; Rom. 15:30; I Cor. 12:11). He is shown to have the attributes of God. He is eternal (Heb. 9:14). He knows what God knows (I Cor. 2:10, 11). He exerts God's power (Luke 1:35). He is everywhere present as God is (Psalms 139:7-10). He is the Spirit of holiness (Rom. 1:4). We have every right to conclude, therefore, that a Bible study of the Holy Spirit is most valuable and essential.

A. THE HOLY SPIRIT WORKED THE WORKS OF GOD IN OLD TESTAMENT TIMES.

1. He was present and active in the creation of the universe (Gen. 1:2).
2. He shared in creating man in the Godhead's image (Gen. 1:26; Job 33:4).
3. He exerted power as from God (Judges 14:6; Mic. 3:8).
4. He convicted men of sin and tried to turn them back to God (Gen. 6:3).
5. He cooperated in confounding arrogant men at the tower of Babel (Gen. 11:7).

B. THE HOLY SPIRIT EMPOWERED AND GUIDED GOD'S LEADERS.

1. During the very unsettled times covered by the book of Judges, God gave assistance to several judges with the presence of His Spirit.
   a. God sent His Spirit upon Gideon, encouraging him to rally the tribes of Israel against the Midianites and the Amalekites (Judges 6:33-35).
   b. God's Spirit enabled Jephthah to defeat the sons of Ammon (Judges 11:29-33).
   c. God's Spirit empowered Samson to slay a lion and to slay thirty men (Judges 14:6, 19).
   d. God's spirit was strong in Samson to prepare him to slay 1,000 Philistines (Judges 15:14).
2. Though Jehovah did not want Israel to have a king, when

granting them their wish, He assisted Saul and David by bestowing His Spirit upon them.

a. When Saul was anointed by Samuel as Israel's first king, the Spirit came upon him to lead him in prophesying (I Sam. 10:1, 6, 10).

b. Once Saul was rejected by Jehovah, David was selected as Saul's successor. As the Spirit came upon David, He deserted Saul (I Sam. 16:12-14).

3. The Holy Spirit's most extensive work of all in Old Testament times is found with respect to God's prophets.

a. Moses expressed the selfless, open-hearted wish that all of God's people could be prophets under the guidance of His Spirit (Num. 11:29).

b. When one understands the Old Testament's concept that the prophet must speak for and represent God to man exactly (Ex. 7:1, 2), he can see the necessity of man's being guided by the Spirit to be qualified as a prophet.

c. In Nehemiah's day, the Israelites stood a fourth of a day confessing their sins. Then they were admonished by Levites to recall the bountiful blessings God had showered upon their ancestors. Among these was the Spirit's instruction of them through the prophets (Neh. 9:20, 30). Sadly, most of the nation would not give heed to the prophetic words spoken.

d. Zechariah observes how the people had hardened their hearts against the former prophets, even though the Spirit revealed Jehovah's law and words through them (Zech. 7:12). Jehovah promised not to listen to them just as they had not listened to Him.

e. The most effective summary of Old Testament prophecy is found in the New Testament: II Peter 1:20, 21. There it is declared that no prophecy of Scripture originates from human will. Rather prophets spoke as they were guided by the Spirit of God.

4. Though there are over 300 references to priests in the Old Testament, there is not one example of the Holy Spirit's

presence to guide them. This is probably best explained by the fact that their duties, mode of dress, and style of life were set down by divine revelation. Their obligation was to obey what God had already told them to do.

C. THE HOLY SPIRIT ASSISTED SECONDARY LEADERS.

1. The leaders previously mentioned furnish illustrations of the major human leadership God provided and equipped for Israel.
2. There was also a back-up or assisting leadership which God prepared with Holy Spirit guidance.
3. During Moses' career of directing people of Israel over a period of 40 years of wandering, God commanded him to select 70 elders from among the population to act as his religious and civil assistants. This would lighten his burden of trying to deal fairly and adequately with almost three million people. God placed His Spirit upon these men, once they were chosen (Num. 11:16, 17, 25).
4. Joshua took Moses' place and led out to conquer Palestine for Israel and to settle the tribes in their new-found home. God had placed His Spirit within Joshua and asked Moses to ordain him to his task by the laying on of hands (Num. 28:17).
5. God endued Bezalel and Oholiab with His Spirit so as to make them skilled tradesmen, fitted to prepare all the artistic designs and accompanying furniture of the Tabernacle. They exhibited superior skills which were worthy of God's "house of worship" (Ex. 31:1-11).

D. THE HOLY SPIRIT STRESSED THAT DEPENDENCE UPON HIM IS THE ONE WAY TO GOD'S VICTORY.

1. Through Isaiah Jehovah chastised the nation of Judah for making its own plans, not accepting His; for making alliances with Egypt and not with His Spirit (Isa. 30:1, 2). See also Isa. 31:1-3. They were adding sin to sin. Their foul attitude is dramatized by the fact that they were refusing to listen to God's instruction. They even bullied God's prophets (seers), telling them not to prophesy what

was right. They wanted to hear pleasant words and deceits (Isa. 30:9, 10).

2. Because Israel rejected God's Spirit in the wildernesss wanderings, He turned against them as His enemies (Isa. 63:7-14).
3. Under the figure of a lampstand holding seven lamps and supplied with lighting fuel by two olive trees, Zechariah conveyed a valuable lesson to Zerubbabel from God: accomplishment of God's work is achieved by God's Spirit, not by human might or power (Zech. 4:1-6).

CONCLUSION:

The presence of God's Spirit has played a fundamental role in His direction of men throughout both the Patriarchal and Mosaic Dispensations. Special men were selected for the Spirit's indwelling so that they might lead God's people correctly. These principles can minister to a better understanding of the Spirit's work in New Testament times.

D. RESTLESSNESS OF ZION (cont'd), CHAPTERS 63 - 64

4. PENITENTLY VEXED

TEXT: 64:1-7

1 Oh that thou wouldest rend the heavens, that thou wouldest come down, that the mountains might quake at thy presence,
2 as when fire kindleth the brushwood, and the fire causeth the waters to boil; to make thy name known to thine adversaries, that the nations may tremble at thy presence!
3 When thou didst terrible things which we looked not for, thou camest down; the mountains quaked at thy presence.
4 For from of old men have not heard, nor perceived by the ear, neither hath the eye seen a God besides thee, who worketh for him that waiteth for him.
5 Thou meetest him that rejoiceth and worketh righteousness,

those that remember thee in thy ways: behold, thou wast wroth, and we sinned: in them have we been of long time; and shall we be saved?
6 For we are all become as one that is unclean, and all our righteousnesses are as a polluted garment: and we all do fade as a leaf; and our iniquities, like the wind, take us away.
7 And there is none that calleth upon thy name, that stirreth up himself to take hold of thee; for thou hast hid thy face from us, and hast consumed us by means of our iniquities.

QUERIES

a. Why has the attitude of the people now apparently changed?
b. Is verse four quoted in I Corinthians 2:9?
c. How does one "take hold" of God? (verse seven)

PARAPHRASE

O Lord we wish you would break open the impenetrable expanse of the skies that seems to be keeping You from coming down personally to us in all Your omnipotence making the whole earth shake and tremble with Your judgment. If you would intervene directly, Lord, Your righteous glory would consume our enemies like fire consumes brushwood and the fiery lava of volcanoes makes the waters boil. Yet, when we think about it Lord, if you came down thus You would do such awe-inspiring wonders that we do not even have language to describe them. Since the world was created no person anywhere has ever seen or heard of a God like You who works for those who patiently trust in Him. Lord, You gladly receive any man who comes to you doing righteousness and joyfully following in Your ways. But we have continued in our sinning; even when You expressed Your hatred of our rebellious ways we went right on sinning. How can we ever be saved? Yes, we all stand in relationship to You as one cut off from the covenant because of our uncleanness; any righteousness we might think we have is really non-existent and we are as legally unclean as the bloodstained rags of a woman at her monthly period. Like the leaves of autumn, we fade, fall and wither; our sins sweep us away like the wind blows away the autumn leaves. In spite of our very apparent condition, no one calls upon Your name and no one ever prods himself to make any firm commitment of his life to Your word. You have withdrawn Your grace from us and we are being consumed by the consequences of our sins.

COMMENTS

v. 1-3 CRY: The complaint of the preceeding passage begins to turn toward a cry of desperation which leads to a confession. The remnant is gradually coming to the attitude God is able to use in His messianic program. Now the cry is that Jehovah will tear an opening in the impenetrable black cloud that is standing in the way of His seeing their predicament and come down to help them. They are begging God to come in direct intervention as He did for their ancestors. God presented Himself as directly as He dared to Isaiah in His theophany in the temple (cf. Isa. 6:1ff). Why could the people not accept Isaiah's testimony to that direct appearance and trust Him to deliver them from the impending captivity? For the same reason men and women today demand a physical appearance from God before they will believe when there is sufficient testimony to His incarnation in the New Testament!

The anticipation of Jehovah's appearance is couched in the experiences of their ancestors—mountains quaking, fire burning, waters boiling, nations trembling, (cf. Ex. 19:16ff; Psa. 144:5; Deut. 32:22; Judg. 5:4-5; Micah 1:3-4; Heb. 1:4-6; 3:3; 15; Psa. 18:8-16, etc.). Should God appear directly He would consume the whole material universe (cf. Heb. 12:18-21; 18:25-29). Instead of coming in His consuming Presence, He sent His Son to give the world a saving Presence. So when the people give more thought to what such a direct intervention of Jehovah would bring, they are moved to cry, "O, Jehovah, if You came down thus You would do awe-inspiring deeds and wonders that not even we could anticipate!" Should Jehovah appear on earth it would be overwhelming—no human language could express it, no human being could guess what it would be like! The great apostle Paul was caught up "into the third heavens" and saw things it was impossible for human language to describe (cf. II Cor. 12:1-4).

v. 4-7 CONFESSION: At last, the remnant, after contemplating the awesome holiness of Jehovah and His unsearchable power, confesses its sin and prepares to be clay in the Potter's hand (cf. 64:8). First, there is the confession of the uniqueness of Jehovah's revelation of Himself and His relationship to those who "wait" (or trust) in Him. The people are at last testifying that Jehovah is quite unlike the idols. In fact, no one in all the world is able to know the mind, Spirit, deeds, personhood of Jehovah unless Jehovah chooses to reveal Himself. And even then, man can know only as much of God's mind as He chooses to reveal through His appointed spokesmen (prophets and apostles, etc.). This is the sense in which the apostle Paul quoted Isaiah 64:4 in I Corinthians 2:9. The nature of the living God is such that the human mind is incapable of *discovering* Him or *inventing* Him—man must humbly "wait" until God reveals Himself and man must humbly accept both the instrumentality by which and the extent to which God reveals Himself.

The uniqueness of Jehovah stands out in contrast to all pretended gods most apparently in His faithfulness to be constantly present with those who seek righteousness and "remember" (walk in) His ways. The holiness of Jehovah was unique in contrast to all the gods of the heathen. At last the people are admitting that Jehovah requires men to "rejoice" in and "work" righteousness to enjoy His presence. They have come confessing as Hosea (Hos. 14:1-9) instructed their northern countrymen to do. This remnant of Isaiah's disciples has been brought to its confession through the preaching of the prophet concerning the atoning suffering of the Servant and the future glory of Zion. They will produce a progeny of faithful servants (by implanting Isaiah's message in their offspring) which will, in turn, bring the Messiah into the world (cf. Mt. 1:18-25; Lk. 1:24-56; Lk. 1:67-80; Lk. 2:1-52; Lk. 4:14-30, etc.).

Once man has been confronted with a revelation of Jehovah's holiness and admits it, then he sees himself as he truly is, a sinner in need of Jehovah's saving grace (cf. Isa. 6:5-6). The remnant here acknowledges it has been "a long time" in its sin and in need of God's grace; else, how shall it be saved? They see their uncleanness. They now realize they are spiritually cut off from Jehovah because He is absolutely holy and they have defiled themselves and are no longer worthy to stand in His presence—even if He should come in answer to their prayer. This is quite different from the attitude expressed by some in Judah when they haughtily dared the Lord to come down and be present with them (cf. Isa. 5:19). They see their uncleanness as a "polluted garment" using the figure of the ceremonial uncleanness of a woman at the time of her monthly period (cf. Ezek. 36:17; Lev. 18:24-28). The Hebrew word *tame'* is translated *unclean* and is the same word the leper is to cry out (Lev. 13:45-46) indicating the confession here is a recognition of having been cut off from covenant relationship by their sin.

Not only are they experiencing the legal condemnation of their sin, they are also experiencing the psychological and social consequences of it. They are all withering and dying like leaves on a tree and their sin is tossing them about and blowing them away like the wind blows the fallen leaves. The tragedy of the situation is that sin is so pervasive in the nation, no one seems concerned enough to call upon the name of the Lord which involves "taking hold" of His word. Perhaps the "none" would be qualified by the fact that a *few* were calling on the Lord (Isaiah and the remnant). But there were so few Jehovah must still withhold His direct intervention ("hid thy face from us") until the captivity comes and the nation is chastened and purified and a larger remnant is formed. The Hebrew word *khazak* is translated *take hold* but is usually more intense and translated *hold fast* as when Hagar was told to *hold fast* to Ishmael (Gen. 21:18) or when Pharaoh was *holding* on to the Israelites (Ex. 9:2). So now their sin is consuming them—they are suffering the due penalty of their sins (cf. Rom. 1:28), and the nation as a whole does not turn to God and hold fast to Him for strength—it is going to be blown away into captivity.

5. PLEA FOR VERIFICATION

TEXT: 64:8-12

8 But now, O Jehovah, thou art our Father; we are the clay, and thou our potter; and we all are the work of thy hand.
9 Be not wroth very sore, O Jehovah, neither remember iniquity for ever: behold, look, we beseech thee, we are all thy people.
10 Thy holy cities are become a wilderness, Zion is become a wilderness, Jerusalem a desolation.
11 Our holy and our beautiful house, where our fathers praised thee, is burned with fire; and all our pleasant places are laid waste.
12 Wilt thou refrain thyself for these things, O Jehovah? wilt thou hold thy peace, and afflict us very sore?

QUERIES

a. Is there a change in attitude here?
b. Is Jerusalem a desolation at this writing?
c. What is their "beautiful house"?

PARAPHRASE

Now, Lord, we are pleading that You will intervene directly and relieve our present circumstances because, First, You alone are our Father. We are clay and You are our Former or Potter, the One who formed us with Your own hand. You should not be so angry with us, or keep on holding our sins against us, Lord, because we are begging You to remember, we are Your children. Second, the cities and villages of Your consecrated land, (even Zion, Jerusalem, the city where Your presence dwells) are being desecrated, profaned and ruined by Your enemies. And if they are not stopped, our beautiful temple, Your house, where our ancestors worshipped You is as good as ruined by the fires of our enemies. All our beautiful, peaceful land will be made a place of desolation and ruin. In view of all this, will You still withhold Your judgment upon our enemies and refrain from intervening for us and allow us to continue to be afflicted?

COMMENTS

v. 8-9 OWNERSHIP: This last section of the petition of Zion, born of her restlessness, is a plea for Jehovah to verify His relationship to her. She offers two motives she thinks should move Jehovah to act and intervene directly to relieve her circumstances. First, the Lord should act immediately and supernaturally, on her behalf, because they have no other Father than Jehovah. The emphasis is on His exclusive Fatherhood. The literal Hebrew syntax would read, "And, even so, Father of us You are, we are clay and You are former of us, and work of Your hand all of us are." Despite their uncleanness and their sin, Jehovah formed them like a potter forms clay. They now fall back upon that relationship as a last resort. This was not always their attitude. Once they refused to admit the potter-clay relationship (cf. Isa. 29:16; 45:9-10)! That was when they thought they needed no help. But now it is a different story! Now they plead for His mercy and His immediate and direct help *because* they have suddenly realized He is the *only* Father they have!

Before we thank God that we are not like those people, let

us remember that we have undoubtedly been as arrogant and then as helpless as they at one time or another in our Christian walk. All of us have tried, with Peter, to walk on the stormy sea of life by ourselves at one time; all of us have probably cried out as we began to sink, "Lord save me!" (cf. Mt. 14:29-31). But actually, this is where God wants us! This is where He wanted Zion! He could not save them until they allowed Him to do so. Of course, most of us want Him to save us right now, and according to our human program. But Jehovah is not only omnipotent, He is omniscient. His knowledge of what we need and when we need it is perfect. He is indeed our perfect Father.

A literal translation of verse nine would read, "Do not be angry, Jehovah, unto strength, and do not eternally remember our sin." In other words, they are pleading that Jehovah not carry out His anger as *strongly* as He is capable of doing. That would obliterate them! Their plea is that they are His *people.* Their appeal is that Jehovah verify their status as His chosen people by intervening and saving them from impending captivity. Jehovah will deliver them from captivity and verify their election as His children when they do their part to verify their relationship to Him by obedience to His will as children should. Will Jehovah claim them as children? Yes, when they claim Him as Father! Will He verify they are His? Yes, when they verify He is theirs! Will He deliver them! Yes, when they allow Him to do so and when it is best for Him to do so! Ezekiel (Ezek. 20:1-49) predicts this very thing! God does have a remnant and He will verify His ownership!

v. 10-12 OMNIPOTENCE: The second motive Zion thinks should move Jehovah to act immediately on her behalf is the continuing plunder of Judah's cities and villages by the Assyrians. This contiuing plunder portends an even more disastrous day when the Temple may be put to the torch and the holy city itself, beautiful Jerusalem, may be overrun and ruined by the heathen hordes. It was evidently so imminent that the prophet spoke of it as if it were already happening! Jerusalem and the Temple were not completely destroyed and burned until 586 when Nebuchadnezzar razed the whole city (cf. Jer. 52:13). Isaiah is not writing after the fact but using the "predictive present."

The statement in verse 12 sums up and presses home the point Zion is pleading—need for immediate, direct intervention by Jehovah to deliver her from her enemies. God must not allow the land and the people who bear His name to be profaned lest His name be profaned throughout the world. Jehovah has acted in the past to vindicate His power and glorify His name; will He now remain silent? The Hebrew word *khesheh* is translated *peace* in verse 12, but more literally means *silence.* The usual Hebrew word for *peace* is *shalom.* The phrase *'ad-me'od* which means, ". . . unto strength . . ." is repeated in this verse. In view of the continued plundering of the cities and the imminent razing of Jerusalem and the Temple, will Jehovah continue to keep silent and continue to afflict Judah so severely? Indeed He will so long as Judah keeps on walking in sin. One has only to read Jeremiah and Ezekiel to know that Judah not only continued but worsened in her sin and rebellion (cf. Ezek. 5:5-6; 8:7-18) until finally Jehovah withdrew His glory from her altogether (Ezek. 11:22-25).

For the sake of His name and the faithfulness of a small remnant, Jehovah delivered His people from their captivity and rebuilt their city and their temple. However, the rebuilt Jerusalem and Zerubbabel's temple were temporary edifices used by the Lord to the ultimate end He sought and that was a "dwelling place of God in the Spirit" (Eph. 2:22), the church of the Lord Jesus Christ. In the church the presence of the Lord dwells now and forever more. An earthly Jerusalem and an earthly temple are now of no consequence to God and His people. Those who worship Him now and forever more worship in Spirit and in truth (cf. Jn. 4:19-26).

QUIZ

1. What is the aim of Zion's petition in these verses?
2. To what relationship does Zion appeal in her plea?

3. Does God want men to come to such helplessness as Zion exhibited here?
4. Why does Zion remind the Lord of what is happening to the cities?
5. Did God ever deliver Zion?
6. What was God's ultimate deliverance?

E. REFINING OF ZION, CHAPTER 65

1. CLEANSED

TEXT: 65:1-12

1 I am inquired of by them that asked not for me; I am found of them that sought me not: I said, Behold me, behold me, unto a nation that was not called by my name.
2 I have spread out my hands all the day unto a rebellious people, that walk in a way that is not good, after their own thoughts;
3 a people that provoke me to my face continually, sacrificing in gardens, and burning incense upon bricks;
4 that sit among the graves, and lodge in the secret places; that eat swine's flesh, and broth of adominable things is in their vessels;
5 that say, Stand by thyself, come not near to me, for I am holier than thou. These are a smoke in my nose, a fire that burneth all the day.
6 Behold, it is written before me: I will not keep silence, but will recompense, yea, I will recompense into their bosom,
7 your own iniquities, and the iniquities of your fathers together, saith Jehovah, that have burned incense upon the mountains, and blasphemed me upon the hills: therefore will I first measure their work into their bosom.
8 Thus saith Jehovah, As the new wine is found in the cluster, and one saith, Destroy it not, for a blessing is in it: so will I do for my servants' sakes, that I may not destroy them all.

9 And I will bring forth a seed out of Jacob, and out of Judah and inheritor of my mountains; and my chosen shall inherit it, and my servants shall dwell there.
10 And Sharon shall be a fold of flocks, and the valley of Achor a place for herds to lie down in, for my people that have sought me.
11 But ye that forsake Jehovah, that forget my holy mountain, that prepare a table for Fortune, and that fill up mingled wine unto Destiny;
12 I will destine you to the sword, and ye shall all bow down to the slaughter; because when I called, ye did not answer; when I spake, ye did not hear; but ye did that which was evil in mine eyes, and chose that wherein I delighted not.

QUERIES

a. What is the practice of "sitting among graves" (verse four)?
b. Where is the valley of Achor?
c. Who is "Fortune"?

PARAPHRASE

This is what the Lord says in answer to Zion's complaint: While some seek Me and do not find Me, others who never before sought Me will find Me! I will reveal Myself to a people I have not chosen. However, the rebellious people I have chosen—with whom I have been continually pleading to come to Me—they have chosen to follow their own evil ideas and desires. These people of Mine insult Me continually, and Blatantly to My face, worshiping in the idol-gardens and burning incense to images on heathen altars. They go out at night to the graveyards and other secret places to hold seances and try to contact the dead; they indulge in the pagan rituals of eating swine's flesh and rotten food. These have so completely given themselves over to pagan ritual and mystery-cults they think they have attained extra-ordinary sanctity and do not wish to associate with their fellow countrymen so they say, Stay away from me, you are not in the same class as I am in wisdom and religion. The Lord says of these, They are as vexatious and repulsive to Me as smoke in the nose from a fire that smolders continually. I have been recording their deeds and I have written down a decree that I will no longer restrain Myself toward these rebels. I am going to pay them with a full penalty for their rebellion. I am going to dump this entire mess of ungodliness they have made right back into their laps. I am going to punish them, not only for their own sins, but also for the sins of their forefathers too, says the Lord, because their forefathers taught them to worship idols on the hilltops and profane My name and insult My name; I will pay them back for the centuries of profanity with which they profaned Me.

But I will not destroy them all, says the Lord; just as one does not want to throw away a cluster of grapes because there are some good grapes mixed with the bad ones, so there are some good people in Zion I do not want to destroy. There are a few in Zion who are My good servants. I will save a small group and these will provide "seed" to form a people who will receive the inheritance and the dwelling I have promised them. This inheritance and dwelling place will be one of prosperity and security like Sharon's plains and the valley of Achor for those who seek Me. But as for the rest of you, who worship the gods of Good Luck and Destiny, and who forsake My temple and forget Me, I will "destine" you to slaughter by your enemy's sword. You are marked for the slaughter because when I plead with you to come to Me you did not answer My pleading; when I commanded, you did not obey. In fact, you deliberately did what I had said was evil and your every desire was what I told you was undesirable to Me.

COMMENTS

v. 1-7 SIN REPAID: It may have appeared up to this point in Isaiah's prophecy that he was pronouncing doom upon the *whole* nation. However, the prayer in chapter 64 shows that there was a small remnant of people who had turned to the Lord for help. This small group had the testimony of Isaiah "bound up and sealed" among them and were the prophet's disciples. They had turned to "the teaching and to the testimony" (cf. Isa. 8:16-20). Chapter 65 is the verification that Isaiah had been declaring all along the *whole* nation was not to be doomed but that there would be a sifting and God would indeed answer the prayer for deliverance by the remnant. Those who blaspheme the Lord will be recompensed with judgment; those who trust Him will become a "seed" and provide heirs to Judah's promises.

The apostle Paul helps us understand that these final verses of Isaiah's book have to do with the Messiah's kingdom (the church) for he quotes 65:1-2 in Romans 10:20-21 as fulfilled at the preaching of the gospel and its reception by Gentiles. Isaiah is predicting that a refining, sorting, culling process is going to take place as a consequence of the Babylonian captivity and the subsequent centuries of the Jewish "indignation" (cf. our comments Daniel, College Press, pages 343-353 and 429-435). From the Babylonian captivity, through the restoration of the Jewish commonwealth, through the Seleucid domination and the Maccabean revolt, and through the early Roman domination the Jewish nation would undergo a *spiritual sifting* until thoroughly prepared (with a remnant of godly servants like Mary, Joseph, Elizabeth, Zechariah, Simeon, Anna, etc.) for the *new creation* (Isa. 66:18-24) (the Messiah's Zion). This sifting must take place because of the abominable rebellion of a majority of Israel in Isaiah's day. Many of these rebels will never find Jehovah even though He has plead with them (through prophets and leaders) for century after century. They would not give up their idols. So it is predicted that God *will* have a people turn to Him in the future who had never inquired about Him before. This will be the *goiy* (singular of *goiym*). Isaiah 65:1 substantiates Ephesians 3:1-6 that Jehovah did not in ancient times make known to the Gentiles the messianic program as He did to the Jews. But Isaiah 65:1 predicts a time when the Gentiles would *find* Him; the Gentiles *will* behold Him and they *will* be called by His name. The time will come, says Isaiah, when God will reveal Himself and invite the Gentiles, "behold Me, behold Me!" That invitation will be through the preaching of the gospel of Christ says Paul in Romans 10:14-21.

But until the time comes for Jehovah to open the messianic kingdom to the Gentiles, He "spreads out His hands all the day to a rebellious people." Jehovah was more than patient, more than merciful, more than just with Israel. Century after century He plead with them through His prophets (cf. II Chron. 24:18-19; 36:15-16; Jer. 7:13; Lk. 11:50, etc.). But they would not listen (cf. Hosea 11:1-2; 12:10-14; Micah 2:6-11; Isa. 30:8-11; Jer. 5:3; 6:16-19; 7:27-28; 8:5-6, etc.). The Hebrew word *soorer* is translated *rebellious* but is more specifically, *stubborn.* They have their own ways and their own ideas and they stubbornly refuse God's thought and ways. With centuries of evidence behind them that God's ways result in good and man's result in evil, they still reject God's ways! The Hebrew phrase in verse three, *ha'am hammake'isiym,* is literally, "the people, the ones *angering* me" to My face continually. The Hebrew word is actually stronger than *provoke*—it emphasizes *anger*! The sin of Israel here depicted is insensitive and blatant. Knowing it angers Jehovah, they persist; not only do they persist, they invent *new* ways to provoke Him.

1. Sacrificing in gardens: making the ritual offerings in the groves of trees and flower gardens dedicated to pagan idols (see comments 57:1-8).
2. Burning incense upon bricks: incense is usually associated with prayer. They were praying to idols by burning incense upon brick altars.
3. Sit among graves, and lodge in the secret places:

apparently this refers to the practice of trying to contact the dead. The Hebrew word *loon* is translated *lodge in in secret places* but means simply, *lodge all night.* They were practicing the common pagan ritual of necromancy which was strictly forbidden by their scriptures (cf. Dt. 18:11; I Sam. 28:3; Isa. 57:9). Jerome refers to a practice called "incubation" in the temples of the idols "where they were accustomed to lie upon the skins of the victims stretched upon the ground, to gather future events from their dreams."

4. Eat swine's flesh, and broth of abominable things: Swine's flesh was offered by the heathen in sacrifice to their idols and then eaten as a ritual of dedication and holiness (cf. II Maccabees 6:18-22; 7:1-2). It was forbidden for the Hebrews (cf. Lev. 11:7ff; Dt. 14:8). The Hebrew word *pigguliym* is translated *abominable things* and according to Ezek. 4:14; Lev. 7:18; 19:7 it is things that are legally unclean. Young calls it "rotten" things; Keil and Delitzsch says the word means *"a stench, a putrefaction,* broth made either of such kinds of flesh or such parts of the body as were forbidden by the law." It was a disgusting and revolting practice evidently a part of pagan cultic worship.

Those who became initiates into the pagan mystery cults did so through secret rituals and orders. They went out in the dark of night to the groves and hilltops; they talked in a cryptic language about mysterious rites and ceremonies; they glanced and smiled knowingly when asked about their worship. All of this made the cult worshipers consider themselves the "in" group, the "wise" people, and religiously above everyone else. Any person not a member of the cult was considered ignorant, unsophisticated and not one with whom to be associated. Therefore, they said (literally), "Be off to yourself," that is, "Stay away from me, you do not know all the secret things I know and we just are not in the same class of people." Such arrogance by men who have rejected goodness and purity for wickedness and rottenness vexes Jehovah (The absolutely righteous One) like the smoke smoldering from a garbage heap in the nostrils of a man.

The Hebrew word *shillametiy* comes from the root *shalam* which primarily means *complete, entire, finish, make good, repay, or requite.* It is translated in verse six *recompense.* The Hebrew *kheygam* is from *khooq* which means *lap,* or *bosom.* Jehovah has written down in His heavenly books the "bill of goods" on these profane, blasphemous people and He is going to pay them back and dump the whole mess into their laps. Sin pays wages (Rom. 6:23). Jehovah has ordered His moral creation so that man and nature may "receive in their own persons the due penalty for their error" (Rom. 1:28). When men plow iniquity, they reap injustice; when they sow falsehood, they eat the fruit of lies (cf. Hosea 10:13). God is not mocked, what a man sows, that shall he reap (Gal. 6:7-10). Generations of men reap the fruit of lies because they follow willingly in the lies of their ancestors (cf. II Chron. 33:9; II Kings 24:3; Jer. 15:4 for the classic illustration of this in Manasseh). The idolatry and blasphemy characterized by Isaiah here was practiced by the Hebrews from the days of Solomon (cf. Hosea 4:13; Isa. 57:7; Jer. 2:20; 3:6ff; 17:2, etc.). Those who "dance" must "pay the fiddler." Israel and Judah paid the consequences of their idolatrous indulgence with sword, pestilence and famine for centuries and centuries until they finally filled up the cup of their iniquity by rejecting Jehovah's Servant, the Messiah, and forfeited their birthright, lost their national identity and surrendered their only salvation.

v. 8-12 SEED REPLANTED: Out of the captivities Jehovah will refine a small remnant. When the husbandman of a vineyard gathers clusters of grapes he does not throw away a whole cluster if he sees some good grapes in it. So Jehovah saw in this rotten nation a few good people who would be a blessing to the world and form the messianic remnant. The Lord did not destroy the whole nation, (cf. Jer. 46:28). Many died of famine, pestilence and the sword during the Babylonian attacks (606, 597, 586 and 582). Many fled into the hills and caves of Palestine from the Babylonian attacks and died there of starvation. Jeremiah says there were approximately 4,600 Jews taken back to Babylon as captives. The number is 10,000 in II Kings 24:14 plus some additional ones later (II Kings 25:8-17). A few of the very poor and physically infirm were left in Judea to farm the land. In addition, some whom the emperor of Babylon gave special favors, such as Jeremiah, and roving bands of deserting soldiers also remained (see comments *Old Testament History,* by Smith & Fields, College Press, pgs. 665-676, and *First and Second Kings,* by James E. Smith, College Press, pgs. 733-755). Altogether, about 15,000 were deported to Babylon from Judea. The Assyrian emperor, Sargon, noted on an inscription (discovered in 1842 by Botta) that he took 27,290 Jews captive from the northern ten tribes (Israel) when that nation fell in 722 B.C. About 42,000 people were taken captive between 722 B.C. and 582 B.C. (140 years). Some 50,000 returned at the release of the captives granted by the edict of Cyrus (536 B.C.). From the fall of the northern ten tribes (Israel) to the return to Palestine was 186 years. The Hebrew nation was begun at the exodus with approximately 2,500,000 people (see *Old Testament History,* Smith & Fields, College Press, pg. 155). After its purging through Assyrian and Babylonian captivities, it was begun again with 50,000. That is about a two-percent remnant!

With those statistics in mind, one is much more impressed with the promise of Jehovah to Isaiah concerning the "holy seed" (cf. Isa. 6:13). Jehovah is going to bring forth a *seed* out of Jacob (65:9) and this seed shall be replanted in the land and it shall *produce servants* to inherit the spiritual blessings which shall come through the messianic kingdom. Isaiah has a goal in mind for the seed of Jacob *beyond* the physical return of the Jews to Judea because the *seed* is to consist not only of Jews but of Gentiles as well (65:1)! Those who came to Jesus, the Messiah, inherited the *rest* God had promised His chosen (cf. Hebrews 3:1—4:13). Those who came to *Zion,* the N.T. church, inherited Jehovah's mountain (cf. Hebrews 12:22-29). Jehovah promised to multiply the *seed* to inherit the messianic promises (cf. II Sam. 7:12-17; Isa. 44:3; 54:3; 59:21; 66:22; Jer. 33:19-22, etc.). And the *seed* was multiplied and did include the *Gentiles* (cf. Rom. 4:1-23; 8:12-17; 9:6-8; Gal. 3:16; 3:28-29).

The restful, prosperous pastoral scene is figurative of the spiritual rest and prosperity that will be inherited by the people of the Good Shepherd (cf. Ezek. 34:1-31; Jer. 33:14-26; Hos. 3:5; Joel 3:1-3; Amos 9:11-15; Obad. 17:21; Micah 5:2-4; Zeph. 3:9-20; Zech. 12:1—14:21). Sharon's plain was well known for its fertility and Achor is probably the same as the Wadi Kelt which descends through a deep ravine from the Judean hills and runs between steep banks south of the modern Jericho to the Jordan river. In all the five places where it is mentioned it is described as the *'emek,* the arable valley of Achor. Hosea pictures the comforting aspect of the terrible event for which the valley is famous (Achan's execution, Josh 7:24-26); it was a doorway of *hope* for chastened Israel (Hos. 2:15).

Gesenius identifies Fortune (Heb. *gad*) and Destiny (Heb. *meniy*) with Jupiter and Venus, the Greater and Lesser Good Fortunes of the astrologers. However, the ISBE (Vol. I, pg. 299) says, ". . . it is more probable that they are the two beautiful starclusters that stand on the head and the shoulder of the Bull at the old commencement of the zodiac . . . the Hyades and Pleiades . . . Both groups were considered traditionally as composed of seven stars; and the two names . . . taken together give the meaning of the 'Fortunate Number,' i.e., seven . . . The . . . spreading of the table and mingling the wine to *Gad* and *Meniy* at the beginning of the year to secure good fortune throughout its course, were therefore held about the time of the Passover, as if in parody, if indeed they were not a desecration of it; heathen rites added to one of the most solemn services of Jehoavh."

Jehovah will save a *seed* through the process of refining and purifying (cf. Mal. 3:1-4), but as for those who make a mockery of His commandments and think they can blaspheme Him by adding heathen rites to their worship, He will arrange for their destiny to be the slaughter of war. There is a very obvious sarcasm in the use of the word *meniy* (destiny) in verse 12. The people worshiped and trusted in the god Destiny; Jehovah will show them who controls destiny! They will receive a *destiny* which they deserve, for when Jehovah called, they did not answer and when He commanded they did not (*shama'* hear) obey. It is well to note here that God came to His people by *words* (a propositional revelation, not mystical and subjective) and those words were to be *obeyed*, not merely noticed or felt. It is also well to note that those to whom the revelation came had the freedom to choose and *chose* to disobey. The Hebrew syntax is interesting in the last phrase of verse 12; the construction (". . . that which I delighted not in, you chose") puts emphasis on that in which Jehovah delighted not! The Lord is justified in His rejection of these people for they have, in fact, rejected, mocked and deliberately chosen against Him.

QUIZ

1. Who are those who found Jehovah having not sought Him?
2. Who are the rebellious people being sought by Jehovah?
3. Name the abominable practices of the rebellious people.
4. Why did they consider themselves holier than others?
5. How does God recompense them?
6. What is the figure of the "new wine" in the cluster?
7. Who were the "seed" brought forth?

2. CHARACTERIZED

TEXT: 65:13-16

13 Therefore thus saith the Lord Jehovah, Behold, my servants
shall eat, but ye shall be hungry; behold, my servants shall
drink, but ye shall be thirsty; behold, my servants shall rejoice, but ye shall be put to shame;
14 behold, my servants shall sing for joy of heart, but ye shall

cry for sorrow of heart, and shall wail for vexation of spirit.
15 And ye shall leave your name for a curse unto my chosen;
and the Lord Jehovah will slay thee: and he will call his
servants by another name:
16 so that he who blesseth himself in the earth shall bless himself in the God of truth; and he that sweareth in the earth
shall swear by the God of truth; because the former troubles
are forgotten, and because they are hid from mine eyes.

QUERIES

a. Who are Jehovah's servants?
b. How will Israel's name be a curse?
c. What is the other name?

PARAPHRASE

On account of the fact that there are a few good people who have chosen to serve Me while the majority of Israel has deliberately chosen to do evil, I will fill My servants with spiritual nourishment and satisfaction but those who rebel against Me will suffer spiritual starvation and shame, says Jehovah. Indeed, those who choose to serve Me will express their joy in singing, but those who disobey Me will weep, moan and wail with sorrow and confusion. The name of this disobedient nation will be forever after used as an illustration of rebellion, mockery and blasphemy by those who are really My chosen people. Jehovah is going to deliver a deathblow to Israel's status as the elect people and He will choose obedient people from every nation on earth and call them by a new name which will characterize their new nature and blessedness. I will so completely and certainly fulfill My promises, the people who are chosen will invoke My name as the source of all truth for those who are My servants will be pardoned forever from the guilt and penalty of sin.

COMMENTS

v. 13-14 NURTURED: Continuing the idea of a refined Zion and the contrast between the "good grapes and the bad grapes" the Lord now pictures the different consequences of the refining process. Those (even of the *goiym* who were not called by His name) who do find Him and call upon Him and become obedient servants, He will fill with spiritual nutrition growth and satisfaction. Of course, Isaiah is using "times coloring" here, i.e., writing of future spiritual things in physical terminology. The New covenant scriptures make it plain that God's richest blessings are spiritual (cf. Eph. 1:3, etc.). Those who hunger and thirst after righteousness will be filled (Mt. 5:6); those who seek the Bread of Life shall have it (Jn. 6:52-65); those who thirst for the Water of Life shall drink of it (Jn. 4:13; 7:37-39, etc.); those who declare joy shall have it abundantly (Jn. 15:1-11, etc.). Eating, drinking, feasting, celebrating and singing merely *symbolize* the blessings God's servants will receive (see comments Isa. 25:6ff). The kingdom of God is essentially *character,* not food and drink (physical things) (cf. Rom. 14:17). Those who rebel and disobey will find their souls and spirits starving and dying of spiritual nourishment. They will suffer sorrow and vexation (cf. Amos 8:11-12). There is no torture more excruciating than spiritual torture (cf. Lk. 16:24-31).

v. 15-16 NAMED: Those of the chosen nation who rebelled against their messianic destiny and their God left their name to the world for a curse. God promised Israel she would become a *proverb* and a *by-word* among the nations if she was rebellious and disobedient (cf. Dt. 28:37; I Kings 9:7; II Chron. 7:20; Psa. 44:14). The Jewish nation became the chief illustration for Christians of the consequences of rebelling against the Lord (cf. Mt. 21:33-43; 22:1-10; Lk. 13:34-35; I Cor. 10:1-13; Heb. 3:1—4:13, etc.).

The Lord will slay the former Israel and create a new Israel (Gal. 6:15-16). Jehovah delivers the deathblow to the former Israel when He cancelled her covenant and nailed it to the cross of Christ. It was definitely prophesied that He would do away with the election of physical Israel (cf. Jer. 3:15-18; 31:31-34, etc.). These verses (Isa. 65:13-16) clearly show that the genetic nation of Israel as such is not synonymous with God's chosen (cf. also Rom. 2:28-29). In the light of this precise statement that God is going to slay the disobedient nation and call His servants by another name, what scriptural reason is there for expecting a future resurrection of genetic Israel? Ezekiel 37 undoubtedly refers to the restoration of Judah after the Babylonian captivity in 536 B.C. Certainly the nation that was restored then cannot be the fulfillment of Isaiah 65:13-16; neither can the present-day Israel! See our comments on Isaiah 62:2 for a discussion of the *new name.*

The Lord will so completely and evidently fulfill His promises in Christ, those who choose to obey Him will invoke His name as the source of *all truth.* They will pray to Him for every need and they will proclaim Him as Infinite answer to man's finiteness. He, Himself will become "the Way, the Truth and the Life" (Jn. 14:6). Those who become His disciples will know the truth and be set free from falsehood (Jn. 8:31ff). The Incarnate Son of Jehovah will become an oath demonstrating in time and space the veracity of Jehovah's promises once and for all (cf. i Cor. 15:1ff; II Cor. 1:20; Heb. 6:17-20; 9:1ff, etc.). Whoever wishes to be blessed from henceforth must be blessed in the name of Jehovah and His Son; whoever wishes to verify the truthfulness, value, reality or meaning of anything must henceforth verify it in the character and will of Jehovah and His Son as revealed in the written record (the scriptures).

The "God of truth" is an extremely significant proposition. Jehovah *is* the truth. In the Person of Jehovah (and His Incarnate Son) is the whole of truth! There is no source of truth outside the character and will of God. He is truth absolute, ultimate, eternal in contradistinction from all that is relative, derived, partial and temporal. All that is true is relative to His character. When we speak of the sanctity of truth we must understand that underlying such a phrase is the sanctity of His character (His love, power, faithfulness, holiness, etc.).

He is the God of truth and all truth derives its sanctity from Him. This is why all untruth or falsehood is wrong; it is a contradiction of what God is! This is why God cannot lie or change His will. To do so would contradict Himself and He cannot deny Himself and be God! The devil's attack upon man was first an attack upon the veracity of God. He accused God of deliberate falsehood and deception in telling Eve that she should not eat of the tree because God knew if she did her eyes would be opened and she would then know something only God knew. Furthermore, the devil said God lied when He told Eve she would die if she ate of the tree. The devil openly assailed the integrity and veracity of God. And here is the important point; in convincing Eve that God was less than faithful, the devil very subtely destroyed Eve's integrity when he seduced her into doubting God's integrity. The only reference point upon which man may build his own integrity, veracity, truthfulness and faithfulness (his own character, as it were) is in unreserved commitment and belief in God's integrity and faithfulness. All of man's unfaithfulness (indeed, all of man's sin) has its affinity with that lie by which Eve was seduced—that God is untrustworthy. Man has only the power to believe or disbelieve. Truth is not in man, but in God. Truth can only be in man when man believes and trusts and obeys God! Therefore, if men are to be formed into the image of God it can only be done by preaching the objectively revealed (in the Bible) character of God (His faithfulness, love, and power). All preaching to convert must center on who God is and what He has done—not in what man feels, or thinks or is able to do. It is not in man to be faithful or to love or to be holy. Man can only be faithful and love and be holy when he believes God is absolutely faithful and absolutely loving and absolutely holy.

All that is false and standing against man has been forever conquered and eliminated through the Son of God. The power, the guilt and the penalty of man's rebellion has been atoned for and truth, ultimate saving truth, is resident in Him. Man can be in Him by faith. That is where God chooses His servants—in Him Who is Truth! This is the new, refined Zion.

QUIZ

1. What kind of eating and drinking is to be given the servants of Jehovah?
2. What did God promise about the name of the Jews if they rebelled?
3. What happened when God slew the rebellious Israel?
4. What is meant about people blessing themselves by the God of truth?

3. CREATED

TEXT: 65:17-25

17 For, behold, I create new heavens and a new earth; and the former things shall not be remembered, nor come into mind.
18 But be ye glad and rejoice for ever in that which I create; for, behold, I create Jerusalem a rejoicing, and her people a joy.
19 And I will rejoice in Jerusalem, and joy in my people; and there shall be heard in her no more the voice of weeping and the voice of crying.
20 There shall be no more thence an infant of days, nor an old man that hath not filled his days; for the child shall die a hundred years old, and the sinner being a hundred years old shall be accursed.
21 And they shall build houses, and inhabit them; and they shall plant vineyards, and eat the fruit of them.
22 They shall not build, and another inhabit; they shall not plant, and another eat: for as the days of a tree shall be the days of my people, and my chosen shall long enjoy the work of their hands.
23 They shall not labor in vain, nor bring forth for calamity; for they are the seed of the blessed of Jehovah, and their offspring with them.
24 And it shall come to pass that, before they call, I will answer;

and while they are yet speaking, I will hear.
25 The wolf and the lamb shall feed together, and the lion
shall eat straw like the ox; and dust shall be the serpent's
food. They shall not hurt nor destroy in all my holy mountain, saith Jehovah.

QUERIES

a. Is this a prediction of the end of time?
b. Why speak of longevity of life in verse 20?
c. Does verse 25 mean the same as Isaiah 11:6-9?

PARAPHRASE

And when this refining takes place I will also create a whole new age or order of things; the former order or age will be considered by the Lord and His new people as no longer valid. None of the Lord's people will regret the passing away of the old; they will be eternally grateful for His new creation. The Lord says, I am going to create a new Jerusalem which will be characterized by and inhabited by a people filled with joy. This new Jerusalem and her joyful people will bring Me joy, too, says the Lord. There will be no more occasions for sorrow and mourning in My new Jerusalem. There will be no more limited life in My new Jerusalem—neither among the very young nor the very old. Every citizen of new Zion will live in eternal joy. The sinner is also going to live forever, but in accursedness and not in new Zion. The citizens of new Jerusalem will no longer labor in vain; whatever they do will prosper and they shall know eternal satisfaction in their service to Jehovah. Nothing shall be able to separate them from their heavenly Father; they shall be the children of God and enjoy eternal fellowship with Him. They shall live in eternal dependence upon Him and He will hear and answer their requests before they even make them! In new Zion man and his environment will be at harmony with one another. There will be nothing to harm the citizen of new Zion—all will be safe and secure. The devil, that old serpent, will be ground into humiliating defeat, and peace shall reign supreme.

COMMENTS

v. 17-19 PERSONALITY: In verse 16 Isaiah promised new Zion, "the former troubles are forgotten." Now the prophet shows why the former troubles will be forgotten; Jehovah is going to create an entirely new order. The Hebrew verb *bara* is translated *create* and is used in the Hebrew *qal* stem only with God as the subject, because it means bringing into existence something absolutely new. This creation is not speaking of a literal, physical new heavens and earth, but of a new era, a new age or a new order in which God will create His spiritual kingdom on the present earth. Young puts it, ". . . heaven and earth are employed as figures to indicate a complete renovation or revolution in the existing course of affairs." It is the *new* Jerusalem, the *new covenant*, and the old will not be remembered (cf. Jer. 3:15-17). In Hebrews 2:5-9 we are told that Christ came to restore man to the dominion over "the world to come" which man lost when he sinned in Eden. God cursed that creation because of man's sin. But Jesus, partaking of human nature, conquered sin in the flesh and has potentially given man's dominion back to him. This was done at the *first* advent of Christ (not the second). What God has done by Christ's redemptive work and establishment of the church is, therefore, the new creation. Hebrews 12:27 indicates that the *old order* (Judaism, or Mosaic covenant) was "shaken" (destroyed) "in order that what cannot be shaken may remain." That which "cannot be shaken" is the *new order* or the kingdom of Christ (Heb. 12:28) which is the church. Paul indicates that *the new covenant relationship* is *the new creation* (cf. II Cor. 5:16-21; Gal. 6:15-16, etc.). The Bible also teaches a *consummation* of the new creation at the *second* advent of the Messiah (cf. I Thess. 4:13—5:11; II Pet. 3:7-18, etc.).

The Jewish Apocrypha (see our comments on chapters 53 and 61), especially those works written after the Maccabean era, speak of the *new age* as being *ushered in* by cataclysmic events, brought about by supernatural powers, taking the form of a cosmic drama in which divine and demonic forces are at work, and involving a remaking of the heavens and earth to form a new beginning free from the corruption which had all along affected creation. It was, of course, to include the judgment of most of the Gentiles and the reign by power and wealth of the Jewish nation over the world. The apocryphal writers were interpreting the prophetic passages of the new order (such as we have here in Isaiah 65) colored by and relative to the persecution and oppression the Jews were having to endure at the hands of Gentile empires. Thus they pictured the messianic age beginning with a great supernatural deliverance of the Jewish nation from its oppressors involving cosmic warfare between God and Satan and demons, followed by creation of a new world order with headquarters in a new Jerusalem. It is easier, in the light of this materialistic interpretation of the prophets, to understand why the Jewish rulers kept insisting that Jesus show supernatural "signs and wonders" to verify His claims to be the Messiah!

What Jehovah is going to create will be eternal because Isaiah exhorts, ". . . be ye glad and rejoice *for ever* in that which I create . . ." Jerusalem, the focus of the new creation, is characterized as both a subject of rejoicing and an object of joy. The *new* Jerusalem (the Jerusalem that is from above, i.e., the church in Gal. 4:26 is *ano* in Greek which means pre-eminent) will be filled with rejoicing as opposed to the sorrow and mourning which will fill old Jerusalem (the physical city). The *new* Jerusalem will also be the exclusive object of God's rejoicing. Calvin wrote, "So great is his love toward us, that he delights in our prosperity not less than if he enjoyed it along with us." Thus the personality of God's newly created Jerusalem is characterized as joyful (cf. comments on Isa. 35:10).

v. 20 PERPETUITY: This verse is portraying in figurative language the *immortality* of the citizens of *new* Zion. It is not as clear as the statement in Isa. 25:8, but nevertheless, in context, is teaching the concept of immortality. The idea of eternal life is taught in the Old Testament (cf. comments Isa. 25:8), but vaguely and gradually. Actually, immortality for both the believer and the sinner is taught here; the believer will enjoy eternal blessedness, the sinner eternal accursedness. The basic idea is, on a level of spirituality commensurate with their immaturity, greatly increased longevity of life will be one of the blessings of the *new* Jerusalem. As we have it in our paraphrase, "There will be no more limited life in My new Jerusalem—neither among the very young nor the very old. Every citizen of new Zion will live in eternal joy. The sinner is also going to live forever, but in accursedness and not in new Zion."

v. 21-25 PROSPERITY: The Lord kept telling His people that when they disobeyed Him, everything they attempted (physically or psychologically) would not reach full fruition or bring them satisfaction (cf. Dt. 28:30; Zeph. 1:13; Micah 6:14-16; Amos 8:9-12, etc.). But in the *new order* (the messianic age of man's reconciliation to Jehovah) the exact opposite will prevail. Everything the citizen of new Zion does, as he conforms to the image of Christ, will produce fruit to Jehovah's glory and satisfaction to the heart of the doer (cf. I Cor. 15:58; Rom. 8:28, 37; II Cor. 9:8-11; Eph. 3:20; I Thess. 1:2-10; 4:9-12, etc.). The picture is one of security, satisfaction and enjoyment. Whatever the citizen in God's new kingdom labors at will glorify God (cf. Eph. 6:5-9; Col. 3:17; 3:22-25; II Thess. 3:6-13). Anything done honestly and within the will of God will be honored by Him and rewarded. Nothing the Christian does (if God can be thanked for it, I Tim. 4:4) will be in vain; nothing he does will be destroyed. The works of the citizen of new Jerusalem "follow after him" (cf. Rev. 14:13).

Those who have been refined and recreated as God's new Israel will call upon Jehovah and He will hear them. In fact, new Israel will be such a joy to Him He will eagerly answer their prayers before they are uttered! Daniel exemplified the faith that such a member of the new Israel would have. While he was still praying (Dan. 9:1-19), the Lord sent an angel to answer his prayer (Dan. 9:20-23). Daniel had hardly begun his prayer before the Lord answered it! Old Jerusalem complained (Isa. 64) Jehovah was not listening to their prayers. It will not be so in the new Jerusalem. He will not only send His angels to minister to new Zion (Heb. 1:14), He will give His Spirit to utter prayers for new Zion when she cannot find adequate ways to express herself to God (cf. Rom. 8:26-27). He knows before we ask what we need (Mt. 6:8). If men know how to answer the requests of others, how much more does a divinely-caring Father know how to answer His children (cf. Lk. 11:5-13; 18:1-8).

Verse 25 is a fitting summation to this chapter. Nothing hurtful will be permitted in new Zion. In God's "holy mountain" (Zion, cf. Heb. 12:22), the place where He dwells, there will be peace, joy and festivity (cf. our comments Isa. 11:6-9; 25:6-9).

QUIZ

1. Is there N.T. teaching to substantiate the interpretation here that the first coming of the Messiah brought a "new creation"?
2. How, according to Jewish apocrypha, did many of the Jews interpret the "new creation" passages in the prophets?
3. How much teaching is there in the O.T. concerning immortality?
4. What will be the end of the labors of citizens of new Zion?
5. What will be the reaction of God to the prayers of citizens of new Zion?

F. EPILOGUE, CHAPTER 66

1. BURIAL OF OLD ZION

TEXT: 66:1-6

1 Thus saith Jehovah, Heaven is my throne, and the earth is my footstool: what manner of house will ye build unto me? and what place shall be my rest?
2 For all these things hath my hand made, and so all these things came to be, saith Jehovah: but to this man will I look, even to him that is poor and of a contrite spirit, and that trembleth at my word.
3 He that killeth an ox is as he that slayeth a man; he that sacrificeth a lamb, as he that breaketh a dog's neck; he that offereth an oblation, as he that offereth swine's blood; he that burneth frankincense, as he that blesseth an idol. Yea, they have chosen their own ways, and their soul delighteth in their abominations:
4 I also will choose their delusions, and will bring their fears upon them; because when I called, none did answer; when I spake, they did not hear; but they did that which was evil in mine eyes, and chose that wherein I delighted not.
5 Hear the word of Jehovah, ye that tremble at his word: Your brethren that hate you, that cast you out for my name's sake, have said, Let Jehovah be glorified, that we may see your joy; but it is they that shall be put to shame.
6 A voice of tumult from the city, a voice from the temple, a voice of Jehovah that rendereth recompense to his enemies.

QUERIES

a. What is the point of stressing the omnipotence of Jehovah?
b. How is one who kills an ox like one who slays a man?
c. How could those who cast others out say, Let Jehovah be glorified?

PARAPHRASE

What arrogance you disobedient ones manifest by thinking I will have anything to do with that building you call My Temple. The wickedness and hypocrisy you are practicing there are abominations to Me. I Am Omnipotent and Absolutely Holy; I am not like the provincial gods of the idolatrous heathen which have to have earthly houses to live in. Neither will I allow My name to be profaned by having it associated with your blasphemies. I created the whole universe; I am omnipresent and I desire an atmosphere of humility where I am worshipped. I dwell in people of afflicted and contrite hearts—those who respect and obey My word. But people like you, arrogant, haughty, rebellious and blasphemous—your hypocritical animal sacrifices are as abominable to Me as if you had made human sacrifices or offered an unclean sacrifice like a dog; your wicked attitudes make your attempts at ceremonial purification as repugnant as if you had offered swine's blood for your cleansing; your burning of incense is as ungodly as if you were worshiping an idol. This is so because you are arrogantly and blatantly doing these things when you know they are against My will. You are not making innocent mistakes; you are doing these abominations because you like them and want to mock Me. You worship the stars because you fear famine and pestilence; you worship pagan idols because you want to trust in the pagan nations of those idols; now I am going to use those very things you fear as a judgment upon you and prove to you that they are delusions. This is the alternative you have left Me, you rebellious people. When I spoke to you through My messengers, you refused to listen and obey. You deliberately did what I told you would profane My name and anger Me. Now, hear Me those of you who do respect and wish to obey My word: Those of this nation who claim to be your brothers but really hate you and make you outcasts of this society and mock you, saying, We have cast you out, but of course, you are Jehovah's so why don't you praise his name and rejoice now!—let Me tell you, says the Lord, it is these arrogant mockers who will be soon put to shame. Very soon now there will be the clash, clatter and din of warfare heard from inside the walls of this very city—yea, even from within the temple you hold so dear shall come the noise of judgment. That noise will be the voice of Jehovah rendering His vengeance upon those who have deliberately declared war upon Him.

COMMENTS

v. 1-3 ABOMINABLE: Chapter 66 contains a three-part summarization of the whole book of Isaiah. First there is capsulation of the abomination of Isaiah's contemporaries and the coming judgment (66:1-6); second, the birth of new Israel (messianic age—church) (66:7-14); third, the proclamation of redemption to the whole world (66:15-24). These are the three major theses of the prophet and thus chapter 66 forms an appropriate epilogue.

These verses are not condemnations of houses of worship as such, nor were they intended to abrogate animal sacrifices for Isaiah's contemporaries. The prophet *is* condemning the arrogant hypocrisy of those who thought an earthly temple guaranteed the presence of Jehovah in their midst regardless of the wickedness of their motives and actions. Many of the Jews fell into the dangerous self-induced delusion that as long as their temple stood Jehovah *must* confine Himself there so their nation would never be without His presence and protection. This delusion is a consequence of spiritual immaturity and this-worldly-mindedness about the worship of God. Most of the Jewish rulers and religious leaders of Jesus' day trusted in their earthly temple, human priesthood and animal sacrifices but not in the Invisible God who made them. It is a common failure of human nature to demand that which can be "handled, touched and tasted" (cf. Col. 2:20-23; II Cor. 4:16—5:5, etc.). When the Pharisees of Jesus day wanted to make an oath by the highest thing they could think of, they made it on the temple or the gold of the temple (cf. Mt. 23:16-21). When Jesus predicted the desolation of the city and the temple (Mt. 23:37-39), His own disciples could not believe it, so He gave an extended lesson to them about the destruction of Jerusalem (Mt. 24:1-35) at the hands of the Romans. The fundamental issue of the entire book of Hebrews in the N.T. is that of "weaning" Hebrew Christians away from the powerful temptation to return to Judaism (abrogated by the new covenant) which appealed to the fleshly desire for a religion that centered in an earthly temple, touchable sacrifices, visible high-priesthood and religious hierarchy. Stephen, the martyr, condemned his Jewish brethren for not accepting the fact that Jesus was the fulfillment of all the temple stood for (Acts 7:44-53). The Jews were not alone in thinking the Creator could be reduced to human level and confined to earthly shrines. Paul reminded the idolaters of Athens that such ideas were illogical (cf. Acts 17:24-28). Young aptly says, "Those who would build a house influenced by such conceptions were seeking to render the infinite finite, the eternal temporal, and the Creator a mere creature."

Jehovah *does dwell* in a spiritual temple composed of people (cf. Eph. 2:11-22; II Pet. 2:5) of afflicted and contrite hearts. The Hebrew word *'anah* is translated *poor* but means literally, *afflicted.* It is from a root word that may also be translated *answer.* The idea is that God dwells in people who are poor in spirit or afflicted in the soul enough to answer God when He calls. God's presence dwells in a people who are humble and penitent, whether they have a "church building" or not. But the most elaborate building and the best well-organized religious system will never enjoy the presence of God if haughty, arrogant, independent and rebellious worshipers gather there. True worship of God is done in spirit and truth (Jn. 4:19-26) and *where* God is worshiped is secondary to that! When truth and righteousness are renounced for the sake of places, things and human traditions, it is an abomination before the Lord!

Rituals and ceremonies are means to an end; they are vehicles of human expressions of faith and willing obedience to a Person —God. When the rituals and ceremonies become the objects of our hope, they become idols! God Himself is the object of our hope; biblical commandments concerning acts of obedience or rituals or worship are revealed as acceptable ways men may express their faith in Him. There are two ways men turn biblically revealed rituals into abominations before the Lord: (a) make the rituals the object of their hope, or; (b) refuse to observe the ritual as the Lord commands it in His Word. The people of Isaiah's day were guilty of both. They were making their ability to keep the rituals the object of their hope which is trusting in self-righteousness, and they were also arrogantly mixing the practices of pagan idolatry with the worship of Jehovah. Sacrifices to God, no matter how often or how affluent, without the proper spirit and contrary to revealed truth are unacceptable to God (cf. Isa. 1:10-20; Ezek. 8:5-18; 14:1-11; I Sam. 15:17-23; Isa. 57:1-13; Micah 3:11; Mt. 5:23-24; 6:1-18; etc.). Observance of rituals contrary to biblical specifications and without humility toward the God who commanded them makes them abominations to God. A man may kill an ox and bring it to the temple for a sacrifice, but with an improper attitude toward God he may as well have offered a human sacrifice—both are equally abominable to God! Do men really realize how serious it is to observe religious ritual in an improper frame of mind and heart?! To give an offering or do any act of worship without a contrite heart is an affront to the Lord and as insulting as offering swine's blood! Such impersonal, rebellious, impenitent behavior exposes the real focus of the heart of a man—the ritual itself—and that is in fact, idolatry! Even people of the new covenant must be on guard against this tendency. Ananias and Sapphira fell—not in the amount given or not given to the Lord, but in the attitude they had in their heart (cf. Acts 5:1ff). Simon, the converted magician, fell—not in what he sought but the purpose for which he sought it (cf. Acts 8:9-13). Even the Corinthian church made the Lord's Supper an abomination before the Lord by the attitude of divisiveness in which they participated in it (cf. I Cor. 10-11). The church at Laodicea was an abomination to Christ—not because she was affluent but because of her attitude toward her affluency.

Men will err and sin. Those who worship God will never be able to do so perfectly. The Lord will forgive those errors when men worship Him penitently, honestly and "trembling at His Word." But when men deliberately choose their own ways against those God has plainly revealed, and when they "delight" in doing what they know is contrary to His revealed will, He will not forgive.

v. 4-6 ABANDONED: What choice do men leave the Righteous and Just God when they delight in their abominations? The only choice God has is to leave them to their choice! God chooses their delusions as the instruments of their judgment. When God called and called, none were poor (*'anah*) enough in spirit to answer. When God spake, none obeyed (*shama'*). They plainly told God they did not want to hear from Him (cf. Isa. 30:9-11; Micah 2:6-11, etc.). They obstinately chose their own way against God's (cf. Jer. 6:16-18; 8:4-7, etc.). So the Lord let them have what they chose! The Lord abandoned them to their sins (cf. Ezek. 11:21-25; 39:23-24, etc.). They are given up to suffer in their own bodies the due penalties of their errors (cf. Rom. 1:27). Judah trusted in human schemes and human allies to keep her safe and prosperous, but her human allies betrayed her and turned on her. Judah's idol gods could not provide anything for her because they were only pieces of wood and stone. Judah's social injustices and political chicanery on the international scene eventually caused her captivity. But it was Jehovah who was exercising His sovereign rule in righteousness over the universe that was the real cause of it. God exercises His sovereign rule through secondary agents both in men and natural means (cf. Isa. 10:5-19; Jer. 27:1-11; Amos 4:6-11; Hab. 1:5-6; Dan. 8:1ff; Rev. 6:1-17; 8:1—9:21; 17:15-18, etc.).

In verse five, the Lord addresses Himself to those few people who were listening to the teaching of Isaiah (cf. Isa. 8:16ff) and being persecuted for their faithfulness. The majority of the people hated the righteous remnant. God's righteous minority will alway be persecuted by the wicked majority because their righteousness acts as a catalyst of judgment in their midst (cf. Jn. 3:18-21; 9:35-40; 15:18-27, etc.). The righteous minority of Isaiah's day had been "cast out" which probably means the haughty, self-righteous majority had ostracized them socially, religiously economically and politically. The poor and humble in spirit and those obedient to the Word of God were oppressed and exploited. The rich and powerful wicked mock them as they oppress them, saying, "Since you are so anxious to praise the name of Jehovah and call on Him for help, we will give you plenty of opportunity to call on Him by casting you out." Such perverse haughtiness in a people who had all the advantages of the miraculous deliverance of God from enemies centuries past and who had the Law of God delivered by angels through Moses, is shocking! It is blasphemous! But such mockery of God's saints in the midst of their persecutions will continue so long as this present order exists. All who live a godly life in this world will suffer persecution (II Tim. 3:12). But God's vindication of His saints will be done—if not in this world, in the next!

As for those of Isaiah's day who were persecuting the righteous, they would themselves be cast out and suffer shame and humiliation for their disobedience to God in the Babylonian captivity. But Isaiah is looking past his own time by many centuries and hears the noise of warfare that comes from Jerusalem, the city that the wicked majority believed would never fall (Micah 3:11; Jer. 6:13-14; 8:11; 26:7-11; 28:1-17). Isaiah's prediction of Jerusalem's judgment refers to her fall at the hands of Rome (70 A.D.) as will be seen from the following text.

QUIZ

1. What did the majority of Isaiah's contemporaries think about God's presence in Jerusalem and the temple?
2. Are these verses intended to condemn building houses of worship?

3. Where does Jehovah dwell in the new covenant age?
4. Just how serious is it to worship with a haughty attitude?
5. How does chapter 66 form an epilogue to the whole book of Isaiah?
6. What is being "poor" and of a "contrite spirit"?
7. Did the people of Isaiah's day and later really think their city and temple would never fall?

2. BIRTH OF NEW ZION

TEXT: 66:7-14

7 Before she travailed, she brought forth; before her pain came, she was delivered of a manchild.

8 Who hath heard such a thing? who hath seen such things? Shall a land be born in one day? shall a nation be brought forth at once? for as soon as Zion travailed, she brought forth her children.

9 Shall I bring to the birth, and not cause to bring forth? saith Jehovah: shall I that cause to bring forth shut the womb? saith thy God.

10 Rejoice ye with Jerusalem, and be glad for her, all ye that love her: rejoice for joy with her, all ye that mourn over her;

11 that ye may suck and be satisfied with the breasts of her consolations; that ye may milk out, and be delighted with the abundance of her glory.

12 For thus saith Jehovah, Behold, I will extend peace to her like a river, and the glory of the nations like an overflowing stream: and ye shall suck thereof; ye shall be borne upon the side, and shall be dandled upon the knees.

13 As one whom his mother comforteth, so will I comfort you; and ye shall be comforted in Jerusalem.

14 And ye shall see it, and your heart shall rejoice, and your bones shall flourish like the tender grass: and the hand of Jehovah shall be known toward his servants; and he will have indignation aginst his enemies.

QUERIES

a. Who is "she" and who is the "manchild" of verse seven?
b. How will Jehovah extend the "glory of the nations" to Jerusalem?
c. How will the Lord combine comfort to Jerusalem and indignation against his enemies?

PARAPHRASE

But a marvelous thing shall happen with Jerusalem. She will fall and this nation will be cast off by God and dispersed all over the world. She will be like a woman pregnant with child but she will miraculously give birth before the travail of labor pains come upon her. Before her time of judgment she shall deliver the predicted Son! At one stroke the nation that is destined for destruction shall produce a new nation. Such a miracle has never occured before—no one has ever seen such an instantaneous birth of a nation! The reason such a miracle will occur is that Jehovah started this work. Will the Lord, having begun this new nation in its germinal form, not be able to bring it to completion? Rest assured that when I decide to bring something into existence, I will certainly do so, says God. Therefore, be jubilant with this news concerning new Jerusalem all you who love the place where God dwells and mourn over old Jerusalem's sin. Rejoice that you will be cuddled to her breast and drink deeply of her sustenance and find security, satisfaction and pleasure. This is what Jehovah says, I will fill her up and running over with goodness and glory from the best people of all the nations of the world and she will be nourished and cared for like a mother cares for her baby. Those who will be citizens of this miraculously-born new Jerusalem shall acknowledge this when it happens and they shall praise Jehovah for having brought them forth and causing them to grow and for manifesting Himself to them. The birth of God's new nation will become His pronouncement of judgment upon all human attempts to usurp His sovereignty over man and the world. When God forms His new kingdom on the earth, it will, in fact, become a judgment upon all other kingdoms.

COMMENTS

v. 7-9 MIRACULOUS: That the pain and travail of verse six predicts the Roman destruction of Jerusalem is evident from what follows in these verses (7-14). Isaiah's prediction here of the birth of a new nation on the ruins of the old closely parallels the predictions of Daniel (see our comments on Daniel 9:24-27) who also looks forward to the Roman destruction of Jerusalem.

The point of verses seven through nine is to emphasize the miraculous nature of what God is going to do *before* He casts off old Zion finally and completely (at the Roman destruction). Before the Old covenant nation is destroyed, the "manchild" and the New covenant nation will be born. The *manchild* can be none other than the *son* and *child* of Isaiah 9:6 and *Immanuel* of Isaiah 7:14. He is the Messiah (the *anointed prince* of Dan. 9:25). The *manchild* of Isaiah 66:7 is the same, we believe, as the *manchild* born of the *woman* in Revelation 12:1-6. In the Revelation John sees the O.T. woman (faithful members of the Old covenant people) give birth to the manchild, the great red dragon (the devil) attempting to devour the manchild, and God catching the manchild up to heaven safe and secure. Just as in Isaiah 66:8, so in Revelation 12, the woman has a plurality of offspring or children. Of course, these children are joint-heirs with the only-unique Son (manchild) by adoption. He is the seed (singular, Gal. 3:16) and they are offspring (plural, Gal. 3:23-29, by adoption).

Old Jerusalem will produce the manchild and the offspring before her travail comes upon her. By a series of rhetorical questions Isaiah emphasizes the uniqueness of the predicted birth of the new nation. Who ever heard of a new nation from an old nation *before* the old nation passes away? But even more unknown is the birth of a nation in one day! The Hebrew word *pa'am* is translated *at once* but means literally, *at one stroke*, as with one stroke of a hammer. A "land" and a "nation" was brought forth with one stroke of God on the Day of Pentecost, June, A.D. 30. Isaiah's figurative use of "land" should help us understand that much of what he (and other prophets, especially, Ezekiel) says about the future of God's "land" refers to the messianic "land" (or church), (cf. Ezek. 37:15-28; ch. 45-48, etc.).

The guarantee of all this is that Jehovah started it (with Abraham) and He will most certainly carry it through. When God promises, He fulfills. God does not lie; He is not a man that He repents or changes His mind or will. God's new nation (the Church) will be born; nothing will stop it (cf. our comments on Daniel 2:44-45, *Daniel*, College Press, pgs. 91-94). Not even the gates of Hades (death) shall prevail against the birth of God's church (cf. Mt. 16:18). God's new nation will be like no other nation ever on the face of the earth. Governments and cultures of human origin come and go, but God's nation (kingdom) will incorporate all races, tongues, cultures and classes, and will last forever. His kingdom is supernatural!

v. 10-14 MATERNAL: Isaiah continues the figure of a mother and her child. He pictures the citizens of the new Zion as hungry children contentedly nursing from the breasts of their mother. Zion's children drink deeply ("milk out") until they are completely satisfied. In contrast to those who rebel against God, who can never be satisfied (cf. Isa. 65:13-14; 9:20; Micah 6:14-15), new Zion will be satisfied (cf. Jer. 31:14; Isa. 25:6-9; 55:1-3; 58:11, etc.). Citizens of new Zion learn to be content (cf. Phil. 4:10-13; I Tim. 6:6-8); they have the peace which passes all understanding (cf. Phil. 4:4-7). It is interesting that this contentment, satisfaction, glory and peace which shall belong to new Zion comes to those in her who rejoice and mourn. It seems incongruous to talk of rejoicing and mourning at the same time. Yet the Lord pronounced those blessed who mourned (cf. Mt. 5:4). Only those who believe in the Lord can comprehend this. Those who think that rejoicing can only come when there is nothing over which to mourn do not understand the meaning of joy as Jesus taught it (cf. John 15:1-11; 16:20-24; 16:33; 17:13-19, etc.). It is possible for the citizens of Zion to *mourn* over sin and all that results from it and at the same time *rejoice* in the salvation and future vindication of the Lord. When the citizen of Zion is able to do this he is at peace. Peace means wholeness (cf. comments Isa. 58:9) and Jehovah is going to fill new Zion's "land" up and running over with wholeness, prosperity and goodness like a river fills up and runs over its banks. Zion's wholeness will come as a result of the best of *goiym* (nations) being brought to her, (cf. our comments 61:5-7). Is there anything more tender and helpful than the comfort a mother gives a distressed child? Nothing except the comfort of God! But our God helps us understand His feeling toward us and His abililty to comfort us in the highest experience of comfort we know—that of our mothers (cf. Isa. 49:15-16; 60:4, etc.). Jesus expressed His tenderness toward Jerusalem often (cf. Mt. 23:37-39; Lk. 19:41-44, etc.).

Those addressed in verse 14 as those who shall see these things are those who shall actually experience them, i.e., those who became the "nation brought forth" at one stroke (verses seven-nine). That generation alive when the Messiah was born (the manchild) and when the nation was brought forth (at Pentecost, A.D. 30), experienced the miracle of God and the maternalness of God (cf. Lk. 1:67-79; 2:29-35; 2:36-38; 24:13-53; Acts 2:43-47; 3:17—4:4; 4:32-37, etc.). The hand of Jehovah was seen and acknowledged in all this, not only by those who believed and became followers of the Way, but also by some who did not follow (cf. Acts 5:27-42; 26:28; 28:1ff, etc.). Not only will the redemptive hand and the providential hand of Jehovah be manifested in the birth of new Zion, but His judgmental hand will also be made known. It is the double-emphasis theme that runs throughout the biblical record of redemption. Whenever God redeems the faithful, He necessarily judges the unfaithful. God cannot reward righteousness without condemning unrighteousness. When He delivered Noah,

He destroyed the world; when He saved Lot, He destroyed Sodom; when He delivered the Hebrews under Moses, He destroyed Pharaoh; when He delivered Israel from captivity, He did so by destroying Babylon. The redemption provided in the atonement of Christ and the establishment of the kingdom, pronounces and gives unequivocal evidence of the final judgment of all who will not surrender to His sovereign rule by becoming covenant members of His church, (cf. Jn. 12:31; 16:11; 17:31; Eph. 4:8; Col. 2:15; Heb. 2:14-15; I Jn. 3:8; Rev. 19:15-16, etc.). God allowed His enemies (Satan and his kingdom) to gather all the power at their disposal and meet Him at Calvary and do battle there. It was at Calvary and the empty tomb that God redeemed the world and judged the world—potentially. Those who wish the redemption He won for them there must appropriate it by accepting His new covenant terms. Those who do not wish it must accept His judgment. The final execution of His redemption and judgment is yet future, but just as certain as the cross and the empty tomb! (see our comments *Minor Prophets,* College Press, pgs. 184-201).

QUIZ

1. Where else in the O.T. and the N.T. are the "woman and the manchild" referred to?
2. Why is the birth of the new nation of God so unique?
3. How can the citizens of the new nation rejoice and mourn at the same time?
4. How did God choose to illustrate His desire to comfort His people?
5. Where did God demonstrate with finality His redemption and judgment of the world?

3. BUILDING OF ZION

TEXT: 66:15-24

15 For, behold, Jehovah will come with fire, and his chariots
shall be like the whirlwind; to render his anger with fierceness, and his rebuke with flames of fire.
16 For by fire will Jehovah execute judgment, and by his sword,
upon all flesh; and the slain of Jehovah shall be many.
17 They that sanctify themselves and purify themselves to go
unto the gardens, behind one in the midst, eating swine's
flesh, and the abomination, and the mouse, they shall come
to an end together, saith Jehovah.
18 For I know their works and their thoughts: the time cometh,
that I will gather all nations and tongues; and they shall
come, and shall see my glory.
19 And I will set a sign among them, and I will send such as
escape of them unto the nations, to Tarshish, Pul, and Lud,
that draw the bow, to Tubal and Javan, to the isles afar
off, that have not heard my fame, neither have seen my
glory; and they shall declare my glory among the nations.
20 And they shall bring all your brethren out of all the nations
for an oblation unto Jehovah, upon horses, and in chariots,
and in litters, and upon mules, and upon dromedaries, to
my holy mountain Jerusalem, saith Jehovah, as the children
of Israel bring their oblation in a clean vessel into the house
of Jehovah.
21 And of them also will I take for priests and for Levites,
saith Jehovah.
22 For as the new heavens and the new earth, which I will
make, shall remain before me, saith Jehovah, so shall your
seed and your name remain.
23 And it shall come to pass, that from one new moon to another, and from one sabbath to another, shall all flesh come
to worship before me, saith Jehovah.
24 And they shall go forth, and look upon the dead bodies
of the men that have transgressed against me: for their

worm shall not die, neither shall their fire be quenched; and they shall be an abhorring unto all flesh.

QUERIES

a. Why repeat the message of judgment?
b. What is the "sign" of verse 19?
c. Who is going to come before Jehovah on new moon and sabbath?

PARAPHRASE

Yes, Jehovah must come with His judgment of wrath to prepare the way for the redemption of mankind. He comes in all the awful consuming fierceness of fire when He judges. His sword of judgment will fall upon the world. Those who have rejected the Lord will suffer His wrath and many will die. Yes, the manifest judgment of God is near upon all, both Israelite and Gentile who dedicate and purify themselves to idolatry, who follow those who indulge in perverseness like eating swine's flesh, mice and other abominable things contrary to My holy Law. I see what they do and I know their secret thoughts, says Jehovah. The time is coming when I will summon all nations and races to behold the ultimate demonstrations of My glory. At this time, men will see My awesome sign of redemption and judgment in its historical certainty, and some of them will escape the judgment I have pronounced upon the world. Those who escape I will send as messengers with the good news of My salvation to the far reaches of civilization to people who have never heard of Me and have never seen My sovereign omnipotence. These messengers will go to Spain, North Africa, Armenia, Greece and other lands beyond these. They shall proclaim My glory among men of all nations and races. All who hear and obey will become brethren and precious gifts to My honor. They will be brought to My New Zion from all over the world; they will come from different directions, by every means possible. Many will come because some of the children of Israel will have accepted My salvation and offered themselves to Me in obedience. They will become messengers, bringing Gentiles to Me with that same faith and obedience; these Israelites will finally have offered Me clean offerings; these Gentiles will also be considered cleansed and I will consecrate them as My servants, says the Lord. For as surely as the new order which I am creating will last forever, so those who accept My salvation shall be My children forever and their relationship to My name shall stand forever. People from all nations will come into covenant relationship to Me and worship Me according to My will forever. These will behold My judgments upon those who were so favored but who rebelliously rejected My will; this will be a constant reminder of the terrible punishment of the rebellious and of the greatness of redemption to the obedient.

COMMENTS

v. 15-17 DESTRUCTION OF THE OLD: We repeat, for emphasis, this chapter (66) is an epilogue. First, judgment upon Israel for disobeying the Old covenant (verses 1-6); second, promise of a new Israel and a new order (verses 7-14); third, building the new order by destroying the old and opening up citizenship in the New order to the whole world (verses 15-24). J. A. Alexander, in *Commentary on the Prophecies of Isaiah,* pub. Zondervan, says these verses are ". . . an integral part of the 'great argument' with which the whole book has been occupied, and which the Prophet never loses sight of to the end of the last sentence. The grand theme of these prophecies . . . is the relation of God's people to himself and to the world, and in the latter stages of its history, to that race with which it was once outwardly identical. The great catastrophe with which the vision closes is the change of dispensations, comprehending the final abolition of the ceremonial law, and its concomitants, the introduction of a spiritual worship and the consequent diffusion of the Church, its vast enlargement by the introduction of all Gentile converts to complete equality of privilege and honor with the believing Jews, and the excision of the unbelieving Jews from all connection with the church or chosen people, which they once imagined to have no existence independent of themselves."

The emphasis of this final prophecy is on the establishment of the New messianic age and the gathering of the Gentiles into covenant relationship. In order to establish its fulfillment the Old order must be abrogated. The abrogation of the Old and the establishment of the New are coincidental— they are to occur at the same time, i.e., within a generation (cf. Mt. 24:34). The generation of the apostles (Peter, James, John, etc.) did not pass away until God had abrogated the Old order and instituted the New!

God's judgments are appropriately likened unto fire. Fire fiercely consumes (cf. Heb. 12:29; II Thess. 1:7-8, etc.). and is often representative of torment and punishment (cf. Lk. 16:24; Rev. 14:10-11). Jehovah abrogated the Old order, in fact, at the cross of Christ (cf. Col. 2:14-15; Heb. 9:15-28, etc.). That was when God judged both the Mosaic system and all other human (Gentile) systems through which men tried to earn righteousness before Him. All human governments, religions, and ideologies are essentially human rebellions against the rule of God. They were all judged, exposed as inadequate, and destroyed in the power they might exercise over men at Calvary and the Empty Tomb. All human deviations from faith in God through His promised Son are idolatrous. They all fall under the generalized picture of abomination in verse 17. They all "came to an end together" in God's great redemptive-judgmental work in Jerusalem, 30 A.D., when Old Jerusalem had run its course and used up the time allotted to it (cf. Dan. 9:24-27). When the Suffering Servant had made atonement for sin and was raised from the dead destroying the ultimate power of the devil, Israel was to turn to Jehovah and accept citizenship in New Zion (the church). Some did, but a majority did not. Jehovah, in His longsuffering allowed the Jewish nation to retain its city and temple for another 40 years (until 70 A.D.), and then, by His own providential design He allowed the city and the temple to be destroyed and burned and the nation dispersed over the face of the earth by the Roman empire. Thus the fire of God's judgment fell both literally and figuratively upon the Old order and consumed it.

v. 18-24 DEVELOPMENT OF THE NEW: Concurrent to the judgment of the Old order, Jehovah will establish the New order. The phrase "time cometh" connects the judgment of those who shall come to an end together and the "gathering of all nations and tongues" to see His glory. All nations would see God's glory in the two-fold accomplishment of the destruction of the Old and establishment of the New. Jehovah's historical *signal* that He was fulfilling His promises made through the prophets about all this was the Messiah! All who saw Jehovah's *signal* that human systems were overthrown believed in the Christ and were saved ("escaped") from that perverse generation (cf. Acts 2:40). These "escaped" ones (the Jews who became Christians at Pentecost and soon thereafter) were sent by the Lord unto the nations (Gentiles) where they announced the great historical events of redemption which glorified God. Perhaps some of the early Gentile converts (e.g., Cornelius) were also among the "sent" ones. Tarshish, if our conjecture is right, is Spain (at the extreme west of the Great Sea); Pul is probably Put in North Africa (the extreme southern boundary); Lud is probably Lydia in Asia Minor (northern boundary); and Tubal and Javan are Armenia and Greece respectively (generally forming a northern bounday). These nations are mentioned to emphasize the extreme distances to which the escapees shall be sent with their declaration of the glory of Jehovah.

Those escapees who are sent are going to bring "brethren out of all the nations." Apparently the apostle Paul had this scripture in mind when he referred to his ministry of bringing the Gentiles to Christ as an *offering* unto God (cf. Rom. 15:16). The prophet's designation of *goiym* from all nations being brought forth as "brethren" of the covenant people is unique! Many of the prophets predicted that the Gentiles would one day be brought to Jehovah, but none (save in this one place) referred to them as "brethren"! The reference to various beasts of burden and vehicles of transportation pictorializes the ease, swiftness and splendor in which the Gentiles will be brought to the Lord. The "holy mountain" is a favorite phrase of Isaiah to designate the messianic age (cf. Isa. 2:1-4; 11:9; 56:7; 57:3; 65:11, 25, etc.).

From the Gentiles Jehovah will take "priests and Levites." In the New age (the church) all citizens are priests (cf. I Pet. 2:5, 9; Rev. 1:6; 5:10, etc.). This may have a more specific reference, however, to the special ministry of those "sent" (even of early Gentile converts) to the extreme boundaries of civilization to "bring brethren out of all the nations." In other words, it may refer to Gentile converts chosen especially by God as ministers and missionaries to declare the glory of God, e.g., Timothy, Luke, Cornelius and others.

The next verses (22-24) emphasize the finality and perpetuity of the establishment of the New order and the judgment of the Old order. We have already established our view that the term "new heavens and new earth" as Isaiah uses it means the New Order (the messianic age) (cf. Isa. 65:17ff). The prophets talk of a whole *new* age to come when the Servant of Jehovah appears:

a. There shall be *new* things told by God (Isa. 42:9; 48:6-7).
b. God's people will sing a *new* song (Isa. 42:10).
c. God will make a completely *new* covenant (Jer. 31:31ff).
d. God will put a *new* heart and spirit in men (Ezek. 18:31; 36:26).
e. They will have a *new* name (Isa. 62:2).

There are many other references to the *newness* of the age to follow the old one where the word new is not specified but inferred. Just as this new creation will be God's final covenant and just as this new order will last forever, so those who enter into the covenant will be His people forever. That was prophesied by Hosea (Hos. 2:16-23; 3:5) and fulfilled according to the apostles (Rom. 9:24-33; I Pet. 2:9-10). The name God gives His New Covenant people will remain upon them forever (cf. Rev. 2:17; 3:12; 14:1; 22:4). Old Israel with its old covenant, old name, and old institutions shall pass away (cf. Jer. 3:15-18) and not even be remembered! But from the old will spring the remnant that survives God's casting off, and together with the remnant will be a great gathering of Gentiles to form the true Israel of God which is a "new creation" (cf. Gal. 6:15-16)!

Isaiah was a preacher-prophet to the people of the Old dispensation. He must communicate his message about the New dispensation in terminology and forms to which those of the old dispensation could relate. So, using the terminology of "new moon and sabbath," Isaiah predicts that in the new order there will be faithful, regular, worship of God which will be pleasing to Him. This brief picture of worship in the new dispensation given by Isaiah is dramatically paralleled and expanded in Ezekiel, chapters 40-48, and in Zechariah 14:16-21. Verse 23 is Isaiah's picture of the situation with new Zion after its creation. Verse 24 is the prophet's description of the relationship of the New, true worshipers, to what they see concerning the Old dispensation which has been judged and destroyed or abrogated. The New citizens of Zion are safe within her walls, worshiping Jehovah gladly and truly. Occasionally New Zion's citizens "look upon the dead bodies" of those who have transgressed against Jehovah and the sight of His judgment upon the sinners reminds Zion of the greatness of its redemption and the awful terror of God's punishment from which she has been saved. The undying worm and the unquenchable fire is figurative use of Gehenna where the Jews disposed of dead carcasses of criminals.

Christians witnessed the destruction of Jerusalem in 70 A.D. and were reminded of the fate of all who disobey God and reject His Son and warned that a similar fate awaits an unbelieving world when Jesus comes back to earth at the end of time (Mt. 24:1-51). New Zion is directed to "look upon the dead" Roman culture of the first and second centuries (Rom. 1:18-32; Revelation, chapters 17-20:6) and rejoice for salvation while also being warned against partaking in Rome's sin.

Isaiah's pictorialization of the great judgment of God upon impenitent Israel and the founding of a new order upon the ashes of the old has parallels: (a) the great battle of Gog and Magog and the new land, city and temple of Ezekiel, chapters 38-48; (b) the great battle in the valley of Jehoshaphat and the escape of those who call upon the name of the Lord in Joel 2:28—3:21; (c) the battle and victory the "king" will win, the purging of the land, and the practice of purified worship depicted in Zechariah 9:9—14:21. So Isaiah closes his great prophecy predicting, not the end of time but the end of the Old dispensation and the creation by God of a New dispensation. Isaiah is predicting the *first* coming of the Messiah and the establishment of the Messiah's kingdom, the church, not the *second* coming of the Messiah.

Essentially Isaiah's message is that God's great plan to redeem the world involves the incarnation of the Word in the person of the Suffering Servant; the atonement for sin by the Servant; the offering of a new covenant relationship of grace through faith; the incorporation into that covenant relationship and the formation of a New Zion from all in the world who will believe and accept its terms; the judgment and punishment forever of all who will not accept it.

QUIZ

1. How is chapter 66 an epilogue?
2. Why use fire as a picture of God's judgments?
3. In what way is the judgment of the old connected to the establishment of the new?
4. Why list the names of the nations in verse 19?
5. What is unique about the term, "bring all your brethren . . ."?

6. Who are the "priests and Levites" of verse 21 and from whence do they come?
7. Who goes forth to look upon the dead (verse 24) and when?
8. How would you sum up the message of the whole book of Isaiah?

And now, dear reader, having lived some portion of each day of our life for the last four years with the majesty and awesomeness of this work from the pen of Isaiah, we are impressed very deeply that the one great necessity for a world of unbelief is it must be brought face to face, mind to mind, heart to heart with the glory of God. Men must be taught, must acknowledge and put their trust in *who God is* and not in what man can do! The focus of the prophets on the character and nature of God is the true focus of all preaching. Now, in the end of the ages, the glory and personhood of God has been revealed incarnate in Jesus Christ and His accomplished redemption. And that is the ultimate focus of all preaching. Now therefore, be wise . . . . . .

PSALM 2

2 Why do the nations rage,
And the peoples meditate a vain thing?
2 The kings of the earth set themselves,
And the rulers take counsel together,
Against Jehovah, and against his anointed, *saying,*
3 Let us break their bonds assunder,
And cast away their cords from us.
4 He that sitteth in the heavens will laugh:
The Lord will have them in derision.
5 Then will he speak unto them in his wrath,
And vex them in his sore displeasure:
6 Yet I have set my king
Upon my holy hill of Zion.
7 I will tell of the decree:

Jehovah said unto me, Thou art my son;
This day have I begotten thee.
8 Ask of me, and I will give *thee* the nations for thine
inheritance,
And the uttermost parts of the earth for thy possession.
9 Thou shalt break them with a rod of iron;
Thou shalt dash them in pieces like a potter's vessel.
10 Now therefore be wise, O ye kings:
Be instructed, ye judges of the earth.
11 Serve Jehovah with fear,
And rejoice with trembling.
12 Kiss the son, lest he be angry,
and ye perish in the way.
For his wrath will soon be kindled.
Blessed are all they that take refuge in him.

EXAMINATION

CHAPTERS SIXTY THROUGH SIXTY-SIX

DEFINITION

(Define the following words or phrases as they were discussed in the comments.)

1. *wealth* of the nations
2. *Spirit* upon me
3. *meek*
4. *liberty*
5. year of Lord's *favor*
6. *strangers*
7. *priests*
8. *covenant*
9. *married*
10. *ensign*
11. *Edom*
12. *Zion*
13. *swine's flesh*
14. *new heavens and earth*

MEMORIZATION

The ______ of the Lord Jehovah is upon me; because Jehovah hath ______ me to preach good tidings unto the ______; he hath sent me to ______ up the broken-hearted, to proclaim ______ to the captives, and the opening of the prison to them that are ______; to proclaim the year of Jehovah's ______, and the day of vengeance of our God; to ______ all that mourn; to appoint unto them that mourn in ______, to given unto them a ______ for ashes, the oil of ______ for mourning, the garment of ______ for the spirit of heaviness; that they may be called ______ of righteousness, the planting of Jehovah that he may be ______. (61:1-3)

EXPLANATION

1. Explain how Zion would be built by foreigners.
2. Explain what the One anointed by the Lord was to declare.
3. Explain the new name Zion was to receive.
4. Explain the Holy Spirit's relationship to believers in the O.T.
5. Explain why God said former things would not be remembered.
6. Explain how God created a land in one day (brought forth at once a nation).
7. Explain how people of Zion look upon dead bodies.

APPLICATION

(In its context every scripture has one meaning—the author's intended meaning. How may the following be applied in the believer's life?)

1. Does Isaiah's prediction of the year of the Lord's favor at the coming of the Messiah apply to our understanding of

biblical eschatology?
2. Does Isaiah's symbolic use of Edom in chapter 63 contribute anything to present day understanding of the relation of Zion to the world?
3. Does the impatient prayer of Zion in chapters 64-65 have any application to New Zion?
4. How can we apply the statement, ". . . bless himself in the God *truth* . . ." to our concept of God today?
5. Does the symbolic use of "new heaven and new earth" in chapter 66 apply to our eschatological understanding of the O.T.?
6. What is the main application concerning the nature of God from the book of Isaiah?

BIBLIOGRAPHY

TEXTS

1. *Biblia Hebraica,* Rudolf Kittel, American Bible Society
2. *Koren,* Koren Publishers Jerusalem Ltd.

LEXICONS

1. *Analytical Hebrew and Chaldee Lexicon,* Benjamin Davidson Bagster
2. *Langenscheidt Pocket Hebrew Dictionary,* Karl Feyerabend, McGraw-Hill
3. *The English and Hebrew Bible Student's Concordance,* Pick, Kregel Publishers
4. *Hebrew and English Lexicon,* Gesenius, Eerdmans
5. *Hebrew and English Lexicon of the O.T.,* Brown, Driver, Briggs, Oxford
6. *Synonyms of the Old Testament,* Girdlestone, Eerdmans

TRANSLATIONS

1. King James Version
2. American Standard Version, 1901
3. Revised Standard Version, 1946-1952
4. The Berkeley Version
5. The New American Standard Version, 1960-1971
6. Living Psalms and Proverbs with The Major Prophets, Paraphrased
7. Four Prophets, Amos, Hosea, Micah, Isaiah, by J. B. Phillips
8. Today's English Version, Good News Bible, 1976, pub. American Bible Society

BIBLIOGRAPHY

COMMENTARIES

1. *The Book of Isaiah,* Three Volumes, Edward J. Young, Eerdmans
2. *Exposition of Isaiah,* Two Volumes, Herbert Carl Leupold, Baker
3. *Isaiah,* John Peter Lange, Zondervan
4. *Isaiah,* Two Volumes, Keil and Delitzsch, Eerdmans
5. *Class Notes on Isaiah,* V. K. Allison
6. *Class Notes on Isaiah,* Chester Williamson
7. *Commentary on the Prophecies of Isaiah,* Joseph A. Alexander, Zondervan Classic Commentary Series
8. *I and II Kings,* James E. Smith, pub. College Press
9. *Old Testament History,* Smith and Wilbur Fields, pub. College Press

ENCYCLOPEDIAS

1. *The International Standard Bible Encyclopedia,* Eerdmans
2. *Pictorial Bible Dictionary,* Zondervan
3. *Handbook to The Bible,* Eerdmans
4. *The International Jewish Encyclopedia,* Isaacson and Wigoder, pub. Prentice-Hall

OTHER WORKS

1. *The Doctrine of The Prophets,* Kirkpatrick, Zondervan
2. *Prophecy and The Church,* Allis, Presbyterian and Reformed
3. *The Grammar of Prophecy,* Girdlestone, Kragel
4. *New Testament Interpretations of Old Testament Prophecies,* Bales, Harding
5. *Prophecy Interpreted,* Milton, Augsburg
6. *The Divided Kingdom,* Pfeiffer, Baker
7. *Exile and Return,* Pfeiffer, Baker

8. *Israel and The Nations,* Bruce, Eerdmans
9. *The Method and Message of Jewish Apocalyptic,* D. S. Russell, pub. The Westminster Press
10. *History of The Jews,* Heindrich Graetz, pub. The Jewish Pub. Soc. of America
11. *The Eternal Spirit,* C. C. Crawford, pub. College Press

Isaiah 62:1-5
For Zion's sake will I not hold
my peace, and for Jerusa-
lem's sake I will not rest, until
her righteousness go forth as
brightness, and her salvation
as a lamp that burneth 2 And
the nations shall see thy
righteousness, and all kings
thy glory, and thou shalt be
called by a new name, which
the mouth of Jehovah shall
name. 3 Thou shalt also be a
crown of beauty in the hand
of Jehovah, and a royal
diadem in the hand of thy
God. 4 Thou shalt no more be
termed Forsaken; neither
shall thy land any more be
termed Desolate: but thou
shalt bc called Hephzibah,
and thy land Beulah; for Jehovah delighteth in thee,
and thy land shall be married.
5 For as a young man
marrieth a virgin, so shall thy
sons marry thee; and as the
bridegroom rejoiceth over
the bride, so shall thy God
rejoice over thee.